HAMAS IN POLITICS

To
Mohammed Rantisi
who taught me so much about Islam, Gaza and
steadfastness in adversity

In memory of my father
Karel Gunning (1926–2007)
who taught me to question dominant 'truths'

Jeroen Gunning

Hamas in Politics
Democracy, Religion, Violence

Columbia University Press
New York

Columbia University Press
Publishers Since 1893
New York   Chichester, West Sussex

Library of Congress Cataloging-in-Publication Data

Gunning, Jeroen.
  Hamas in politics : democracy, religion, violence /
Jeroen Gunning ; foreword by James Piscatori.
    p. cm.
  Includes bibliographical references and index.
  ISBN 978-0-231-70044-3 (cloth : alk. paper)
  ISBN 978-0-231-70045-0 (pbk : alk. paper)
  1. Harakat al-Muqawamah al-Islamiyah. 2. Palestinian National Au-
thority. 3. Palestinian Arabs—Politics and government—1993- 4.
Democracy—Gaza Strip. 5. Democracy—West Bank. 6. Islam and
politics—Gaza Strip. 7. Islam and politics—West Bank. I. Title.
  JQ1830.A98H3739 2008
  324.25695'3082—dc22
  ∞   2007044194

CONTENTS

FOREWORD

Considerations of Islam and politics have moved from the periphery of studies on Middle Eastern politics to the centre, but well-defined, contesting explanations have hardened over time. The electoral victory of Hamas in January 2006 has particularly excited opinion, startling observers both within and outside Palestine and giving new urgency to debates over its aims and the future of the Palestinian-Israeli conflict. It has also renewed longstanding questions about the evolutionary potential of Islamist movements. Some have seen its participation in national elections as purely tactical, even cynical – a means to power without a commitment to democratic values; others have interpreted it as evidence of at least pragmatic, and perhaps principled, accommodation. However interpreted, isolation abroad and fragmentation at home have ensued. The security, political, economic, and social conditions within Palestine have markedly deteriorated, civil war between Fatah and Hamas has pitted the West Bank against Gaza, and outside powers such as the United States and the European Union have had urgently to reconsider their policies. Not for the first or the last time, the unfolding of Muslim politics has cast wide circles of controversy, and *Hamas in Politics* explores them in a manner that could not be timelier or better informed.

The history of Harakah al-Muqawamah al-Islamiyyah, the Movement of Islamic Resistance, cannot be separated from the momentous events of the recent Middle East, especially the Intifada of the late 1980s. Religious sentiment had been on the rise for at least a decade before then as Islamic revitalisation took hold throughout the region and as political despair at both the Israeli occupation and the seeming ineffectiveness of the Palestine Liberation Organisation (PLO) grew. Between 1978 and 1987, for example, Islamist groups won 40 per cent of the student vote in the West Bank, and 65 to 75 per cent in the Gaza Strip. Gaza, mired in poverty and political neglect, was the fertile ground on which Shaykh Ahmad Yassin (1937-2004) and others, such as 'Abd al-'Aziz al-Rantisi (1947-2004), mobilised anti-PLO sentiment and laid the foundations for a cohesive movement. The precipitous advent of a popular uprising crystallised developments, and within a few short months of the Intifada's outbreak in December 1987, the Muslim Brotherhood formally adopted Hamas as its branch in Palestine.

Hamas' covenant offers a number of guiding principles, but their exact meaning and the degree of commitment to them have been questioned over time. In presenting an interpretation of history that views Palestine as a sacred trust (*waqf*), it is at odds with the secular nationalism that was once dominant. Its principles are pegged high: no one can negotiate away any part of the sacred trust, and everyone has a solemn duty to participate in jihad to liberate Palestine. The covenant is thus nothing less than an alternative constitution for Palestine, one that acknowledges fraternal relations with the PLO but fundamentally differs from the Organisation's charter. Hamas' ideology guides followers and makes it difficult for them to be seen to deviate from it, but whether it constitutes a straightjacket remains controversial and occupies well-needed attention in this volume. Since the 2006 election and the ensuing international pressure on Hamas to come to terms with Israel, the issue of whether or not it can rise above its formalised core principles has become particularly important. This was seen in the often arcane debate over the degree to which the Islamic legal concept of *hudnah*, which Hamas proffered in late 2004, was tantamount to a 'ceasefire' or merely a very temporary, tactical halt to hostilities without larger strategic significance.

The analysis that Jeroen Gunning skilfully develops thus speaks directly to one of the great debates of our time: is an Islamist movement capable of evolution? The evidence suggests an uneven trajectory and variable levels of support for Hamas, but, like other political groups, it was naturally both responsive to public opinion and intent on protecting its own interests. Around 1993, Hamas could command the support of perhaps 30 to 40 per cent of the Palestinian population, but opinion polls up to mid-2000 indicated that its popularity had declined to around 10 per cent. The slow institutionalisation of the Palestinian Authority (PA) added a considerable dilemma for the movement: it could not afford to oppose the emergence of the new state and so marginalise itself, but nor could it afford to cede moral and political ground to the PLO as the leaders of the PA. Its attitude towards elections was largely ambivalent, in part because of suspicions that Israel would manipulate them. Hamas was successful in student and professional association elections, and Mahmud al-Zahhar, a Gazan leader, argued that an Islamic movement must adapt to realities, including self-rule elections, and did not appear to reject democracy. Yet the election to the Legislative Council of January 1996 was especially awkward. If, on the one hand, Hamas were to participate, it would appear to endorse the peace process, specifically the Camp David, Madrid, and Oslo agreements that had called for elections, and to enhance the legitimacy of its main rival, the PLO. Yet, on the other hand, if it were to boycott the elections, it might be left behind in the building of the Palestinian state and appear as self-centred and preoccupied with its own ideological purity. Changes in class, state formation, and civil society provided the larger backdrop to this political calculus, and, as Gunning makes clear, Hamas could no more escape the shifting landscape than could the PLO.

For a variety of reasons, then, Hamas came slowly to engage with the political process, though reluctantly and with uncertain long-term effects. While it did not directly contest the 1996 election, it made known its support for sympathetic independent candidates. Five of these candidates were elected (out of a total Council membership of 88), and an exit poll showed that 60 to 70 per cent of Hamas supporters eligible to vote had taken part in the voting. In effect, then, it had chosen what Mishal and Sela call 'unofficial participation' in the election. Hamas and Islamic Jihad boycotted the presidential election of January 2005 that was to elect Mahmud 'Abbas. In the West Bank, about half of the eligible voters took part. Despite boycotting the presidential election, Hamas participated, and did well, in the local elections that took place between January and May 2005. Fatah won control of 50 out of 84 municipalities in the West Bank and Gaza, while Hamas won 28. It had not gained the upper hand, nor could one simply say that it had been socialised into becoming democratic. But electoral participation was emerging as one of the two pillars, along with unflinching opposition to the Israeli occupation, of its political programme.

The degree of organisational cohesion has had, as one would expect, some impact on the group's ability to implement its programme. Hamas had become, on the one hand, an efficient machine, running schools and health clinics and channelling financial assistance to members and the families of 'martyrs'. Yet, on the other hand, it was riven at times by internal divisions. Leaders inside the Occupied Territories appeared generally, for example, to favour electoral participation whereas those in Amman were opposed to it. Ultimately, the instability that followed the death of Yasir 'Arafat in November 2004, the growing irritation with the corruption and ineffectiveness of the political class, and widespread discontent at the economic and political *status quo* produced a clear majority for Hamas in 2006 in the first parliamentary elections in ten years, an election that saw a turnout of nearly three-quarters of the estimated 1.3 million Palestinian voters. Whether this was due to the success of Hamas or to the failure of the PLO was a matter of interpretation, but there was no doubt that Hamas had now momentously moved from an oppositional movement to government.

The resort to violence seems most at odds with the obligations of rule and goes to the heart of public views of Hamas. In Gunning's balanced perspective, violence – terrorism to some; resistance to others — is neither irrelevant to the Hamas story nor religiously predetermined. It is an integral part of its political make-up and may, even, move in tandem with its policy of electoral participation. Many would argue, rather, that it is a militant organisation masquerading as democratic, but what this volume persuasively does is to move us away from the kinds of essentialist analysis that have portrayed Hamas as fundamentally violent or inevitably democratic. Rather, it uncovers the complex layers of Palestinian Islamic identity and an evolving normative framework. Ambivalence and fragmentation may thus appear to lie at the movement's centre, but a more rounded and subtle depiction such as that presented here can serve as an antidote to the polarised and stark pictures that have commonly emerged.

It may also remind us that, as the pitched battles in Gaza in June 2007 between Hamas and Fatah, formal partners in a government of national unity, demonstrated, the resort to arms is not reserved solely for the Israelis.

Blending a consideration of Hamas' political theory with its conduct, informed by conceptual prisms from several disciplines but avoiding jargon, *Hamas in Politics* provides a reliable and discerning guide to one of the most important actors in contemporary Middle Eastern politics. Interviews with officials and supporters supplement an examination of official texts, and together they provide a window on to context — the self-understandings of Hamas supporters and its political record. What emerges is a movement that is the product of its values and behaviour but also the consequence of circumstances, most notably today the radicalisation of a population after forty years of occupation. And therein is Hamas' greatest challenge in power: it must lead but cannot greatly outpace popular sentiment. In such a fluid and dangerous situation, summary labels like 'terrorist' or, indeed, 'democratic', often applied to the organisation by critics or admirers, scarcely capture the complexity of Muslim politics — a complexity that, by contrast, unfolds dispassionately and compellingly in the pages to follow.

James Piscatori
Wadham College, Oxford, October 2007

ACKNOWLEDGEMENTS

My first thanks go to the many in Gaza, the West Bank, Lebanon and Syria who were willing to talk to me and gave their time generously to be interviewed, often repeatedly. For incisive feedback I am indebted to Charles Tripp, Suha Taji-Farouki, James Piscatori, Menachem Klein, Khaled Hroub, Jan Selby, Kirsten Schulze, Andrew Linklater, Michael Williams, Alastair Finlan, Lucy Taylor, Elena Korosteleva, Linda Herrera, Harmonie Toros, Frazer Egerton, Ilan Zvi Baron and Luca Mavelli. The animated debates with colleagues at the NUPI-SSRC workshops on political violence were invaluable, as were the verbal sparring with Emanuele Ottolenghi, and Asef Bayat's encouragement to continue exploring social movement theory. Ali Khalil, Ahmad Lutfi, Samer el-Karanshawy, Sara Ababneh, Nida Shoughry and Mohammed Rantisi all helped at various stages with the difficult labour of translation. Mohammed Rantisi, Samer Abu Ghazaleh, Taher, Kamil, Sara Ababneh, Graham Henderson, Ilan Zvi Baron and Angela Setterlund did sterling jobs as part-time research assistants. I am particularly indebted to Mohammed for his untiring willingness to help.

This project would have been impossible without the financial support given by the Sir Richard Stapley Educational Trust, the Rens-Holle Stichting, and my parents during my PhD, and the various research grants provided by the University of Wales, Aberystwyth, to conduct additional fieldwork and pay for translation subsequently. The British Academy, by granting me a Postdoctoral Research Fellowship, though awarded for research into the Lebanese Hizballah, offered me precious time to reflect further on how to study Islamist organisations engaged in both violence and politics, and to learn from the community of Middle East scholars in Oxford, chiefly Avi Shlaim and Eugene Rogan. The Department of International Politics in Aberystwyth has been invaluable by providing both a stimulating academic and postgraduate community, and giving me time off from teaching and administrative duties to finish my research and write up the book. Finally, I would like to thank Michael Dwyer of Hurst Publishers for his incisive editorial help and his unwavering commitment to this book.

My thanks also go to those in both the Palestinian territories and Israel who gave me their friendship, offered a glimpse into what it is like to live in that beautiful yet war-torn part of the world, and helped me to see the people and pain behind the conflict.

Most important of all has been the support given by my wife, Janet. Thank you for your never-ending practical help and for maintaining faith. And thanks to my sons for sharing their dad so patiently with this book, even though it was hard at times.

Aberystwyth, 15 August 2007   J.G.

GLOSSARY

'alim (pl. *'ulama'*)	scholar, expert (often with reference to religion)
amanah	trust
'aqd ijtima'i	social contract
barakah	God's blessing (equiv. to Weber's 'gift of grace')
da'wah	lit. summons: the call to Islam (equiv. to preaching)
dawlah Islamiyyah	Islamic state
DFLP	Democratic Front for the Liberation of Palestine (leftist PLO faction)
Falastin al-Muslimah	Hamas' overseas publication, published in London
fiqh	Islamic jurisprudence
fitnah	disorder, sedition
Hadith	Saying or tradition of the Prophet
Hamas	Harakah al-Muqawamah al-Islamiyyah (Islamic Resistance Movement); acronym means: zeal
haram	religiously prohibited
hijab	headscarf
Hizb al-Khalas	Hizb al-Khalas al-Watani al-Islami (Islamic National Salvation Party), political offshoot of Hamas in Gaza
hudnah	ceasefire
hudud	Qur'anicly prescribed penal laws
'ibadat	Islamic principles regulating worship
IDF	Israeli Defense Forces
ijma'	consensus

ijtihad	legal deductive reasoning, independent opinion
Islamic Bloc	Hamas' student wing (al-Kutlah al-Islamiyyah)
Khalifah	Caliph (vicegerent)
Majlis al-Shura	lit. Consultative Council: Legislative Council
al-Mithaq	Hamas' 1988 Covenant
mu'amalat	Islamic principles regulating social interaction
al-Mujamma' al-Islami	Islamic Complex, Hamas' main charity in Gaza, founded by Ahmad Yassin
mujtahid (pl. *mujtahidun*)	religious scholar, qualified to perform *ijtihad*
PA	Palestinian Authority
PFLP	Popular Front for the Liberation of Palestine (leftist PLO faction)
PLO	Palestine Liberation Organisation
al-Risalah	Hizb al-Khalas' newspaper, unofficial Hamas organ
shari'ah	Islamic law
shura	consultation
shura democracy	Hamas' form of democracy
tahdi'ah	period of calm, less formal and binding than ceasefire
takfiri	engaging in the practice of accusing other Muslims of apostasy or unbelief (*kufr*); label given to particular ideological trend within Islamism (cf. Egypt's *Takfir wa'l-Hijrah*, al-Qaeda)
tawafuq	harmony
ummah	global community of Muslims; loose equiv. to 'nation'
usrah (pl. *usrat*)	lit. family: lowest organisational unit within Hamas
waqf (pl. *awqaf*)	religious endowment
zakah	religiously-ordained alms tax

1

ON STUDYING HAMAS

In January 2006 Hamas, an organisation classified by Western governments as 'terrorist' with a long history of political violence against both civilians and military personnel, was democratically elected to govern the Palestinian territories. The apparent contradictions in this situation has left many observers at a loss. Hamas has used political violence against both Israel and its main political rival, Fatah, yet it won the 2006 election on a law, order and social welfare ticket. It pursues an Islamic state, yet holds internal elections and champions democracy. It campaigns for *shar'iah* law, yet its leaders are predominantly secular professionals rather than religious scholars. It calls for the destruction of Israel, yet has shown (limited) readiness to consider honouring previous peace agreements.

One view of Hamas, dominant in the rhetoric of Western politicians and some academics, is that the organisation has certain inherent characteristics and that it cannot, and will not, change. This view—which Klein labels the 'static approach' (Klein, 2007: 442)—is neither interested in contradiction nor in the possibility of change. Violent and so-called 'fanatical' behaviour is highlighted as an innate characteristic while contradictory evidence is marginalised as irrelevant or duplicitous. Hamas' welfare network is depicted as solely dedicated to funding, promoting and supporting terrorism without much consideration of what other purposes this network may serve, and what contradictions this introduces (cf. Levitt, 2006). Tensions between Hamas' political theory and democratic principles are explained away by pointing to the fundamental incompatibility between political Islam and democracy (cf. Nüsse, 1998: 180). Evidence of transformation is ignored, enabling Dennis Ross, former U.S. envoy to the Middle East, to state with certainty that Hamas is unlikely "to undergo … a transformation" ('Foreword' in Levitt, 2006: x-xi).

Within such a framework, Hamas is typically cast as the primary obstacle to the successful resolution of the peace process, and the creation of a democratic state in the West Bank and Gaza. In conflict resolution terms, it is depicted as an innate 'total spoiler' (Stedman, 1997: 7-16), an actor with "immutable preferences", implacably opposed to the peace process. The notion that Hamas might act both as a total and as a 'limited spoiler', whose preferences are negotiable, and which can potentially be brought into the peace process given a change in the political calculus of violence, is hardly entertained.

Such an analysis, though appealing in the black-and-white context of the War on Terror, is deeply unsatisfactory. Politics is never static. Neither are political organisations. Hamas has changed since its inception, and will continue to change. The question is merely how fast and in which direction.

Whether Hamas is categorised as a total or a limited spoiler has serious policy implications—just as labelling it anti-democratic, 'terrorist', or religious fundamentalist has policy implications. Total spoilers are not expected to respond to inducement (meeting some of the spoiler's demands) or socialisation (changing the behaviour of the spoiler through a mixture of inducements and coercion), while the threat of violence or of withdrawing the support of external 'sponsors' of a peace process is expected to strengthen them (Stedman, 1997: 7-16). The strategies proposed as effective by Stedman's spoiler model are the actual use of force or the 'final train' scenario (continuing with the peace process without recognition or participation of the spoiler)—although he warns that if the total spoiler has a popular following, as is the case with Hamas, even these strategies may backfire. However, if Hamas is categorised as a limited spoiler, Stedman's model advocates the use of inducement and socialisation, and the careful calibration of force to prevent "counterescalation of violence by the limited spoiler" and increase in its popular support.

Hamas is here to stay. It has too large a following for it to be readily marginalised. Whether we like it or not, indeed whether or not Hamas signs up to a two-state solution, the international community, Israel and Fatah must come to terms with Hamas as a central political player. Yet the series of negotiations between Fatah and Israel designed to resolve the nearly sixty-year-old conflict, has been premised, at least rhetorically, on the notion that Hamas must be neutralised or eradicated for peace to work (Milton-Edwards and Crooke, 2004a: 43, 9-51). The same attitude has informed the West's myopic focus on President Mahmud 'Abbas and Fatah since Hamas' 2006 election victory. Such a static approach fails to understand how Hamas works beyond the narrow focus of peace and violence, or to consider what wider (contradictory) societal factors influence Hamas.

This book is based on the premise that Hamas will endure, that it is subject to change, and that contradictions within it must be explored rather than dismissed. It proposes that Hamas cannot be reduced to its use of violence, that it must be studied in the wider context of Palestinian society and politics, and that any analysis must include (though not stop at) an attempt to understand Hamas on its own terms. It also assumes that how we study a phenomenon affects both our premises and what we find, obliging us to adopt a critically self-reflective methodology.

The focus of this book is the role of democracy, religion and violence in Hamas' political thought and practice. Each of these themes is central to Hamas' political future and our understanding of Hamas' role in Palestinian politics. Together they encapsulate the contradictions alluded to above. They overlap in numerous ways. But one thing that concerns all three, and offers a useful—though by no means exhaustive—prism through which to study Hamas, is the question of authority. How does Hamas approach the issue of authority? Is authority derived from God or the people? Is there room for dissent? What makes a Hamas leader authoritative? What role does violence play? What role religion, elections? How does this affect Hamas' attitude towards the electorate or towards the peace process?

To answer these questions, Hamas' rhetoric, organisational structure and political practices are analysed at three different levels: internally (Chapter 4), domestically within the Palestinian arena (Chapter 5) and vis-à-vis the peace process (Chapter 6). Chapter 2 provides a brief contextualisation of Hamas' origins and evolution. Chapter 3 introduces Hamas' political theory. Chapter 7 concludes with a reflection on Hamas from the perspective of democratisation studies.

A 'Critical' Methodology

Hamas has been studied from a variety of perspectives and disciplinary traditions. Two of the most prominent fields that study (aspects of) Hamas are 'terrorism' studies and what might be termed Islamism studies—the study of political and social organisations advocating the creation of an Islamic state and society. Neither of these fields is homogeneous. Within terrorism studies, there are a variety of approaches veering from traditional or problem-solving to critical (cf. Gunning, 2007c). Within Islamism studies, one can distinguish between essentialists, modernists and pluralists (cf. Gunning, 2000: 10ff).

The 'static approach' described above is typically found among the more traditional terrorism scholars and the essentialists within Islamism studies. Their conceptual framework and methodology are characteristically incapable of capturing the complexity of Hamas. To explore this complexity, and the contradictions inherent in it, a more nuanced, 'critical' methodology is required—if 'critical' is understood as being self-consciously self-reflexive about methods and assumptions.[1] In constructing such a methodology, valuable lessons can be learned from existing critiques of traditional terrorism studies and essentialist approaches to Islamism.[2]

Both traditional terrorism studies and essentialists among Islamism scholars have been critiqued for relying too much on secondary sources and too little on fieldwork and interviews. Schmid and Jongman, Silke and Horgan all observe that terrorism research too often simply recycles secondary sources (Silke, 2004c: 59-65; Schmid and Jongman, 1988: 137-8, 79-80; Horgan, 2004: 30-4). O'Leary

---

1 I here follow Krause and Williams' approach (Williams and Krause, 1997: x-xi). See also Gunning, 2007d.

2 For a fuller analysis, see Gunning, 2007d; Gunning, 2000. See also S. Hunter, 1995; Salvatore, 1997; Nieuwenhuijze, 1997; Said, 1978; Salamé, 1994; Sayyid, 1997; Crelinsten, 1987; Silke, 2004a; Schmid and Jongman, 1988; Horgan, 2006; Ranstorp, 2006; O'Leary and Silke, 2007.

and Silke go one step further, arguing that "much of what is written about terrorism … is written by people who have never met a terrorist, or have never actually spent significant time on the ground in the areas most affected by conflict" (O'Leary and Silke, 2007: 393). Critics of essentialist studies of Islamism similarly warn against being "overly textual" and "insufficiently sociological" (Norton, 1995: 8). "Direct observation, interaction, and study", Esposito remarks, "are particularly critical, since many Islamic activists write comparatively little and their writings are often mere ideological tracts or public relations documents. What they write or say must be placed within the context of what they actually do" (Esposito, 1999: 263). Research should thus both include interviews (interaction), and close analysis of practice (observation)—as exemplified, in the context of Hamas, by the studies of Hroub (2000), Jensen (1998), S. Roy (1995a) and Holt (1997).

There are numerous practical reasons for why both terrorism research and students of Islamism rely heavily on secondary sources. But one factor is arguably the political bias often present against the subject of study, resulting in an *a priori* demonising of the 'other' and an unwillingness to try and understand what motivates 'them' (see also Ilardi, 2004; Zulaika, 2006). A critical methodology problematises such rigid us-them dichotomies, adopting the far more challenging approach described by Richardson in the context of terrorism research, and exemplified by Mishal and Sela (2000) and Klein (2007) in the context of research on Hamas:

When I consider a terrorist atrocity I do not think of the perpetrators as evil monsters but rather I think about the terrorists I have met, and the people I have known who have joined terrorist groups … I grapple with how a young idealist can believe that in murdering innocent people he or she is battling injustice and fighting for a fairer world. I think, as the Protestant martyr John Bradford said 500 years ago, 'There but for the grace of God, go I' (Richardson, 2006: 2).

Following this approach, I have self-consciously sought to engage with my research subjects with the purpose of 'humanizing the other' (Roy, 2006: viii). This means moving beyond the images dominating the Western press—the shocking violence, the public rhetoric, some of it vitriolic—to try to understand what motivates Hamas members.

It means trying to live into their situation, demanding extensive field visits, close interaction and what Euben calls a "dialogic approach", beginning with taking Hamas' own discourse and explanations seriously before subjecting them to critique (1999: 155-8).

For this study, I lived in Gaza City for nine months in 1998 to conduct fieldwork, and visited Israel and the occupied territories on numerous occasions both before and since. I interviewed scores of Hamas members, visiting them in their offices and occasionally their homes. Security concerns limited the number of interviews I could conduct, particularly with ordinary members. Nevertheless, this book's analysis is based on well over 100 interviews with well-known Hamas leaders, ordinary Hamas members, political opponents of Hamas, and local analysts.[3] Similarly, Hamas texts, ranging from make-shift publications of the Palestinian Muslim Brothers in the early 1980s to the electronic news analyses of the mid-2000s, have been studied extensively.

A second critique is that traditional terrorism studies and essentialist scholars tend to ignore historical and socio-political context (cf. Silke, 2004d: 209; Crenshaw, 1995b: ix, 12-9; della Porta, 1995b: 4-7; Wolff, 1998; Zubaida, 1989: ix; Esposito, 1999: 263). In terrorism studies, this leads to a fixation on violence, and a disregard for the wider political and socio-economic conditions that facilitated it. A similar critique may be levelled at Islamism studies.

A critical methodology places Islamism within its historical and socio-political context (cf., with regard to research on Hamas, Mishal and Sela, 2000; Hroub, 2000)—though, importantly, without reducing it to a purely "mechanical response to structural pressures", such as changing socio-economic structures, while ignoring "its inherent power as an ethico-political vision of the modern world" (Euben, 1999: 154). It situates violence within a whole array of practices, violent as well as non-violent, and considers to what extent violence is a function of external factors, such as state violence against Islamist movements, rather than simply a manifestation of some supposed 'Islamic' essence (cf. Burgat, 2003: Ch. 5; Hafez and Wiktorowicz,

---

3   For list of interviews cited, see References; for full list of interviews conducted in 1998, see Gunning, 2000: 362-8.

2004; Dalacoura, 1998: 200-5). It moves away from reifying Islam, from positing it as the chief explanation for Islamist behaviour, to conceptualising Islam as an evolving tradition which, while influencing people's worldview and responses, is itself affected by new interpretations and wider structural changes (cf. Eickelman and Piscatori, 1996; Zubaida, 1989; Halliday, 1996; Dalacoura, 1998; see also Hasenclever and Rittberger, 2003: 109-13).

Within such a framework, religion has a life of its own, in that political entrepreneurs have to operate within existing social practices and discourses. But it is always interpreted, and can be re-interpreted by political entrepreneurs. Consequently, as Hasenclever and Rittberger (2003: 115) note, "the impact of religious traditions on conflict behaviour is deeply ambiguous: They can make violence more likely, insofar as a reading of holy texts prevails that justifies armed combat; on the other hand, they can make violence less likely, insofar as a reading of holy texts prevails that delegitimizes the use of violence ....".

It is particularly important to meticulously distinguish between different trends within Islamism, rather than conflating them and dismissing all as hostile, violent and anti-democratic on the grounds that they are 'Islamic' or 'Islamist' (cf. Esposito, 1999: Ch. 6; Halliday, 1996: Ch. 4; Wiktorowicz, 2004b; Farsoun and Hajjar, 1990). This is important for academic reasons, but it also affects policy. Quoting Sara Roy,

The West, in demonizing Hamas and, by extension, all parts of the Islamic movement in Gaza, is committing a potentially fatal error. Instead of ... lumping all Islamic groups together, the Western powers should differentiate between radical and moderate (and productive) Islamic forces and actively assist the latter. [...] The key question in Gaza, as elsewhere in the Arab world, is not whether Arab society will be religious or secular, but whether people will eat, develop, and progress (Roy, 1995a: 33-4).

To aid contextualisation, this study has adopted a social movement approach,[4] which includes a focus on changing socio-economic

---

4 Although social movement theory emerged to study primarily secular, non-violent, Western movements, it has been applied to religiously-motivated, violent and/or non-Western movements (cf. Tarrow, 1988; della Porta, 1995b; della Porta, 1992; Wiktorowicz, 2004a; Robinson, 2004).

structures, the political system and the wider social movement of which Hamas is a part. Violence will receive less attention than it has received in other studies, not because it is less significant but because it has too often obscured other aspects of the organisation. The political apparatus of Hamas will be studied alongside affiliated charities, women's organisations and student associations, even though not all who are members of the latter categories are Hamas members. To focus too narrowly on the political organisation, would be to underestimate its dependency on the wider social movements from which it draws its strength. Both the political organisation and the wider social movement will be studied within the context of wider socio-economic changes.

In much of the analysis, this social movement approach is implicit. It nevertheless informs how Hamas is conceptualised; what units of analysis are deemed relevant; and what categories of analysis are employed.[5] Within this framework, personnel of affiliated charities, student leaders and supporters with no known position within Hamas but who identify with it and expound its theories, become relevant 'units of analysis'—which goes some way in overcoming the methodological problems inherent in studying semi-clandestine organisations, whose members may not feel free to identify themselves as such. Taking the three levels of analysis proposed by McAdam, McCarthy and Zald (1996), this study considers among other things the wider political and socio-economic structures within which Hamas

---

5   To be clear, Hamas is not a social movement which Diani defines as "a network of informal interactions between a plurality of individuals, groups and/or organizations, engaged in a political or cultural conflict, on the basis of a shared collective identity", but a social movement organisation which is part of a number of overlapping social movements. A political party may be considered part of a social movement if it considers itself "as part of a movement and be recognised as such both by other actors in the movement and by the general public" (Diani, 1992: 13-5). Goldstone similarly justifies using social movement theory to study political parties, arguing that "there is only a fuzzy and permeable boundary between institutionalized and noninstitutionalized politics. ... one cannot understand the normal, institutionalized working of courts, legislatures, executives, or parties without understanding their intimate and ongoing shaping by social movements" (Goldstone, 2003: 2).

operates ('political opportunities'), organisational strength ('mobilising structures'), and ideological factors ('framing processes').

A third useful critique is that terrorism studies are too often uncritical of both their methodology and wider theoretical framework. Essentialist scholars of Islamism can be similarly guilty of this. In response, I have sought to enhance the empirical research of this study by engaging relevant theoretical paradigms, and allowing these to highlight details and questions that might otherwise not have come to prominence. Chapter 7, for instance, sheds an innovative light on Hamas' relationship to democracy by approaching this question through the prism of various democratisation theories, thus both broadening the study by placing Hamas within the broader (comparative) context of observed paths towards democratisation elsewhere, and deepening it by making the study more rigorous. Social movement theory plays a similar role, as do the comparisons drawn between Hamas' political theory and various Western and Islamic political theorists.

The strength of this comparative approach lies in the theoretical rigour it brings to the research. The danger is that local particularities can be overlooked or misinterpreted. Clergy, for instance, do not necessarily occupy the same position in Catholic and Muslim societies, rendering parallels between the two problematic. Similarities, conversely, can obscure underlying differences. Electoral systems operate in both the Middle East and Europe. Yet clan loyalties play a far greater, and not always readily visible, role in the former.

This is precisely the critique offered by another trend in Islamism studies which warns against the wholesale application of theoretical models developed within a Western (or Westernised) context (cf. Burgat, 1993; Esposito, 1999; Holt, 1997: 74; Roy, 1995a: 34). Like the comparativists, they assume that there are human universals that hold true for different societies. Where they differ is that they do not presume to know for certain what these universals are, or how they will be translated within a particular culturally-specific manifestation (Dalacoura, 1998: 29-32)—not unlike Butler's notion of a 'not-yet-arrived' universality (Butler, 1996: 46-9, 52). As a result, they are more open to consider alternative modernities and democracies (which is why I have called them 'pluralists' elsewhere; Gunning,

9

2000), and to reflect on the possible cultural specificity of those universal concepts that have their roots in Western political history.

To minimise the bias that comes from applying models developed within a (predominantly) Western social science to a historically, culturally and politically different situation, key concepts need, within the confines of time, to be subjected to a critical reflection on their historical and cultural specificity, and how they have been used to create binary divisions between the 'accepted' and the 'unacceptable'.[6]

The term 'religion', for instance, is rooted in the specific historical trajectory of the Christian and post-Christian West, and is part of its particular hegemonic project. Within this framework (cf. Asad, 1993; Salvatore, 1997: 29-32), religion is a private, symbolic thought system, posited as irrational in opposition to the secular and allegedly rational worlds of politics, civil society and science. Through this demarcation, religion is effectively banned from secular politics and public space and, as such, Western conceptualisations of religion serve to maintain a particular political order in which the secular is privileged over the religious (cf. Asad, 2003)—even though, in practice, the West is far from the secularised entity it purports to be (cf. Burgat, 1993: 129-32).

6　To facilitate the problematisation of key assumptions, this study has borrowed from Derrida the notion of 'traces' (cf. Derrida, 1981: 17-36, 8-47; see also Derrida, 1982; Derrida and Spivak, 1976; Silverman, 1989). Western social science, according to Derrida, is deeply shaped by binary opposites such as modern-traditional, democratic-terrorist or liberal-intolerant. These binary opposites act not only to suppress crossover elements ('traces') of the opposite term, but they are also usually linked in clusters that serve to further obscure 'traces'. 'Modern' is associated with terms such as 'liberal', 'democratic', 'non-violent', while 'traditional' is more readily associated with 'intolerant', 'authoritarian' or 'violent'. Un-problematised usage of these clusters serves to obscure 'traces' of their opposites, and encourages one to assume that the sighting of one element of a cluster of binary pairs means that the whole cluster applies. The result is a reifying of expectations which discourages further questioning. Terms tend to be clustered together for historical reasons. Their clustering is not meaningless and can offer valuable insights. But it can equally obscure understanding. I have sought to move beyond the dichotomous 'either-or' to a "*simultaneously* either *or*" perspective (Derrida, 1981: 43).

When applied to contemporary Islamism, such a definition both obscures our understanding of the phenomenon and serves to delegitimise it. As Esposito observed, "the modern notion of religion as a system of personal belief makes an Islam (or any world religion ...) that is comprehensive in scope, in which religion is integral to politics and society, 'abnormal' ... and nonsensical. Thus Islam becomes incomprehensible, irrational, extremist, threatening" (Esposito, 1999: 257-8).

Recognition of this allows us to problematise the 'secularisation credo'—the belief that modernisation and democratisation must go hand in hand with secularisation[7]—which underpins much of Western social science. In social movement theory, this credo has for long prevented the study of religious social movements, regarded as 'false' alternatives to 'real' social movements (Hannigan, 1991: 317-8; see also Riesebrodt, 1993: Ch. 1). In Middle Eastern studies, the secularisation credo has led scholars to unproblematically regard Islamists as rigidly dogmatic compared to their secularist counterparts (cf. Waterbury, 1994: 36, 9), ignoring both the existence of persistent dogmatism among secularists (cf. Keane, 2002; Inayatullah and Blaney, 2004), and the capacity of Islamists to reinterpret their sacred texts in response to changes in political opportunities (cf. Burgat, 1993: 132).

Recognition of the cultural specificity of the term 'religious'—and its corollary, 'secular' (cf. Asad, 2003)—also allows us to look afresh at what constitutes the religious and the secular. Use of mosques is not necessarily proof that a movement is defined by its 'religious' commitment if mosques are among the few 'secular' public spaces available. Those called 'shaykh' are not necessarily clerics in a culture where respect is expressed through calling people by the honorary

---

7   Historically, the secularisation credo is rooted in the Durkheimian (or more precisely Parsonian) notion that secularisation is the inevitable next step in a unilinear process of religious evolution (Swatos Jr., 1989: 148-51; Salvatore, 1997: 31-2). This notion feeds the belief that Islamism, and religious resurgence in general, is a throw-back to medieval times. Durkheim himself was more ambiguous about the unilinearity of this evolution.

title of 'shaykh'.[8] While recognising their fundamentally problematic nature, I will continue to use the terms 'religious' and 'secular', to denote the presumed distinction between the 'transcendent' and the 'immanent' (cf. Laustsen and Waever, 2003)—although, as we will see, this distinction breaks down in the way the transcendent is implicated in the immanent, for instance in the notion of 'civic piety'—and that between 'religious' and 'political' structures and practices—although, here too, the distinction will prove unsatisfactory. 'Religious' is here used to denote anything from the institutions, communities, traditions (legal, moral, political, cultural), values, ideas, and dispositions usually associated with religion in the context of Palestinian politics (thus side-stepping the debate over whether 'religion' refers to all practices involved in shaping the self through reference to a universe of sacred meanings, or only to manifestations of historical religious traditions or, more specifically still, to those actively involved in transforming society; cf. Hervieu-Léger, 2000: 30-41). More broadly, religion is considered to be a socially and historically situated "body of more or less organized beliefs and practices relating to a transcendent supra-empirical reality" (Campiche and Bovay, in Hervieu-Léger, 2000: 39-40), a definition which can encompass both traditional and new forms of 'religion'.

'Democracy' and 'violence' are similarly culturally situated. Space does not allow me to reflect more fully on these terms. Suffice it to say that within a secular Western framework, 'democracy', 'religion' and 'violence' are characteristically considered antithetical and that this assumption must be problematised if the terms are to be of any use to this study. Democracy is usually considered non-violent, even though violence has often been integral to the development and maintenance of democracy while the ability to inflict violence can be a key component of an elected leader's authority (cf. Rustow, 1970; Rapoport and Weinberg, 2001; Carter, 1979: 45-9; Tilly, 1992; Eckstein and Gurr, 1975: 203). Democracy is also typically posited as inherently secular, even though the development of secular modernity,

---

8 Hamas founder 'Shaykh' Ahmad Yassin was a school teacher whose title was a mark of respect, as is common practice in Palestine. Compare this to Schiff and Ya'ari's depiction of Israel waging war on Hamas by arresting "clerical figures" (1990: 237).

of which democracy is a part, is profoundly rooted in developments in 'religion' (cf. Salvatore, 1997; Asad, 2003). Democratic systems, moreover, are invariably less secular than they are typically depicted (cf. Burgat, 1993: 129-32) while religion has in many instances continued to be one of the factors sustaining democracy, for instance, by encouraging civic responsibility (cf. Stout, 2004).

In the same way, the presumed connection between Islam and violence must be problematised. Those who assert that Muslims are inherently more prone to violence typically do so on the basis of deeply flawed methodologies. One of the most-quoted 'authorities' in this field, Huntington, comes to this conclusion on the grounds that, during the 1990s, Muslims were involved in more wars than any other religious grouping—without considering the nature and context of these conflicts, or the role socio-economic, ethnic and other factors played (Huntington, 1998: 254-65). It has also been argued, in the context of terrorism studies that 'religious terrorists' are inherently more violent and less capable of compromise because for them violence, rather than being primarily a considered political tool—as is presumed to be the case for other 'terrorists'—is "foremost a sacramental act or divine duty" (Hoffman, 1998: 94-5). However, Hoffman ends up contradicting his own model by linking the occurrence of violence to, among other things, tactical, this-wordly calculations, and inter-factional rivalry over constituency support (cf. 145-65; see also Hoffman and McCormick, 2004).

Rather than assuming that 'religion' makes political groups more violent, this study follows Hasenclever and Rittberger's above-quoted observation that 'religion' can both facilitate and prevent violence. The relationship between 'religion' and violence must thus be investigated rather than assumed.

A fourth and related critique that has informed this study concerns the observation that much of the literature on terrorism takes the legitimacy of the *status quo* for granted, without sufficiently questioning its origins, premises and the extent to which it has contributed to the problem of political violence (cf. Herman and O'Sullivan, 1990; George, 1991; Schmid and Jongman, 1988: 182; Silke, 2004b: 15-9; O'Leary and Silke, 2007).

In response, I have sought to go beyond the problem-solving approach that has dominated the study of terrorism and adopted a self-consciously critical approach to the notions of the state, the insurgents and political violence. This has meant, among other things, questioning the legitimacy of the state and the *status quo* (which is not the same as adopting a dogmatically anti-state position), and moving beyond state-centric security notions which equate individual security with state security, to a notion of human security, which places equal emphasis on the security of the individual and the community—and the effect of state actions upon them (cf. Heiberg, Tirman and O'Leary, 2007; Crenshaw, 1995a; della Porta, 1992). It has also meant moving beyond a paradigm which seeks the eradication of violent non-state actors, presumed to be inherently illegitimate, to one which contemplates the possibility of a political solution through political transformation on all sides.

A similarly critical approach has been adopted vis-à-vis evidence. Rather than seeing 'reality' as something 'out there' which can be known objectively, 'reality' is here regarded as mediated through our conceptions, experiences and theories. Within this framework, theory becomes part of the 'shaping' of reality rather than a conceptually separate tool to better 'see' reality, rendering it all the more imperative to make explicit what theories underpin one's research (in this sense, Tarrow's observation, that terrorism research is 'innocent of theoretical apparatus' is misleading, as the field is imbued with theoretical assumptions).

Such a framework has consequences for the way 'causality' is interpreted. The notion of causality implies a level of knowledge, objectivity and determinism that sits ill with the interpretive framework adopted in this study. Instead, this study uses the looser notion of 'facilitating conditions', and focuses more on dynamic processes, interaction and the 'how', rather than the 'why', although the two are implicated in each other (cf. also Horgan, 2006: 77-84).

More fundamentally, research becomes a contribution to an ongoing conversation, rather than a definitive verdict. This study is premised on Ricoeur's observation that social science resembles judicial proceedings, following a 'logic of probability' which can always be challenged, as new effects, interpretations and evidence come to light, rather than the 'logic of empirical verification' (Ricoeur, 1971: 210-5). Thus,

> To show that an interpretation is more probable in the light of what is known is something other than showing that a conclusion is true. ... Validation is an argumentative discipline comparable to the juridical procedures of legal interpretation. It is a logic of uncertainty and of qualitative probability. [...] In front of the court, the plurivocity common to texts and to actions is exhibited in the form of a conflict of interpretations, and the final interpretation appears as a verdict to which it is possible to make appeal. Like legal utterances, all interpretations in ... the social sciences may be challenged ... Only in the tribunal is there a moment where the procedures of appeal are exhausted. ... Neither in literary criticism, nor in the social sciences, is there such a last word (Ricoeur, 1971: 212, 5).

Adopting such a 'critical' methodology is particularly difficult when analysing a movement such as Hamas. Not only is Hamas situated in the minefield that is the Israeli-Palestinian conflict, but it is also discursively implicated in the War on Terror. Both these conflicts have a tendency to impose an 'either-or' framework on those who study them: either you are with us, or you are with the enemy. A critical approach seeks to break out of such a dichotomy, and subject both 'them' and 'us' to a critical analysis. To attempt to understand 'the other' one needs to empathise—which is mistaken for sympathy in a dichotomous framework. To understand why there is conflict one needs to explore how both 'we' and 'they' have contributed to the conflict. My attempt to better understand Hamas should not be mistaken for condoning all that Hamas does. Ethically, to be clear, I hold violence directed at non-combatants to be unjustifiable—regardless of whether this violence is perpetrated by Hamas, the Israeli army, the IRA or British Special Forces. However, this ethical position need not, and should not, prevent me from trying to understand what Hamas does, what reasons it gives for doing so, and how structural and ideational factors affect its behaviour.

Scope and Sources

The focus of this study is Hamas' political practice, and the role played in this by democracy, religion and violence, particularly over

15

the period 1997-2007. Its primary concern is how Hamas conceptualises and practises authority, which corresponds to the first aspect of Hadenius' three-way definition of democracy as "a general principle of popular sovereignty, a principle of freedom, and a principle of equality" (Hadenius, 1992: 9; see also Diamond, Linz and Lipset, 1995: 6-7). Other aspects of democracy, such as equality and freedom, are touched upon, where relevant, but for reasons of space, not explored in their own right.

One of this study's core premises is that Hamas' political behaviour cannot be fully understood without a thorough understanding of its political theory (loosely defined). As an activist movement, Hamas is not given to producing detailed theoretical tracts. It is, nevertheless, a self-consciously ideological organisation which has sought to create a vanguard of activists who exemplify 'genuine' or 'authentic' Islamic behaviour. As with all human organisations, Hamas' practice is influenced by human shortcomings, manipulation and the exigencies of the actual. Actual practice does not therefore necessarily reflect utopian theory. But in the eyes of Hamas' core supporters the organisation is considered to be a living example of an attempt at 'authentic' Islamic behaviour. As such, political theory—and in particular utopian conceptions of what constitutes 'authentic' Islamic political behaviour—self-consciously informs actual practice. Analysis of Hamas' political theory is therefore a useful tool for interpreting the meaning of Hamas' practice, and complementing functionalist and structural explanations.

Comprehending Hamas' utopian vision, combined with an understanding of how it approaches politics in practice and how both have been affected by wider socio-political structures, will furthermore help us to gain a deeper insight into what underpins Hamas' current policies: from its position on Israel and its refusal to give up arms to its domestic policies and its relation with other players in the Palestinian arena. This study will do so by analysing how, beyond the populist and often vitriolic rhetoric of its public rallies, Hamas members think about politics, what principles they most value, and how they propose to translate these into practice. It will also do this by showing how utopian ideals inform current practice, and *vice versa*.

That this point has to be argued in the context of terrorism studies is an indictment of the field in itself. If the subject had been state elites and their formulation of foreign policy, it would have been accepted as normal practice to pour over their every word, in an attempt to understand what they meant by a particular decision.[9] Similarly, the notion that one has to understand what value framework underpins a particular policy in order to understand its meaning is relatively uncontroversial in the study of international politics, particularly among those who operate within a constructivist framework. Margot Light articulated this point persuasively in her study of Soviet foreign policy, when she observed that "all policy reflects theory, whether or not that theory is articulated or recognized by those who make policy" (Light, 1988: 1). This is the position adopted in this study.

The subject of this study is the political organisation of Hamas, from its Muslim Brotherhood origins prior to Hamas' creation in 1987-88, to its winning the 2006 national elections. The goals and activities of the 'Izz al-Din al-Qassam Brigades, the resistance wing created by Hamas in the early 1990s, are discussed insofar as they illustrate a wider point about the practices of the larger political organisation. But they do not feature centrally as they represent a paramilitary, underground operational logic, rather than that of a political organisation with social and political goals. The activities of the numerous charities that are loosely affiliated to Hamas are similarly only discussed to the extent that they illustrate aspects of Hamas' political framework.

Much of the existing literature on Hamas focuses either on documents (if the focus is on ideas) or on practice (if the focus is on behaviour). Relatively few have focused on both, and those who do, have tended to concentrate on the peace process, rather than Hamas' political practice more broadly.[10] Some studies have used personal

9 O'Leary made this point at the NUPI-SSRC Workshop on 'Political Violence' in Cuenca, Spain, November 2004.

10 Hroub (2000), Nüsse (1998) and Milton-Edwards (1996) discuss Hamas' ideology in some detail. Nüsse ignores practice, thus providing no insight into how discourse affects practice and *vice versa*. Hroub's otherwise masterful analysis does not engage much with Hamas' underlying political theory. Milton-Edwards likewise focuses overly

interviews with Hamas leaders but their focus is typically on current affairs. Fewer still have interviewed ordinary members to gain a better understanding of the internal dynamics of the movement.[11] This study is distinct in the breadth of sources it has sought to use, in the central place accorded to interviews, and in its dual focus on the movement's political theory and practice.

I have used six types of sources: primary texts, interviews, personal observation, surveys and statistics, newspaper reports and secondary texts. Primary texts include Hamas' Charter (*al-Mithaq*), its 2006 election manifesto, newspaper articles and conference papers by Hamas leaders, articles in affiliated magazines (e.g. *Falastin al-Muslimah* and *al-Risalah*) or on affiliated websites (e.g. www.palestine-info.co.uk), and Hamas pamphlets. Also included are influential texts by Islamist thinkers such as the Indo-Pakistani founder of Jamaat-e-Islami, Abul A'la Mawdudi (1903-79), and the Egyptian Muslim Brotherhood ideologue, Sayyid Qutb (1906-66), on whom Hamas draws.

Primary texts, surveys and statistics and newspaper reports are drawn, where possible, from the entire period under investigation. They span rare copies of the first editions of *Falastin al-Muslimah* and documents written by the founding board members of the Islamic University in Gaza in 1979, Hamas' 2006 election manifesto and the latest commentary on Hamas' various websites (covering both Arabic and English versions).

Interviews span a decade (1997-2007) and range from Hamas leaders, members, and supporters to Fatah leaders, political rivals and civil society actors.[12] Included are interviews with Hamas' assassinated leaders, such as Ahmad Yassin, 'Abd al-'Aziz al-Rantisi and Ismail

---

on grand ideology and is more interested in practice. Mishal and Sela (2000) provide an in-depth practice analysis but do not analyse Hamas' political theory.

11 Hroub (2000), Holt (1997), Jensen (1998) and Roy (1995a) use interviews relatively extensively but Jensen alone focuses specifically on interviews with ordinary members.

12 The bulk of interviews were conducted between November 1997 and July 1998 when I lived in Gaza City. Subsequent interviews were carried out over the course of numerous field trips.

Abu Shannab, Hamas' three most senior leaders in Gaza during the 1990s (featured on the book's cover), as well as interviews with its current leaders, including Prime Minister Ismail Haniyyah, Mahmud al-Zahhar (Minister of Foreign Affairs in the first Cabinet), and Head of Hamas' Political Bureau, Khalid Mish'al. Most of the interviews have been carried out in Hamas' heartland, the Gaza Strip. Where interviewees requested anonymity, I have changed their names to fictional names, which is indicated by the use of inverted commas (e.g. 'Muhammad').[13]

The decision to focus my fieldwork primarily on one site was inspired by both methodological reasons (to conduct an in-depth ethnography) and practical reasons (limited time and resources). The Gaza Strip was chosen because it, rather than the West Bank, has traditionally been Hamas' intellectual and political centre of gravity. The fact that the Gaza Strip, unlike the politically fragmented West Bank, has functioned as a more or less integrated political unit since the arrival of the Palestinian Authority in 1994 also makes it a better candidate for exploring Hamas' (domestic) political practice, in terms of how it interacts with political others and the authorities. To ensure nation-wide representation, interviews with members from the Gaza Strip have been complemented by interviews with West Bank members as well as exiled leaders abroad, analysis of practices observed in the West Bank and findings from secondary literature regarding the West Bank.

Because Hamas is a grassroots activist movement, not given to lengthy theorising, textual analysis has its limitations. Published documents are an important source as the official interface between a movement and the larger political arena, but not only are they abstractions and momentary snapshots (cf. Said, 1978: 300), they are not necessarily representative of the entirety or the complexity of the movement. Hamas' 1988 Charter, for instance, neither does justice

---

13 I have transliterated Arabic names and terms into English following a much simplified version of the system adopted by Brill's Encyclopaedia of Islam (new Edition), taking into account both common transliterations used by the mainstream media (if the divergence was too great, as in 'Hamed Bitawi') and personal preferences of transliteration as expressed by the interviewees themselves.

to the political thinking of Hamas' leaders (it is weak on specifics) nor does it adequately reflect the views of the present leadership, few of whom would quote it or regard it as reflecting their positions (it was written in 1988 by the then old guard of the movement).[14] *Falastin al-Muslimah* is published in Britain and thus is typically more reflective of the outside leadership than the movement's Palestinian-based leadership.[15] *Al-Risalah* tends to reflect the movement's pragmatists' views while pamphlets are typically populist in nature.

If we are to have any chance of grasping Hamas' self-understanding, textual analysis must be complemented by personal interviews. There are three compelling reasons for taking this approach. Palestinian culture, like others under occupation, is heavily biased towards the oral (Scott, 1991: 160). Secondly, one cannot cross-question the written word to understand its underlying logic (which is particularly important when studying Islamism, since so much of what is written in the West is based on erroneous assumptions).[16] Thirdly, official texts do not reveal what ordinary members think, how much of their leaders' thinking they have absorbed, or how they evaluate their leaders' claims to legitimacy.

Besides clarifying public statements, interviews can also enhance one's insight into what Scott (1991) called the 'hidden transcript' (the discourse members use with each other)—particularly when one is in a position to build up some level of trust in the course of multiple interviews. 'Hidden transcripts' are unavailable to outsiders. However, when grievances and beliefs are strong and anonymity can

---

14 According to Tamimi, author of *Hamas: Unwritten Chapters* and long-standing member of the Palestinian Muslim Brotherhood living in London, debates about replacing the *Mithaq* have taken place since the late 1990s, and a new document is being prepared for Hamas' 20th anniversary in December 2007 (Tamimi, 2007). Very few of those I interviewed referred to the *Mithaq* at all.

15 When I lived in Gaza (1997-1998), it was almost impossible to obtain a copy of *Falastin al-Muslimah* locally.

16 Cf. Nüsse's assumption that Hamas' thinking on Muslim-Christian relations is represented by the 1960s writings of Sayyid Qutb (Nüsse, 1998: 101-4), which, had she tested it in interviews, would have been shown to be overly simplistic.

be guaranteed, interviewees can provide a glimpse into this internal discourse in a way that published documents seldom do.

Group discussions with ordinary members in particular provide a glimpse into how internal debates are conducted and how authority is expressed, legitimated and challenged. However, because ordinary members have more to lose than well-known Hamas leaders if their membership becomes public knowledge, the sample of ordinary members I have been able to access in this way is relatively small.

For surveys, I rely predominantly on the Ramallah-based Palestinian Center for Policy and Survey Research (PSR),[17] the Jerusalem Media and Communication Centre and Near East Consulting. Though the methodology used follows international polling guidelines, there are persistent complaints among Hamas activists that Hamas sympathizers are systematically under-represented in polls (Hroub, 2000: 229-33). There has indeed been a persistent discrepancy during the 1990s between electoral outcomes in student and professional bodies—until the resumption of municipal and national elections in 2004-6, the main barometer of political opinion in Palestine—and poll findings regarding the percentage of support Hamas enjoys. Exit polls at the 2006 election similarly under-represented the percentage Hamas eventually received, although the discrepancy was far less than had been the case previously. There are various explanations for this—ranging from differences in the average educational and socio-economic background of the student and professional samples to the possibility that Hamas supporters are less likely to declare their allegiance to a pollster for fear of harassment by the security services.[18] Whatever the reason, when using polls, it is important to bear this in mind.

I also use the findings of two surveys I carried out during Student Council elections at the Islamic University in Gaza (December 1997)

---

17 Formerly the Center for Palestine Research and Studies in Nablus.

18 PSR blames the discrepancy in its 2006 election findings on Hamas members actively discouraging voters from filling in questionnaires ('Results of PSR's Legislative Elections' Exit Poll', January 2006). Others blamed it on Hamas voters' reluctance to declare their preference (Associated Press, 'Palestinian pollsters bewildered', Globeandmail.com, 26 January 2006).

and the neighbouring Al-Azhar University (April 1998).[19] For logistical reasons, the samples are smaller than those typically used by professional pollsters (though still substantial). Not having access to databases which could be randomised, I polled students as they emerged from the election hall, ensuring that all who filled in surveys were indeed students and that no student could fill in the survey twice. Consequently, the surveys only provide a rough indication to what voting students at Gaza's two main universities thought (or, for the more calculating, wished me to think) during their 1997-8 elections.

The growing secondary literature on Hamas contains some fascinating material. However, not all findings can be taken at face value. There are a number of methodological pitfalls authors have fallen into, often unconsciously. Some over-privilege accounts of Palestine's Westernised elite, in particular those who are hostile to Hamas, without adequately triangulating these with insider accounts of Hamas members (cf. Milton-Edwards, 1996; Shadid, 1988; Hammami, 1990; to a lesser extent Usher, 1995a; regarding 'elite bias' generally, see Miles and Huberman, 1994: 263-4). Others over-privilege practice analysis without sufficiently juxtaposing this with discourse analysis or at least an analysis of internal meaning (cf. Schiff

---

19 The surveys are based on a sample of 4.8 per cent and 13.4 per cent of the Islamic University's male and female students respectively, and about 10 per cent of al-Azhar's male and female students. Against 3081 female students registered in 1997-1998 at the Islamic University (http://www.iugaza.edu), I received 412 filled-in questionnaires and 224 for the 4628 male students (my aim was to cover 10 per cent of the student body; however, 50 per cent of the questionnaires were not returned). For al-Azhar, the exact gender breakdown for 1997-8 was not known. Judging by later figures, the ratio of men was approximately 55-60 per cent (http://www.alazhar-gaza.edu). In 1997-8, 5500 students were registered (of which only 1811 voted; see *Al-Ayyam*, 19 April 1998). I surveyed 311 men and 265 women (10-11 per cent of the male and female student bodies respectively, 30-34 per cent of those who voted). In both instances, the percentage of votes for each party recorded by my survey corresponded to within a 5 per cent margin of the official election results, indicating that the composition of my respondents was relatively representative. For al-Azhar, official results and my findings respectively were: al-Kutlah al-Quds (Shabibah) 83 per cent (82.6 per cent), al-Kutlah al-Islamiyyah 6.5 per cent (6.2 per cent), al-Nizam al-Islami 1.0 per cent (1.2 per cent).

and Ya'ari, 1990; Hammami, 1990). Still others have allowed their analysis to be overly coloured by Western models and their value expectations, thus missing important clues (cf. Nüsse, 1998; to a lesser extent Milton-Edwards, 1996; Shadid, 1988; Usher, 1995a).

In other instances, ideological agendas have coloured findings. Reports published by Israeli intelligence agencies tend to focus overly on Hamas' violent activities—for instance, by depicting charities as mere fronts for terrorist operations—and usually do not explicitly reflect on the veracity of their evidence (cf. ITIC, 2005). Levitt (2006) displays a similar ideological agenda, resulting in a methodology that conflates all of Hamas' multiple facets and fails to reflect on whether the evidence provided can be read differently, or whether it is sufficient to draw the conclusions reached. Pro-Zionist American Evangelical websites typically post articles which are equally one-sided, ignoring counter-evidence or alternative explanations to the ones promoted. An example of this is the link posted on Christian Action for Israel's website (http://christianactionforisrael.org) to Raab's one-sided analysis of Christian-Muslim relations in Palestine (Raab, 2003). Evidence contained in these sources may be useful but needs to be scrutinised carefully.

The fieldwork for this book spans the period 1997-2004, with additional telephone interviews carried out in 2006-7. Most of the interviews and observations were conducted in 1997-8 when I lived in Gaza City, not far from the Islamic University, Arafat's residence and Hamas' political office. Since then, the political situation has changed dramatically, from a faltering peace process through a five-year uprising to the current uneasy stalemate. Hamas itself has moved from unremitting resistance to (grudging) acceptance of the utility of a ceasefire (although this has not prevented its members from supporting others not bound by the ceasefire), and from boycotting the 1996 national election to participating in, and winning, the 2006 election.

However, despite these changes, much of Hamas' underlying political theory appears to have remained the same, as have many of its practices. Changes in the make-up and socio-economic fortunes of its supporters, and in Israel's and Fatah's policies, have reinforced certain aspects and diluted others. But most of what interviewees said in 1998 still holds true today.

Many of those interviewed now occupy central positions in Hamas' hierarchy, suggesting continuity rather than fundamental change—especially when contrasted to the leadership changes of the late 1980s. Ismail Haniyyah, Dean of the Islamic University in 1998, was Prime Minister of Hamas' first Cabinet. Mahmud al-Zahhar, a medical doctor and lecturer at the Islamic University in the 1990s, was the Minister for Foreign Affairs. Sami Abu Zughri, a student and former head of the Student Union at the Islamic University, was one of Hamas' most-quoted spokesmen in 2006. Mish'al remains the head of Hamas' Political Bureau. Others have since gained iconic status through assassination, giving their political thinking an even greater level of authority among Hamas' membership. Ahmad Yassin, 'Abd al-'Aziz al-Rantisi and Ismail Abu Shannab, the three most powerful leaders in Gaza before their assassinations in 2004-5, all fall into this category and feature prominently in the following analysis.

2
ORIGINS AND EVOLUTION

It is central to the argument of this book that Hamas is a product of its changing environment. This is not to deny the role played by agency and chance. But to comprehend why and in what form Hamas emerged, and how it subsequently evolved, we need to understand the socio-economic, political and ideological environment against which this occurred. This chapter provides a brief overview of the main socio-economic, ideological and political factors that helped to shape Hamas.

The following analysis is (loosely) informed by the political process or opportunity structure model of social movement theory which focuses on three different levels of analysis: the state and wider socio-economic structures, organisational strength, and ideological factors (cf. McAdam, McCarthy and Zald, 1996). Of particular importance in the first category are the level of openness of the political system, the state's attitude towards protest and repression, elite re-alignments, and how wider socio-economic changes affect the organisational potential of activists. The second category considers the relative strength of competing social movement organisations and political parties, as measured by their success in mobilising activists, accessing resources, utilising pre-existing networks and creating new ones. The third category concerns the relative strength of competing ideologies, and how successful movement entrepreneurs are in making their message resonate with existing master frames, life experiences and ideologies.

The political opportunity structure within which Hamas operates is not typical of those found in most social movement studies. It does not operate in a unitary sovereign state where the chief opponent is the ruling state elite. Rather, it operates in a political structure where formal power is divided between different state and non-state actors, local authority structures are subject to the actions of an occupation army, and the chief opponents include both an indigenous elite and the ruling elite of a neighbouring state which claims sovereignty over the territory where Hamas is active. The occupying state, Israel, does not use police forces to maintain order but the army. The indigenous elite uses police forces as well as the 'paramilitary'[1] militias it has created to fight occupation, as do Hamas and other opposition factions. An additional factor is the extent of the Palestinian Diaspora which numbers more than the 4 million Palestinians living inside the occupied territories, and which has played an important role in the development of both the ruling elites and their opposition. However, each of these factors can be accommodated within the political opportunity structure model.

Early years of the Palestinian Muslim Brotherhood

Hamas was established as the 'paramilitary' wing of the Palestinian Muslim Brotherhood, the roots of which, in turn, lie in the Egyptian Muslim Brotherhood. The latter was founded in 1928 by the school teacher Hasan al-Banna with the twin goals of re-Islamising Egyptian society, and liberating Egypt, and the Muslim world more broadly, from colonial rule (cf. Mitchell, 1993). From its inception, the Egyptian Brotherhood had shown concern for the fate of Palestine. But it was not until the mid-1940s that branches were established in Palestine, facilitated by the emergence of a more autonomous Palestinian lower middle class, and a nascent Islamist trend which had grown as a result of, among others, the preach-

---

1   I will use the term 'paramilitary' to denote those organisations whose chief task is to perpetrate political violence against Israeli targets. In the context of the Israeli-Palestinian conflict, this term is less ideologically loaded than either 'terrorist' or 'resistance'.

ing, institution-building and 'paramilitary' activities of 'Izz al-Din al-Qassam (after whom Hamas named its Brigades).[2]

The Palestinian Brotherhood spread quickly. By 1947, there were thirty-eight branches and over 10,000 registered members, drawn from both the ruling elite and the lower classes (Mishal and Sela, 2000: 16). But its branches became severed by the creation of Israel in 1948. The Gaza Strip came under Egyptian control. The West Bank was incorporated into Jordan. The branches inside Israel—comprising three quarters of British Mandate Palestine—became largely defunct as a result of the mass exodus of refugees who fled due to the conflict (cf. Barghouti, 1996: 170-1).

The Gazan branches became the largest political organisation in the Strip, though never exceeding an estimated 1,000 members (its main rival, the Communist Party, was estimated at around 200; Sayigh, 1997: 51). One of their main foci were the 220-250,000 refugees who had flooded the Strip, tripling the population (Roy, 1995b: 15; Tessler, 1994: 279-80). Refugees became an important part of the Brotherhood's constituency as, unlike the traditional elite, it succeeded in establishing a presence in all the major refugee camps (Milton-Edwards, 1996: 43). The Brotherhood was initially involved in (limited) armed resistance against Israel. Though largely ineffective, their efforts served as the training ground for some of those who would later found Fatah (Hroub, 2000: 22-9; Hart, 1984: 100-3, 6-10).

From 1954 onwards, the Gazan Brotherhood became caught up in both the power struggle between Egypt's new President, Gamal 'Abd al-Nasser, and the Egyptian Muslim Brotherhood, and in Nasser's clampdown on autonomous Palestinian resistance groups (Hroub, 2000: 23-4, 8-9; Milton-Edwards, 1996: 46-55). Within this hostile climate, the Brotherhood decided to turn its back on resistance—but to little avail. By the late 1950s, its members were in prison or in exile, leaving only a handful of supporters at large, and Arab Nationalism became the dominant ideology. However, the decision to renounce resistance—which led activists such as Khalid

---

2 For details, see el-Awaisi, 1998: 28-89; Hroub, 2000: 11-7; Milton-Edwards, 1996: 10-35; N. Johnson, 1984 [1982]; Lachman, 1982; Schleifer, 1993.

al-Wazir (Abu Jihad) to leave the movement and set up their own, Fatah, in the late 1950s—would have profound consequences in the period after the 1967 Arab-Israeli war.

The West Bank branches similarly had some 700-1,000 members. But they were overshadowed by the estimated 2,300 members of the (Palestinian) Communist Party and the larger Jordanian Brotherhood, into which they were integrated (Cohen, 1982: 55, 162; Milton-Edwards, 1996: 60-1). The Brothers paid lip service to the idea of resistance, but beyond organising weapons training, they were largely inactive (Hroub, 2000: 22-3; Milton-Edwards, 1996: 61-2). They focused on welfare and local politics, participating in municipal and national elections, and winning parliamentary seats for Hebron and Nablus. They catered for the estimated 400,000 newly-arrived refugees (UN estimate, quoted in Tessler, 1994: 279-80; Cohen, 1982: 163-4). But following the Jordanian Brotherhood's decision to be a 'loyal opposition' to the King, they subjugated calls for the liberation of Palestine to the King's agenda, focusing more on anti-imperialist and moralist themes, although they did champion some specifically Palestinian issues such as the the right of return for refugees (Milton-Edwards, 1996: 59; Cohen, 1982: 179, 206-8). This subjugation was facilitated by the dominance of members of the traditional elite in the organisation who, unlike the predominantly lower middle class Gazan leadership, had a greater stake in preserving the *status quo*.[3] This, and the Brotherhood's record of toeing the King's line, was to deeply affect their re-emergence in the aftermath of the 1967 Arab-Israeli war.

The re-emergence of the Palestinian Muslim Brotherhood

The Six-Day war of 1967 profoundly changed the political opportunity structure facing the Palestinian Brotherhood. Gaza and the

---

3 Compare the notables listed by Cohen for the West Bank with the list of predominantly (lower) middle class teachers listed by Milton-Edwards for Gaza, although Cohen also lists non-notables and the Gazan branch included notables such as Shaykh Hashim al-Khozondar and members of the Qeshawi family (Cohen, 1982: 162-6; Milton-Edwards, 1996: 43-5, 62-3; M. Rantisi, Gazan research assistant, pers. comm., 2006).

West Bank were re-united under one sovereign power, facilitating the emergence of an indigenous, territories-wide Palestinian leadership. Arab Nationalism was discredited as the scope of the Arab defeat sank in, creating space for the re-emergence of both Palestinian nationalism and Islamism. Meanwhile, the partial integration of Gaza and the West Bank into the Israeli economy triggered a socio-economic revolution which weakened the traditional class of notables, accelerated the emergence of a new counter elite, and resulted in the strengthening of civil society which became the central site for political contestation (Robinson, 1997: 8-37; Younis, 2000: 148-50; Sahliyeh, 1988: 42-9).[4]

The re-emergence of the Palestinian Muslim Brotherhood, and the way it happened, was to a large extent a function of this changing political opportunity structure. Both the new nationalist factions and the nascent Brotherhood were dominated by the emerging counter elite. But the nationalists, led by Arafat's Fatah, had a head start. They had emerged in exile during the 1950s and 1960s and had been able to recruit and network among the Palestinian Diaspora and its regional allies, while the Gazan Brotherhood was being suppressed, and the West Bank branches were pre-occupied by Jordanian politics. The 1967 Arab defeat allowed the nationalists to take centre-stage, and continue the resistance against Israel through guerrilla attacks across the river Jordan, and from within the Gaza Strip. By 1969, the various nationalist and Marxist-nationalist factions had succeeded in taking over the, until then, elite-dominated Palestine Liberation Organisation (PLO) which provided them with an over-arching organisational structure, legitimacy and, ultimately, the foundation for building a state-in-exile. They were briefly set back by their forceful eviction from Jordan, and by the Israeli army's success in suppressing the Gazan insurrection in the early 1970s. But in 1974, the PLO was recognised by the Arab League as the sole, legitimate representative of the Palestinians, and by 1976, it had succeeded in winning over sufficient allies inside the territories to defeat the traditional elite in municipal elections (Sayigh, 1997: 195-216; Sahliyeh, 1988:

---

4   Cf. also Roy, 1995b: 136-50, 263-87; World Bank, 1993a: 15, 26; World Bank, 1993b: xiv.

42-86). In this, they were aided by the socio-economic changes that had swept the territories, resulting in the transformation of a largely peasant economy into an economy dominated by wage labourers who were far less dependent on the patronage of the traditional elite (cf. Younis, 2000: 148-53).

That the Brotherhood re-emerged as a modest charitable network, rather than a political faction, was a function of its relative weakness vis-à-vis the nationalists. Islamism was only just beginning to regain ground regionally. The Egyptian Muslim Brotherhood had only begun to re-emerge in the early 1970s, following Nasser's death. Saudi Arabia had not yet benefited from the rise in oil prices in 1973, and the Islamic revolution in Iran would not come until 1979.

Locally, the political arena was dominated by the power struggle between the traditional elite, the nascent nationalists and the resurgent Communist Party. The Brotherhood was in no position to compete. In Gaza, it had no organisational structure, and in the West Bank, its leadership was in disarray, having been severed from its headquarters in Jordan. Civil society, however, was not saturated with social movement organisations. While the traditional elite's hold over civil society was weakening, the only faction seriously engaged in local institution-building was the Communist Party. Fatah and the PLO's leftist factions (chiefly the PFLP and the DFLP) were still too pre-occupied elsewhere, and it was not until the late 1970s that they began to invest in institution-building inside the territories (Sahliyeh, 1988: 98-107; Sayigh, 1997: 470-84).

The Brotherhood stepped into this gap, facilitated by the rapid growth in national disposable income, and the increasing pool of available activists. In 1973, under the leadership of school teacher Ahmad Yassin, and a number of recently graduated students from the lower middle classes it founded what was to become the hub of the Gazan Brotherhood, al-Mujamma' al-Islami (Islamic Centre), to be followed in 1976 by al-Jam'iyyah al-Islam'iyyah (Islamic Association), both of which focused on educational, social and welfare activities in areas neglected by others: refugee camps and poor urban quarters. In 1981, the Mujamma' helped to create al-Jam'iyyah al-Jam'iyyat al-Shabbat al-Muslimat (Young Women's Islamic Association), laying the foundations for the popularity Hamas was later to enjoy among women

(Milton-Edwards, 1996: 94-102, 25-7; Mishal and Sela, 2000: 19-20).

Leaving aside the presence of charismatic leaders such as Yassin, the fact that the Brotherhood re-emerged faster and stronger in Gaza than in the West Bank was similarly influenced by socio-economic, ideological and political factors. The Brotherhood's main institutional competitor, the Communist Party, was much weaker in Gaza than in the West Bank (Sayigh, 1997: 476)—as were the nationalists, leaving more space for an alternative ideology to develop. Gaza offered a much more conducive combination of urbanisation (which, across the Middle East, has been one factor behind the emergence of Islamism; cf. Robinson, 1997: 132-6; Zubaida, 1989: 155-62; Saad-Ghorayeb, 2003; Kepel, 2002: 65-9), concentrated poverty, an emerging lower middle class, and conservative culture for the Brotherhood's activist approach to Islam to flourish.[5] Its greater population density and smaller geographical spread also made it easier to concentrate resources.

The Gazan Brothers were better prepared for activism under occupation than their West Bank counterparts. Not only did they have more experience of operating clandestinely but they had never been subservient to a larger sister organisation as had been the case in the West Bank. Because Gaza had not been integrated into Egypt, Gazans generally were also better accustomed to operating in a specifically Palestinian framework (Younis, 2000: 103-4), facilitating the convergence of nationalist and Islamist themes. The West Bank branches had been used to privilege pan-Islamic over specifically Palestinian themes, and their leadership was too wedded to the *status quo* to know how to adapt quickly to the new situation (Milton-Edwards, 1996: 84-90; Cohen, 1982: 154, 78-208). The Gazan Brotherhood was moreover dominated by the lower middle classes, which meant that they were both less caught up in the power struggle between the nationalists and the traditional elite, and abler, and more determined, to branch out into the poorer areas of the Gaza Strip, building on the record of their predecessors.

---

5   Gaza had, for instance, undergone further 'proletarianisation' than the West Bank (cf. Graham-Brown, 1984: 241-2).

The Brotherhood's entry into politics in the late 1970s can similarly be partially explained by changes in the political opportunity structure. It was facilitated by the organisation's rapid institutional growth, the shift away from municipal politics to new arenas of political contestation, and the growing power struggle between Fatah and the Palestinian Left. By the late 1970s, the Brotherhood had established itself as a notable civil society actor. By 1981, its Mujamma' charity was in a position to help rebuild over a thousand homes damaged by a storm, and the Brotherhood had come to control the Islamic University in Gaza (Mishal and Sela, 2000: 20, 3-4; Milton-Edwards, 1996: 108-10).[6] Its overall membership had grown exponentially, facilitated by ongoing socio-economic changes.

Similar socio-economic changes had occurred across the Middle East, enhancing the pool of activists and resources available to Islamist movements elsewhere. Of particular importance was the effect of the re-emergence of the Egyptian Muslim Brotherhood and its more radical offshoots on the many Palestinian students (particularly from Gaza) who went to study in Egypt during the early 1970s (Tamimi, 2006: 22-9). The phenomenal increase in oil prices following the 1973 oil boycott meanwhile enabled Saudi Arabia and other Gulf states to fund Islamists, including the Palestinian Brotherhood, in a bid to counter the influence of the (more secular) leaderships of Syria, Iraq, Egypt, and the PLO (cf. Cleveland, 1994: 383).[7] In 1979, Islamism was given a further boost by the Islamic revolution in Iran and the Muslim response to the Soviet invasion of Afghanistan (cf. Sahliyeh, 1988: 141). The regional resurgence of Islamism was reflected in a surge in mosque-building inside the occupied territories, and increasing levels of religiosity, particularly among the expanding student population (cf. Robinson, 1997: 136; Sahliyeh, 1988: 144-7; Shadid, 1988: 662-3; Barghouti, 1991).

---

6 The Brotherhood's 'take-over' of the university was, however, not as dramatic as these accounts suggest, since the nationalists had never fully controlled it (Jensen, 1998: 203; Gunning, 2000: 119-27).

7 The links forged between Saudi and other Gulf nationals, and Egyptian and Palestinian Muslim Brothers during the latter's exile following Nasser's clampdown, were important in channelling money into Brotherhood projects inside Palestine.

By the late 1970s, the focus of political factions had begun to shift from municipal politics to the professional and student unions. The rapid increase in disposable income and population numbers had fuelled the establishment of a university sector. Within a decade, the occupied territories went from having no local universities to having six. The Communist Party had concentrated its efforts on expanding professional, student and trade union organisations. When the PLO shifted focus to civil society organisations inside the occupied territories, these unions became the primary focus of political contestation. This shift was accelerated by the rise of the Likud in Israel, and its strategy of weakening the PLO by decapitating its local political leadership and suspending municipal elections, until then the main focus of politics (Robinson, 1997: 21-2; Hiltermann, 1991: 47-53; Sahliyeh, 1988: 63-86, 98-107, 20-33).

The emergence of this new arena of political contestation created new opportunities for the Brotherhood. Many students were of lower class origins and had grown up in the more conservative urban areas, the villages or refugee camps. The Brotherhood's religious focus appealed to them, as did their greater institutional presence. But so did the lack of any concrete successes by the PLO, especially following Egypt's 1978-9 decision to make peace with Israel which left the PLO sidelined. Secular Palestinian nationalism had failed to deliver, despite a decade of dominance, and Fatah's decision to opt for a two-state solution and explore diplomatic channels was beginning to be resented. The Brotherhood, with its insistence on a one-state solution, a return to Islam and on meeting people's local social and communal needs (Sahliyeh, 1988: 148-51), could capitalise on this discontent.

The Brotherhood's resurgence was helped by the Likud's increasingly explicit religious claims to the West Bank and Gaza (compared to its secular predecessor, the Labour Party), and the rapid expansion of Jewish settlements, particularly of religiously-inspired settlements, rendering Fatah's lack of success more glaring, and increasing the appeal of a religious response (Mishal and Sela, 2000: 26; Sahliyeh, 1988: 40-1); Hroub disputes this claim, 2000:32). It was also helped by the Likud's attempts at fostering an alternative Palestinian leadership. While nationalists were deported or imprisoned, Brotherhood activists could act with relative impunity. State funds were channelled into mosques and religious schools, and the Brotherhood's institutions found fewer obstacles in their way (Sahliyeh, 1988: 81-5; Sayigh, 1997: 483-4; Milton-Edwards, 1996: 124, 8-9).[8] Another factor was the rivalry between the PLO and Jordan, and the Brotherhood's long-standing links with the pro-Jordanian elite in the West Bank (cf. Jensen, 1998: 203; Abu-Amr, 1994: 14; Turk, 1998). The decision to unite the two separate Brotherhood branches in Gaza and the West Bank under one umbrella with the Jordanian branch further consolidated the Brotherhood's position (Tamimi, 2006: 40-1).

By 1980-1, the Brotherhood briefly eclipsed Fatah, winning eight of the ten student union elections that year (Sahliyeh, 1988: 145; Abu-Amr, 1994: 17). In Gaza, it continued to dominate student politics throughout the 1980s. In the West Bank, it typically gained no more than a third of the vote, after the various PLO factions united against it following its early electoral success in 1980-1 (Robinson, 1997: 23-5). The emergence of Hamas was in part a direct outcome of this continuing rivalry between the Muslim Brotherhood and the other factions.

The emergence of Hamas

Hamas' establishment at the start of the 1987 Intifada (uprising) was similarly driven by the convergence of a series of socio-economic and political changes. The traditional elite continued to be eclipsed by the newly emerged, and still expanding, lower middle classes. However, the expectations raised by the economic growth of the 1970s were eroded by the recession of the 1980s, Israel's policy of de-development vis-à-vis the territories, and growing economic pressures arising from the expansion of Israeli settlements in the West Bank and Gaza, and the limits imposed on Palestinian agricultural produce to protect Israel's economy (Sayigh, 1997: 607-8, 10; McDowall, 1989: 112; Kimmerling and Migdal, 1994: 259-61; Roy, 1995b: 117-287). Society as a whole was affected. But it particularly affected university

---

8   This was more so following the Likud's 1977 rise to power. For instance, the Brotherhood's first Gazan charity, the Mujamma', established in 1973, was refused a permit until much later – 1982 according to its director (Shamma', 2006); 1978 following Mishal and Sela (19-20).

graduates who made up the bulk of activists for all political factions. Those entering university in the 1970s could expect to find jobs after graduation, and improve their family's living conditions. From the mid-1980s, only 20 per cent of school-leavers and university graduates found jobs, and many had to accept being un(der)-employed (Sayigh, 1997: 608). Such a situation, of frustrated rising expectations and an acute sense of status inconsistency stemming from graduates remaining un- or under-employed, has been found elsewhere to provide fertile ground for political violence (Davies, 1975; Gurr, 1975)—although not on its own (cf. Piven and Cloward, 1977: 208; Lia and Skølberg, 2005; Krueger and Malečková, 2003).

The sharp drop in job opportunities combined with continuing population growth. By 1987, around half the population was less than fourteen years old (Adlakha, Kinsella and Khawaja, 1995; F. R. Hunter, 1991: 52). Though such 'youth bulges' similarly do not inevitably lead to political violence, they do increase the opportunities of such a process occurring (Urdal, 2006; Goldstone, 2002). In the occupied territories, the increasing percentage of youth, and in particular of educated youth—by 1987, student numbers had reached 20,000 inside the territories alone (Robinson, 1997: 21), most of which came from lower socio-economic backgrounds, had lesser stakes in the *status quo*, and thus were more open to the increasingly radical tactics proposed by the nationalist factions—coincided not only with recession, but with an increasingly violent contestation between Palestinian factions, increasingly brutal occupation tactics, the forced removal of a more experienced leadership, and an increasing belief that the territories had been abandoned by the external leadership.

The Brotherhood's success in the 1980-1 student elections set in motion a decade of violent clashes between the PLO's factions and the Brotherhood, hardening activists on both sides (cf. Milton-Edwards, 1996: 108-16, 32-9; contrary to Milton-Edwards' and other accounts, the nationalists were not just victims but also instigators of violence; cf. Gunning, 2000: 113-41). The Likud's decapitation policy meanwhile had resulted in the removal of the older PLO cadres, enabling a younger, more militant leadership to emerge, many of whom had been radicalised by the clashes between the nationalists and the Israeli army in the late 1970s and early 1980s, and by their time spent in Israeli prisons (Frisch, 1993; Robinson, 1997: 22; Sayigh, 1997: 608-10). The introduction of 'Iron Fist' policies by the Israeli government in 1982 and 1985 further radicalised activists while the relative quiet in between allowed the building of semi-legal support networks which served to mobilise thousands of activists who might not have joined the clandestine factions, and were vital in later sustaining the general population during the Intifada. It was this younger, radicalised leadership that was involved in the clashes between the PLO and the Brotherhood and that, from 1987 onwards, led the Intifada. In this, they were spurred on by the belief, following the PLO's ignominious defeat in Lebanon in the early 1980s that liberation would only come through armed struggle within the territories (Sayigh, 1997: 608-10; Tessler, 1994: 554-68, 684-6; Smith, 1992: 293; Hiltermann, 1991: 173ff).

The Brotherhood's decision to create Hamas must be seen against this background. The passing of the initiative from the outside PLO leadership to local cadres created both opportunities and pressures. Already in the early 1980s, the Brotherhood had been rocked by the creation of Islamic Jihad, a militant Islamist break-away faction that challenged the Brotherhood's refusal to join the resistance (Hroub, 2000: 32-6; Milton-Edwards, 1996: 116-23). The Brotherhood's policy of not engaging in resistance had its roots in the events of the 1950s and 60s when both the Gazan and West Bank branches, for different reasons, had decided to focus on social and political activities. This position had hardened over the years due to a combination of political rivalries with the nationalist camp, ideological justifications (that resistance was futile unless society had been fortified by a return to Islam), and the Brotherhood's initial lack of institutional strength. The creation of Islamic Jihad challenged the Brotherhood's position.

The wider process of radicalisation had similarly begun to undermine the Brotherhood's position, as its activities were eclipsed by the feats of nationalist, and Islamic Jihad, activists. The situation became worse when the PLO's factions buried their differences (briefly) in April 1987. On the eve of the Intifada, both Fatah and Islamic Jihad were making inroads even in the Islamic University, the Brotherhood's stronghold, gaining 650 and 200 votes respectively of the 1650 votes cast in the 1987 elections (Abu-Amr, 1994: 17; Sahliyeh, 1988: 133). By the time the Intifada broke out in December 1987, there was thus a real chance of the Brotherhood becoming marginalised. Internal pressures also played a part. The Brotherhood's membership had become increasingly dominated by young activists of a lower class background—even in the West Bank, where the organisation's policy of targeting students from lower (middle) class backgrounds had paid dividends (Robinson, 1997: 137, 44-5). Overshadowing the Brotherhood's other key constituency, the quietist, socially conservative supporters of (often) rural descent (a high proportion of which were women), these young (male) activists had experienced many of the same pressures their nationalist counterparts had, and were subject to the same forces that were facilitating the emergence of a national(ist) consciousness. Many were from refugee camps that had formerly been Arab nationalist strongholds (Robinson, 1997: 145) and from 1981 onwards, when nationalist demonstrations reached a new level of intensity, (some) Brotherhood activists had begun to participate in nationalist demonstrations (Hroub, 2000: 33-6; Mishal and Sela, 2000: 33-4).

The PLO's defeat in Lebanon had created an opening in the wider opportunity structure. Suddenly, the Brotherhood could envisage a future where the PLO might be eclipsed by an 'Islamist-nationalist' resistance (Mishal and Sela, 2000: 33-4). They were simultaneously pushed in this direction by the radicalisation of their own members and the competition their younger members experienced from the nationalists. The combination of these external opportunities and internal pressures led elements of the leadership to begin discussing, and preparing for, armed struggle from 1983 onwards. By the mid-1980s, a few militant cells had been set up although, officially, the Brotherhood still opposed resistance (Hroub, 2000: 33-6; Mishal and Sela, 2000: 33-4; Levitt, 2006: 31). Despite greater grassroots participation—the Brotherhood had (re-)introduced internal elections in the late 1970s/early 1980s,[9] although it had yet to develop the elaborate consultation mechanisms that Hamas adopted in the

---

9   Al-Rantisi (2002a) and Abu Shannab (1998d) dated the introduction of elections to 1983-4, Tamimi to 1978 (2007).

1990s—control of the organisation's agenda remained firmly in the hands of the older, more cautious leadership who did not wish to jeopardise the Brotherhood's social institutions, particularly in the West Bank, where the leadership was still more dominated by the pro-*status quo* middle classes (Robinson, 1997: 145).

When Hamas was established, it was pushed through by a coalition of the more militant among the older leadership, chief among them Yassin, and representatives of the (younger) generation who had been instrumental in re-launching the Brotherhood in the 1970s. This younger leadership carried the support of the student and youth leadership—but not that of the more conservative leaders. The result was a compromise: the younger leadership was given the go-ahead to establish a dedicated resistance wing, as long as it was separate from the Muslim Brotherhood (Robinson, 1997: 144-50; Sayigh, 1997: 630; Abu-Amr, 1994: 63-5).

The Brotherhood's turn to violent resistance was facilitated by the fact that it had done so before. The shift, from prioritising Islamic revival to privileging armed struggle, was made both imperative and possible by the fact that it resonated more closely with the life experience of the Brotherhood's changing constituency.

The Brotherhood's shift from a pan-Islamic emphasis with patriotic overtones to a specifically Palestinian nationalist focus was similarly assisted by the presence of patriotic themes in the Brotherhood's ideological repertoire since its inception (cf. Litvak, 1996). However, as with the shift towards armed struggle, it was facilitated by changes in the Brotherhood's constituency and the wider socioeconomic political changes affecting it. Many of the changes occurring during the 1970s and 1980s, from the expansion of universities to the shift towards wage labour in Israel, and the expansion of trade unions and ideological factions, had worked together to break down class and geographical barriers, facilitating the emergence of a national consciousness which (partially) replaced the geographical, clan and class loyalties that had preceded it.[10] The shared experience

---

10 Cf. the emphasis in nationalism studies on the role of socio-economic changes wrought by industrialisation and modernisation (for a critical overview, cf. Özkirimli, 2000).

of occupation, curfews and collective punishment accelerated this process as did the rapid expansion of Israeli settlements, competition over water resources, attacks on religious sites, and public calls for the transfer of Palestinians out of Palestine, which made Palestinians fear that both their land and identity were under threat. The proliferation of newspapers similarly played a part, as did the fact that economic grievances were subsumed by the struggle between Israelis and Palestinians, particularly for those working inside Israel (Sahliyeh, 1988: 7, 40, 69, 105; Younis, 2000: 155; Kimmerling and Migdal, 1994: 253; Tessler, 1994: 562-3, 679-80).

Hamas' evolution

The establishment of Hamas had a profound impact on the evolution of the Islamic movement as a whole. Within years, Hamas had eclipsed the Muslim Brotherhood as the central Islamist political actor. Its leaders became the leaders of the Islamic movement, inheriting the movement's welfare network, and the more conservative among the Brotherhood leadership receded into the background.[11] With the creation, for practical reasons, of a two-tier system of Hamas activists and full-blown Brotherhood members, aspiring members were no longer required to undergo as arduous an ideological training as Brotherhood members had had to complete ('Muhammad', 1998; Hamas Cell, 1998a; Tamimi, 2007),[12] facilitating the gradual influx of an ideologically more heterogeneous membership.

This process was accelerated when Fatah committed itself to the US-led peace process in 1991. With the Left weakened by internal divisions, waning grassroots support, and the collapse of the Soviet Union (Sayigh, 1997: 643-50; Younis, 2000: 155), Hamas became the faction of choice for those opposed to the peace process—even if

---

11 Both Yunis al-Jarro' (PFLP-affiliated lawyer; 1998) and, more implicitly, Yusuf 'Abd al-Haq (PFLP-affiliated lecturer al-Najah University; 1998) linked Hamas' pragmatic turn to the receding influence of more conservative, dogmatic Brothers. Robinson similarly described Hamas' creation as a coup by younger leaders who prioritised politics over morality (Robinson, 1997: 149).

12 Cf. also fears of older leadership (Sayigh, 1997: 630).

they did not wholly subscribe to the Brotherhood's ideological programme. By the mid-1990s, Hamas' constituency had become both broader and more heterogeneous than the Brotherhood's had been prior to the Intifada.

Heterogenisation and the difficulties inherent in operating a widely dispersed, clandestine organisation facilitated the evolution of a more consultative political culture. The tumultuous creation of Hamas in 1987 had brought home the need for greater internal consultation. The incarceration of much of Hamas' senior leadership in the late 1980s, and the deportation of 415 Islamist leaders in 1992, similarly emphasised the need for developing mechanisms for maintaining contact with a dispersed leadership while preserving unity (Mishal and Sela, 2000: 56-9, 64-5, 160-7).

In response to these pressures and to safeguard against 'decapitation', the organisation was restructured. The political, social and resistance wings were separated (although the charities had always been somewhat autonomous, as they included non-members in their advisory boards). In 1991-2, the 'Izz al-Din al-Qassam Brigades were established, and by then, a leadership structure had been created in the Diaspora, initially under the umbrella of the joint Palestinian-Jordanian Brotherhood, to ensure continuity when the internal leadership was in prison (Mishal and Sela, 2000: 58-9, 64-5, 160-7; Tamimi, 2007).

One of the tasks of this external leadership, initially led by Musa Abu Marzuq and later Khalid Mish'al, was to expand Hamas' embryonic regional network, built on the Brotherhood network, for raising funds for the resistance. Its success in doing so increased the tensions between the internal and external leaderships as the latter came to *de facto* control the Qassam Brigades through their control over funding. Unlike the internal leadership, the external leaders neither suffered the consequences of resistance inside the territories, nor did they have to consider the response of Hamas' wider constituency, allowing them to be more militant than the inside leadership. Militancy, through control of the Brigades, also became a tool to prevent marginalisation by the internal leadership. These tensions became especially acute during the 1995-6 attempts at rapprochement between the internal leadership and the newly-established

Palestinian Authority, and the internal debate over whether or not to participate in the 1996 legislative elections (Mishal and Sela, 2000: 75-81; Klein, 1996: 124-5).

The relationship between the internal and external leaderships was further complicated by the increasing autonomy of the Qassam Brigades. Established with the specific purpose to prevent detection, the Brigades were highly decentralised. Already during the first Intifada, this created tensions when individual cells carried out actions without authorisation from the leadership (Mishal and Sela, 2000: 159-60)— particularly against suspected collaborators (Abu Shannab, 1998d).

Hamas' internal heterogenisation strengthened the organisation, by enhancing its capacity to gain support from a larger section of society. But it also served to weaken it. For much of the 1990s, Hamas was embroiled in internal debates over its future, which limited its ability to act decisively. By the mid-1990s, a number of internal fissures had become apparent, chief among them those between the internal and external leaderships, and between the political and 'paramilitary' leaderships. A third tension was between members of the political wing, who disagreed over how Hamas should proceed vis-à-vis the PA, and which aspects of its ideological programme to prioritise. A fourth tension was between different cells within the Qassam Brigades (Robinson, 1997: 192-5).

More broadly, Hamas' political fortunes were affected by changes in the wider political opportunity structure. As Hamas became more adept at carrying out resistance activities during the first Intifada, its political influence increased. By the time Fatah embarked on the Madrid peace process, in the wake of the 1991 Gulf war, Hamas had become a formidable opponent. Its position was greatly enhanced by its deft handling of the Gulf crisis. Unlike Fatah, which unequivocally sided with Saddam Hussein, Hamas both condemned Hussein's invasion of Kuwait (with a nod to its Gulf state sponsors) and condemned the US's offensive against Hussein (with a nod to its grassroots constituency). While Fatah lost the financial support of its Gulf state sponsors, Hamas' financial support increased (Legrain, 1991; Mishal and Sela, 2000: 88-9).

Hamas was also strengthened by its newfound proximity to the PLO's Left. Reflecting both the greater heterogeneity and pragmatism within the organisation, and the weakened position of the Palestinian Left, and following a series of prison encounters which had led to a mutual re-appraisal, Hamas joined the Left's alliance against the peace process (Hroub, 2000: 119-25; Gunning, 2000: 324-9). Although in practice this alliance meant little, at a symbolic level it marked the entry of Hamas into mainstream Palestinian politics. Until then, Hamas had operated outside, and often in opposition to, the PLO. It had not been part of the United National Leadership of the Uprising which had orchestrated the PLO's strikes, and resistance activities, and had openly competed with it by declaring alternative strike days marking the Islamic calendar (Legrain, 1990: 183-5; Mishal and Sela, 2000: 53-5). On numerous occasions, activists from both sides had sought to disrupt the other's strikes, as the extent of a strike became a measure of political influence. When Hamas agreed to enter an alliance with its former foes (whom it had in the past described as 'forces of falsehood'),[13] and its former foes agreed to ally themselves to Hamas, this marked a watershed.

By 1992, Hamas was in a position to defeat Fatah electorally, repeatedly. In 1992, it won the elections for the Chambers of Commerce in Gaza, Hebron and even Ramallah, despite the latter being a Fatah stronghold and having a high proportion of Christian businesses. Fatah only narrowly achieved a victory in Nablus' Chamber of Commerce (by 3 per cent), and although it succeeded in winning elections for the engineers', physicians', and lawyers' associations in Gaza, it did so only by enlisting the support of the PLO's Left (Mishal and Sela, 2000: 90). In 1993, Hamas beat Fatah for the first time in the secular nationalist stronghold of Bir Zeit University, ending Fatah's sixteen-year dominance (Schad, 1994: 164). By 1993, Fatah, financially still vulnerable, faced the prospect of Hamas eclipsing it—which was one factor pushing Israel and Fatah into the Oslo process (Sayigh, 1997: 656-62; Robinson, 1997: 189; Tessler, 1994: 754-5 ; Beilin, 1999: 61-3, 81, 269-70; Usher, 1995b: 5-8). In this sense, the Oslo agreement was in part a response to Hamas' growing strength, and designed to enable Fatah to regain the up-

---

13 Cf. depiction of nationalist opponents in 1981 al-Najah student elections (*Falastin al-Muslimah*, Issue 6, March 1982: 20-4).

per hand. Hamas' opposition to the agreement, though ideologically motivated, must be seen in this context.

The establishment of a Fatah-led Palestinian Authority drastically changed local politics. It changed the balance of power within Fatah, as Arafat installed the cadres who had been with him in Tunis at the top of the Authority and systematically sidelined local Fatah leaders with a grassroots following (Amundsen and Ezbidi, 2004: 152-4; Robinson, 1997: 179-81; Roy, 1994: 86). It changed the balance of class power as the new Palestinian Authority forged alliances with members of the traditional elite to bolster its position vis-à-vis the grassroots, and bound the growing middle class to it through financial and employment incentives (Robinson, 1997: 178-9; Hilal and Khan, 2004: 94-7). And it changed the balance of power between Fatah and Hamas, providing the former institutions and funding that far outstripped what Hamas had access to.[14]

More broadly, the relationship between the PA and the general population was affected by the specific characteristics of the peace process and Arafat's entourage. The Oslo agreement had been brokered by a small elite, which, apart from Arafat, did not have a grassroots following. It was premised on Arafat being able to suppress domestic dissent, and implement whatever final status negotiations would result in, in return for being given international support to rule—or what Robinson has called a 'hegemonic peace' (Robinson, 2001; cf. also Robinson, 1997: 197-200; Roy, 2002). Given the power imbalance between Israel and the PA, and the reluctance of 'the Quartet' sponsoring the peace process (the United States, the European Union, Russia and the United Nations) to put pressure on Israel, it was unlikely that the PA would be able to wrest significant concessions from Israel. Yet what Israel was willing to offer—a fragmented Palestinian entity, divided up in 'cantons', separated by settlements, without sovereignty over Jerusalem, and with no right of return for the millions of Palestinian refugees—was unlikely to

---

14 Against an Israeli intelligence estimate putting Hamas' annual total budget at $10-20m in the late 1990s, the PA received $1,527m in donor funding alone between 1994-7 while its budget for 2000 was $1,363m (Roule, 2002: 17; United Nations, 2001: 22-3.

be acceptable to the majority of Palestinians, particularly once it became clear that the process would not usher in the economic 'miracle' promised by its proponents.

From the start, therefore, the logic of the peace process demanded that, in the absence of an immediately visible economic 'peace dividend', the PA be both sufficiently strong and sufficiently independent from popular support, to control its own population. International aid was the instrument by which the PA could lessen its dependence on grassroots support, creating a (quasi-)'rentier state' (Robinson, 1997: 198-200; Hanafi and Tabar, 2004).[15] The security forces were the instrument by which it could maintain control. By the late 1990s, an estimated 60,000 personnel were employed by over ten security services, providing a 'police'-to-population ratio of a staggering 1:150 (Hilal and Khan, 2004: 84). Despite its emphasis on elections, therefore, the peace process required an autocratic rather than a genuinely democratic regime, a dynamic which was reinforced by Arafat's autocratic leadership style and the absence of genuine competitors.

The establishment of the PA particularly affected the balance of power between (quasi-)state and civil society—with significant consequences for Hamas. Prior to its arrival, local state structures had been in the hands of the Israeli government, funded in part by Jordan. Most of the activities of the nationalist movement, meanwhile, had been limited to civil society. Although these activities had been conducted under the auspices, and often with the funding, of the PLO, local civil society actors had been relatively autonomous from the Tunis-based external PLO leadership. With the return of the PLO's leadership to the territories, and its acquisition of quasi-state structures in the areas under its control, the boundary between civil society and state began to blur (Giacaman, 1998). In addition, because much of the international aid was now channelled through the PA, funding for civil society organisations dropped drastically. What funding was still available, became increasingly concentrated in the hands of fewer, professionalised NGO actors. The result was a

---

15 A 'rentier state' does not primarily depend on raising taxes from its population, but has independent resources (such as oil, or international aid); for details, cf. Beblawi and Luciani, 1987.

weakening of civil society, and, because the new professional NGO actor was typically pro-peace and more connected to international aid circles than local civil society, grassroots support for the NGOs withered (Hanafi and Tabar, 2004; Hilal and Khan, 2004: 91-100).

Hamas' affiliated charities were the exception to this rule. Hamas affiliates were far less dependent on Western donors than the nationalist and leftist NGOs (although during the 1990s, a number of Hamas charities were funded by Western donors; Gunning, 2000: 217n53), and could thus maintain a greater level of autonomy vis-à-vis both the peace process and the PA. Hamas had developed a network that surpassed that of the other factions in both size and efficiency. In a field where corruption was rife, Hamas' charities had established a reputation of accountability and transparency, ensuring enduring grassroots support and donations. This reputation also facilitated enduring regional support, which itself was a function of regional rivalries and opposition to Fatah or the peace process. Because the PA, for fear of empowering local leaders, had decided not to use existing nationalist networks, instead opting to build a new parallel infrastructure (Hanafi and Tabar, 2004: 226-7), it remained inordinately dependent on the successful operation of Hamas' charities to complement its incomplete state institutions—a dependency which was exacerbated by the weakening of civil society and the worsening of the economy as a result of border closures (Roy, 2001: 98-103). A striking illustration of this dependency was Arafat's having to allow Hamas charities to re-open after having closed them at the behest of the Israeli government following a series of suicide operations by the Qassam Brigades in 1997 (Robinson, 2004: 128; Gunning, 2004: 244-5). Hamas' ability to continue expanding its grassroots support through its charitable network was a major factor in its eventual electoral victory in 2006 (Chapter 5).

Hamas' aptitude to continue to win student and professional union elections similarly took on added significance. Though Fatah sought to limit opposition, it could ill afford to end union elections or prevent the opposition from winning. Not only did the international sponsors of the peace process insist on expanding democracy inside the territories, but Fatah itself sought to legitimise its authority in the eyes of the Palestinians by invoking democracy.[16] In addition, union elections had been a well-established practice in the territories. Fatah's leadership, which had been in exile for decades, had to hold a careful balance between extending its control and maintaining local legitimacy. Though rich in symbolic capital, winning a union election brought little real power beyond the remit of the union. Fatah could thus afford to allow union elections to continue, and even to allow opposition factions to win.

In the absence of an alternative political arena for contesting Fatah, and given the vast discrepancy between the PA's security forces and the Qassam Brigades (60,000 vs. less than 1,000),[17] undermining the peace process through political violence against Israelis became a particularly attractive option. Hamas' decision to continue the armed struggle in spite of the Oslo agreement was in part driven by ideological opposition. But an additional factor was that this was a sure way to weaken Fatah (Usher, 1995a: 69-71). Fatah had staked its political future on the Oslo agreement. If Hamas could 'persuade' Israel to renege on its commitments—helped by Israel's own internal divisions, and the vulnerability of the peace camp to continued Palestinian violence (Kydd and Walter, 2002)—and limit the economic growth opportunities envisaged by the architects of Oslo, it would both undermine Fatah and, so it hoped, rally people around its resistance platform by demonstrating the futility of the peace process.[18]

Hamas' increasing resort to terrorist tactics, and in particular its adoption of suicide bombings from 1993 onwards (which typically led to border closures which negatively affected the Palestinian

---

16 Cf. also Savir's observation regarding the importance of Palestinian public opinion for the peace process (Savir, 1999: 34).

17 A special report in *The St. Petersburg Times* estimated in 2003 that it had 200-500 "hard-core members", although this was probably a conservative estimate ('Special Report: Terror Groups', *St. Petersburg Times*, St Petersburg, FL, http://www.sptimes.com/2003/webspecials03/alarian/terror.shtml).

18 Cf. similar developments at the end of protest cycles, following the 'cooptation' of the mainstream leadership by the *status quo* (della Porta, 1995a: 110-17; Ross and Gurr, 1989: 414-5; Piven and Cloward, 1977: 252-5).

economy), must be seen both in the context of this intra-Palestinian rivalry and its ideological opposition to the peace process. But these were not the only factors. The Intifada had had a radicalising effect on Hamas' members, as resistance and Israeli counter-insurgency tactics had fed off each other, becoming increasingly violent. By 1993, Hamas had 'professionalised' its resistance wing by separating it from its other wings. For security reasons, those involved in the resistance had become increasingly isolated from the rest of Hamas' infrastructure, as well as from each other. This exacerbated the process of radicalisation,[19] as did increasing economic hardship, expansion of settlements, and Israel's occupation policies. By 1993, moreover, helped by the expulsion of 415 Palestinian Islamist leaders to Lebanon in 1992 and the rapprochement between Iran and Hamas, Hamas had developed a closer working relationship with Hizballah, the pioneer of suicide tactics in the Middle East (Mishal and Sela, 2000: 65-6).

Although the regularisation of union elections, the convergence of opposition around Hamas candidates, the weakening of civil society and the vulnerability of the peace process to continued violence strengthened Hamas, the PA's arrival and the peace process ultimately limited Hamas' options. Despite disillusionment with the PA, increased Israeli settlement expansion, prolonged border closures and the absence of a clear economic 'peace dividend', opinion polls recorded high support for the peace process for much of the 1990s (CPRS Polls 1-48, 1993-2000). Hamas' violent opposition to the peace process thus had to be justified with reference to specific, clearly discernible flashpoints—the killing of thirty worshippers in a mosque, the assassination of a Hamas leader, prolonged border closures, the building of a controversial settlement (Bloom, 2005: 24; Hroub, 2000: 249 50). Because of the discrepancy between the security forces and Hamas' Qassam Brigades, maintaining public support (as measured in union elections and to a lesser extent in opinion polls) was paramount to Hamas' political survival. Lack of popular support for political violence was indeed one of the factors

---

19 Cf. the effect of isolation on the Italian Left's radical fringe (della Porta, 1995a: 134-8).

leading Hamas to focus on social and political activities towards the end of the 1990s, although the weakening of the Brigades also played a significant part (Roy, 2003: 296-301).

Under the PA's autocratic structures, and in the absence of municipal elections, Hamas lacked the opportunity to capitalise on its welfare network, or its electoral wins in student and professional elections. Throughout the 1990s, Hamas continued to score low in opinion polls, although actual support was arguably higher than the average of 18 per cent returned in the polls (Hroub, 2000: 229-33). Support in student and professional unions was much higher—in the West Bank, Hamas won more student elections than it lost in the main universities (Amayreh, 1999; Parry, 1999; Regular, 2004)—but this did not translate into actual power. The one opportunity to participate in national elections—the one-off 1996 legislative elections—Hamas decided, against strong internal opposition, to boycott, fearing both that participation would legitimise the peace process, and that the PA would not allow Hamas to win a significant share of the vote (Mishal and Sela, 2000: 119-38).

Hamas nevertheless scored two political 'victories' which helped lay the foundation for its subsequent rise to prominence. Support for suicide bombing increased from around 20 per cent in the mid-1990s, to some 40 per cent in the late 1990s, and disillusionment with the Oslo peace process, if not with the idea of a peace process, rose to the point that only a third of respondents to polls conducted in 1999-2000 believed that a final settlement was possible within the Oslo framework (CPRS Polls 40-48, 1999-2000). In both these cases, Hamas could only take part of the 'credit'. Israeli border closures, controversial settlement expansions and lack of progress in the peace process, coupled with PA corruption and lack of Palestinian leadership, had similarly contributed to this state of affairs.

The al-Aqsa Intifada and Hamas' electoral victory

Hamas' victory in the 2006 legislative elections was the outcome of a changed political opportunity structure. Fatah had been weakened by a number of factors. Corruption, nepotism and an autocratic style of governing meant that by the end of the 1990s, the PA had lost much of the popular goodwill it had received upon its arrival (CPRS Poll 40, 1999). The Oslo process, meanwhile, had become thoroughly discredited, further undermining Fatah's authority. Not only had it not brought the promised prosperity—by 2000, many believed themselves worse off economically after Oslo than before (CPRS Poll 48, 2000)—it had also not appeared to lay the foundations for a credible two-state solution. Between 1994 and 2000, the number of Israelis settling in the occupied territories had tripled, while the Israeli government had confiscated land worth over $1 billion to facilitate the expansion and accessibility of Israeli settlements (Rabbani, 2001: 76; Roy, 2001: 95). Unemployment, meanwhile, had increased nine-fold between 1992 and 1996, while the Gross National Product had decreased by 18 per cent (Roy, 2001: 91-2). There was a brief upsurge in the economy towards the end of the 1990s. But by mid-2000, approximately one in five Palestinians lived below the 'poverty line', defined as "a household with two adults and four children with a yearly consumption of less than $2.10 per day" (91, 95, 101).

The al-Aqsa Intifada which began in September 2000 further weakened Fatah. It allowed internal tensions to re-emerge as the sidelined grassroots cadres of the first Intifada regained centre-stage (Robinson, 2001: 121-3). It contributed to Arafat's marginalisation, and, following his death, to the high levels of disunity within the movement, which was one of the factors behind Fatah's 2006 election loss (Chapter 5). But it also resulted in a weakening of the PA's infrastructure, as Israel began targeting the PA's security services and withholding Israeli-controlled revenue income in response to Palestinian acts of resistance (Roy, 2007: 266-7; Bickerton and Klausner, 2007: 346-7, 51). This, and the increasing levels of lawlessness that resulted from the deterioration of the security services, the spread of weapons and the emergence of clan militias and armed gangs, further undermined people's faith in the PA, and in Fatah's ability to re-establish law and order, or improve its service record.

Hamas, meanwhile, benefited directly from the al-Aqsa Intifada. Not only did the Intifada allow it to carry out resistance activities with impunity, but it also enabled it to cement its place as one of the central political players. Where it had been in opposition to the PLO's leadership structures during the first Intifada, it was now an integral part of the popular resistance committees, and its tactics—such as suicide bombing—became the model for other groups, including Fatah's al-Aqsa Martyrs' Brigades. Popular opinion had begun to shift in favour of suicide operations, with opinion polls regularly returning figures of 70-80 per cent support (PRS Polls 2-15, 2001-5). Unlike the 1990s, when Hamas had to carefully calibrate its suicide operations, and justify them with reference to Israeli intransigencies, suicide operations had become a measure of political influence, and factions began to compete with each other in carrying out operations (Bloom, 2005: 29-31; Gupta and Mundra, 2005: 584; Hoffman and McCormick, 2004: 268-71). Israel's decision to assassinate Hamas' political leadership only served to increase the organisation's popular appeal, as mass funerals increased Hamas' visibility and public anger led to an increase in volunteers and political support (Gunning, 2007a: 141).

Hamas also profited directly from Fatah's internal power struggles. Under Arafat, Hamas' political influence was limited to the student and professional unions. The waning of Arafat's power, the PA's overall weakening and the increasing level of tensions within Fatah contributed to the latter's leadership decision to start negotiations with Hamas over entry into the PLO, and, more generally, into mainstream politics (Chapter 6). Fatah needed Hamas' participation to increase the system's legitimacy, while it could ill afford Hamas' continued opposition to the system, given the changed balance of power. Fatah's decision to hold municipal and legislative elections in 2005 was similarly driven by the need for greater legitimacy, and encouraged by the peace process's international sponsors (cf. Roadmap, 2003). This process was accelerated by the threat of Fatah's grassroots cadres, led by Marwan Barghouthi and the al-Aqsa Martyrs' Brigades, opening up parallel negotiations with Hamas.

This radically changed political opportunity structure strengthened the hands of those within Hamas who advocated electoral participation. Participation in the municipal elections was never in doubt, as Hamas had always argued that municipal elections were not part of the Oslo process (Hroub, 2000: 219). But the question of participation in the second legislative elections re-opened the debate preceding the 1996 elections. By now, however, the Oslo process was all but dead. Participation in the legislative elections could no longer be regarded as a legitimisation of Oslo. With Arafat gone, Fatah in disarray, and Hamas scoring only marginally less than Fatah in opinion polls, the chances of securing a significant percentage of the vote had increased drastically. At the time these discussions took place, regional support for continued resistance was moreover looking shakier than ever, with both Syria and Iran weakened by a variety of factors (although this would soon change for Iran; see Chapter 6). Unlike 1996, therefore, Hamas' 'politicos' and the more pragmatic among the 'radicals'—to borrow Irvin's terms to describe the IRA's internal dynamics (1999: 25-30)—won the debate against the absolutists among the 'radicals' and the hard-line 'ideologues'. Hamas' gains in the municipal elections in which it typically received a third of the vote only served to strengthen their hands.

Hamas' 2006 election victory was, however, also a function of longer-term socio-economic and structural changes. The socio-economic shifts of the 1970s had continued, although muted by the outbreak of the first Intifada and the economic downturn of the 1990s. Many of the lower middle classes continued to send their children to university—the number of university students more than doubled between 1994 and 1999 (Hilal and Khan, 2004: 92)—thus steadily increasing the pool of available activists. The 1990s furthermore saw the expansion of the middle classes. Yet, this expansion was not translated into autonomous political influence, as the middle classes became increasingly dependent on the PA (Hilal and Khan, 2004: 91-100).

By 2005-6, the PA's overall weakening enabled the middle and lower middle classes to express their resentment towards the PA more openly. Hamas, meanwhile, was in a position to offer a credible alternative, building on a record of efficiency and accountability, and a decade of relative autonomy from the PA. One of the factors shaping the 2004-6 elections was precisely the (lower) middle classes' opposition to the PA's monopolies policy, and a reaction to the effects of the PA's corruption and nepotism on their business opportunities (Selby, 2006; for background, see Hilal and Khan, 2004: 87-109). Even those who were less dependent on the PA because they received international aid directly resented the PA's repeated attempts to circumscribe their autonomy (Robinson, 2001: 119-20). Hamas could, and did, capitalise on this.

The failure of Oslo to halt Israeli settlements and improve the Palestinian economy had furthermore made Hamas' principled opposition to the peace process more popular. The al-Aqsa Intifada and Israel's subsequent 2005 withdrawal from the Gaza Strip had fuelled the belief—already on the rise since Israel's May 2000 withdrawal from Lebanon which Palestinians believed was the result of Hizballah's armed campaign—that violence was necessary to force Israel into concessions (PRS Polls 1-2, 2000-1; 17-8, 2005). Thus, Hamas could not just build on its social services record, but its resistance record was also seen by a significant number of Palestinians as having done more for Palestinian state-building than the peace process. Hamas' decision to abide by a ceasefire from early 2005 onwards meanwhile re-assured those in favour of a two-state solution that Hamas would not insist on continued resistance once a two-state solution acceptable to a majority of Palestinians had been achieved, enabling them to vote for Hamas for domestic reasons. Hamas' decision to downplay its long-term goal of total liberation in the lead-up to the elections facilitated this process (Chapter 5).

Hamas won the 2006 election in part because it succeeded in securing the vote of the middle and lower middle classes, well beyond its core Islamist and anti-peace process constituencies. Its ability to benefit from the above opportunities was enhanced by its social network, its newly acquired access to municipal institutions and the exposure this gave it to wider society. But it was also a function of its attitude towards consultation, and a decade of experience in securing electoral victories at union level amongst heterogeneous constituencies. Far more so than Fatah, Hamas focused its energy on canvassing people's opinions, and fine-tuning its election message accordingly (Chapter 5).

Concluding Remarks

A number of themes emerge from this brief overview, which inform this book's argument. First, Hamas is to a large extent a product of its environment. The timing of its emergence, where it emerged, and how it evolved can all in part be explained with reference to changes in the wider political opportunity structure. This is not to deny the role played by activists in affecting this opportunity structure and making the choices that they did. The Brotherhood's decision in the late 1970s/early 1980s to hold internal elections, for instance, was facilitated by external changes, such as the emergence of a university-educated, more autonomous lower middle class, and the introduction of elections in professional and student unions. But equally important was the leadership's decision to actively (re-)embrace this practice, rather than pandering to the more radical amongst the activists who, around that time, approvingly quoted the argument that "all attempts to reconcile, synthesise, or bring into harmony the notions of nationalism, socialism, capitalism, democracy and Islam, even if this is done in the name of Islam, must be rejected. The point of view of the Muslim world must be rooted in Islam alone."[20] Similarly, Oslo's failure was facilitated by Hamas' actions, although Israel's response to these actions, Fatah's lack of moral leadership, and contradictions within the process, also played their part. But Hamas' evolution cannot be fully understood outside the context of wider socio-economic and political changes.

Second, both in terms of the wider structures which have helped shape it, and its internal dynamics, Hamas is subject to a number of conflicting pressures. The tensions that emerged during the 1990s between internal and external, political and 'paramilitary', and different wings of the political leadership still haunt Hamas, and go some way in explaining why Hamas has been unable to act more decisively in the wake of its electoral victory. Similarly, a fundamental tension exists between Hamas' focus on institution-building and its commitment to armed struggle. At one level, the two reinforce each other, since both serve as recruiting agents and increase the organisation's overall political profile. At another level, though, they contradict each other, as presaged by the reluctance of the 1980s Brotherhood leadership to engage in armed struggle. In the same vein, Hamas'

---

20 Quoted from *Magazine Imam* [majallat imam] in 'Nationalism is the cause of the wounds of the Muslims', *Falastin al-Muslimah*, 1 December 1980, p. 4.

refusal to recognise Israel since coming to power in January 2006 has prevented it from honouring its domestic promises of increasing overall social welfare because of the international boycott that has been the response to its refusal.

Finally, if democratisation and social movement theories are to be believed (Chapters 1 & 7), Hamas' participation in electoral structures is likely to have affected its members' attitude to democracy. Repeated participation in social practices can induce a favourable disposition towards such practices, even if they have been entered for purely tactical reasons. Given that Hamas has participated in elections since before its inception, both internally and within the wider Palestinian arena, one can expect members to have been socialised, at least to some extent, into the principles of electoral competition and representative authority. However, since Hamas has simultaneously continued to be involved in political violence, which can similarly be expected to have had a socialising effect, there are likely to be tensions between its commitment to democracy, and its involvement in violence. Given its involvement in religious structures, and the conservative background of many of its activists, tension is also likely to exist between Hamas' commitment to democracy and commitment to its particular interpretation of Islam, although, as we will see, a commitment to Islam is one of the factors driving Hamas' commitment to democracy.

3

HAMAS' POLITICAL PHILOSOPHY

To make sense of Hamas' political practices we must understand how its members think about politics. Not only, as Light says, does "all policy reflects theory, whether or not that theory is articulated or recognized by those who make policy" (Light, 1988: 1) but, despite not having produced great philosophical tracts, Hamas is also a self-consciously ideological organisation which paints itself as the van-guard of the Islamic state it hopes to establish. Although pragmatic and confined by necessity and opportunity, its practice is nevertheless self-consciously informed by political theory.

Political theory informs both Hamas' utopian worldview, and its day-to-day decisions. What Hamas thinks to be the appropriate bal-ance between religious authority and authority derived from elections (representative authority) affects how it critiques Fatah, how it inter-acts with Palestinian society, and what position it takes on the peace process. Since its electoral victories in 2004-6 at both municipal and national level, how Hamas thinks about politics has become of even greater significance as it is now in a position to directly influence legislation and policy-making.

This chapter provides a rough outline of the Islamic state Hamas advocates, and what role religion and representation play in it. Key questions include what constitutes legitimate authority for Hamas? How does it conceptualise the relationship between the state and the individual? What state structures flow from its conception of authority? What role do revelation, *shari'ah* law and religious authorities play?

Neither Hamas nor its ideology are static. Both are affected by changes in the wider political opportunity structure. At the same time, certain ideological commitments have remained the same. Political theory, or ideology more broadly, is malleable, but not infinitely so. Political entrepreneurs can re-interpret it, over time. But once formulated, it constrains what political entrepreneurs can do with it.

The following is an analysis of attitudes observed during the period 1996-2006, as expressed in over sixty semi-structured interviews with Hamas leaders and members, innumerable informal conversations, and a selection of official publications. Although much has changed in the political opportunity structure in which Hamas operates, a number of fundamental aspects have remained the same. Hamas is still one of two dominant factions, dependent in part on wresting popular and electoral support from a secular Fatah with a reputation for corruption and autocratic behaviour. Its constituency is still a mixture of members of the lower and (lower) middle classes, with a high percentage of university graduates amongst its leadership, both of which factors are likely to affect its approach to politics. Religion still plays an important role in its identity, just as it does in society more generally. So does Hamas' ability to perpetrate violence. Regionally, a number of Islamist organisations are still practising electoral participation and, if anything, the rise of al-Qaeda-type splinter groups has pushed mainstream Islamist groups further into forging a synthesis between Islamist interpretations of Islam and democracy. It is thus not surprising that the rough outlines of Hamas' political theory have remained more or less the same—although the radically changed balance of power in Gaza since June 2007, and the loss of so many of Hamas' political founders to Israeli assassinations, may profoundly alter its future trajectory.

Hamas is not a monolithic organisation. Its constituency is relatively heterogeneous, with varying degrees of commitment to the project of creating an Islamic state, and varying interpretations of what this entails. Nevertheless, although much still remains to be determined, there are some principles, drawn from the Sunni traditions of Islam on which most agree. The following is my interpretation of what these are.

Structure of Hamas' utopian Islamic State

When Hamas talks about an Islamic state, what exactly does it mean? Although interviewees differed on details or indeed had not always fully thought them through, the general outline of such a state is agreed upon.

The government of the state Hamas advocates consists of an executive, a legislative and a judicial branch. Legislative power rests with a *Shura* (consultative) Council[1] whose members would be elected in regular elections which would be open to all citizens (including Christians, Jews, communists and secular Muslims).[2] Executive power rests with a government to be formed from the *Shura* Council but possibly including unelected technocrats and experts. Judicial power rests with judges and the law courts, and would be independent of the executive and legislative branches.[3] No member of any branch of government would be above the law while in office.

The principal source of legislation would be Islamic or *shari'ah* law. But, because Hamas recognises that the *shari'ah* is primarily a set of general principles, it acknowledges that it is not a sufficient source of law. Other legal systems and scientific knowledge would have to complement the *shari'ah*. A number of interviewees specifically emphasised that legislators would need to be familiar with Western legal traditions as well as Islamic law (cf. Abu Shannab, 1998d; Abu Zughri, 1998). Others implied it with their emphasis on needing to learn from all human experience (cf. Yassin, 1998a; Hamad, 1998a; Musa, 1998b; Bahr, 1998). Where the *shari'ah is* specific, as in the description of a penal code for offences such as theft or adultery (the *hudud*), the *shari'ah* would override all other concerns although it would not

---

1 Called variously *majlis al-shura* or *ahl al-shura* . Some took *majlis al-shura* to mean the Cabinet, others reserved it for the historical *shura* councils.

2 Only three interviewees did not adopt the principle of elections for all (Dukhan, 1998; one member of Women's Islamic Bloc II, 1998; Head Islamic Bloc al-Azhar, 1998).

3 I did not discuss the details of how judges were to be selected. However, a poll conducted by JMCC (May 1995) found that 54 per cent of Islamists polled believed judges should be elected, against 24 per cent advocating appointment by Parliament and 13 per cent advocating appointment by the President.

become law until legislated by the *Shura* Council, which would be expected to consult the general population before doing so. The *Shura* Council would be the ultimate authority on legislative issues. But its authority would be derived from having been elected, not primarily from having religious or other expert knowledge (see further).

In recognition of the fallible nature of human beings and the corrupting influence of power, Hamas proposes a number of checks and balances. It proposes regular elections to ensure that legislators and the government remain accountable to the electorate who must "watch over the performance of their representatives" (Musa, 1998b; cf. also Abu Shannab, 1999; Haniyyah, 1998a; Shamma', 1998; al-Bardawil, 1998).[4] It advocates a separation of power between the executive, legislative and judiciary branches and expects each branch to scrutinise the other two (cf. Yassin, 1998b; Abu Shannab, 1998c, 1998d; Musa, 1998b; Hizb al-Khalas, 1997a: 24-5, 1997b). If the executive branch has lost the trust of the *Shura* Council, the latter would have the right to disband the former following a (weighted) majority vote (Yassin, 1998b; Abu Shannab likened this to the American Presidential system which he called "close to the Islamic system"; Abu Shannab, 1998c).[5] If any member of the executive, legislative or judiciary branches is accused in a court of law, that member would have to undergo trial like any other citizen (cf. Yassin, 1998b; Bahr, 1998; Musa, 1998b; implied by Abu Shannab, 1998c). The notion of political immunity is condemned because those in power are believed to be particularly prone to power's corrupting influence (cf. Yassin, 1998b; Abu Shannab, 1998d; Haniyyah, 1998b; Musa, 1998b; Hizb al-Khalas, 1997b, 1997c).

---

4 Though frowning on self-nomination, particularly within Hamas (see Chapter 4), interviewees generally recognised that Islam's traditional condemnation of self-nomination as a manifestation of self-seeking egotism was unpractical in a modern state. In this, they break with earlier Islamist thinkers (cf. Maududi [Mawdudi], 1960b: 47; Maududi [Mawdudi], 1960a: 20-2, 36-7; al-Turabi, 1983: 248).

5 Cf. also the early Egyptian Brotherhood's argument that the *Majlis* "commands the obedience of both ruler and ruled" (Mitchell, 1993: 248).

Hamas proposes two further sets of checks and balances. One involves the establishment of a clear moral code for politicians and legislators derived from religion and the notion of piety. Politicians are thus expected to internalise the religious principles of their faith and lead by example (cf. Yassin, 1998b; Abu Shannab, 1998d; Bahr, 1998). The other check concerns the proliferation of political parties—although some believed, no doubt influenced by the experience of Palestinian politics, that this would promote partisanism, elite manipulation and civil strife (cf. al-Rantisi, 2002a; al-Zahhar, 1998a).[6] Those in favour argued that multi-partyism embodied the right of people to express their views freely (Hamad, 1998a; implied by Musa, 1998b; al-Na'ami, 1998) and, with a clear dig at Fatah, to hold government accountable (Hamas Cell, 1998c; implied by Taha, 1998). Others saw multi-partyism as a recognition of the inherent plurality of views in society (Abu Shannab, 1998c; Bahr, 1998). All, however, demanded that parties operating in an Islamic state, once it had been consented to by a majority, should not be allowed to actively undermine the Islamic basis of the state.

The two terms that sum up Hamas' approach to decision-making are *shura* (consultation) and *ijma'* (consensus). One of the conditions of legitimate authority in Hamas' Islamic state is that a leader consults the people. Hamas roots this in various Qur'anic injunctions where either the Prophet exhorts his followers to consult or God exhorts the Prophet to consult his companions. So significant does Hamas deem this command that it often calls its version of an Islamic state '*shura* democracy' (cf. Abu Shannab, 1998). It considers elections central to the consultative process, since elections are believed to guarantee "the freedom to choose ... the right of every individual to express their opinion" (Taha, 1998; cf. also Abu Shannab, 1999; al-Bardawil, 1998; Haniyyah, 1998a; Shamma', 1998; Musa, 1998b). But it also advocates that legislators and governors practise *shura* daily so as to remain in touch with what the general population

---

6   That interviewees generally supported multi-partyism is intriguing. Previous Islamist thinkers have condemned multi-partyism (cf. Maududi [Mawdudi], 1960b: 43-4). Hanf and Sabella (Hanf and Sabella, 1996: 121-6) found that 41 per cent of Islamist respondents to their survey in the occupied territories preferred a dominant party model.

thinks and feels. It is this *shura* model that informs much of Hamas' internal practice as well as its behaviour during the municipal and legislative elections.

Shura also underpins the process of creating an Islamic state. Interviewees emphasised that a genuine Islamic state cannot come into being through force—although all interviewees simultaneously argued that, in extreme situations, force might be necessary to remove dictators (which takes on added significance following the June 2007 events in Gaza).[7] An Islamic state must be 'willed' by the people, and can only come about if a clear majority support its establishment. If it is enforced, it ceases to be an Islamic state. For Hamas, an Islamic state promotes the three principles of freedom, equality and justice. If it is enforced, people are neither free nor equal, nor is it a just system. An Islamic state which is forcefully imposed by a minority is thus, at least in theory, a contradiction in terms. The preferred path towards such a state, therefore, is through a process of consultation, education and socialisation, creating the right conditions for people to voluntarily will this state. Here we begin to see one of the tensions that runs through much of Hamas' political theory, namely between respecting the popular will as a source of authority and seeking to educate the very same popular will into wishing for an Islamic state.

For Hamas, a decision is more likely to be 'right' if it is the product of consensus. This condition is similarly grounded in Islamic tradition, in particular in the promise by the Prophet that "my community shall never agree on an error" (Kamali, 1991: 178-9). The principle behind this notion is that, given humanity's fragmentary understanding of 'truth', the right decision is more likely to emerge

---

7   Abu Shannab's (1998c) qualified support for Turabi's Islamist coup in Sudan was typical. Asked to comment on the coup, he said: "It is not Islamic. [...] but you know, this is real life. If the military coup succeeded, in bringing Islam, I accept it ... if this is the only way. And if popular riots bring Islam, then it is Islam. But one important thing, we should notice, that Islam is a clean ideology, and also needs clean ways to achieve it. This way, you, we can criticise, the Sudanese system. [...] This is why we reject this kind of getting power. Shaykh Qaradawi spoke openly and on many occasions ... about this, saying: by doing this you encourage others to make a coup against you. ... So we do not need to encourage the wrong methods."

if all agree. Personal preferences and factional interests are believed to be less influential if a decision is arrived at through consensus-building. Over the centuries, scholars have debated who the Prophet meant when he said 'my community' (178-82). Most traditional scholars concluded that the Prophet only meant the community of Islamic scholars. Hamas breaks with this tradition and follows the interpretation of al-Shafiʻi (d. 820), founder of the school of law which forms the basis for the legal system in Gaza, who insisted that the Prophet had meant "the people at large" and not just the scholars (181). Because Hamas holds that 'the people at large' cannot be involved in the everyday deliberations of government, the burden of this command falls on the people's representatives.[8] For Hamas, 'my community' is therefore the elected legislature. Because consensus is seldom achieved, Hamas has interpreted the demand to mean achieving a majority. For significant or constitutional decisions, a weighted majority of two-thirds is demanded. For everyday decisions, a mere 50 per cent majority suffices. In both instances, full consensus remains the ideal.

Views differed on how elections should be conducted.[9] Some argued for a bottoms-up approach, with local communities electing their leaders who would in turn elect the national representatives (cf. Abu Shannab, 1998c; al-Rantisi, 2002a). Most argued for direct national elections (cf. Yassin, 1998b; Hamad, 1998a; Hamas Cell, 1998c; Bahr, 1998; Musa, 1998b; al-Naʻami, 1998).[10] A handful of ordinary members and student leaders argued for candidates to be

---

8 Representation for Hamas means both having a contractual relationship with one's constituency, and representing the different facets of society so that the representative body reflects 'the people' in both composition and their opinions (Abu Shannab, 1998c; cf. also Abu Shannab, 1999; al-Bardawil, 1998; Haniyyah, 1998a; Shammaʻ, 1998; Musa, 1998b). For discussion of representation in Western political theory, cf. Birch, 1993: 69-79.

9 Only a few ordinary student members ('Ahmad'; Women's Islamic Bloc II, 1998) wavered between elections and the notion of "someone wise in religion", "like Qaradawi", appointing an assembly.

10 Abu Zughri (1998) could be interpreted as either supporting national elections, or supporting the bottom-up approach. His main concern was that people did not nominate themselves.

vetted by a council of scholars to ensure that candidates had the right characteristics to maintain a truly Islamic system (one of Hamas and Khalas members, 1999; al-Masri, 1998; more ambivalently, 'Ashraf', 1998; Taha, 1998), but this view was not shared by any of the leadership, and roundly condemned by Abu Shannab (1998c) and Yassin (1998b).

Citizenship would be granted to all those who live in the Islamic state, regardless of religious affiliation. All citizens would have the right to vote, including women and non-Muslims. Women would have the right to run for the *Shura* Council and occupy ministerial posts. But, with the exception of two interviewees, one of whom has since been assassinated by Israel (Salim, 1998; Y. Hamdan, 1998),[11] all insisted that women could not be Head of State or Commander-in-Chief—with some arguing that women were physically unfit for the job, and others justifying their position with reference to a saying by the Prophet.

Interviewees disagreed over what rights non-Muslims would have. The majority held that non-Muslims, including lapsed Muslims who had become communists, had the right to stand for election, and occupy ministerial posts but that they did not have the right to become Head of State or Commander-in-Chief (Gunning, 2000: 285-99, 308-24).[12] They justified their position by appealing to the notion of inalienable human rights and argued that non-Muslims and Muslims alike had a right to participate in the political process. That Christians would be barred from the highest position was justified with the argument that the Head of State had to both represent the majority of the citizenry (at present, Palestinian Christians make up less than

11 Salim was assassinated on 31 July 2001.

12 Twenty-three of the thirty-six I interviewed regarding Christians advocated this position, including Abu Shannab, Haniyyah, al-Zahhar, Shamma', Bahr and Hamad. Yassin argued for a separate Christian assembly. Dukhan believed this to be unnecessary. Thirteen of the nineteen I interviewed regarding communists advocated the same, including Abu Shannab, Shamma', Hamad. Though I did not discuss this issue with Haniyyah, his logic concerning Christians suggests he would belong to this group. Dukhan, Bahr and Musa argued against communists participating in the legislative process.

2.5 per cent of the population) and defend the Islamic nature of the state. A minority, including Yassin (1998b), advocated a return to a modernised version of the traditional *dhimmi* model according to which Jews and Christians are treated as separate political communities, with their own representatives and their own 'personal status' laws (family laws and laws pertaining to one's religion). The majority similarly upheld the right of non-Muslims to a separate personal status law, but in their case the motive was to facilitate exemption from the personal status aspects of Islamic law.

Dual Contract

A number of tensions underpin the above account: between freedom and morality, popular will and revelation, representative and religious authority. Central to many of these is the tension between free will and divine design. On the one hand, Hamas defends the right of people to express their opinions, and select their leaders. On the other, it insists that politics must be safeguarded from self-interest, baser human instincts and anything that is threatening to Islam. This tension is embodied at the very heart of Hamas' political theory in the form of a dual contract: one between the people and their representatives (safeguarding free will), and one between the people and God (safeguarding divine design).

To understand where this tension stems from and how it is played out we have to turn to Hamas' understanding of humanity's purpose on earth and what this means for its approach to authority and freedom. Humanity, according to Hamas, has one overriding purpose: to be God's representative on earth. Following Yassin (1998a),

God has created the human being and provided him with a brain, thus increasing his value above that of other creatures, ... so that he can be vicegerent [*khalifah*] of God on earth. God has made him a *waqil* [authorised agent] to do his work—just as a merchant appoints a trustee to do his business in a different country (cf. also Hamas and Khalas members, 1999; *al-Risalah*, 12 February 1998: 16).

This, however, introduces a tension. Being an agent presupposes free will. Yassin, for instance, explicitly defined freedom as meaning "that the human being should be left to do what he wishes to do" (Yassin, 1998b). Yahya Musa, head of Hizb al-Khalas' Political Bureau in the late 1990s, similarly characterised the Islamic state as one "where people who are part of this state can say and believe in whatever they wish; they can practise their personal beliefs in any way they want, socially or politically" (Musa, 1998b). Hamas' emphasis on consultation is rooted in this understanding of freedom.

Yet, freedom, for Hamas, is not simply 'to do as one pleases'. As God's agents, humanity has an obligation to God, namely to further his business interests (to stick with the merchant metaphor which in itself says something profound about Hamas' view of its constituency). Thus, to be free means both being able to do as one wishes and submitting oneself to God's will.

In a 'secular' context, these statements appear contradictory. For Hamas, there is no contradiction. Because God has created humanity, submitting oneself to his will means acting in accordance with one's higher nature. Sayyid Qutb (1906-66), one of the most influential Egyptian Muslim Brotherhood thinkers and a source for Hamas' political theory, encapsulated this aspect of freedom, saying that "He Who has created the universe ... has also prescribed a Shari'ah for [man's] voluntary actions. If man follows this law, then his life is in harmony with his own nature. [...] Only [through obedience to the Shari'ah] does man's personality, internal and external, become integrated" (Qutb, 1964: 164-5; cf. also Yassin, 1998b; Abu Shannab, 1998a, 1998d; Bahr, 1998; Musa, 1998a, 1998b). On this reading, freedom means to rise above one's baser instincts, to fulfil one's divine destiny by being "in harmony with one's own nature". By being God's agent one is fulfilling one's destiny, and is thus free.

When moving beyond the individual to the community, the tension between free will and submission becomes more complex still. In addition to the potential for friction between individual free will and submission to God's will there are tensions between individual freedom and communal order. For Hamas, only a state rooted in divine law will preserve freedom. Echoing Jean-Jacques Rousseau's famous statement that "man is born free; and everywhere he is in chains" (Rousseau, 1762: 181), Yassin (1998a) asserted that

The human being is born free. But when human-made systems come into existence, in many cases these systems exploit and subjugate the human being. Revelation and religion have come to preserve this freedom and to protect [him] against enslavement by human-made systems. When a human being becomes a Muslim, he protects his freedom by subjugating himself to God alone, ... and by fearing none but God. God's religion thus preserves the freedom of this human being.

'Religion', here, must be read in the context of Yassin's cultural framework, as a comprehensive system of beliefs and institutions, rather than the private, personal belief system typically implied in Western parlance. For Yassin, religion is both a privately liberating force, enabling one to stand up against repression and occupation by removing fear, and a political system which preserves freedom because it is in harmony with God's purpose for humanity on earth.

These two sets of tensions, between individual free will and submission to God's design, and between freedom from tyranny and submission to a divinely-inspired political system, come together in the dual contract, part divine, part social. The divine contract is to ensure that people behave in accordance with God's laws, and thus remain free from following their baser instincts. But it is also believed to guarantee the creation of a system that preserves true freedom, and prevent self- or factional interest from leading the system to corruption, inequality and tyranny.

Only if the system is based on God's laws, Hamas holds, will the right balance be struck between individual and communal needs, between individual freedom and social harmony, and between freedom and equality. Here Hamas draws on the thinking of the Indo-Pakistani founder of Jamaat-e-Islami, Abul A'la Mawdudi (1903-79), who argued, along with other Islamists such as Sudan's Hassan al-Turabi (cf. al-Turabi, 1983: 245-7) that, in an Islamic state, "the relations between the individual and the society have been regulated in such a manner that neither the personality of the individual suffers any diminution, ... nor is the individual allowed to exceed his bounds to such an extent as to become harmful to the community ..." (Maududi, 1960a: 33; cf. also Yassin, 1998a; Abu Shannab, 1998a; Hamad, 1998a; Bahr, 1998; Musa, 1998b). That this is possible is down to the fact that the *shari'ah*, like the universe and humanity, is God's creation, and thus in harmony with his overall design.

However, in Hamas' political theory, a leader's obligations do not end there. If they did, Hamas' Islamic state would simply be a theocracy, or to be more precise, a nomocracy—the rule of (divine) law. Instead, Hamas insists that a leader's obligations are just as much to the governed as to God. Because, within Hamas' framework, everyone is an agent of God, no one has the right to govern over anyone else. To impose a system, law or leader on anyone against their will is to negate their freedom, and create inequality. To obtain the right to govern, and preserve freedom, a governor needs the active and voluntary consent of the governed. Without this, there would be tyranny—even if their rule were based on divine law.

This is the social contract, or *'aqd ijtima'i* as the founder of the Egyptian Muslim Brotherhood, Hasan al-Banna, labelled it in the early part of the 20th century (Mitchell, 1993: 247)—a temporary and voluntary transferral of sovereignty from those of God's agents who agree to be ruled, to those of God's agents they consent to be ruled by.[13] Under such a contract, the governed remain free because they have consented to being governed, even if the government's policies or the legislature's laws restrict their freedom.

Those who govern and legislate are, in Hamas' terms, representatives of those who are governed. Their authority rests on having a mandate to rule—which, in practical terms, means being elected in regular, nation-wide elections. Significantly, their authority is not

---

13 Yassin, 1998b; Abu Shannab, 1998a, 1998b, 1998c; Shamma', 1998; al-Zahhar, 1998a; Haniyyah, 1998a; Salim, 1998; Hamad, 1998a, 1998b; Muslih, 1998; 'Muhammad', 1998; 'Ibrahim', 1998; Hamas Cell, 1998c; Hamas and Khalas members, 1999; 'Iyad', 1998; 'Nasr', 1998; 'Ashraf', 1998; Muslim Girls Association, 1998; Director Women's Training Centre, 1998; Bahr, 1998; al-Bardawil, 1998; Musa, 1998a, 1998b, 1999; Y. Hamdan, 1998; al-Na'ami, 1998; *al-Risalah*, 12 February 1998: 10; Hizb al-Khalas, 1997a: 24-5, 1997c, 1997d; al-Masri, 1998; Taha, 1998; Abu Zughri, 1998; 'Yusuf', 1998; Women's Islamic Bloc I, 1998; half of Women's Islamic Bloc II, 1998. For intellectual sources of these ideas, cf. Mitchell, 1993; Maududi [Mawdudi], 1960a; Maududi [Mawdudi], 1960b; Ghannouchi, 1993; al-Turabi, 1983; Kotb [Qutb], 1953: 93.

derived from having religious knowledge, or from being appointed by God or being God's representatives. Ismail Abu Shannab, one of Hamas' three most senior leaders in Gaza before his assassination in August 2003, summarised this as follows:

In the Islamic system, the Head of State [*al-khalifah*] represents the nation, not God. The community does not choose *al-khalifah* except to be their representative [*na'ib*]; so he does not derive his authority except from representing the community which has ... the right to watch him and forbid him from getting beyond the borders of his brief (Abu Shannab, 1998).

Those who govern derive their authority from representing the nation. Theirs is representative authority, not religious authority.

Abuse of authority negates the contract. Hence, Hamas' emphasis on trust and on regarding leadership as a burden, to be accepted reluctantly, rather than a prize to be won (Chapter 4). When trust is abused, the ruled have the right to reclaim the sovereignty that belongs to them as God's agents. *In extremis*, this means they have the right to rebel—but only when all other mechanisms have failed. Authority is therefore never an inherent right, but has to be earned. Once earned, those who have consented to being governed have an obligation to obey.

The dual contract is the foundation of Hamas' political theory. Neither prong is sufficient by itself. A divine contract without a social contract negates people's sovereignty. It may guarantee that the political system is run according to God's laws. But it negates one fundamental aspect of those laws, namely that every human being is God's agent. A divine contract by itself does not solve who is to rule in God's stead, or how to interpret his laws for the specific context within which people live. Without a social contract, those who govern are dictators, however divinely inspired (which is one of the dilemmas facing Hamas in the wake of the violent ousting of Fatah from Gaza in June 2007).

A social contract without the divine contract, conversely, negates God's sovereignty. It may guarantee that the governed remain free from tyranny in the sense that they have elected those who govern them. But by itself, it does not guarantee that the government governs according to God's laws, thus negating one fundamental aspect of freedom, as Hamas sees it: only in a system governed by God's laws will humanity have the freedom to live in harmony with its intended purpose, and strike the right balance between individual and communal needs, freedom and equality. Without the divine contract, the popular will may threaten the very conditions of freedom.

Sovereignty, for Hamas, is thus neither wholly God's, nor wholly belonging to the people. Following Abu Shannab (1998: 6),

in an Islamic system, the authority of the people is not unlimited but is constrained by the *shari'ah*, even though the collective will of the *ummah* [here meaning 'the people'] is one of the sources of the law. This will should adhere to the moral laws [of Islam]. Thus, sovereignty in Islam is dual, one part belonging to the *ummah*, the other belonging to the *shari'ah*, so that the *shari'ah* sets the boundaries which God has established to balance a human being's life.

Hamas' system is neither a theocracy nor a democracy but a hybrid, in which citizens have the sovereignty to elect who legislates and rules over them, and God has the sovereignty regarding morality and the principles on which legislation is to be based. In Hamas' state, the authority of legislators is thus circumscribed twice: once by those who elect them (to whom they are answerable in the next elections), and once by God (to whom they are answerable in the afterlife).

Islamic vs. Western Sources of Inspiration

Hamas' contractual theory is grounded in the Qur'anic verse: "Allah has promised those of you who believe and do good works to grant them viceregency in the land..." (24:55; see also verse 2:30: "I will create a *khalifah* on earth").[14] It was Mawdudi who developed an Islamist contractual theory on the basis of this verse (Maududi, 1960a: 29-32). That Hamas has adopted Mawdudi's framework is instructive in itself, since Mawdudi's interpretation is far from incontestable. It departs from the classical view that the legislative process be reserved for *mujtahidun* (religio-legal experts). It also stands perpendicular

---

14 I use Khurshid Ahmad's translation (Maududi [Mawdudi], 1960a: 29) rather than Yusuf Ali's (*The Holy Qur'an*, 1946) because Ahmad's better expresses the notion of being granted viceregency that is implied by the Qur'anic term *iastakhlifannahum*.

to Qutb's argument that there is no need for a legislature since, for Qutb, the *shari'ah* is complete and only needs to be administered (Qutb, 1964: 165). That Hamas has distanced itself from such views is significant, particularly as they have been taken up by the more radical *takfiri jihadi* groups, of which al-Qaeda is an outgrowth.

However, Hamas differs from Mawdudi in three significant ways. Where Mawdudi depicts vicegerency as a 'gift', Hamas regards it as a right—though a right which brings obligations. Mawdudi limits this 'gift' to Muslims. Hamas extends it to all humanity, thus in effect broadening the definition of "those of you who believe and do good works" to include Christians, Jews, and, in theory, even atheists. And Hamas diverges from Mawdudi in placing more trust in 'the great mass of the common people'. Although Hamas believes, with Mawdudi, that the 'common people' are easily "swayed by emotions and desires" (Maududi, 1960a: 21-2), it nevertheless squarely places temporal sovereignty with 'the people'. This stands in sharp contrast to Mawdudi who, his vicegerent argument notwithstanding, justified, at least in his earlier speeches, the use of coercion by a just and enlightened ruler to save the common people from their own mistakes (Maududi, 1960a: 34-7; he later modified this position; Maududi, 1960b: 29-33). Mawdudi could make this argument because for him vicegerency was a gift, rather than a right.

Although Hamas roots its political theory in Islam, it is also indebted to Western political theory—a point leaders such as Abu Shannab (1998; 1998c) and Musa (1998b) readily acknowledge. The early Egyptian Muslim Brothers, despite their critical stance towards Western ideologies, specifically studied Western political models for inspiration (Al-Husaini, 1956: 89-93; see also Mitchell, 1993: 224-5, 33-4, 41-2). The adoption of the notion of the social contract was a direct result of these studies. Hamas leaders similarly study Western models and borrow what they regard as compatible with their interpretation of Islam. Rather than rejecting Western models, they argue for making them their own, after critique and reflection. Following Shafiq (1998), "those who are concerned with issues of democracy have to rid themselves from looking at it from the outside". Rather, "democracy should be spoken about after we truly know Western democracy and have analysed it to the smallest detail, and criticised it severely". For, "critising modernity is necessary to create our own modernity". Hamas is thus neither anti-modern nor anti-democratic, nor inherently anti-Western.

A closer look at Hamas' dual contract reveals a striking number of similarities with Western contract theories, and in particular with foundational ones such as the theory of John Locke. Although Hamas leaders themselves do not explicitly make this link, it is instructive to briefly reflect on the similarities, if only to illustrate that Hamas' thinking shares themes central to Western democratic theory (cf. Euben's analysis of Qutb; 1999) and to probe Hamas' philosophy further by drawing on political analysis of Lockean themes (see also Kerr's use of the natural law tradition in studying the thinking of Muhammad 'Abduh; 1966: 103-44).

Locke, like Hamas, insisted that humans are "by nature, all free, equal and independent" (§II.95),[15] and that this freedom can only be preserved if the individual is "under no other legislative power, but that established, by consent" (§II.22). No edict, argued Locke, has "the force and obligation of a law, which has not its sanction from that legislative, which the publick has chosen and appointed" (§II.134). Conversely, if the people "find the legislative act contrary to the trust reposed in them", the latter's power becomes "forfeited, and ... devolve[s] into the hands of those that gave it". "Supream power" thus always remains "in the people" (§II.149).

Like Hamas, however, Locke believes authority to be legitimate only within the context of God's law. Mirroring Hamas, Locke argues that "God hath given the World to Men in common" (§II.26:1) and that, accordingly, human beings, including their leaders, are accountable to God and his law. This, Locke insists, means that freedom is not "liberty for every man to do what he lists" (§II.57:22) but rather to learn to choose the "greater good" by way of our reason (*Essay Concerning Human Understanding*, §II.21:35, 48; quoted in Tully, 1984: 70). A true law, therefore, should direct the individual "to his proper interest" (§57:10-12). Thus, "the municipal laws of countries are only so far right, as they are founded on the Law of Nature, by which they are to be regulated and interpreted" (§II.12:16-

---

15 All references, unless specified, are to Locke and Laslett, 1960.

9). "Though the legislative ... be the supream power in every com-mon-wealth", Locke insists, "it is not, nor can possibly be absolutely arbitrary over the lives and fortunes of the people". Rather, "the law of nature stands as an eternal rule to all men, legislators as well as others. The rules that they make for other mens actions, must, as well as their own ..., be comfortable to the law of nature, i.e. to the will of God" (§II.135).[16]

Like Hamas, Locke suggests two sources for political author-ity: one divine, one contractual. Intriguingly, he solves the tension between the two in much the same way as Hamas does—at least, on Riley's interpretation of Locke. Rather than accusing Locke of subordinating consent to natural law (as, for instance, Barker does; Riley, 1982: 64), Riley argues that "natural law and contractarianism, far from being simply antithetical in Locke, necessarily involve each other". For, "given human imperfection and corruption", Locke's social contract "is necessitated by natural law's inability to be liter-ally "sovereign" on earth" (69). Because natural law cannot command political obligation, for lack of both political power and specificity, it needs human agents to turn it into codified law and enforce it. For this, consent is needed, as without it, those subject to the law would be robbed of their freedom. Or, following Riley, consent is the mechanism needed to make natural law "sovereign" on earth. Yet, because consent does not have the authority to contradict natural law, it must always operate within the framework of natural law. The end result is an "equilibrium between the naturally and the consensu-ally right" (72).

That such similarities exist between Hamas and Locke is not to ar-gue that Hamas is wholly Lockean. Hamas' organic approach to the state, for instance, is, as we will see, more Hegelian than Lockean, with its emphasis on socialising citizens into willing God's will or its belief that the Islamic state is the fulfilment of God's will on earth (in Hegel's words, "the way of God in the world")[17], and that only by

---

16 I here follow the argument that Locke's 'Law of Nature' is in essence 'divine law' (cf. Riley, 1982: 83-91; M. Johnson, 1977: 23-45; Simmons, 1992: 14-67).

17 Hegel, *Philosophy of Right*, §258 (addition) as translated by Kaufmann

partaking in such a state will individuals be truly free. Hamas is also much more prescriptive than Locke, and although it accords reason a central place, it appears readier than Locke, and certainly than his contractarian descendants, to override reason with revelation (even though Hamas acknowledges that revelation must be rationally interpreted). It is important, however, to acknowledge that Hamas' political theory closely echoes aspects of the Western contractarian tradition.

Some of the tensions in Hamas' model arguably derive from Hamas' attempt at marrying Western and Islamic traditions. The proposed separation of powers, for instance, is derived from both Western tradition (where the idea was explicitly formulated) and Islamic tradition (from which Hamas has taken the notion that rulers should be subject to the law). The tensions between these two traditions derive from the fact that one is rooted in a model where authority has traditionally been derived from religio-legal knowledge (although not exclusively), while the other conceptualises authority as derived from a popular mandate (although, again, not exclusively). In the Western tradition, the legislature is the highest legislative authority because it has a direct popular mandate. In the early Islamic tradition on which Hamas draws, the highest legislative and executive authorities were combined in the Prophet because of his privileged access to religio-legal knowledge. As we will see, Hamas has resolved this tension by placing representative authority above religious authority—on the ground that the Prophet's successors derived their authority from having a popular mandate (which is itself a modern interpretation)—while allowing representatives to draw on religio-legal expertise where needed.

However, at times, this tension re-emerges, for instance when Yassin, despite advocating a separation of powers and calling the *Shura* Council the highest legal authority in the state, referred to the Head of State as *mujtahid mutlaq* (most learned religio-legal expert) and insisted he have the right to overrule the *Shura* Council in matters where he was more learned. No other interviewee used this term, suggesting that this was a tension within Yassin himself, who, after

(quoted in Avineri, 1972: 176-7).

all, was a generation older than the other Hamas leaders and had grown up in an era when religious authority was still more prevalent. But it shows the potential for tension in those areas where the two traditions diverge, and in particular regarding the relative roles of knowledge and popular mandate. This is not to argue, as Nüsse does, that the two traditions are so inherently contradictory to make convergence problematic (Nüsse, 1998: 180). There is sufficient ambiguity and room for alternative interpretations in both traditions to allow convergence to take place, aided by the fact that Islamic and Western thought have common roots in ancient Greek philosophy and in the exchange of ideas at the time of the Renaissance (cf. M. Watt, 1972; Abu Shannab, 1998: 7).

The influence of Western ideas can also be seen in the way Hamas interprets Islamic traditions. The various Qur'anic verses and Prophetic traditions enjoining leaders to consult, for instance, do not inevitably lead to a democratic system of elections, checks and balances, as Hamas has it. Not only is it left unspecified in the original texts as to who should be consulted or on what subjects (Kamali, 1991: 33) but it is unclear whether the outcome of a consultation is binding on the leader, let alone whether consultation is obligatory (cf. el-Awa, 1980: 86-97). Consultation, moreover, does not automatically imply nation-wide elections. And yet, that is how Hamas has interpreted the command to consult.

The traditional jurisprudential notion of *ijtihad* (scholarly interpretation) has similarly been recast—from describing a practice reserved for religious scholars, to describing the practice of elected legislators, whose authority rests on having a popular mandate, rather than on religio-legal knowledge. The notion of *ijma'* (consensus), once reserved for the process by which religious scholars turned a legal interpretation into binding law with as much authority as revelation, has been re-interpreted to describe the decision-making process of the elected *Shura* Council and give it the weight traditionally reserved for scholarly consensus.[18] That Hamas has interpreted Islamic tradition in this particular way is significant, and may say something

---

18 Here Hamas draws on the thinking of, among others, Muhammad Iqbal (Iqbal, 1930: 173-4).

about the socio-economic and political context within which Hamas has evolved (see Chapter 7).

Freedom vs. Popular will

One tension that needs further probing is that between freedom and popular will. In Hamas' model, the popular will cannot be left unrestrained. Following Abu Shannab, "in [a situation of] unlimited freedom, there is a way out of Islam's binding rules which God legislated to organise morals, life and relations between people" (Abu Shannab, 1998: 5). If a people flout these rules, they are no longer free, according to Hamas, as their system will no longer be in harmony with God's design for humanity. In this sense, Hamas is against the notion of popular sovereignty since "Islam perceives the sovereignty of the *umma* [literally 'community of believers' but here meaning 'the people'] as a usurpation of the sovereignty of the law (*shariah*) descending from God" (*ibid.*). Popular sovereignty is thus circumscribed by God's law.

To better comprehend what Hamas means when it says that the unrestrained popular will may undermine freedom, we must turn to its critique of Western secular democracies. There are various reasons why Hamas believes secular democracy to be detrimental to freedom. But the two chief threats to freedom come, Hamas believes, from powerful interest groups (in particular 'big business' and those with power and connections) and the misguided masses.

To start with the latter, Hamas is not confident that the masses always know what is best for them. Though its theory of vicegerency implies that, as God's agents, everyone has the potential to know what is best, and although Hamas invokes the notion of 'the popular will' to critique Fatah and calls on leaders to 'trust the people' (cf. Shafiq, 1998; Abu Marzuq in Hroub, 2000: 91), it simultaneously fears that the masses will be misled, whether by ignorance, arrogance or manipulation. The 1998 president of the women's Islamic Bloc (Hamas' student wing) at the Islamic University in Gaza, for instance, warned that "normal people cannot just be given the right to decide because they may look at the surface only" (Women's Islamic Bloc I, 1998). Unscrupulous elites might manipulate them, or they might wilfully decide to do the wrong thing. As a member of the men's Islamic Bloc at the Islamic University put it, "democracy says that people should govern themselves by themselves or by electing others. This is right. But suppose that these people are bad? They would elect bad people like them. So this contradicts with Islam" ('Ashraf', 1998).

The other threat to freedom comes from what Hamas calls 'the strong'—those who can manipulate the democratic process to their own advantage. Hamas' critique of Western democracies (as well as of Fatah) is precisely that they allow such manipulation to occur—whether by elites controlling the levers of power or by manipulating public opinion (which is where this threat overlaps with the threat from the masses). Using an almost Gramscian framework of analysis (Gramsci, 1929-35: 5-23, 210-76), Abu Shannab for instance observed that

[though] in theory, the vote of big landowners, the elite, media moguls, ... is equal to the vote of the unemployed and the cheap labourers who represent the majority ..., in reality this majority follows the direction of the former who use their influence to form public opinion and distort the facts for the public. [...] When the masses vote for the elite, is it a free, mature representation, or is it a representation of the ignorant, the misled, the forced? Western democracies have ... abolished aristocratic privileges. However, they have gradually created an economic inequality which is in the process of founding a new aristocracy based on ownership and massive monopolies that exert broad control over parties, journalism and public opinion (1998: 3; cf. also Shafiq, 1998).

Musa (1998b) put this equally forcefully:

Take for example the Congress of the United States of America. No one can become a Senator until they have money in the range of $250 million. The regular man from the street cannot reach that level, ... and this money will of course give access to the media and to different centres of power. So it becomes the democracy of the strong and the rich, not the democracy of everyone. ... Under such circumstances, morals become abstract and everyone can decide what a moral standard is. ... Then those in power can rule over society in wicked, crooked ways. ... [Regarding] the mechanism of achieving power, we do not differ on this: let it be democratic. But the problem exists when equality is not achieved. ... The main objective is [thus] equality, not rulership (cf. also Abu Shannab, 1998: 4).

Particularly intriguing is the way Musa links the absence of controls over the rich to the absence of a divinely-ordained, and thus by definition supra-factional, moral code. Without such a code, Musa (1998a) insists, values are created "according to cost and ... benefit", subjectively, and in the interests of the powerful. For both Musa and Abu Shannab, democracy becomes tyranny if the rich are allowed to control the thinking of the masses (in Gramscian terms, to establish hegemonic control), and thus manipulate them into voting in the interests of the rich. Significantly, though, while this is a critique of secularism and its human-centric instrumental rationality, it is not the more sweeping denunciation of modern rationality which Qutb appears to have advocated (cf. Euben, 1999). For reason is still regarded as the central interface between God's moral laws and human interpretation of these laws.

Both the threats from manipulative elites and from popular ignorance are, in Hamas' scheme, countered by the dual contract. The social contract serves to safeguard freedom, equality and leadership accountability. The divine contract serves to ensure that the law is just, the weak are protected, and the rich will not have a free hand to manipulate the process. It does this by providing a moral-legal reference point, like that provided by 'natural law' in Western thought, independent of both the rich and the masses (although some Hamas leaders recognise that God's laws are subject to interpretation, and thus not independent of those who do the interpreting). But the divine contract also acts on the individual by creating an internalised set of checks and balances, an internal 'big brother', to complement the institutional checks and balances of elections, consultations and a separation of powers.

Following Yassin (1998b),

It is to be expected that the Head of State or the government can become corrupted. But there are various 'security valves'. The first of these is the fear of God. A leader must be pious and must understand that he will be held accountable before God—that, if he deviates from the just path, his destiny will be hell-fire. That fate should be rejected by any sane person.

Abu Shannab (1998d) similarly named a leader's relationship with God as one of the key instruments for keeping him or her accountable:

First, you devote yourself to your cause for the sake of God. This means that you do not want any reward from anybody. Second, you know that God is watching you, so you have to be straight. Third, you wish for a reward from God, so you expend maximum effort so that God may reward you abundantly.

This aspect of the divine contract is best encapsulated in the notion of piety or virtuous behaviour (cf. also Stout, 2004: 20ff) which plays a central role in what makes a Hamas leader authoritative (Chapters 4 & 5). In this emphasis on pious behaviour, Hamas echoes Stout's reading of Whitman that in an American context, "character is important ... precisely because we are not self-evidently fit to perform the tasks that our circumstances demand of us if we want to live democratically" (21). Piety is what distinguishes a virtuous community from a non-virtuous one, and it is piety, embraced voluntarily, which should restrain the popular will.

Revealed Law vs. Legislated Law

Before further exploring the tension between piety and freedom, it is important to recognise the far-reaching consequences of Hamas' notion of the dual contract, and in particular its emphasis on consent, for the process of legislation. God's laws, or revealed law, define the legislative landscape. But without consent, revealed law cannot become law. Hamas members typically make a sharp distinction between *shari'ah* law, which it regards as a body of general principles, and actual codified law, as passed by the legislature.[19] Because God's law is not legislated law, it lacks both the detail and the political authority to be legally binding. It may be morally binding, but only when transformed from divine revelation (typically cast in general

---

19 Cf. Yassin, 1998a, 1998b; Abu Shannab, 1998c, 1999; Shamma', 1998; al-Zahhar, 1998a; Hamad, 1998b; Muslih, 1998; Musa, 1998b; al-Na'ami, 1998; al-Masri, 1998; Abu Zughri, 1998; Women's Islamic Bloc I, 1998; Hamas and Khalas members, 1999; 'Ashraf', 1998; 'Nasr', 1998.

terms) into legislated law (of necessity precise and context-specific) does it become legally binding. This can only be done by elected legislators who, because they have a popular mandate, can perform the task without compromising the freedom of those who will be subject to the law.

The exception to this rule are the *hudud* (revealed penal laws concerning for instance theft and adultery), and to a lesser extent family law. Because here revelation is highly specific, consent becomes less essential. God's will is already clear, and there is little room for alteration (cf. Yassin, 1998b). Consultation and consent are still needed to legitimise the process, and ensure compliance. But they are more about recognition (recognising something that is already 'true') than about shaping legislation. Consent has to be brought into harmony with the *hudud*, not *vice versa*.

However, even here, consent plays a role. It does not have the power to fundamentally alter the *hudud*. But it is needed to ensure that the *hudud* are not implemented prematurely, and that when they are implemented, they are regarded as legitimate by the electorate. In part, this is about preparing the electorate by helping them to recognise the *hudud* as 'true'. But it is also about creating the right conditions for consent, so that the *hudud* are considered legitimate. For instance, Hamas leaders such as Ghazi Hamad, chief editor of *al-Risalah* and spokesperson of Hamas' first Cabinet, insist that one cannot adopt the ruling against theft unless poverty has been eradicated (Hamad, 1998b; cf. also al-Fenjari, 1998; Abu Marzook and Gaess, 1997: 126). Consent is thus a mechanism to ensure that the majority of the electorate agrees that the conditions are right for the *hudud* to be implemented. I will return to this when discussing Hamas' approach to creating an Islamic state. What matters here is that, at least in theory, Hamas grants the electorate (or its representatives) a veto over the *hudud*. Whether Hamas would allow this veto to be exercised is an open question. But it is significant that, in theory, Hamas places consent over divine law (in terms of turning the *hudud* into law, rather than changing the content of the *hudud*).

With this emphasis on consent, Hamas has introduced a further tension. Although the *hudud* need no justification, since they are believed (including by Hamas) to be God's word revealed, Hamas has developed a series of what in a Western context would be considered 'secular' arguments to legitimise the *hudud* in the eyes of the general public. The punishments proposed in the *hudud* for adultery and theft are defended, for instance, on the grounds that they are beneficial to society by acting as a deterrent. Theft and adultery are considered harmful to society. The *hudud* are thus presented as increasing overall welfare.

The religious injunction to wear the *hijab* (headscarf) is similarly defended, not just by invoking religious texts, but with reference to the *hijab*'s perceived utility or to arguments about the right to wear a *hijab*. Hamas argues, for instance, that the *hijab* enables women to operate more freely in a male-dominated public space, while at the same time averting social corruption (cf. Women's Islamic Bloc I, 1998; Abu Shannab, 1998d, 2002). It insists that, precisely because an institution such as the Islamic University demands that girls wear the *hijab* and be taught separately, daughters from conservative families have been able to persuade their parents to allow them to go to university, with the effect that women typically outnumber men among the university's student body (Abu Shannab, 1998d).[20]

Once utility, or inalienable rights, become the justification for a religious imperative, the command's absoluteness is eroded. Whether or not to continue the practice becomes a function of its perceived utility, or its effect on people's rights—both of which are human-, rather than God-centric, arguments. If hand-cutting fails to deter thieves, the divine command to cut off a thief's hand comes under severe strain if a utility argument had been used to justify it. This does not necessarily imply the demise of the command. It may still carry sufficient intrinsic authority to remain intact. However, over time, the command's authority is likely to be undermined, increasing the scope for re-interpretation with a focus on human needs, rather than divine will.

Hamas denies that such a tension exists. According to Abu Shannab (2002), increasing utility is a fundamental goal of Islam. Every religious imperative is believed to increase human welfare. Utility, however, is not the primary reason for obeying religious imperatives. A Muslim's

---

20 For enrolment figures, see http://www.iugaza.edu.

duty, for Abu Shannab, is to obey, regardless of whether a command appears utility-enhancing. The command not to eat pork, for instance, made little sense to Abu Shannab, until he heard scientists declare that pork fat and certain bacteria that thrive in pork meat are particularly detrimental to human health. Thus, "[though] all Islamic teachings are based on usefulness, you practice them as a believer first of all out of obedience for God. Because if you practice them for their usefulness, then you will forget your God." Or, as *Falastin al-Muslimah* asserts: "The human being in the view of Islam has both a mission from God [*mukhalaf*] and is to rule earth for God [*mustakhlaf*], whereas the human being according to the Western conception is a person who has passions and wants to fulfil his monetary and physical desires. The starting point is therefore different from that of Islam" (January 1998: 40). This, according to Abu Shannab, is what distinguishes a secular utilitarian from a Muslim utilitarian.

Abu Shannab's argument notwithstanding, the adoption of arguments from utility or human rights in the debate about how to interpret revelation subtly shifts the balance of authority. Once utility is used to justify a religious imperative in the context of gaining a popular mandate, whether or not the argument is persuasive to the electorate becomes more important than whether the argument is divinely ordained—thus strengthening the veto power Hamas has tentatively assigned to the mechanism of consent.

Where the Qur'an is less specific or silent, consultation and consent play a far more central role in Hamas' proposed state. General principles have to be interpreted. Silences have to be filled. Rational debate and consultation are the primary sources of authority. Here, Hamas' model approaches the contractarian model so familiar in Western political theory, although the Qur'an's general principles are typically more prescriptive than the natural law principles underpinning Western contractarianism.

Because the number of Qur'anic verses dealing with legal matters is relatively small, the scope for interpretation and human reasoning is great. Out of the over 6,000 verses contained in the Qur'an, less than a tenth concern legal matters. Just 350 are considered 'legal verses' in the strictest sense of the word (Kamali, 1991: 19-20), and even these contain speculative aspects in need of clarification and interpretation.

That Hamas accords such a central place to consent is directly related to its approach to decision-making. As we saw earlier, Hamas models the Islamic state's decision-making process on the jurisprudential principle of *ijma'* (consensus) and the Prophet's promise that 'my community shall never agree on an error'. Because Hamas interprets this promise as pertaining to the wider electorate, it needs the consent of that electorate to ensure that legislated law is as close to God's will as humanly possible (see also Klein, 2007: 444). However, because Hamas simultaneously fears that the electorate may be too ignorant or too easily swayed to be able to discern truth from falsehood, this introduces a tension which Hamas proposes to resolve by creating a balance between expertise and popular mandate.

Knowledge vs. Popular Mandate

The dual contract invokes two types of authority: the popular will (representative authority) and divine law or revelation (religio-legal authority). The first values individual opinion, regardless of expertise, and is derived from the notion that each person is God's representative, and thus a (potential) source of divine wisdom. The second values expertise and knowledge. On this view, individuals are only considered a source of divine wisdom if they are knowledgeable.

Although Hamas holds that authority comes from having a popular mandate, it also demands that legislators work within God's law. As such, they are expected to be familiar with God's law, which in Hamas' case is Islamic law. Significantly, though, Hamas refrains from insisting that legislators be qualified religious scholars (*mujtahidun*), thus placing representative authority and having a popular mandate above religio-legal authority—although some junior interviewees were more ambiguous about this (al-Masri, 1998, 'Ahmad', 1998; 'Ashraf', 1998). In this, Hamas breaks with the dominant tradition within Islamic jurisprudence, and indeed with the earlier Muslim Brothers—although the Brotherhood's founder, al-Banna, was more flexible on the issue (Mitchell, 1993: 248).

A significant number of interviewees explicitly placed having the trust of the people above all other characteristics they sought in a legislator. Yassin put this most forcefully, saying: "Elections bring up individuals who the people themselves want. Thus the people decide who should be in the *majlis al-shura* [*Shura* Council]. It is not necessary that this person should be a *mujtahid* ... Those who are elected by the people, those who are the favourites of the people should be in this position and they should be representing the majority of the people" (Yassin, 1998b). Hamad similarly stated unequivocally: "don't say: this man is not an Islamist and he is not an expert, so we should exclude him; no, I don't think so. It is according to the election of the people" (Hamad, 1998a; cf. also Abu Shannab, 1998c; Haniyyah, 1998a; Shamma', 1998; Musa, 1998b; Bahr, 1998; Abu Zughri, 1998; Hamas Cell, 1998c). Or, as Klein concluded from his analysis of Hamas' political practice, "the voice of the masses, in its view, is the expression of God's will" (2007: 444).

Apart from a few (see above), interviewees also insisted that candidates for the legislature should not be vetted by an election tribunal of religious scholars, to ensure their legal and moral credentials. In this, it breaks with Mawdudi (1960b: 45-7) and, less surprisingly, with the Iranian Islamic state model (which is inspired by the more hierarchical structure of Shi'i Islam, that is absent from Sunni Islam which informs Hamas' thinking). Hamas thus appears to believe it more important that representatives have the trust of their constituency than that they are judged acceptable by a committee of religious scholars.

At the same time, Hamas expects elected representatives to have enough background knowledge of the *shari'ah* to ensure that God's principles are not violated (cf. Abu Shannab, 1998c; Yassin, 1998b; Abu Zughri, 1998; al-Masri, 1998; Hamas and Khalas members, 1999). Yassin himself expected at least some of the elected representatives to be *mujtahidun* and an examination of Hamas' elected legislators indeed suggests that Hamas regards knowledge of Islamic law as one of the more important qualifications (though by no means the most important) for becoming a legislator (Chapter 5). Political authority, however, remains rooted in having a popular mandate—to the extent that some argue that if the electorate prefers a communist over an Islamist their judgement must be respected ('Nasr', 1998; implied by Hamad, 1998a; Abu Shannab, 1998c).

Though Hamas argues that religion and politics are one, and should not be separated, it recognises, *de facto*, that the 'religious' and the political realms are different. Its proposed legislature has no authority to pass *fatwas* ('religious' rulings), and 'religious' scholars have no automatic right to sit in the legislature. In its political theory, if not its rhetoric, Hamas thus differentiates between religion and politics and recognises that 'religious' authority does not imply political authority and *vice versa*.

The tension between religio-legal and representative authority also plays itself out in the wider question of how to ensure that the legislature has sufficient expertise if one allows people to choose freely. Although Hamas insists that it is down to the electorate to decide who to elect to the *Shura* Council, it is also conscious that an open electoral process does not necessarily return the nation's most knowledgeable people to the legislature. Significantly, Hamas is here concerned with ensuring that the *Shura* Council has expertise in all fields of knowledge, not just Islamic law (which, again, is reflected in the make-up of Hamas' elected legislators; Chapter 5). To solve this dilemma, Hamas proposes a partnership between experts and representatives, in which the latter have the final word as the representatives of the people.[21]

Some (cf. al-Rantisi, 2002a) argued that elected representatives should be allowed to appoint a limited number of experts and representatives of different sections of society to the legislative body to ensure that sufficient expertise be present. This, according to al-Rantisi, is how Hamas operates internally, ensuring that its *Shura* Council has both the needed expertise and represents the spectrum of interests across Hamas. Others (cf. Yassin, 1998a, 1998b; Abu Shannab, 1998b, 1998c; al-Zahhar, 1998a, Haniyyah, 1998a; 'Ibrahim', 1998; 'Iyad', 1998; Bahr, 1998; al-Masri, 1998) stipulated that legislators appoint special expert committees to advise the legislative body on issues ranging from divine law to the latest scientific discoveries. The final

---

21 Cf. Yassin, 1998a, 1998b; Abu Shannab, 1998b, 1998c; al-Zahhar, 1998a; Haniyyah, 1998a; 'Ibrahim', 1998; Hamas Cell, 1998a; 'Iyad', 1998; Muslim Girls Association, 1998; Bahr, 1998; Y. Hamdan, 1998; al-Masri, 1998.

decision rests with the elected legislature, not the experts, since the latter lack a popular mandate. The role of the experts is thus confined to proposing amendments and alternatives, until the legislators agree on a mutually acceptable law (Abu Shannab, 1998c; al-Zahhar, 1998a).

Significantly, neither approach amounts to an expertocracy. Rather, Hamas' solution resembles the one suggested by Western political theorist Giovanni Sartori who proposed that, given the increasing complexity of state bureaucracies, governments should allow experts to help shape policies (Sartori, 1987: 426-33). To minimise the 'democratic deficit' this arrangement creates, Sartori drew a distinction between "democracy in input" ("how much the voice of the people counts") and "democracy in output" ("how much the people benefit"). The former remains subject to the popular will. The latter is to be shaped by experts. As long as "democracy in output" is held accountable to "democracy in input", the democratic deficit will be kept to a minimum.

Where Hamas and Sartori diverge is in the limits the latter sets on the government's sphere of action. Sartori insists that to safeguard democracy, the 'government of experts' must limit itself to decisions on means, leaving decisions regarding ends to the electorate. In theory, Hamas similarly maintains that a government's ends are determined by the electorate. In practice, however, a tension may emerge between Hamas' particular understanding of what is right, and allowing the electorate to choose freely. Hamas, after all, believes strongly that one can only find true freedom in an Islamic state, and it regards it as one of its main tasks to call people to a truer understanding of the Islamic faith (*da'wah*). With such an ideological disposition, the temptation will be to lead from the front, and shape the ends of government, rather than to allow the electorate to do so.

Positive vs. Negative Freedom

One tension that needs further exploration is between notions of what constitutes 'proper' or pious behaviour and freedom. Underpinning this tension are two, at times contradictory, conceptions of freedom. On the one hand, Hamas condemns any form of human tyranny and insists that people in an Islamic state should be able to "say and believe in whatever they wish" and "practise their personal beliefs in any way they want, socially or politically" (Musa, 1998b). This corresponds to what Isaiah Berlin (Berlin, 1969: 122-34) called a 'negative' conception of freedom—a *freedom from* constraints. On the other hand, Hamas insists that one can only be free if one obeys God's laws, corresponding to Berlin's 'positive' conception of freedom—the *freedom to* realise one's higher destiny. This second conception brings with it a particular set of expectations of what this higher destiny is, and what freedom should be used for.

The tension between these two conceptions manifests itself in numerous forms. It appears in the tension between consultation (allowing citizens to shape policies) and education (socialising citizens into willing the Islamic state). It shows in the tension between Hamas' defence of individual rights and its subjecting these to the rights of its particular understanding of community. It reveals itself in Hamas' simultaneously insisting that laws have a popular mandate, and that they are God's law.

The tension is most visible in Hamas' approach to establishing an Islamic state. On the one hand, Hamas argues that it will accept the will of the people, as expressed in elections. On numerous occasions, its leaders have stated categorically that they would abide by the outcome of a referendum, even if this went against the establishment of an Islamic state (cf. Hroub, 2000: 85-6, 210-2; Abu Shannab, 1998c; Haniyyah, 1998a; Hamad, 1998a; Bahr, 1998; see also Hamas Cell, 1998c; 'Nasr', 1998; al-Masri, 1998; Abu Zughri, 1998; 'Yusuf', 1998; Gunning, 2000: 246). On the other hand, however, Hamas has an explicit programme of socialising people into willing the Islamic state. Hamas' extensive charity network is part of this programme of *da'wah* (calling people to Islam), as is its network of Kindergartens, orphanages, and schools, including the Islamic University in Gaza.

Underpinning Hamas' approach to state-building is an almost Hegelian belief that membership of the ideal state is the only way for individuals to be genuinely free and become fulfilled. Or, using Hegelian language, only in a state ordered according to the universal (divine) will, shall individuals come into "possession of their ... own inner universality" (§153)[22] and so become free. True freedom, for both Hegel and Hamas, is "[to] know and will the universal ... [and] recognise it as [one's] own substantive mind" (§260; see also Cullen, 1979: 73-7; Schacht, 1976: 325). Both only believe this to be possible in the context of a state ordered according to the universal-divine will. This is what drives Hamas' positive conception of freedom, and its very definite ideas on what constitutes 'the good life', from its advocacy of the *hijab*, charitable work and, within the context of occupation, martyrdom, to its condemnation of corruption and nepotism.

The belief that individuals can only be free in an Islamic state profoundly affects the relationship between individual and state. Unlike the Western liberal notion that the state's primary function is to protect citizens (at least in theory), the state, for Hamas, is about human fulfilment. Rather than simply facilitating the individual's pursuit for private happiness, Hamas' Islamic state is meant to create the right legal and communal framework for both the individual and the community to discover and fulfil their divine destiny. Hamas' state is about membership and participation through which the right disposition is created in its citizens. Consultation, for Hamas, is part of this process of socialisation, of educating people to recognise the benefits of the Islamic system (cf. Hamad, 1998b; Abu Shannab, 1998c). The same holds for charitable work in the community.

This perspective is in part a function of the culture of which Hamas is an integral part, and which is much more community-oriented than most Western societies. It is also a function of the emphasis in Islam on community. Emphasis on community does not, however, mean that Hamas wholly neglects the needs of the individual. Rather, Hamas believes that by protecting the community and creating the divinely-ordained state, the individual's needs will be better met than by focusing solely on the individual. Because the *shari'ah* is God's creation, both the individual's and the community's needs are believed to be embedded within it. Submission to the *shari'ah*, moreover, is believed to transform both the individual and the community so that their needs will be brought into balance (cf. Abu Shannab, 1998a; Hamad, 1998a; Bahr, 1998). This argument closely mirrors Hegel's

---

22 Hegel, 1942.

that the individual can only find fulfilment in the universal will, and that this will does not neglect the needs of the individual because it contains the individual (cf. §141, §147, §260, §260A).

A positive conception of freedom informs Hamas' attitude towards the state. It informs Hamas' emphasis on education and *da'wah*. It strengthens Hamas' resolve that Islamic law is the only basis on which to create a state. Taken to its extreme, this conception of freedom leaves no room for popular consent. Freedom would be guaranteed by the fact that the law is God's law. Dissent in such a system would be meaningless as it could only emanate from the irrational and the misguided. Those who are not yet consenting simply need education to recognise what is best for them.

Significantly, though, this positive conception is kept in check by a negative conception of freedom. From this conception flows Hamas' insistence on consent in the establishment of an Islamic state—thus departing from Hegel who considered the popular will both normatively inappropriate and too capricious a basis for establishing the divine state (cf. Benhabib, 1984: 163ff; Houlgate, 2005: 208-9). A negative conception informs Hamas' argument that there be a private sphere outside the state's reach in which the law has no power and alternative visions of the good life are tolerated, on the ground that this is between God and the individual[23]—a position Hegel shared (§213, §270).

Hence the distinction between sin and illegality, between the moral and the legal, between the 'religious' and the political. Thus, though a Muslim voting for a communist candidate is considered to be sinning, he is not necessarily acting illegally (cf. 'Nasr', 1998). A Muslim drinking alcohol in his home is sinning but should be allowed to do so if he does not corrupt or harm society (cf. 'Muhammad', 1998). Similarly, a citizen should be free to practise atheism at home and participate in society but not actively proselytise for atheism (cf. Musa, 1998b; Bahr, 1998; Hamas Cell, 1998b).

---

23 Yassin, 1998a, 1998b; Abu Shannab, 1998a, 1998b, 1998c; Dukhan; Hamad, 1998a; 'Muhammad', 1998; 'Ibrahim'; Hamas and Khalas members, 1999; 'Ashraf', 1998; 'Nasr'; 'Iman'; Islamist and leftist women, 1998; Bahr, 1998; Musa, 1998b; 'Yusuf', 1998.

Views differ within Hamas over where exactly the line should be drawn between private and public, law and morality. Some would like to legislate against unmarried men and women meeting each other in the dunes behind Gaza's beach, although they insist that the law has to be passed by majority vote (implied by al-Zahhar, 1998b). Or they would like to restrict what satellite channels people can watch in the privacy of their homes because what they watch is believed to be potentially harmful to the wider community.

The majority, however, appear to see the role of the state as less intrusive. They oppose legislating on the *hijab*, even while actively promoting it (cf. Hamas legislators Maryam Farhat and Houda Naim al-Qrenawi; NPR, "Mothers of the Martyrs' Joins Hamas Parliament', 20 March 2006; WINEP, 2007). They are less restrictive regarding what people watch in the privacy of their homes. They insist that communists should have the right to organise a political party in an Islamic state, as long as they do not actively preach atheism (cf. Abu Shannab, 1998c; Musa, 1998b). However, wherever the line between private and public is drawn, all agree that any public action believed to undermine the Islamic basis of the state should be forbidden, once the electorate has come out in favour of an Islamic state.

Creating an Islamic state

Hamas sees the establishment of an Islamic state as an organic process, where people are gradually educated to see the benefits of an Islamic state so that, when a referendum is held, people will naturally choose the Islamic state over any other form of polity. In this, Hamas closely mirrors Hegel's approach to the state—and with it come the same types of accusations of harbouring totalitarian designs which Hegel is accused of (cf. Singer, 1983: 41; Riley, 1982: 261n89).

This is not the place to embark on a detailed comparison of Hegel and Hamas, query the argument that Hegel's system is necessarily totalitarian (cf. Schacht, 1976: 312-27; Singer, 1983: 41-4; Riley, 1982: 261), or underline that Hamas differs from Hegel precisely in its emphasis on the role of consent (Gunning, 2000: 207-21). But there is one element in Hegel's theory, at least on Stillman's interpretation, that helps to illuminate Hamas' approach to the state, and how it differs from the more Lockean ideas underpinning Western models of liberal democracy. For, as Stillman rightly observes (even though his analysis ignores the positive elements in Locke's conception of freedom; cf. Inayatullah and Blaney, 2004: 37-8; Berlin, 1969: 147; Tully, 1984: 70-1):

> Locke jumps from the natural man with his arbitrary will to the civil state which makes laws but otherwise lets man's arbitrary will have full play. In other words, Locke generally assumes (or ignores) all those institutions and ways by which the natural man ... becomes a civilized man ... But Hegel is surely correct in his argument that men plucked from the state of nature would not be able to maintain or govern a Lockean state. [...] [Hegel] spends much ... of the *Philosophy of Right* dealing not only with the political order and arbitrary freedom, but also with those various attitudes (like morality) and those various institutions (like the family, and the pluralistic group) by which men become fully developed men who have freedom, culture, and individuality, men who can give reasoned consent to a reasonable political order, men who are mature enough to be able to exercise their freedom (Stillman, 1974: 1086-7).

For Hegel, as for Hamas, structures shape people, and both insist that the ideal state cannot be realised without a lengthy preparatory process during which structures and institutions are altered so as to socialise people into the type of citizens the ideal state needs to function. In this, Hamas echoes Whitman who, in the context of 19th century American politics, emphasised the Hegelian notion of creating virtuous citizens precisely because, in Stout's words, constitutional checks and balances are, after all, in themselves insufficient to "prevent a wealthy and powerful class from rigging the electoral system to favor the wealthy and the powerful" (Stout, 2006: 21-2).

In this, Hamas is indebted to Mawdudi who in turn influenced Qutb (Maudoodi 1955: 3, 17-9, 31-6, 40-7; Qutb, 1964: 42-52). Taking the evolution of the first Islamic community around the Prophet as his example, Mawdudi observed that the Prophet did not establish an Islamic state overnight. Rather, he sought to gradually create the practices and institutions which would produce genuine Muslims capable of running an Islamic state according to the divine principles they had internalised. An Islamic state, Mawdudi concluded, could thus never materialise out of a secular nationalist project since its civil servants would not have internalised Islam's principles.

Following Mawdudi, Hamas compares the creation of an Islamic state to the evolution of the first Islamic community and the gradual revelation of the Qur'an. Hamad, for instance, likened the introduction of *shari'ah* law to the gradual way in which the Islamic prohibition against alcohol was revealed (Hamad, 1998b). Following Hamad, this prohibition was revealed in stages and did not become law until the community around the Prophet had understood—had 'recognised as their own substance', to use Hegelian terminology—why they should abstain from alcohol. In the same vein, "Islamic law should not be imposed in one instance—there are thousands of issues which need an answer before we can implement them. ... So I think at this point, the Islamic movement should not ask to implement Islamic law but first of all prepare society ...".

However, preparing society, in Hamas' view, is not just about socialising people into recognising the principles of *shari'ah* law as true. It also means creating the right socio-economic conditions. The ruling on theft, for instance, cannot become law until poverty and inequality have been eradicated so that no citizen has to steal to survive (al-Fenjari, 1998: 16, 9; Hamad, 1998b; Abu Marzook and Gaess, 1997: 126). The ruling on adultery similarly cannot be enforced until advertising and customs have been changed to reduce the sexual stimuli that permeate public life. Thus, only once the 'good society' has been established—where leaders subject themselves to the law, children are taught the values of religion, poverty is eradicated, and the moral environment offers "no causes for deviation, like wines and drugs and places for corruption and inciting sexual desire" (al-Fenjari, 1998)—can *shari'ah* law be implemented. Arab states who have imposed Islamic law overnight, without eliminating economic inequality and preparing society spiritually and morally—the Saudis are usually singled out—are condemned as acting "surely against Islam and God" (al-Fenjari, 1998; cf. also Hamad, 1998b).

The same attitude informs Hamas' attitude towards state-building. It believes an Islamic state can only emerge out of a long process of preparation and consultation involving the entire citizenry. Mirroring Hamas's own internal process of instilling a particular set of (pious) dispositions in its members, by inculcating fear of God, respect for morality, and a notion of servant-leadership (see also Chapter 4), the process of creating an Islamic state is conceptualised as a process of internalisation through discussion and participation. The very process of consultation is believed to inculcate a disposition towards consultation and thinking for the good of the community. Following Abu Shannab (1998d), "a group decision is better than an individual decision—even if the individual is right. This encourages democratic behaviour". Participation in mosques and charities is similarly seen as a way to inculcate the right disposition in citizens (al-Zahhar, 1998a), as is developing a social consciousness or what Abu Shannab (1998a) called 'societal interdependence' (*takaful ijtima'i*; cf. also Kotb, 1953: 30-67; Yassin, 1998b).

Although such a process of socialisation sits uncomfortably within a liberal framework, Hamas does not see a tension between freedom and socialisation. Rather, like Hegel, it believes that becoming socialised into recognising God's laws as true means becoming liberated. Because God is the creator, his laws are not, in Hegelian terms, 'alien' to the individual. Rather, they are an expression of his 'own essence', so that by recognising them, the individual is no longer alienated from his true self, but becomes fulfilled (Hegel, 1942: §147). Significantly—at least in theory—Hamas follows Hegel by arguing that this process cannot be forced. Only when the individual freely and independently recognises God's or the universal will as his own, will he be free (cf. Hegel, 1942: §213, 60A, 70; Schacht, 1976: 312-27; Singer, 1983: 41-4). In practice, however, the more one believes to know the truth, the greater the temptation to 'force people to be free'.

Rhetorically, Hamas desists from imposing 'divine justice' on Palestinians, insisting instead that any move towards an Islamic state must be a consensual one. Yet the emphasis here is not necessarily solely on finding out what people think but also on socialising them into internalising the principles of Islam. Consultation, then, becomes a process of socialisation, rather than an exercise in empowerment and direct democracy (cf. also Harb's study of Hizballah's municipal practices; Harb el-Kak, 2001). From Hamas' perspective, this process is benign since the end result is genuine freedom. For those who disagree with Hamas' interpretation, this process may well seem threatening.

In this regard, it is unsettling that many Hamas leaders seem to suggest that the creation of an Islamic state will be a smooth, harmonious process in which dissent will gradually dissipate (cf. also Euben's critique of Qutb's understanding of freedom; 1999: 158). Many of those who argued, for instance, that communists should have the right to stand for election in an Islamic state simultaneously believed that a genuinely Islamic state would persuade even the most ardent communist of its superiority, thus minimising the threat from communism (cf. Abu Shannab, 1998c; Hamad, 1998a). Similarly, some of those who opposed multi-partyism seemed to believe that in a genuine Islamic state there was no need for multiple parties (cf. al-Rantisi, 2002a). In this sense, despite Hamas recognising that truth is not unitary and that multiple interpretations of truth can exist side by side, Nüsse (1998: 78) is right to point out that Hamas' political theory insufficiently concerns itself with conflict "within [the] "will of the people"" as opposed to conflict "between the people and the ruler". In the absence of any realistic anticipation of dissent, such an approach increases the likelihood that Hamas will regard opponents as irrational or, worse still, apostates—although it has so far largely refrained from doing so.

Concluding Remarks

In this chapter, I have focused on Hamas' political theory, as presented to the outside world, and on the tensions inherent in it. I have shown that Hamas' theory echoes key themes from Western political theory, such as the notions of popular will, social contract and representative authority, and that these notions have come to overlay Islamic traditions, changing how the latter are interpreted. The notion of popular sovereignty is counter-balanced by the notion of divine sovereignty but, importantly, not negated, except in those instances where revelation is highly specific, as in the *hudud*. This has important implications for the role of religion and religious authority in politics, although the fact that Hamas' theory insists that popular mandate is more important than religious knowledge and reason is central to the process of legislation, suggests that the role of religion in politics may not be as large as is often assumed in

Western discourse. But even this counter-balancing of popular and divine sovereignty has parallels in the early modern natural law tradition in Western political philosophy, some significant differences notwithstanding.

One of the key differences between Western liberal models and Hamas' political theory is in the emphasis Hamas places on community and the (ideal) state. Here, Hamas' theory displays decidedly Hegelian elements, for instance in the notions that freedom can only be found in the divinely-ordered state, and that individuals need to be socialised, through engagement in the community and the state, into becoming truly free citizens. This introduces a fundamental tension between two different conceptions of freedom and humanity's purpose on earth, a tension which we will find runs through much of Hamas' political practice.

Whether the above interpretation of Hamas' theory corresponds with the organisation's 'hidden transcript' cannot be stated with certainty, although analysis of the organisation's internal structure and political culture suggests that this theory plays an important role both in how members wish Hamas to be perceived, and in their internal practices (Chapter 4). Analysis of Hamas' behaviour in the domestic arena similarly suggests that the above theory informs much of how the organisation has sought to present itself towards the electorate. At the same time, as will become clear, significant tensions exist, not just within Hamas' political theory, but also between theory and practice.

Even if an alernative, 'hidden' discourse operates in parallel, the logic of the public discourse is likely to have influenced the way members see themselves and value certain practices over others. This is even more so for Hamas' non-affiliated supporters who are less likely to have access to this 'hidden' discourse. That all interviewees, ranging from media-savvy leaders to media-shy supporters who had never been interviewed before, expressed roughly the same set of ideas suggests furthermore that this public discourse is pervasive within the organisation, or at least among its general support base.

If Hamas' theory is anything to go by, it values both 'religious' and representative authority. Of particular interest in the following chapters is how these two types of authority manifest themselves in practice, whether in the way Hamas leaders claim authority, in

Hamas' approach to elections, or in its attitude towards the peace process. Of similar interest is what role violence plays in both the creation of authority and in its maintenance, given that, in theory, and despite its prescriptive approach to freedom, Hamas condemns the use of violence to coerce people into obeying Islamic injunctions or submitting to illegitimate authority (although it does reserve a role for violence for upholding legitimate authority and, in extreme situations, for disposing of an illegitimate ruler).

4

AUTHORITY WITHIN HAMAS

Contrary to its western image as a 'terrorist organisation' pursuing a Taleban-style theocracy, Hamas is considered by its supporters as an organisation of pious, upright citizens who defend the interests of their grassroots constituency. Among them, it is celebrated for its consensual decision-making, its readiness to consult its support base and its emphasis on self-sacrifice and integrity. How are we to make sense of these contradictory images?

This chapter will explore the internal authority structures and political practices of Hamas. It will consider what makes a Hamas leader, or a particular policy decision, authoritative within the organisation, formally and informally, and what role popular mandate, 'religious' authority and violence play in this.

Because Hamas portrays itself as a precursor of an Islamic state, the type of authority structures it has created internally reflect some of the central aspects of its political theory. As with any human organisation, Hamas' practice both imperfectly reflects its ideals and suffers from the contradictions inherent in those ideals. But it is perceived by its supporters as genuinely trying to be true to these ideals. Hamas' internal practices are thus a rich source for gaining a fuller understanding of both its political theory and what factors shape its policy decisions and behaviour (for instance, why Hamas has been unable to rapidly develop innovative policy responses since coming to power).

Conceptualising Authority

Authority is a form of social control (cf. Friedman, 1990: 59-60; Barnett, 2001: 55). Within both Western political science and Islamic political philosophy, it is usually understood—though not always consistently used as such (Friedman, 1990: 62)—as a form of non-coerced control. Authority is a relational phenomenon; one cannot have authority unless someone else recognises and consents to it. It is thus both inherently subjective and inter-subjective, and must be understood within a particular framework of shared values.

One of the most influential models of authority within Western political theory is that of Max Weber who identified three archetypal forms of authority: charismatic, traditional and rational-legal (Weber, 1964: 328-63). Charismatic authority engages the emotions, and is found in heroes and prophets, both of whom have what Weber calls the 'gift of grace' (or what Palestinians call '*barakah*', God's blessing). Traditional authority is derived from "the sanctity of the [traditional] order" and is found in, for example, feudal lords. Rational-legal authority is derived from occupying a position in a bureaucracy that is ruled by formal rules and hierarchies. In the first two cases, loyalty and obedience are owed to the person in authority. In the third, they are owed to the rules and the office of authority.

However, Weber's typology is inadequate for our purposes because it does not adequately address the relationship between personal and institutional, and between formal and informal authority (cf. Lukes, 1990: 207). Hamas leaders both contribute to the organisation's political standing through their personal reputation, and derive authority from their position in the organisation. Their authority rests in part on election, but this in itself says little about the type of authority they wield, or what role 'religious' authority or violence play. To unravel this, we must look beyond the formal at what ordinary members believe makes their leaders authoritative.

Authority is often characterised as coming in one of two forms: one derived from a person's place in the hierarchy of an organisation (institutional or *de jure* authority), the other derived from a person's individual characteristics (personal or *de facto* authority). A person can be 'in authority', 'an authority' or a mixture of both (cf. Friedman, 1990; Lukes, 1990; Carter, 1979; Barnett, 2001).

One way to conceptualise this distinction is through Pierre Bourdieu's notion of 'symbolic capital' (Bourdieu, 1991: 194; see also Bourdieu and Passeron, 1973; Bourdieu, 1986). 'Personal capital', in Bourdieu's schema, is the authority that comes from personal characteristics such as fame, popularity, charisma, heroism, knowledge, skills, or a good reputation. It can be 'cultural capital' (knowledge, skills, piety, experience), 'social capital' (social standing, family connections, social networks), or 'economic capital' (with which both 'cultural' and 'social capital' are intertwined). It often concerns informal authority, recognised by those in its thrall, but not necessarily made explicit in formal structures. As such, it is more about being 'an authority' than being 'in authority'.

'Delegated capital' is the authority derived from one's position in an organisation (Bourdieu, 1991: 190-6). It is "capital held and controlled by the institution", and consists of both "objective structures" and the "symbolic capital of *recognition* and *loyalties*" that has accumulated over the years "through the action of its officers and its militants" and their personal capital. Delegated capital requires authorisation from the organisation to represent it. It is representative authority—but it does not necessarily involve elections. Members of Parliament have delegated capital. But so do (unelected) priests, academics and diplomats. Where there are elections, delegated capital is controlled by both the institution and those entitled to elect. However, as Bourdieu notes, "the elected member of a party apparatus depends at least as much on the apparatus as on his electors".

Wielding symbolic capital is impossible without "the collaboration of those it governs" (Bourdieu, 1991: 113, 205-15). It is in this process of collaboration that representative authority can become manipulative. For Bourdieu, authority is based not primarily on recognition but on "misrecognition": on usurpation of power achieved through the concealment of what actually occurs in the process of authorisation (cf. also Weber's critique of the origins of elective democracy; Weber, 1964: 386-92). The exercise of such power Bourdieu calls 'symbolic violence' (209-10). It is discursive, not physical violence, and is considered legitimate by those against whom it is used—and thus typically invisible to them.

Where authority is based on superior expert knowledge, the terms 'misrecognition' and 'symbolic violence' are less applicable. But they do highlight one of the core tensions in relationships of authority, namely that between self- and group interests. Those who lead typically present themselves as pursuing the collective interest. They try to change others' behaviour by appealing to this notion (or closely related variants such as God's will) while concealing, often also from themselves, the extent to which they pursue their self-interest. To the extent that their followers accept this claim to self-less leadership, they are complicit in this 'misrecognition', and undermine the effectiveness of the electoral process to scrutinise and hold accountable.

Partially overlapping with this dynamic is the tension between representation as formally given consent, and representation as identification or recognition. In the first instance, representation is contractual, and, because it is formally 'tested', contains the explicit possibility of scrutiny. In the second instance, the source of authority lies elsewhere, whether in knowledge, moral rectitude, embodiment of national identity or divine designation—closely resembling forms of 'religious' authority (cf. also E. D. Watt, 1982: 67). It still involves consent since the exercise of authority requires collaboration. But because the formal source of authority is not consent itself, scrutiny becomes less central.

Formal Authority Structures

Formal authority within Hamas is derived from elections. At the bottom of the hierarchy are small 'cells' or '*usrat*' (families) which consist of a cell leader and cell members. At the next level are regional consultative or *shura* councils, which consist of representatives elected biennially by established Hamas members[1] within a particular

---

1   The boundary between established members (who are formally consulted) and new recruits (who are not) is unclear but it appears that (some) rank and file members who have pledged their loyalty to Hamas and shown their commitment participate even if they have not reached the position of cell leader. According to one former cadre leader ('Muhammad',

region.[2] In addition, each prison appears to have the equivalent of a *shura* council (cf. Abu Shannab, 1998a; Hamad, 1998b; Abu Zughri, 1998; 'Ashraf', 1998). The regional *shura* councils elect representatives to a national *Shura* Council, which in turn elects the Executive Council or Political Bureau (cf. Mish'al, 2002; Yassin, 1998a; al-Rantisi, 2002a; Abu Shannab, 1998d; Haniyyah, 1998a; Hamad, 1998b). Both the *Shura* Council and the Political Bureau consist of members drawn from the various geographical regions. But the Political Bureau is dominated by those living in exile, primarily in Lebanon and Syria—although it has representatives of the Executive Councils in Gaza and the West Bank (Mish'al, 2002; al-Rantisi, 2002a; Tamimi, 2007).[3]

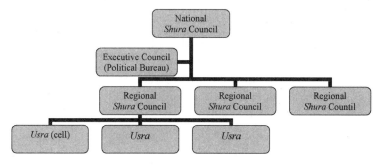

Figure 1. Schematic depiction of Hamas' organisational structure

The *Shura* Council is the equivalent of the legislative power at state level. It has final authority over formal policy decisions, and

---

1998), the voting was initially restricted to those who had been with Hamas for five years and had become Muslim Brothers. But the pool appears to have been subsequently widened since a number of rank and file members I interviewed acknowledged they had voted.

2   Mishal and Sela (158) list seven regions in Gaza, and five in the West Bank.

3   According to Mishal and Sela (157-63), the Political Bureau consists solely of exiled leaders; they do not mention the existence of a movement-wide *Shura* Council. Hroub (2000: 58-9; 2006: 117-20) concurs with my finding that the Bureau and *Shura* Council consist of leaders from both inside and outside, as does Levitt (2006: 9-10).

determines the strategy and political aims of the organisation. The Political Bureau is the equivalent of the executive at state level and is charged with the day-to-day implementation of the *Shura* Council's strategy (Mish'al, 2002; Yassin, 1998a; al-Rantisi, 2002a). It does not have the mandate to set overall policy and if it oversteps its mandate, the *Shura* Council has the authority to disband the Executive Council (although, in practice, and despite members of the Executive Council seeking to influence overall policy, this has, as far as we know, never happened).

Policies are developed by what Mishal and Sela call a "bureaucratic hierarchy" of different committees. Each committee has several sub-committees which, according to Khalid Mish'al (2002), the Damascus-based head of the Political Bureau, involve 'the base' of the movement so that policies are "made from below" (although, as we will see, the reality is somewhat more complex). Mishal and Sela, Hroub and Levitt all mention the existence of such a hierarchy of committees, each with its own Weberian 'sphere of competence' (such as social welfare, media relations, political activities, Islamic preaching, finance, internal security and 'paramilitary' activities) and, crucially, involving the grassroots (Mishal and Sela, 2000: 155-60; Hroub, 2006a: 118; Levitt, 2006: 9-11).

Constitutionally, women cannot be Hamas members—although Hamas seems to have allowed women to become part of the *Shura* Council since its 2006 election victory (Hroub, 2007). Women play a central part in the Islamic movement's overall success. The population group with the second highest percentage of Hamas voters (47 per cent) in the 2006 election were 'housewives' (PSR PLC Exit Poll, February 2006).[4] A number of Hamas legislators and municipal councillors are women (WINEP, 2007; see also Chapter 5). Among Hamas' most active supporters are the female branches of its student wing, the Islamic Bloc, who operate independently from their male counterparts. Women are similarly active in numerous affiliated women's charities. In most instances, these organisations are run by women and their authority structures resemble those of Hamas (see further).

---

4   See also NEC (January 2006); Hilal, 2006.

Formal Structure and Representative Authority

Both the *Shura* Council and the Political Bureau derive their formal authority from elections. They are mandated to act on behalf of the collective and as such, their authority is representative both in a contractual and a delegated sense (Birch, 1993: 69-79). They also represent (both symbolically and physically) the different regions and interest groups within Hamas, from affiliated charities and elected officials to the Qassam Brigades.

Only if leaders are believed to be speaking on behalf of the organisation are they considered authoritative by the membership (cf. Hamas Cell, 1998c; Islamic Bloc members, 1998). They may be 'an authority' on the basis of their acquired personal or cultural capital. Those who have studied Islamic law, for instance, are considered more authoritative on matters pertaining to Islamic law. But, true to Hamas' political theory (Chapter 3), their views are not politically binding.

Hamas leaders readily recognise that their authority is derived from membership of the *Shura* Council and that it is circumscribed by the Council's decisions. Al-Rantisi, for instance, stressed that "if the *Shura* Council says that Hamas should do something, then we, as leaders here, and Khalid Mish'al [abroad] will say what the *Shura* [Council] said. ... So the last word will be for the *Shura* [Council], not for Khalid Mish'al or Shaykh Ahmad Yassin" (al-Rantisi, 2002a). Mish'al similarly insisted that decisions are never made "by one man", adding that "the age of the hero is over" (Mish'al, 2002)—a sentiment echoed by Ismail Abu Shannab, one of Hamas' three most senior leaders in Gaza before his assassination in 2003, who argued that "the group decision is better than the individual decision, even if the individual is right" (Abu Shannab, 1998d).

Ordinary Hamas members also insist that decisions are only authoritative if representative of the *Shura* Council's will. Leaders suspected of presenting their personal view as the collective will or of creating a personal power base within Hamas are seriously frowned upon (cf. Hamas Cell, 1998a; 'Ashraf', 1998). Even those leaders with the added authority of greater 'personal capital', such as Ahmad Yassin or 'Abd al-'Aziz al-Rantisi (the two most senior leaders in Gaza before their assassination in 2004), are not deemed to have the authority to go against the collective will of the *Shura* Council (Hamas Cell, 1998a). Despite Yassin having championed the notion of a *hudnah*, or long-term ceasefire, since the early 1990s, for instance, the *Shura* Council never formally adopted his position (Tamimi, 2007). Formal authority is thus derived from occupying an elected position and representing the collective will. It consists of 'delegated capital'.

Both leaders and ordinary members emphasise that a Hamas leader's authority is contractual. According to Khalid Mish'al,

We in Hamas ... use democracy and rely on it ... for this gives every man in Hamas the right to have a vote, to choose this one and not that one and to hold [whoever he chooses] accountable, to ask about his behaviour ... We have no atmosphere of dictatorship, no fear. I am now in a leading position, however, for example, I do not control the salary or the money or privileges of a member of Hamas ... When people choose me or anyone else it is not because they are afraid of me or because I control their position within the movement or their money ... No, he chooses me as a result of conviction ...: who is more capable, who is more trustworthy, who is more suitable. These are the aspects we look for when we choose the leaders. And this, I believe, is the right direction: it is what protects the movement and guarantees that those who climb up [the ranks] are the most efficient (Mish'al, 2002).

This self-description is significant in what it says about how Hamas' leadership wishes to present itself. It must be read in the context of Hamas' rivalry with Fatah. What Hamas is depicted as 'not being', is typically what ordinary Palestinians have accused Fatah of being (dictatorial, nepotistic, corrupt). It must also be read as a self-justificatory statement that seeks to downplay tensions in the practice of authority. Despite Mish'al's claim that he does not control the salaries of Hamas members, for instance, he and the external leadership around him control the funds raised internationally for the Qassam Brigades, enabling them to influence overall policy (cf. Mishal and Sela, 2000: 160-9; Robinson, 1997: 193).

However, the available evidence does suggest that internal elections are contests with no guarantee of re-election, and that no individual leader has the power to impose his views on the movement. Abu Shannab and al-Rantisi claimed that up to a third of the *Shura* Council is not re-elected (a claim I have not been able to verify although ordinary members implied the same), and Abu Shannab insisted that in the 1980s Yassin had not always been re-elected as head of the organisation (Abu Shannab, 1998d; al-Rantisi, 2002a; cf. also Tamimi, 2007). Similarly, a number of observers have underlined the collective nature of decision-making in Hamas, and the absence of autocratic leaders (cf. ICG, 2007a: 26-7; Hroub, 2000: 58-9; Mishal and Sela, 2000: 121-35).

Furthermore, ordinary members do not appear afraid to criticise their leaders or express dissent. Al-Zahhar's position that *zakah* tax (a religiously-sanctioned annual tax) would be sufficient in an Islamic state was typically dismissed as unrealistic. Abu Shannab's lenient attitude towards atheists in an Islamic state was challenged, though not dismissed. Critique was facilitated by members knowing that al-Zahhar's and Abu Shannab's positions were not shared by all Hamas leaders. But the fact remains that interviewees felt free to openly disagree with their senior leaders—even in their presence.[5]

Members criticised aspects of the *Shura* Council's policies. Some disagreed with the decision to boycott the 1996 elections. Others disagreed with the continuation of suicide operations in the late 1990s. But, as long as they believed that the decision had been taken by the Council, they accepted it as authoritative and binding (cf. al-Rantisi, 2002a; Hamami, 1997; 'Ahmad', 1998; Hamas Cell, 1998a; ICG, 2006a: 5n25).

Part of the *Shura* Council's authority rests on the way decisions are made. As its name suggests (*shura* means 'to consult'), it is expected to consult—among *Shura* Council members, but also with the grassroots where fundamental decisions are concerned. A number of organisation-wide consultations preceded the decision to boycott the 1996 elections, the ceasefire declarations in 2003 and 2005, and the decision to participate in the 2006 legislative elections (Mishal and Sela, 2000: 121-35; Gunning, 2004: 250-1; Kalman, 2006b). The list of legislative candidates was similarly compiled through organisation-wide consultations (Kalman, 2006b). Though final decisions rest with the *Shura* Council, these are considered more authoritative when taken after consultation with the wider membership. In this

---

5 Most such instances involved cell members disagreeing with their cell leader. On a few occasions, though, I observed members and supporters challenging Hamas' senior political leaders.

sense, the *Shura* Council's authority is derived from its representing the collective will (although, in practice, members have no formal mechanism beyond word-of-mouth for ascertaining that the *Shura* Council's decisions are indeed representative; see further).

Decisions within the *Shura* Council are determined by majority vote; those which fundamentally affect the movement's direction require a two-thirds majority (cf. al-Rantisi, 2002a; Shamma', 1998; Hamad, 1998b). A decision is thus only authoritative if both taken by elected representatives, and representative of the movement's collective will (on the understanding that a two-thirds majority among elected representatives is likely to reflect this will).

In the many affiliated organisations that together make up the wider 'Islamic movement' authority is similarly derived from elections. The Islamic Bloc student organisations, Hamas' political affiliate Hizb al-Khalas and the affiliated charities I investigated in Gaza all hold elections as a means to both selecting and legitimating the leadership. Charities operate two-tiered hierarchies, with registered members electing an Executive Board or Administrative Council of typically around 7-9 members (al-Yazuri, 1998; Muslih, 1998; Muslim Girls Association, 1998; Director Women's Training Centre, 1998; 'Ibrahim', 1998; al-Kurd, 1998). As the law under which charities are registered does not stipulate how Boards are to be selected, the fact that charities have chosen to adopt this model is highly significant.

The Islamic Bloc and Hizb al-Khalas operate multi-tiered hierarchies. Student members of the Islamic Bloc elect a twenty-member *Shura* Council which elects a seven-member Administrative Council (al-Masri, 1998; Taha, 1998; Abu Zughri, 1998; 'Yusuf', 1998). The Administrative Council oversees day-to-day affairs and is tasked with appointing an election committee to select nine candidates for the university-wide student council elections whose candidacy has to be ratified by the Administrative Council. Hizb al-Khalas members elect regional *Shura* Councils which then elect representatives to the party's 250-member General Assembly who, in turn, elect the fifty-one-member *Shura* Council out of which the fourteen-member Political Bureau is chosen (Musa, 1998b; al-Bardawil, 1998; Y. Hamdan, 1998). In all these cases, formal authority is derived from election to a representative body which is invested with the institutional authority to make binding decisions.

The centrality of contractual authority in Hamas' self-depiction—and of the role consultation plays in its maintenance—is further illustrated by the way female activists responsible for running a women's branch of Hamas' flagship charity in Gaza, al-Mujamma' al-Islami, described their relationship with the Mujamma''s all-male General Assembly. When asked whether they believed themselves to be part of the charity's decision-making process, they said:

> We are part of the *shura* [consultation] process. We tell them what we think. If we weren't listened to, we wouldn't have the motivation to continue working for them. Of course we are asked. ... We don't feel the need to be members of the General Assembly. ... As long as our opinions are being represented, we are happy (Director Women's Training Centre, 1998).

These women were not formally part of the Mujamma''s decision-making structures. Nevertheless, they described their relationship with the General Assembly as one of representation. For them, the General Assembly had authority because their views were represented. Here, too, the relationship is conceptualised as contractual and based on trust, although not via the mechanism of elections.

The dominance of this contractual model is further underlined by the relative absence of alternative models. Formal authority within the organisation has little to do with 'religious' knowledge or 'religious' authority. This does not mean that 'religious' authority plays no role for, as we will see, it is central in the creation of personal capital and the legitimisation of representative structures. But in a formal sense, authority is derived from elections.

Charismatic authority, particularly of the ego-centric, rule-transcending kind, is actively condemned. Charismatic qualities are only admired if put to the service of the movement. Any hint of self serving posturing undermines a leader's authority (cf. Hamas Cell, 1998c; Islamic Bloc members, 1998). Unlike Fatah, where Arafat long dominated decision-making, Hamas has succeeded in creating a 'collective leadership' culture. No individual Hamas leader has the authority to impose his will on the organisation. This held true for its founder, Yassin who, despite being revered, was overruled by the

Shura Council on numerous occasions, most notably regarding participation in the 1996 legislative elections (Tamimi, 2007; Mish'al and Sela, 2000: 132-6; Hroub, 2000: 222-9). But it also holds for Ismail Haniyyah, the current Prime Minister, and Khalid Mish'al, the Damascus-based head of the Political Bureau (ICG, 2007a: 26-7). Although the organisation's consensual model has come under severe strain since Hamas' 2006 election victory and the movement is more internally divided than it has been to date, there is no evidence yet that Mish'al or any other leader has been able to impose his will on the wider organisation.

Hamas condemns nepotism, patronage and all forms of inherited authority—although this condemnation must be seen in the context of its rivalry with Fatah, and the widespread perception that Fatah is guilty of gross nepotism. Where leaders are believed to have gained a position through patronage Hamas members are typically scathing (cf. Hamas Cell, 1998c). The promotion of family members is categorically condemned.[6] Conversely, that two of Yassin's sons worked as cleaners at the Islamic University is applauded, as is the fact that the sons of senior leaders have had to earn their positions of authority on the basis of their own achievements.

Hamas leaders are typically unrelated to the families that have dominated Palestinian politics for much of the 20th century. This is not to say that Hamas does not exploit traditional authority structures to further its political goals (Chapter 5), or that, within Hamas, patronage plays no role (see further). In some cases, geographical links can be found between Hamas leaders, begging the question whether familiarity based on origin played a background role in the ascent of some. Al-Rantisi, Musa Abu Marzuq (first head of the Political Bureau in Amman), and Ghazi Hamad (currently spokesperson for the Hamas-led government) are all refugees from the village of Yubna (situated between al-Majdal/Ashkelon and Yaffa/Tel Aviv), while Yassin and Abu Shannab come from Joura and Jeyeh, villages close to Yubna (Milton-Edwards, 1996: 98; M. Rantisi, research assistant,

---

6 For security reasons, blood relationships appear to play a more prominent role in the Qassam Brigades (cf. Roy, 1995a: 30; Post, Sprinzak and Denny, 2003: 172-3).

pers. comm., 2007; *Hamas Leaders*, n.d.; *Palestine Report*, 'Straight from the mouth', 16 January 1998; Lynfield, 2003). Similarly, some sons of political leaders have become prominent within the Qassam Brigades. Ayman Taha, son of Muhammad Taha, is a case in point as are some of his brothers (*Birmingham Post*, 'Israelis capture Hamas founder', 4 March 2003; Rosenberg, 2003). Without further research, these facts are insufficient to prove that patronage plays a decisive role. Available evidence suggests that ability and rapport with the wider membership are more decisive and that instances of patronage are limited and not systemic.

Tensions within Hamas' Representative Model

The notion of representation dominates Hamas' formal authority structure. However, there are a number of tensions which seriously undermine its structure's representative function.

One derives from Hamas' practice of nominating candidates from above. According to Hamas' ethos, those actively seeking power are suspect because they are believed to be motivated by self-interest—a view rooted in early Islamic tradition (cf. Maududi, 1960b: 47) with which members are inculcated (cf. through posters on the walls of the Islamic University's Student Union office; Islamic Bloc members, 1998; Abu Zughri, 1998; Hamas Cell, 1998c). Self-promotion is disapproved of, although Hamas leaders recognise that in a mass society worthy candidates may have to promote themselves to become noticed (Abu Shannab, 1998c; Yassin, 1998b; al-Zahhar, 1998a; Muslih, 1998). In itself, such an approach is not antithetical to representation. Indeed, the way Hamas sees it, candidates should be nominated by their communities, thus enhancing the representative function of elections. In practice, however, the relative absence of public arenas in which to observe leadership potential, coupled with the deference junior members exhibit towards their elders (despite their readiness to criticise them) means that nominations appear to come from above rather than below.

Interviewees were reluctant to discuss this issue for security reasons. But the available evidence suggests that nominations are more likely to be from above. The elected leadership of Hamas' student wing in Gaza, for instance, appoints a committee which selects a list of potential candidates for the universities' Student Council elections which is then ratified by the Administrative (or Executive) Council (al-Masri, 1998; Abu Zughri, 1998; Taha, 1998). Students do not normally nominate themselves because "they have been educated not to ask for [leadership]" (Abu Zughri). The way the members of the former Intifada cell discussed the trajectories of individual leaders similarly suggests that endorsement by the existing leadership is key to a candidate progressing upwards (Hamas Cell, 1998c). That a disillusioned ex-cadre leader accused the leadership of meddling in elections by limiting the choice of candidates available underlines this point ('Muhammad', 1998).

If a candidate cannot progress without leadership endorsement, Hamas' representative structure may not be as open to the grassroots as its leaders suggest. Members might be able to hold candidates accountable by withholding their vote. But their ability to nominate candidates appears to be limited. Elections seem to be more about conferring authority than about an open competition for leadership.

Significantly, the ex-cadre leader did not deny that candidates needed membership support to become elected, and acknowledged that he still had a choice of "five or six" candidates for three positions. According to the former Intifada cell (1998c), whose views were typical of those I encountered generally, someone can only become a leader in Hamas "when he is trusted by both the people and the leaders, and because of his skills and activities—all three of these are needed". Conversely, "if the base loses trust in a leader, they don't wait for the leadership to say that this is right". They cited only one case where they suspected a candidate was elected because of his proximity to a senior Hamas leader, remarking that the candidate had since vindicated his promotion to leadership. They also insisted that young members with leadership potential had rapidly risen through the ranks if they had the support of both members and leaders.

Coupled with the claims by Abu Shannab and al-Rantisi that up to a third of the existing *Shura* Council is not re-elected, and that almost all interviewees stated that they believed their leaders to be trustworthy, the available evidence intimates that, despite the need for leadership endorsement, elections perform a contractual function by serving as a reminder that leaders are accountable to the grassroots membership. They do not, however, appear to offer free and open competition.

A second set of tensions lies in Hamas' consensual decision-making model. At one level, this model increases the organisation's contractual-representative, and indeed, democratic, credentials. It encourages leaders to consult the grassroots and to express their, or their constituency's, opinions freely. The result is a lively, often heated, internal debate between competing positions (see also Klein, 2007: 445, 449-50).

In the lead-up to both the 1996 and the 2006 legislative elections the *Shura* Council was divided over the question of whether to participate. Prior to the first legislative elections, the wider membership was consulted, both inside and outside the occupied territories, including those in prison (Abu Shannab, 1998a; Haniyyah, 1998a; Hamad, 1998b; Bahr, 1998; 'Muhammad', 1998; Mishal and Sela, 2000: 120-35; Milton-Edwards, 1996: 163-6). A summary of the first stage of consultation was distributed amongst senior leaders who were then asked to "consult with knowledgeable people in your area" with the purpose of reaching "a decision acceptable to the widest possible basis of our ranks, which, at the same time, would preserve the movement's achievements and remain faithful to its goals and principles" (Mishal and Sela, 2000: 123; for full text of memorandum, see 122-30). Even interviewees who had been too junior to be consulted knew of the consultation and knew which leaders advocated which set of arguments (Hamas Cell, 1998a; 'Iyad', 1998; 'Ashraf', 1998; 'Nasr', 1998). The consultation thus appears to have been relatively inclusive, and relatively transparent (to the extent that a clandestine organisation can be transparent).

Although interviewees invariably stated that they believed the final decision to have been representative, in the absence of meticulous records it is impossible to corroborate this claim. Since the final decision was made by delegates attending negotiations with Fatah and other factions in Khartoum and Cairo (Mish'al, 2002; Kristianasen, 1999: 27; Mishal and Sela, 2000: 134), the consultation seems, in practice, to have served to register the concerns of the wider movement, rather than to reach a definite decision. However, the delegates did appear to derive their authority from being mandated by the *Shura* Council to negotiate on the basis of a set of recommendations arrived at by majority vote. Regardless of how representative the decision was, it was explicitly legitimated by the notion of representation—and not with reference to 'religious' or other forms of authority (cf. Mishal and Sela, 2000: 121-2). Furthermore, the leadership had a pragmatic incentive to heed the consultation's findings as this would increase the likelihood that the final decision would be accepted by the membership as legitimate.

However, it is precisely Hamas' cumbersome consensual model which can both prevent the expression of dissent and tempt elements within the Hamas leadership to manipulate it. If Hamas were a legal organisation operating in the open, these tensions would not be as pronounced. But, because Hamas has operated for most of its life in a clandestine environment, it is difficult for potential dissenters to know whether their position is shared more widely.

Because Hamas' political culture emphasises the ideals of unity, consensus and harmony, there is enormous pressure to conform. On sensitive or emotive subjects, such as whether to recognise Israel, it takes courage to depart from what is believed to be the dominant view, particularly as the one public arena where Hamas members hear each others' views is the mass rally where populist themes dominate. It is no surprise, therefore, that those few who publicly dissent on emotive issues are typically leaders who feel sure of their grassroots support. Abu Shannab's tireless advocacy of a long-term ceasefire is a case in point, as is Ismail Haniyyah's decision to (briefly) stand in the 1996 legislative elections. Both leaders had a wide support base which enabled them to take political risks.

Haniyyah's decision to withdraw his 1996 candidacy illustrates the power of this consensual dynamic well. In December 1995, Haniyyah and a handful of colleagues decided to stand for election, despite the leadership's decision to boycott the elections (Haniyyah, 1998a).[7] Haniyyah's dissenting position was widely shared (Mishal

---

7   Reports differ over how many leaders declared their candidacy. Six names have been mentioned in total, one from the West Bank (Jamil Hamami), five from Gaza: 'Imad al-Faluji, then chief editor of Hamas' official mouthpiece *al-Watan* and the most senior among the five, Ismail Haniyyah, Khalid al-Hindi, Sa'id al-Namruti, and Nasser Muzaini (Hroub, 2000: 224; Andoni, 1996: 7; Segal, 1995; Mish'al,

and Sela, 2000: 132-5; Hroub, 2000: 225-7), suggesting that the decision to boycott the elections was not as representative as claimed by interviewees. Not only had a significant number of leaders argued for participation but voter turn-out in Hamas-controlled areas was allegedly high (Mishal and Sela, 2000: 136; Zogby, 1996: 5; *Jerusalem Times*, 26 December 1996: 3), despite edicts by the external leadership not to vote (which were countered by the internal leadership who declared that Hamas members should follow their own conscience in deciding whether to vote; *Jerusalem Times*, 'Hamas refuses to join', 29 December 1995: 2). According to Haniyyah, he had sought, and obtained, authorisation from the leadership to stand for election in a personal capacity (Haniyyah, 1998a). However, his actions were not unanimously supported, opening up the possibility that Haniyyah had only been authorised by a section of the leadership. Some of those who disagreed distributed leaflets calling Haniyyah and his colleagues traitors (Mish'al, 2002; 'Ashraf', 1998; 'Ahmad', 1998; 'Khalid', 2000; Pro-Hamas Students, 1998). Others, such as al-Rantisi, sent letters from prison to persuade them to stand down, arguing that if they did not do so, the general population would think that Hamas had effectively split (al-Rantisi, 2002a).

In the end, all but one withdrew their candidacy—because, in Haniyyah's words, they believed their candidacy "would endanger the unity of the Islamic movement" (Haniyyah, 1998a; see also Dunn, 1996). Note that he did not say 'because my position was wrong'. That Haniyyah and his colleagues agreed to withdraw on the grounds of 'preserving unity' underlines how difficult it is for leaders to dissent and how the demand for 'unity' can be used to enforce compliance, particularly in a situation where the organisation's future appears to be at stake. This is a typical case of 'symbolic violence'—though, significantly, not physical violence (see further).

Even without overt coercion, the consensual model can thus be (ab)used to impose a unanimous position even if the dissenting position has technically been authorised and may have represented the majority view of the grassroots members. If the majority did indeed support Haniyyah's candidacy, and if a majority of the *Shura* Council

2002; Dunn, 1996).

opposed it (both of which are, in the absence of hard data, mere suppositions), this would be an example of the tension between representative models of democracy (where the electorate appoints representatives to make the decisions) and direct democracy (where the majority of the electorate determines the decision). As such, it would not have contradicted the principle of representation, since the membership had authorised the *Shura* Council to decide as it saw fit. If, however, a minority within the *Shura* Council 'persuaded' the majority to comply by threatening to break away (which would be particularly 'persuasive' if this minority controlled the finances to fund the resistance effort, as the external leadership did), this would have contradicted the principle of representation.

Too little is known regarding the level of support for different positions within the *Shura* Council. According to numerous sources, the external leadership was more opposed to participation than the internal leadership (Mish'al, 2002; Hamad, 1998b; Musa, 1998a; 'Muhammad', 1998; Mishal and Sela, 2000: 134, 64-66; Kristianasen, 1999: 27; see also interview with Ghawshah, *Falastin al-Muslimah*, October 1992). However, a significant number among the internal leadership and the grassroots similarly opposed participation (Mishal and Sela, 2000: 134; Kristianasen, 1999: 28).

This consensual leadership model both strengthens and weakens the organisation. It has prevented the fragmentation of Hamas—in sharp contrast to the splits experienced by other Palestinian factions. Precisely because authority is believed to be derived from representing the collective, once a decision is taken by the *Shura* Council, it is accepted as authoritative by the membership, regardless of whether they agree with it. This process is aided by the trust members have in the leadership. But it also makes the decision-making process slow, unwieldy, and conservative. Because leaders have few channels through which to debate new positions or canvass support, the dynamic of the consensual process favours conservative views. Prolonged consultation and collective decision-making (complicated by the dispersed nature of Hamas' leadership) mean Hamas cannot respond quickly to external developments. One of the reasons that has been cited for Hamas' inability to agree to implicitly recognise Israel—despite public promises by Haniyyah to that effect—is precisely this 'collective leadership' culture which militates against flexibility and developing new positions (ICG, 2006b: 6).

The unwieldy nature of the decision-making process also presents an opportunity to manipulate it, either by presenting a decision as more representative than it is, or by creating situations on the ground that foreclose certain options. Significantly, none of the interviewees expressed doubts about their leadership's commitment to report back the findings of consultations faithfully. This is in striking contrast to Fatah, whose grassroots members, for instance, violently protested against their leadership's manipulation of the internal primaries for the 2006 legislative elections (Aljazeera.net, 'Fatah fighters storm police offices', 13 December 2005; 'Fatah fighters clash with police', 28 December). Hamas members, by contrast, trusted the process of grassroots canvassing by which the movement's smallest units, the *usrat*, suggested candidates to the central *Shura* Council and its specially appointed High Election Committee (Kalman, 2006b; *Daily Star*, 'Hamas to conduct secret primaries', 14 March 2005). Trust is clearly Hamas' strength. However, in the absence of transparent checks and balances, such a level of faith in the leadership's integrity can undermine the membership's ability to scrutinise their leaders.

There is some evidence that members of the leadership have occasionally tried to force a decision by changing facts on the ground. The external leadership's support for the 1996 suicide operations following bomb-maker Yahya 'Ayyash's assassination appears to be such an instance, since the suicide operations effectively put an end to the tentative rapprochement between the internal leadership and the Palestinian Authority (Mishal and Sela, 2000: 75-6). A number of interviewees indeed acknowledged that the *Shura* model was under severe strain during the late 1990s (Hamad, 1998b; Musa, 1998a; 'Muhammad', 1998; hinted at by al-Rantisi, 2002b; Mish'al, 2002). Similarly, if elements of the leadership are found to have encouraged the June 2006 kidnapping of Israeli corporal Gilad Shalit or the inter-factional violence between Fatah and Hamas in 2006-7, with the specific purpose of jeopardising national unity talks, this would similarly constitute such an instance, although there is insufficient evidence to support either claim (cf. ICG, 2007a: 27).

A third and related set of tensions is between formal structures and actual ability to enforce authority. Since the *Shura* Council lacks a direct coercive mechanism, its authority is primarily symbolic. It is, moreover, unclear to what extent the ideal of the *Shura* Council is translated into practice, given the movement's geographical fragmentation, threat of assassination and imprisonment. However, the combination of Hamas' collective leadership culture, and the *Shura* Council's status as authorised by and representative of the collective, has meant that, whether or not it actually operates as claimed, its symbolic authority has been relatively effective.

Its ability to impose authority most often breaks down in the area of political violence. A number of suicide operations, for instance, appear not to have been authorised by the *Shura* Council. The suicide operation that ended the ceasefire of 2003 seems to fall into this category as does the latter part of the 1996 campaign to avenge the death of Hamas bomb-maker 'Ayyash (*Guardian*, 'Muted feelings for martyr with a grudge', 21 August 2003; *Globe and Mail*, 'Deadly bus blast shatters fragile ceasefire', 20 August 2003; Mishal and Sela, 2000: 75-81, 159-60). Inter-factional violence, such as that seen in 2005-7, is another instance where the *Shura* Council's authority appears to be limited.

Tensions can also be seen in the occasionally contradictory nature of public statements, particularly since Hamas' 2006 election victory (cf. Associated Press, 'Hamas official says group ready for 'two-state' solution with Israel', 7 April 2006; *Independent*, 'Can Hamas and Fatah ever agree on how to negotiate with Israel?', 30 May 2006). Some of these contradictions are the result of Hamas seeking to appeal to different audiences, without alienating others. But public tensions have existed between different factions within Hamas for years (cf. Robinson, 1997: 192-5; Hamami, 1997; Klein, 2007).

These tensions between formal structure and observed practice are in part explained by Hamas' clandestine character. The fact that, for security purposes, the movement's decisions are clouded in secrecy undermines the capacity of elections and consultations to hold leaders accountable. Because no one who is not a member of the *Shura* Council is privy to its deliberations, there is considerable leeway for leaders to interpret the Council's position in their own way. Since elections have to be carried out in secret, there is little opportunity for public debates between candidates and members. Tensions are exacerbated by the geographic spread of Hamas leaders and the fact that the *Shura* Council cannot meet collectively in one place due to travel restrictions on Hamas members (Tamimi, 2007; al-Rantisi, 2002a; Mish'al, 2002).

The ability of the *Shura* Council to exercise authority is further undermined by the fact that much of the fundraising for resistance and welfare activities occurs outside its control. The Qassam Brigades have traditionally been funded by Hamas' external leadership, often by-passing the internal leadership (Mishal and Sela, 2000: 162, 7; 'Muhammad', 1998; 'Ahmad', 1998; al-Rantisi, 2002b). Affiliated charities raise much of their funding individually, and are technically only accountable to their own membership (which often includes non-Hamas members).[8]

Another factor undermining formal authority structures concerns the (intentionally) ambiguous relationship between the political leadership and the Qassam Brigades. In principle, the Brigades answer to the political leadership. There is evidence to suggest that political leaders have personally given the go-ahead in numerous operations (cf. Levitt, 2006: 35-47). However, because the Brigades have, for security purposes, been set up as a separate organisational entity, with a separate (though overlapping) leadership, and a highly secretive, de-centralised cell structure (Mishal and Sela, 2000: 75-81, 159-60), there is considerable leeway for Brigades cells to operate independently or on behalf of a particular faction within Hamas (particularly if that faction provides the money as has been the case with the external leadership).

Whether these tensions between formal structure and actual practice are indicative of a lack of commitment to the formal structures, or purely a function of the clandestine character of the organisation,

---

8   Levitt (52-106) argues that charities are an integral part of Hamas' resistance effort. However, although there is considerable overlap in personnel and interests, each charity is operated by its separate Administrative Council. While charity representatives sit on Hamas' *Shura* Council, the charities do not appear to be directly controlled by Hamas. See also Gunning, 2007c.

cannot be determined with certainty. Significantly, though, it is precisely the negative effect of secrecy on Hamas' accountability mechanisms which has been one of the key factors behind the decision of some Hamas members to join its legally authorised political offshoot, Hizb al-Khalas (Musa, 1998a; al-Bardawil, 1998; al-Na'ami, 1998). Although Hizb al-Khalas has since become largely insignificant, the fact that it operated regular and apparently transparent elections during the late 1990s—and, incidentally, that its leaders included women—had an important exemplary effect on the Hamas movement as a whole, preparing the ground for the Change and Reform umbrella (and the formal inclusion of women therein) which Hamas established for the municipal and legislative elections of 2004-6.

A final set of tensions derives from the tension between formal and informal authority. Informal authority plays an important role and, to the extent that it operates independently from the electoral system, it can undermine it. Authority stemming from 'religious' knowledge or piety falls into this category, as does authority stemming from the capacity to inflict violence on the Israeli 'enemy'. It is significant, though, that Hamas' structures make it difficult for informal authority to be translated into actual power unless one is formally elected.

'Religious' Authority

Claims that Hamas advocates a cleritocracy or theocracy, modelled on Iran, are both simplistic and erroneous with regard to Hamas' internal practices. Most Hamas leaders are not 'religious' authorities, as would be the case in a cleritocracy, and Hamas does not operate a council of 'religious' authorities to vet its leadership candidates, as is the case in Iran. Mishal and Sela mention the existence of an Advisory Council abroad which they argue functions as a 'supreme religious authority' (2000: 161). However, this Council's remit appears limited to provide "normative backing and moral justification for Hamas' political conduct and major decisions". It does not have politically binding authority (none of my interviewees credited this Advisory Council with any political authority) but fulfils the role of experts described in Hamas' political theory. Hamas' practice thus seems to comply with its political theory in that 'religious' authority can only become political authority through elections.

However, although formal authority within Hamas is derived from elections (the social contract), religion (the divine contract) plays an important informal role. It informs Hamas' political culture and legitimates its political structures. It influences the way Hamas members vote and what they expect from their leaders. It affects the moral and legal framework within which leaders are expected to make their decisions, and influences which topics are considered taboo.

The custodians of this culture are not just the *Shura* Council. Cell leaders play an important role, as do those who preach or teach classes in the mosque. Ordinary members play their part by expecting a certain behaviour of their leaders, and censuring them if they feel their leaders do not comply (which I observed in all group interviews).

The emphasis on religious authority must be seen within the context of a relatively religious wider Palestinian society. Religious themes have been central to both Islamist and nationalist parties (cf. Frisch, 2005; N. Johnson, 1982). Since the 1970s, Palestinian society as a whole appears to have undergone a process of Islamisation. Mosques have more than doubled since then while surveys have shown increasing levels of religiosity (cf. Robinson, 1997: 136; Sahliyeh, 1988: 144-7; Shadid, 1988: 662-3; Barghouti, 1991).

For Hamas' core constituency, religion is particularly important. In the 1997 student survey I conducted at the Islamic University of Gaza, 73 per cent of respondents supporting Hamas stated that 'all' of their family members were 'religious', against 0.2 per cent saying that 'none' were 'religious'. Similarly, 78 per cent of pro-Hamas respondents stated that they considered themselves 'religious' while 68 per cent said they never missed morning prayers. By contrast, the figures for Fatah were 57 per cent, 12 per cent, 65 per cent and 54 per cent.

In the Palestinian context, religiosity does not necessarily mean the same thing as it does in a 'secular' Western, or Western academic, context. Asked to name "the most important issue facing Palestine now" in the same survey, 38 per cent of pro-Hamas respondents selected 'Islamisation'. But a combined 44 per cent chose one of the three 'secular'/'immanent' issues of 'peace', 'human rights'

117

and 'economy'; 56 per cent stated that they believed modernity to be 'very' to 'moderately good' for Palestine; and only 5 per cent said that 'religious people' were the institution most influencing their political views.[9] In other words, religiosity does not necessarily mean a neglect of 'secular' concerns or an aversion to politics or modernity.

Within Hamas, 'religious authority'—defined loosely, and in the context of blurred boundaries between religion and politics—is derived primarily from three sources: 'religious' knowledge, pious behaviour (understood as virtue; see also Stout, 2004: 20ff) and affiliation with mosques or religiously-inspired charities. Religious knowledge plays an important part in the creation of a leader's personal and cultural capital. All senior Hamas leaders I interviewed were well-versed in Islamic history and had a good understanding of the principles of Islamic jurisprudence. Yassin's personal authority was in part derived from his religious knowledge, or more specifically, the way he applied it. Al-Rantisi and Abu Shannab used their time in prison to expand their religious knowledge (Abu Shannab, 2002). Al-Zahhar used his spare time to write a book on aspects of Islamic political theory (al-Zahhar, 1998a).

Religious knowledge is particularly valued if it concerns Islamic jurisprudence (see also Chapter 5). Studying Islamic law enhances a leader's authority. A telling illustration of this dynamic is the respect shown by ordinary members to the views of Yusrah Hamdan, a female Hizb al-Khalas leader who had studied Islamic jurisprudence. When I told them that Hamdan believed a woman could head an Islamic state, they took her views seriously even though they were shocked by her interpretation of Islam (Hamas and Khalas members, 1999). When one member dismissed Hamdan's interpretation, others rebuked him by saying that Hamdan's views were authoritative because she had studied jurisprudence (rebuke being a form of 'symbolic violence').[10] Another illustration is Abu Shannab's self-

---

9 Fatah supporters accorded 'peace' the highest importance (37 per cent), with economy a close second (31 per cent).

10 Hamdan based her views on a re-interpretation of a *hadith* which has traditionally been taken to mean that the Prophet held women to be unfit to lead an Islamic state (Y. Hamdan, 1998). For a discussion of *hadith* and its context, cf. Mernissi, 1991.

conscious practice of enhancing his authority by tracing his views back to internationally renowned scholar-activists such as Yusuf al-Qaradawi or Rashid al-Ghannouchi who are respected among Hamas members (Abu Shannab, 1998c).

Formal religious training is relatively rare among Hamas' senior leaders. Of the thirteen leaders identified by the former Intifada cell (Hamas Cell, 1998b) as most senior in Gaza in 1998, only one was the official imam of a mosque (Ahmad Nimr Hamdan). One other had studied Islamic law and taught Islamic *shari'ah* at the Islamic University (Sayed Abu Musamah).[11] But his authority was largely built on having been the chief editor of Hamas' official newspaper in the early 1990s, *al-Watan* (cf. WINEP, 2007). In its internal practices, therefore, Hamas seems to value 'secular' political and administrative expertise more than 'religious' expertise.

Internal arguments about political strategies similarly focus on secular, this-worldly as opposed to theological or other-worldly concerns. The internal memorandum that was circulated prior to the 1996 legislative elections makes no reference to religious texts, symbols or knowledge and employs a 'secular' political cost-benefit analysis (Mishal and Sela, 2000: 121-2, 2-30). Interviewees deployed what in a Western context would be considered secular arguments in policy discussions and typically only referred to religious arguments or revelation when discussing the more theoretical aspects of the utopian Islamic state. Articles in *al-Risalah* and *Falastin al-Muslimah* show a similar pattern although they are more likely to employ religious arguments to support otherwise secular concerns. Hamas thus appears to recognise that to run a political organisation one primarily

---

11 Because the exact positions of Hamas leaders are shrouded in secrecy, I use the proxy of Hamas' senior leadership as defined by the members of the former Intifada cell: Sayyid Abu Musamah (Rafah), Ismail Abu Shannab (Gaza City), 'Abd al-Fattah Dukhan (Deir al-Balah), Ahmad Nimr Hamdan (Khan Yunis), Ismail Haniyyah (Gaza City, Beach Camp), Ahmad al-Ja'abari (Gaza City, Beach Camp), Ibrahim al-Maqadmah (Rafah), 'Abd al-'Aziz al-Rantisi (Khan Yunis), Muhammad Shamma' (Gaza City), Muhammad Taha (Burej), Ahmad Yassin (Gaza City), Ibrahim al-Yazuri (Gaza City), Mahmud al-Zahhar (Gaza City).

needs 'political', rather than 'religious', expertise (insofar as one can distinguish between these).

Hamas supporters similarly distinguish between 'religious' and political authority. Against the 5 per cent of pro-Hamas students polled at the Islamic University in 1997 who cited 'religious people' as the institution that had most influenced their ideas, 17 per cent cited political party, 19 per cent television and 10 per cent newspapers. That the majority of those surveyed were Hamas supporters, rather than Hamas members, probably affected these figures, since Hamas supporters may be less committed to a particular religiously-inspired ideology than Hamas members. However, all members I interviewed similarly made a *de facto* distinction between political and religious authority, and the vast majority only considered religio-legal scholars authoritative if these were judged authoritative by the political leadership.

This is not to say that religious scholars have no influence. The fact that Qaradawi, the Kuwait-based, internationally renowned Muslim Brother scholar, issued an official verdict (*fatwa*) that suicide bombings are justified in Islamic law in the case of Palestinians fighting Israeli occupation played a significant role in legitimating this practice—although it must be underlined that Hamas had already engaged upon this practice well before Qaradawi's pronouncement. In the campaign against the 1996 Marxist-led consultation on women's rights, religious scholars similarly provided much of the ammunition for those opposed to the project (cf. al-Zahhar, 1998b; Sarraj-Mattar, 1998; Scheindlin, 1998), although those in Hamas who entered into dialogue on women's rights were more willing to focus on social and political dilemmas, away from religious dogma (Abu Shannab, 1998d; Hamad, 1998b; Shamma', 1998; Musa, 1998a; al-Bardawil, 1998; Y. Hamdan, 1998; more ambivalently Women's Islamic Bloc I, 1998; see also Hammami and Johnson, 1999). In the same vein, most ordinary Hamas members tend to respond to specialist questions regarding Islamic political theory by saying 'ask the *'ulama*' ['religious' scholars]'. Imams also play a significant role in spreading, and up to a point shaping, Hamas' message to the masses.

Religious knowledge also informs how Hamas conceptualises politics and legitimises its internal structures. The emphases on consultation, unity and consensus-building are all explicitly grounded in religious revelation (Chapter 3). Mish'al explicitly linked Hamas' consultation exercises to the notion of *ijma'*, according to which truth is guaranteed if the entire community agrees (Chapter 3), insisting that "the more important and dangerous the decision, the larger the circle of consultation about it, so that we undertake proper decisions that are as close to right as possible ... and that express the opinion of the base in Hamas" (Mish'al, 2002). However, consultation also serves the very pragmatic purpose of maintaining unity in an increasingly heterogeneous organisation, and augmenting the loyalty among ordinary members to the ultimate compromise. It similarly serves to differentiate Hamas' reputation from Fatah's and is particularly attractive to aspiring, well-educated members of the lower middle classes who are not part of the traditional ruling elite. The particular interpretation of religion that is adopted is thus as much shaped by Hamas' position in the political spectrum as it informs Hamas' response (see also Chapters 2, 7; Gunning, 2007a: 129-33), just as it is shaped by Western notions of representation, human rights and majority rule (Chapter 3).

Piety, and mosque or charitable involvement also enhance personal capital. For Hamas members, piety means living a frugal lifestyle, putting the needs of the community above one's personal needs and putting one's beliefs into practice. The austerity of the reception room in Yassin's home or of al-Zahhar's clinic increases the personal capital of these leaders. The same holds for Abu Shannab driving around in a dilapidated car and Haniyyah not even owning a car during the 1990s (and continuing to live in the impoverished Shati' refugee camp despite being Prime Minister).

Piety affects personal capital in at least two ways. Pious behaviour is seen as an indicator of a leader's attitude towards leadership. Members believe, for instance, that shunning earthly riches, handling money honestly, or refraining from self-serving behaviour are desirable leadership qualities since they make leaders more effective and trustworthy. As such, they constitute a form of ('secular') cultural capital—what Stout in a different context calls 'civic piety', or the promotion of religion "not for its own sake, but rather as a convenient means of support for this-worldly virtue" (2004: 26).

121

At another level, piety generates charismatic authority. By show-ing that one is serious about one's religious beliefs, and placing the community's welfare above one's own, a leader is more readily re-garded as God's representative on earth, and therefore likely to both have *'barakah'* (Weber's 'gift of grace', central to charismatic author-ity) and the authority to discipline aberrant behaviour. In this sense, piety is a proxy for religious devotion, and thus serves to increase 'religious' authority—although here, too, with a distinctly civic, 'secular' spin-off.

In the context of occupied Palestine, and in the eyes of Hamas members (and many besides), piety also means being ready to kill and be killed in what Hamas members believe to be the national interest, 'religious' duty or the organisation's interest. Part of the symbolic capital of paramilitary leaders lies in their willingness to risk being killed. The authority of Hamas' political leaders has been enhanced by Israel's assassination campaign and the way leaders have responded, by declaring their readiness to die and refusing to be dis-suaded from taking up leadership positions within Hamas. Indeed, the reverence with which both the victims of occupation and suicide bombers are held in much of Palestinian society is based precisely on the belief that this is the ultimate pious act.

Involvement in mosques or religiously-inspired charities similarly enhances symbolic capital. The leadership of the early 1970s Gazan Brotherhood worshipped at Yassin's local mosque, affiliation to which increased their personal capital (Milton-Edwards, 1996: 100). Thirty years later, the mosque is still the key location where potential leaders are observed, or rise to prominence. More generally, mosques are one of the chief recruiting grounds for Hamas. Most interview-ees mentioned the mosque as the place where they were drawn to Hamas, or where they learned about Hamas in study groups. Post, Sprinzak and Denny similarly found that 50 per cent of the jailed Islamist activists they interviewed cited "the mosque, the Muslim Brotherhood or other religious influence as central" to their recruit-ment process (Post, Sprinzak and Denny, 2003: 173).

The capital derived from mosque involvement is, however, only partially 'religious' (in the Western sense of the word). Much of it is 'secular' social or cultural capital, an indicator of one's organisational and networking skills and the kind of social standing and connections one brings to the organisation. Mosques in Palestinian society function both as places of worship and as one of the few readily accessible public spaces. Those who attend religious study circles may do so because they are interested in religion. They may equally do so because it is an available social thing to do—and, in the absence of cinemas and theatres and the relative scarcity of restaurants in Gaza, and due to the pervasiveness of Israeli checkpoints in the West Bank, often one of the few available things to do. The mosque thus has an added social function which cannot be reduced to its religious aspects. At the same time, the capital derived from being a regular prayer leader or from giving the Friday sermon has an authority that cannot be equated with the personal capital acquired through secular community involvement.

Illustrating how interwoven the social and the religious are in the eyes of Hamas members, the members of the former Intifada cell observed for instance that

most of the leaders in Hamas are people who give speeches on Fridays (*khutaba'*), they are important in society in general, people trust them—so that creates the trust between base and leaders. In general, we trust these people from [the way they behave in] society, before talking about political issues. I trust such and such because he is nice and trustworthy—so, if it comes to politics, this feeling is increased (Hamas Cell, 1998c).

Involvement in religiously-inspired charitable work or student activism similarly increases 'symbolic capital' in both a 'religious' and a 'secular' sense. Charities are often associated with mosques or operate from their premises. Participation signifies both piety and public-spiritedness as well as social networking capital. For women, charities offer a particularly attractive route to gaining social and cultural capital since involvement in the mosque is typically reserved for men. It is this cultural and social capital, which has enabled a significant number of women to run successfully in the municipal and legislative elections of 2004-6 (Chapter 5).

The combination of 'religious' knowledge, piety and mosque and community involvement has enabled Hamas leaders to claim some of the capital traditionally reserved for shaykhs, 'saints' and 'religious' functionaries (drawn, in the past, from the notable class). Whether it concerns community leadership, welfare distribution, piety as a proxy for wisdom and proximity to God, or dispute mediation,[12] Hamas has come to perform some of the vital functions once performed by these traditional authority figures (cf. N. Johnson, 1982; Peteet, 1987; or, more historically, Heller, 1994).

To the extent that it has come to fulfil these roles, Hamas leaders have been able to acquire both the personal and the delegated capital that comes with such functions. The authority that flows from this capital has charismatic, traditional as well as rational-legal aspects. But it is perhaps the charismatic and traditional aspects that are the most interesting. For, beyond the rational-legal, Hamas appears to be able to tap into a deep-seated need for, and identification with, religion which can reduce rational scrutiny, and increases the organisation's ability to elicit obedience and emotional loyalty. I will return to this when discussing Bourdieu's 'mystery of ministry'. Suffice it to say here that Hamas has been aided in this process by the fact that it, more than the existing religious hierarchy, has been able to address the needs of ordinary people and make religion relevant to their daily lives. Here the widespread perception of Hamas as being 'of the people' plays an important role (Milton-Edwards, 1996: 100-1), as does the fact that many have re-discovered religion, or have come to see their religion in a new, activist light, through Hamas.[13]

---

12 Each time I interviewed Yassin, for instance, he was delayed because of having to mediate between disputing parties (cf. also Mishal and Sela, 2000: 21).

13 Some interviewees suggested that they had become religiously observant through Hamas. Most suggested that they were already religiously observant because of their upbringing (cf. most members of the Hamas Cell, 1998b; 'Ashraf', 1998; 'Ibrahim', 1998; 'Muhammad', 1998; 'Yusuf', 1998; Women's Islamic Bloc I, 1998). But because this observance was traditional, rather than activist, interviewees would have had to shift from a traditional to a more explicitly ideological-activist understanding of religion which would have included a 'salvational' element, giving traditional forms of observance, and indeed their lives, a new meaning and vigour, and inspiring a personal devotion to the people who inspired this "internal reorientation" through their "call" (or what Hamas calls *da'wah*) to action (cf. Weber, 1964: 359-63). This in turn would have enhanced Hamas' symbolic capital.

Besides enhancing a leader's personal capital, religion also plays a disciplinary role. It does so indirectly, through the symbolic capital stemming from being believed to know God's will, as well as more directly by setting the limits of what can be discussed. I will address the former later in this chapter. Concerning the latter, religion is used to circumscribe debates and strengthen taboos. One of the reasons debate about the possibility of recognising Israel has been relatively successfully suppressed is because Hamas leaders have been able to cast the conflict in religious terms, and assert that Palestine belongs to (Palestinian) Muslims by divine decree (Chapter 6)—although this argument has been partially replaced with a contractual argument. This has both served to enhance Hamas' authority (by linking its ideological position to a religiously-rooted command) and enabled it to portray any questioning of this premise as disrespectful to God—though, significantly, not usually as heresy. More often than not, this has been inferred, rather than blatantly stated, and as such is a classic example of 'symbolic violence'.

More generally, religion is used to set the parameters within which debate is acceptable. Whether it concerns the Israeli-Palestinian conflict, domestic legislation (for instance, regarding apostates) or morality, religion is expected to frame the debate—at least in those relatively few areas where religious revelation is specific (cf. concerning family and penal laws). This is where the 'divine contract' is most clearly visible, partly circumscribing the 'social contract'. Leaders play a role in this by ostensibly studying religion. But members also play a part by expecting their leaders to have religious knowledge, by referring complicated moral and legal issues to the *ulama*, and by electing leaders who display such a religious disposition.

This is not to say that religion wholly determines what leaders say and do. Religion, or rather how it is interpreted at a particular point in time, sets the parameters. Within these parameters, debate can range freely (as we saw in the absence of religious references in the internal pre-1996 memorandum). The parameters themselves, moreover, are not static but change in a dynamic process, where religion and politics mutually shape each other. A telling illustration is the way interpretations of Islam have changed from legitimising the labelling of communists as 'the forces of falsehood' to condoning the inclusion of communists in the body politic of an Islamic state by a significant number of Hamas leaders (Gunning, 2000: 308-33). Islam remained the same, but changes in the political and ideological climate meant that different interpretations became more imperative. As such, we should be careful not to overstate the role of religion in circumscribing practice.

'Authority' arising from Violence

Authority within Hamas cannot be fully understood without an appreciation of the role of violence. In Western political theory, violence is usually considered separate from 'authority'. Authority revolves around questions of legitimacy, and "the maintenance of cohesion not simply by force" (Friedman, 1990: 59-63). It involves respect and identification rather than fear. Authority may be linked to violence by the Weberian notion that a legitimate authority has the right "to use force to secure compliance". But it is usually considered as separate.

Yet, violence can be both a source of legitimacy and necessary for the maintenance of authority. Particularly in the context of the modern state, theorists recognise that (the threat of) coercive force is needed for the smooth functioning of authority (cf. Carter, 1979: 45-9; see also Tilly, 1992). 'Coercive ability', or the ability to inflict violence, can be a source of legitimacy, particularly when people feel under threat. Under such conditions, a leader with the ability to increase security, or the perception of security, through force is likely to be more authoritative than one without this ability. As Eckstein and Gurr observe, "when minimal security is lacking or when just directives ... cannot be enforced", the ability to use violence can be a valued commodity in a leader (Eckstein and Gurr, 1975: 203; see also Tilly, 1985).

In the eyes of many Palestinians, 'minimal security' is lacking as a result of the continuing occupation of Palestinian land, Israel's occupation practices, and the perceived inability of the Palestinian Authority to provide security in the face of these challenges. Similarly, a number of what Hamas members consider 'just directives' (such as ensuring the return of refugees to their ancestral homes, or ensuring justice for those whose family members were 'collaterally' killed by Israeli forces) cannot be enforced because neither the Palestinian Authority nor the Palestinians have the power to do so.

That Hamas has been one of the factors contributing to this lack of security does not feature in members' opinions. Instead, they interpret Hamas' ability to hurt Israel as a 'valued commodity', whether for strategic, political or psychological reasons (cf. el Sarraj, 2002). In this, they are not alone. A June 2005 poll (PSR Poll 16, June 2005) found that 66 per cent of Palestinians polled believed that political violence had served to achieve 'national objectives'.

The ability to commit violence against Israelis is thus an important source of legitimacy. This is so at an individual level for 'paramilitary' leaders such as Yahya 'Ayyash, 'Imad 'Aql or Muhammad Deif.[14] But the same dynamic operates at an institutional level, with political leaders deriving authority from the ability of the organisation's armed wing to inflict violence on Israelis. This is particularly true for leaders such as Yassin, al-Rantisi and Mish'al who are or were considered centrally involved in decisions regarding the use of violence (Levitt, 2006: 35-47). But it also contributes to the authority of leaders who are not considered directly involved (a form of 'delegated capital').

Intriguingly, this 'authority' is typically intertwined with other strands of personal capital, such as a reputation for piety, modesty and self-sacrifice, and the skills to lead. Deif, for instance, has a reputation for "calmness, patience, deep belief and caution" and has been described as someone who "does not know leisure, and loves simplicity and constantly prays" (*PalToday*, 'Mohammed Deif', 12 July 2006). 'Ayyash was known as a "devout scholar of the Koran" (Redford, 1996). In addition, leaders gain authority from their readiness to risk death or imprisonment (which is linked to the notion of piety)—as well as from their skills in evading these two fates. The personal authority of Deif and 'Aql would not have been as great if they had not narrowly escaped death so often (*PalToday*, 2006;

---

14 'Ayyash was one of the Brigades' chief bomb-makers (assassinated in 1996); 'Aql was one of the Brigades earliest leaders (killed in 1993); Deif is the current head of the Brigades in Gaza.

Chehab, 2007: 47-50), adding to their charismatic capital in a mixture of '*barakah*' or grace, and a mythical sense of invulnerability.

However, for an organisation founded as a resistance wing, strikingly few Hamas leaders are commanders in the Qassam Brigades. Of the thirteen most senior political leaders in Gaza identified by the former Intifada cell, only three—Sayyid Abu Musamah, Ahmad al-Ja'abari and Ibrahim al-Maqadmah—were believed to be Qassam commanders. Though all had been involved in organising violence at some time or other, and some, like Yassin and al-Rantisi, were believed to be closely involved at the strategic level, the majority of those leading Hamas in Gaza did not derive their authority from being Qassam commanders. The same holds for the West Bank although there Qassam commanders appear to play a larger role. This is not to deny violence's symbolic role. Most leaders increased their authority by calling on the Brigades to inflict violence on Israeli civilians, or whipping up emotional support for violence. In some cases, their personal capital was enhanced by their having sons in the Brigades (for instance Muhammad Taha, 'Abd al-Fattah Dukhan). But their direct involvement in perpetrating violence was minimal.

The ability to use violence against Palestinians also plays a role. Especially before the arrival of the Palestinian Authority, and after it was weakened as a result of the al-Aqsa Intifada and Hamas' rise to power, security considerations played an important role in the positive value members attached to Hamas' ability to punish criminals and moral 'deviants'. During the early stages of Hamas' existence, at the height of the first Intifada, the readiness and ability to punish what was considered moral deviancy increased Hamas' standing in its members' eyes, and through this, the standing of individual leaders. The reputation of Salah Shehadah, one of Hamas' senior leaders in the late 1990s, was in part built on his heading the Organisation of Jihad and Da'wah (Majd), set up in 1986 to deal with collaborators and enforce Islamic rules in society with a particular emphasis on punishing drug dealers and prostitutes (Mishal and Sela, 2000: 34).

Part of the reason that punishment of moral deviancy is valued lies in its being linked in popular perception to collaboration. Underground texts circulated during the first Intifada suggested that Israel's intelligence agencies used drug dealers and prostitutes to undermine Palestinian morale and lure people into compromising situations which could then be used to blackmail them into collaboration (cf. Hamas Cell, 1998b; 'Ashraf', 1998; Be'er and Dr 'Abdel-Jawad, 1994: 41-2). Whether these allegations were true is a moot point. What is significant is that many Palestinians had come to associate moral deviancy with collaboration, thus rendering the ability to punish moral deviants an even more valued commodity.

The other role of violence, its capacity to strengthen authority and ensure compliance, is less obvious within Hamas. The organisation's ability to punish criminals and moral deviants—although this has been less prominent during the al-Aqsa Intifada—has an indirect effect on the movement's members. But as far as internal coercion is concerned, Hamas appears to be largely capable of ensuring compliance through a combination of the political legitimacy derived from its representative authority structures and the authority derived from being 'representatives' of God.

Unlike Fatah, which is popularly believed to have carried out numerous internal assassinations (cf. Usher, 1995b: 18; Jarbawi, 1994: 147), and has seen a steep increase in internal violence since the death of Arafat, Hamas has not, as far as is known, resorted to internal violence to discipline its members or settle internal disputes—although the current climate of near-anarchy may usher in a new era. According to both popular rumour and informed opinion, there is no conclusive evidence of any internal assassination prior to the 2006 election, unless the death of bomb-maker Muhyi al-Din al-Sharif in 1998 was the result of an internal feud, rather than a political assassination by Israel or Fatah, as claimed by Hamas (Mishal and Sela, 2000: 79-80). Hamas and Qassam squads have killed a significant number of suspected collaborators within Hamas' own ranks, particularly during the first Intifada, and political rivalries or moral differences probably played a part in some of these. However, compared to other political factions, Hamas is typically considered by informed observers to have been more meticulous in its investigations (less so towards the end of the first Intifada), and less prone to killing suspected collaborators for other reasons than intelligence cooperation (cf. Be'er and Dr 'Abdel-Jawad, 1994: 145-7; al-Sourani, 1998; 'Khalid', 1998; Hamas Cell, 1998b).

The mere ability to inflict violence may have played a more invisible role in strengthening authority. However, members I interviewed did not display any signs of fear for their senior political leaders or their paramilitary counterparts, even when criticising them. Moreover, those who found their views to be irreconcilable with the organisation's have been able to leave the party and have not subsequently been prevented from playing a political role elsewhere. 'Imad al-Faluji, formerly chief editor of Hamas' *al-Watan* publication and subsequently Communication Minister under Arafat, is a case in point, as are, less prominently, Khadr Mahjis and Mahmud Abu Dan, who both set up ill-fated splinter groups supported by Arafat (Hamas Cell, 1998c).[15]

The apparent absence of internal violence—particularly striking given the high levels of violence within Fatah and within Palestinian politics more generally, and given the important role of internal violence in violent organisations elsewhere—suggests that Hamas' alternative mechanisms are sufficient to both maintain legitimacy and ensure compliance. Elections and consultative mechanisms play a role, as does the 'religious' authority leaders can draw on. But the centrality of trust in members' perception of the movement and its leaders is equally central. This is the focus of the next section.

Symbolic Capital and the 'Mystery of Ministry'

One of the key terms members used to describe their relationship with their leaders is 'trust'. Trust is vital for representation to function. However, trust can also serve to hide any less representative aspects of authority, or what Bourdieu calls 'misrecognition'. Ordinary members felt free to criticise their superiors. But they also exhibited an almost deferential trust in their leaders' commitment to represent their best interests and were extremely reluctant to entertain the thought that their leaders might have manipulated the articulation of Hamas' collective interests to further their own agenda.

---

15 Cf. also Hijaz Burbar who allegedly led the 1980 attack on the Gazan Palestinian Red Crescent Society and was ousted from the movement (Abu Shannab, 1998d); 'Muhammad', the disillusioned ex-cadre leader, continued to be on good terms with local Hamas members.

Bourdieu highlights trust as the key characteristic enabling politicians to have authority, and it is in Bourdieu's analysis of the role of trust in representation that we may find an explanation for why Hamas members are so loyal to their leaders—and how this loyalty can undermine the ability of the electoral process to ensure equal competition, leadership accountability, and independent thinking.

For Bourdieu, 'political capital' is fundamentally "founded on credence" (Bourdieu, 1991: 192). A politician has power to the extent that he can make people "believe in his truthfulness and his authority" (194). His power is derived "from the trust that a group places in him" (190). At one level, the creation of trust between leaders and led is a rational process of scrutiny and assessment. The more leaders are seen to deliver and defend the interests of the organisation, the more members will trust them. To the extent that this is a process of rational scrutiny, it strengthens the social contract between leader and led. However, trust is also the product of a complex process of emotional identification, and at this level representation can lead to usurpation and a suspension of individual judgement.

Bourdieu calls this phenomenon the 'mystery of ministry', in reference to the dynamic between priest and congregation which inspired his observations (although he expands his analysis to encompass any representative relationship, including that between political leaders and their followers). For Bourdieu, the suspension of individual judgement is encouraged by two mutually reinforcing processes. The very process of authorisation serves to disempower the group that has authorised a spokesperson. Though the spokesperson is created by the group, it is the spokesperson that comes to signal the group's existence, becoming the group's substitute. In the process of authorisation, the group's members become "isolated, silent, voiceless individuals" who "are faced with the alternative of keeping quiet or of being spoken for by someone else" (204-7). Consultation and elections may convince people that they are not 'voiceless'. But through the process of delegation they become effectively 'voiceless' as the only person authorised to speak on their behalf is the spokesperson.

This process is reinforced by another, the "self-consecration of the delegate". To increase "his capacity to make people believe in his truthfulness and his authority", a delegate must "abolish himself in the group". This involves acting modestly, sacrificing himself, and being seen to serve the group. It involves "giving everything" to the group. But it also involves becoming the embodiment of the collective—becoming not only the "symbolic substitute of the people", but also, and especially in the case of Hamas, God's representative. Bourdieu puts this rather boldly by saying that "it is in abolishing himself completely in favour of God or the People that the priest turns himself into God or the People. ... I am nothing but the delegate of God or the People, but that in whose name I speak is everything, and on this account I am everything" (209-12). A Muslim (or Christian or Jew, for that matter) cannot accept this statement as turning oneself into God would be blasphemy. But, phrased differently, by becoming nothing but God's representative, by abolishing their individual personality "in favour of a transcendent moral person", Hamas leaders can increase their capacity to command obedience.

The more a leader can inspire followers to believe that he is both God's delegate and an embodiment of the collective "in the sense that everything he says is the truth and life of the people", the more authoritative he will be and the more difficult it will be to dissent. For, "if I am an incarnation of the collective ... and if this group is the group to which you belong, which defines you, which gives you an identity, ... you really have no choice but to obey" (211-12). This is even more the case if the group's identity is bound up with a particular understanding of God and his will.

It is this process of self-consecration that facilitates eliciting obedience and silencing dissent, *without*, importantly, *being seen to do so*. It also increases the distance between (idealised) leader and led, thus making it more difficult for potential contenders to put forward their candidacy. In one of his more scathing descriptions of this dynamic, Bourdieu argues:

The mystery of ministry works only if the minister conceals his usurpation ... It is possible for such a person to confiscate the properties associated with his position only in so far as he conceals himself—that is the very definition of symbolic power. A symbolic power is a power which presupposes recognition, that is, misrecognition of the violence that is exercised through it ... by denial, by those on whom that violence is exercised (209-10; see also Lukes, 1990).

The terms 'usurpation' and 'symbolic violence' sit ill with the high regard Hamas members accord their leaders. But they do allude to the fact that authority is derived from a concealment of both its origins and its benefits to the authority-holder, and that this authority is maintained through the subtle application of what Bourdieu calls 'symbolic violence'.

As Bourdieu is at pains to point out, this is not necessarily a self-conscious, cynical manipulation of power—although it often is. A leader's self-sacrifice may well be genuine, and come at great cost. The interests of the leader often overlap with the interests of the led, so that both can sincerely believe that the leader "has no interests outside those of his mandators" (214-5). But this does not diminish the fact that the more a leader is perceived to be both God's representative and the incarnation of the collective, the greater his capacity to elicit voluntary compliance by persuading his followers that he understands their interests better than they do. The more this is so, the more dependent the group becomes on the leader's articulation of their interests, and the more difficult it is for dissenters to articulate interests differently, or for junior contenders to claim this mantle of authority without support from the present leadership.

A stark illustration of this dynamic is the way Haniyyah and his colleagues were leant on to withdraw their candidacy in the 1996 elections (see above). Through appeals to unity, reinforced by the unspoken understanding that 'true' Muslims do not engage in *fitnah* or brotherly strife, they were forced to accept the narrative that they, rather than their detractors, were causing dissension (even though they had sought permission from the leadership, while some of their detractors had resorted to publicly calling them traitors)—illustrating what Bourdieu called "the quasi-physical impossibility of producing a divergent, dissident speech against the enforced unanimity which is produced by the monopoly of speech and the techniques for creating unanimity" (213). Those responsible for 'disciplining' Haniyyah did not, as far as we know, resort to physical force (the traitor leaflets were the closest they came to coercion). Instead, they used the far more insidious 'symbolic violence' of appeals to unity, of nods to the Muslim ideals of harmony and consensus, and of blaming Haniyyah and colleagues for the discord that ensued. That the most senior of Haniyyah's colleagues,

'Imad al-Faluji, was ousted from the movement must also have played a cautionary role—even though his expulsion was linked to his proximity to Arafat rather than his refusal to stand down *per se* (Haniyyah, 1998a; Andoni, 1996: 7; Kristianasen, 1999: 27; Hroub, 2000: 105). To the extent that such a dynamic is at work, it clearly undermines the ability of both electoral and consultative processes to hold leaders accountable as dissenters are silenced *with their full compliance* (thus maintaining the perception of unity).

This 'mystery of ministry' occurs in all political parties. It is indeed why Weber insisted that elections encourage demagoguery and undermine the rational process by evoking an emotional response to charismatic authority (386-92). But Hamas leaders appear to be particularly good at harnessing its power—which in part explains why members are so loyal and deferential to their leaders, and why so few schisms have occurred within the organisation.

There are a number of reasons why Hamas leaders are particularly well-placed to harness the power of this dynamic—more so than Fatah. As a long-time opposition movement, and a resistance organisation, it offered ample opportunity for self-sacrifice. Its leaders were seen to suffer for their beliefs, whether in prison, or through political assassinations. Because membership of Hamas was, and is, relatively dangerous, a deep bond of trust is created through a shared sense of political persecution as well as dependence on others not betraying one's membership to the authorities.[16] Even now that Hamas is officially in power, its leaders continue to be seen to suffer—whether through incarceration (at the time of writing, half of Hamas' legislators were in Israeli prisons) or through the decision of the international community to boycott the Hamas-led Palestinian Authority. That this suffering is in part the result of Hamas' own actions does not diminish the significance of its leaders' perceived suffering, as long as followers believe that their leaders had no other choice and acted in their followers' best interests.

Hamas is also better placed than Fatah because its ideology and, crucially, the practice of its leaders, places greater emphasis on self-

---

16 Cf. also della Porta on affective bonds and persecutory narratives created in Italian clandestine groups (della Porta, 1995a: 144-53).

sacrifice, piety and service, and on the acquisition of religious knowledge. Through the former, Hamas' leaders can claim the authority that comes from 'abolishing oneself in the group'. Through the latter, they can reinforce their claim to be God's delegates. Through this combination of self-sacrifice (a form of inflicting 'symbolic violence' on oneself) and 'religious' knowledge, they can augment their authority to judge 'aberrant' behaviour, and establish a particular regime of truth. Fatah's close links with the traditional religious and political establishment similarly enables its leaders to augment their authority but its reputation for corruption and its lesser emphasis on religious knowledge places it in a weaker position than Hamas which is moreover perceived by many as closer and more relevant to the interests of ordinary people than the traditional religious establishment.

This dynamic is further enhanced by Hamas' assumption of the role previously filled by shaykhs, local 'saints' and notables in charge of the main religious institutions through its capacity to offer both material and religious support. To the extent that Hamas has inherited this mantle, members (and supporters more generally) are almost sub-consciously encouraged to put their trust in their leaders, mirroring the way those described by Weber's traditional authority model expect unquestioning obedience from their subjects (Weber, 1964: 341-2). Here again, Hamas is better placed than Fatah because of its more explicit emphasis on religion and its greater involvement in grassroots charitable work.

The power that religious knowledge accords a Hamas leader is largely derived from the centrality of the afterlife, and particularly the Day of Judgement, in the consciousness of Hamas supporters. Considerations of the afterlife were prominent in many of the conversations I had with Hamas members. Hamas leaders similarly emphasised how an increased awareness of divine judgement serves to keep both members and leaders honest and self-sacrificing. Charity directors mentioned awareness of divine judgement, and the desire to please God, as one of the means to ensure that charity personnel remain incorruptible. This dynamic does not have a ready equivalent in the 'secular' realm since it allows Hamas leaders to elicit compliance, even when members are unobserved. Their monitor, after all, is an omnipresent God. Leaders themselves, however, are also subject to this pressure.

In this context, the symbolic power derived from a percieved knowledge of God's principles is an important ingredient of a Hamas leader's authority. It allows him to project himself as able to protect people from God's wrath. It enables him to judge on God's behalf and be recognised as doing so. And it enables him to portray his interpretation of God's principles as more authoritative than the interpretations of scholars who do not subscribe to Hamas' ideology (although to do this, he typically needs to bolster his authority by referring to established religious scholars who do subscribe to Hamas' ideology; cf. Abu Shannab, 1998c).

The dynamic of this 'mystery of ministry' does not negate the principle of representation. Rather, it is an essential part of representation, and corresponds with the charismatic aspect of elections highlighted by Weber. The emotional and affective bonds that it inspires dramatically increase the sense of being represented in a way that rational deliberation cannot match. However, to the extent that it discourages criticism, scrutiny and autonomous reflection, it undermines the capacity of elections to hold leaders accountable. To the extent that it makes it harder for potential candidates to compete without leadership endorsement, it also impedes open electoral competition. That a Hamas leader's authority is in part derived from having personal 'religious' capital exacerbates the situation as fear of God's wrath or of not being sufficiently pious or knowledgeable further restricts competition, dissent and independent judgement (especially concerning issues considered taboo by ordinary members, such as whether the revelations regarding the penalties for adultery, theft and apostasy can be re-interpreted; cf. Hamas Cell, 1998b).

Much of this concerns a general criticism of the principle of electoral representation, and is thus more about the electoral model than about Hamas *per se*. But because Hamas is particularly adept at harnessing this dynamic, it is especially applicable to Hamas.

Significantly, though, critical scrutiny still occurs, even though this is circumscribed by the loyalty members feel towards their leaders. Members clearly feel free to criticise their leaders, and genuine debate appears to take place in both the *Shura* Council and the various movement-wide consultations. That Hamas has known less internal dissension and violence than Fatah is not in itself an indication that there is less internal debate. Rather, it is an illustration of the effectiveness of the combination of electoral and consultative mechanisms, and Hamas' emphasis on self-sacrifice and integrity. Indeed, during group interviews, ordinary Hamas or Islamic Bloc members were markedly more comfortable challenging their superiors in their presence than ordinary Fatah members, and less in awe of their superiors. They were respectful but far from submissive.

Moreover, despite Hamas' success at harnessing the power of the 'mystery of ministry', it has not used it to persuade members that it is in their interest to abandon the electoral process. Representation can be achieved through non-electoral mechanisms. The archetypal priest on which Bourdieu models his theory does not derive his authority from elections but from a complex process of identification, sublimation and fear. For Hamas, however, the process of election appears to be central to the acquisition of legitimate authority, and indeed to the proper functioning of the 'mystery of ministry'.

The dynamic of the 'mystery of ministry' has furthermore allowed Hamas leaders to break previously established taboos. The shift from regarding communists as 'forces of falsehood' to seeing them as fellow nationalists was facilitated by leaders such as Abu Shannab whose words and actions carried authority precisely because he had been seen to sacrifice himself (he spent eight years in prison) and devote himself to the movement (thus becoming its embodiment). Similarly, the shift from denouncing any form of compromise with Israel to considering interim solutions short of total liberation was facilitated by leaders like al-Zahhar (during the first Intifada), Yassin, Nazzal and Abu Marzuq starting to discuss these alternatives (cf. Hroub, 2000: 74-86). Other factors played a part. But these shifts were facilitated by the agency of leaders who could mobilise people around topics previously considered taboo precisely because they could harness the power of the 'mystery of ministry'.

The 'mystery of ministry' can undermine the voluntary aspect of elections in one further way, namely to the extent that leaders create the conditions that make their particular style of leadership seemingly imperative. As Bourdieu observes, "in order to consecrate himself as a necessary interpreter", a leader "must produce the need for his own product. And in order to do that, he must produce the difficulty that he alone will be able to solve" (210). In the case of Hamas, leaders are partially complicit in creating the conditions of fear, suffering, violence and counter-violence which render their particular brand of leadership imperative. External factors outside the control of Hamas have obviously contributed to creating these conditions. But through its own actions, Hamas is at least in part responsible for, to name but a few, Israel's closure policy of the 1990s and its economic ramifications, Fatah's incarceration policy, and the socio-economic and political conditions that facilitated the emergence of the al-Aqsa Intifada (although Fatah and successive Israeli governments played significant roles too). In this too, though, Hamas is far from unique.

Concluding Remarks

Comparing Hamas' political theory to its internal political practices, one is struck by the extent to which the two overlap. Both emphasise the importance of consultation and representative authority on the one hand, and the centrality of religion, and in particular religiously-inspired piety and religio-legal knowledge, on the other. In both, representative authority is placed above religious authority in the determination of political office. In both, authority is formally dependent on elections while religion is expected to shape both candidates and the prevailing political culture. Both emphasise the importance of a separation of powers between legislature and executive.

As in any political movement, tensions exist between the ideal and the actual. The *Shura* Council's ability to exercise authority is undermined by the geographical spread of Hamas' leadership, the relative political and financial autonomy of the external leadership, and the particular problems thrown up by Hamas being a clandestine organisation engaged in political violence. Especially detrimental are the need for secrecy, and the lack of public platforms to debate positions and canvass the wider membership, providing extra scope for leaders to interpret *Shura* Council decisions in line with their own, sometimes contradictory, agendas.

The ability to inflict violence—both on Israelis and on Palestinians considered a threat to society—is an important source of authority. As long as Palestinians lack basic security, the ability to use violence is likely to remain a valued commodity. However, for an organisation specifically established to perpetrate violence, the percentage of Hamas' senior political leaders who are also commanders in the Qassam Brigades is remarkably small. While the capacity for violence provides important symbolic capital for Hamas as a whole, the majority of its political leaders derive the bulk of their authority from other sources—increasing the possibility of a transformation away from violence if Hamas members believe their basic security will be guaranteed through different means.

Much of Hamas' internal practice follows democratic principles. Formal authority is derived from regular elections. Formal decisions are taken by elected representatives who are expected to consult the wider membership on particularly important policy issues. Disagreement is expected to be resolved through debate, consultation and bargaining, until a majority of representatives agree on a compromise position. However, apart from tensions between the ideal and the actual, and its engagement in violence, Hamas' internal practices ostensibly differ most from Western liberal democratic models in the role accorded religion in the creation of authority (although religion plays a greater part in Western liberal models than is usually acknowledged).

It is partly religious authority that has enabled Hamas to harness the power of Bourdieu's 'mystery of ministry' (although elections, consultation, occupation, violence and perceived political persecution similarly play a part). This is both a strength in that it militates against internal splits by increasing trust, loyalty and discipline, and a weakness in that it makes open debate and dissent on contentious issues harder. The explicit links made between Hamas and Islam, such as the notion that Hamas represents the Islamic ideals of unity and consensus, make it more difficult for dissenters as they can be more readily categorised as a threat to unity and thus not 'true' Muslims. Religion, as it is interpreted and used, thus helps to reinforce the notion that the community is more important than the individual, and that freedom can only come from total abandonment to the (divinely-ordered) community. At the same time, religion is used to justify internal elections and the notions of leadership accountability and consultation, thereby increasing the importance of individual opinion and locating authority in the individual, as well as in the community and in God.

It is important not to exaggerate the role of religion in the creation and maintenance of authority, or in the decision-making process. Religion affects certain types of decisions, particularly those related to legal and moral principles that are derived from precise revelations, by circumscribing what is permissible to say. But by and large, decisions appear to be primarily made in the 'secular' realm using this-worldly justifications, with religion serving as a cultural-moral overarching framework—although more research needs to be done to determine in more detail how exactly religion affects political decisions. Similarly, those aspects of authority that are derived from religion revolve mostly around attributes and skills that are important in a secular, civic sense. Religious knowledge is valued primarily as it relates to legal issues. Piety is valued primarily in terms of encouraging personal integrity, community service and the administrative skills and social standing thus acquired.

Elections serve to hold leaders accountable and so increase trust between leaders and led. As such, they embody the social contract central to Hamas' political theory. However, they do not enable the level of open competition typically envisaged by Western political theorists (though not always practised by Western political parties). While there is some competition and re-election does not appear to be guaranteed, without leadership endorsement a candidate has little chance of success. Hamas' religiously-inspired objection to self-promotion discourages potential candidates from stepping forward, as does its emphasis on piety, self-sacrifice, religious knowledge and social capital. Consequently, even though leaders cannot succeed without members' trust, elections are more about conferring legitimacy and maintaining accountability than about open competition.

The emphasis on consensual decision-making and consultation, while preventing schisms, simultaneously prolongs the decision-making process, privileging conservative positions. The necessity for consultation, coupled with Hamas' geographic spread and security problems, makes decision-making laborious and prevents Hamas from responding swiftly to new situations. While this is less problematic when in opposition, for an organisation in power it is debilitating. Because Hamas operates in a hostile security environment with few public platforms to debate, it is difficult for innovators to assess how much support their position enjoys among the wider membership. The emphasis within Hamas' political culture on unity, coupled with the political importance of unity to survival, discourages dissent—particularly if it involves political risks.

Nevertheless, Hamas' internal electoral practice and movement-wide consultations are potentially of great significance for the future of democracy in Palestine. Various democratisation theories posit that such internal policies facilitate the socialisation of members into the practices of democracy, and as such contribute to the process of democratisation in society more generally. This process is partially undermined by the way religion is sometimes used to prevent discussion of contentious topics and to the extent that it introduces an alternative source of authority to that of popular consent. Hamas' continuing resort to political violence, and the lack of basic security in Palestinian society, similarly weakens this process. I will return to this theme in Chapter 7.

5

HAMAS AND ELECTIONS

In the previous chapter, we saw how authority within Hamas is formally derived from elections, and how religion, reputation, skills and the capacity to perpetrate violence all play a role in the creation of a leader's symbolic capital. In this chapter, we shift our focus to Hamas' behaviour in the Palestinian domestic arena to examine what it says about the organisation's attitudes towards representative authority, religion and violence. How does it present itself to, and interact with, wider society? What role do public opinion, religion and violence play in this? What type of candidates does it put forward for election, and what can be inferred from this?

Hamas' behaviour in the municipal and legislative elections of 2004-6 will be used as a prism through which to reflect on these broader questions. Hamas' interaction with society clearly goes beyond electoral campaigns, and much could be gleaned from a more comprehensive study. However, the 2004-6 elections provide a rich case study from which to draw broader conclusions on the role of representation, religion and violence in Hamas' behaviour.

Hamas, Representative Authority and Elections

From its inception, Hamas has participated in electoral politics. Its predecessor, the Palestinian Muslim Brotherhood, had already actively taken part in elections in the 1950s (Milton-Edwards, 1996: 57-64; Cohen, 1982: 144-59). When the Brotherhood re-emerged in the 1970s, it re-entered the electoral fray when it believed itself sufficiently strong to contest the other political factions in professional and student union elections. Hamas inherited the Brotherhood's political network and built on it. By 1992, it had become a significant threat to Fatah's dominance across the territories, winning a number of significant victories in professional and student union elections, including those that had hitherto been Fatah strongholds (Mishal and Sela, 2000: 90; Hroub, 2000: 216-7). Hamas continued to succeed in defeating Fatah in key student and professional elections for much of the 1990s, winning, for instance, all elections between 1995-2006 at the key universities of al-Najah (Nablus), Hebron and the Islamic University (Gaza). But even at the secular stronghold of Bir Zeit, Hamas lost only three times to Fatah during this period (Amayreh, 1999; Parry, 1999; Regular, 2004; http://birzeit.edu/news). By the time the municipal and legislative elections were held in 2004-6, Hamas could build on twenty years of electoral experience, and a decade of executive experience (longer in Gaza), including working in coalition with other political factions.

Although elections have a long history in Palestine, a number of different authority models operate alongside each other in the occupied territories, chief among them the traditional authority structures of the clan and, to a lesser extent, the various religious institutions. Prior to the 1967 war, electoral politics was still largely dominated by the traditional elite of land-owners and notables. By 1976, however, party affiliation had come to partly replace the clientelist networks of the traditional elite (see Chapter 2). Clan affiliation, though, has continued to play an important role, particularly at the municipal level.

Between 1976 and 2004, professional, labour and student union elections were the main site of electoral contestation. Election victory at this level, though considered important as a barometer of political influence, did not result in control over the fragmentary offices of state (such as there were). Until 1994, those offices were controlled by the Israeli military administration. With the establishment of the Palestinian Authority, Fatah—or to be more precise, Arafat and his entourage—took over these offices in the areas under its control. In Area A, it had sole control. In Area B, it shared control with the Israeli occupational authorities (see map). Following the establishment of a Legislative Council in 1996, Fatah maintained control over the executive and judiciary arms of the Palestinian Authority, and suc-

'Areas under Palestinian control in the West Bank following Oslo II (source: http://www.passia.org/palestine_facts/MAPS/Oslo-2.html; for a map of post-Oslo II Gaza, see http://www.passia.org/palestine_facts/MAPS/gaza-2000.html).

ceeded in marginalising the legislative arm (Hilal and Khan, 2004: 86-7). Municipal offices continued to be filled by appointment (cf. Robinson, 1997: 178-9), following Israel's decision to indefinitely suspend municipal elections in 1980.

While culturally and politically central, elections did not offer real power beyond the unions. The (re)-introduction of municipal and legislative elections in 2004-6 changed all that. For the first time, opposition factions could compete electorally with Fatah and gain real access to the structures of state. Hamas' election campaign must be seen against this backdrop.

Municipal and Legislative Elections, 2004-6

Hamas' 2004-6 electoral campaigns can be read in countless different ways. Three observations, however, are particularly noteworthy for our analysis. Hamas' campaign strategy suggests that it is acutely aware of what constitutes power within an electoral system, and that, more than Fatah, it recognises that in such a system, power is fundamentally linked to gaining, and maintaining, votes. Secondly, echoing Hamas' internal practices and political theory, grassroots consultations and heeding public opinion played a central role in Hamas' election campaign and victory. And thirdly, Hamas' election results suggest that it is stronger in urban areas, with important implications for its attitude towards religion and democracy (see also Chapter 7).

Between December 2004 and December 2005, four rounds of municipal elections were held. Overall, Hamas—or rather the lists Hamas supported (at municipal level, clan affiliations and local politics dominate who is put forward, thus making alliances with non-members a necessity)—won around a third of the seats. During the first round, when elections were held in carefully selected municipalities where Fatah was expected to do well (Ephron, 2005; *New York Times*, 'Hamas Surprisingly Strong', 25 December 2004), Hamas won an overall 43 per cent of the council seats up for election, 64 per cent in the Gaza Strip, and 36 per cent in the West Bank (*Times*, 'Hamas makes electoral breakthrough', 27 December 2004). A year later, during the fourth municipal round, Hamas won 26 per cent of the seats, against Fatah's 35 per cent (*New York Times*, 'Hamas Surges In West Bank', 17 December 2005).

These figures, however, only tell part of the story. Significantly, they conceal the fact that Hamas' electoral victories typically occurred in the more highly populated urban districts. In the second round of municipal elections, for instance, Fatah won control of a greater number of municipalities than Hamas. However, as the

Israeli newspaper *Ha'aretz* noted, "only seven of the 38 authorities in which Fatah won have more than 4,000 voters ... In contrast, of the 30 authorities in which Hamas won, 11 have more than 4,000 voters ... In the Gaza Strip, Hamas won the three largest authorities [with a combined total of 112,000 voters and 284,000 residents]" ('Fatah takes most councils', 8 May 2005).[1] The same dynamic could be observed in the fourth round of municipal elections. While Hamas only gained 26 per cent of the overall vote, a PSR December 2005 exit poll found that 59 per cent of respondents in the four main cities where elections were being held—three of which went to Hamas—had voted for Hamas. By then, as Litvak observes, despite Fatah having won control over 121 municipalities against Hamas' eighty-one, "over 1,000,000 Palestinians now live in municipalities governed by Hamas, compared with about 700,000 in municipalities controlled by the hitherto dominant Palestinian movement, Fatah" (Litvak, 2005a).[2]

In the legislative elections, this dynamic was less obvious as villages and towns were merged in larger electoral districts. Nevertheless, one of the explanations given for Hamas losing in the district of Qalqilya—having trounced Fatah's municipal slate in the previous year—was precisely the fact that the district boundaries for the legislative elections had been drawn in such a way that the inhabitants of the surrounding villages outnumbered the inhabitants of Qalqilya town (FCO Official, 2006), although other factors, such as disgruntlement with the municipal council also played a role (cf. *Christian Science Monitor*, 'One town doubts Hamas', 28 February 2006).

The legislative elections also tell another story. Voters were asked to cast two votes: one for a national list, in which parties would gain

---

1   NDI (2005b) sets the number of authorities won by Fatah and Hamas at 29 and 20 respectively. The discrepancy lies in the ambiguity of party affiliations of candidates.

2   According to *Ha'aretz*, "another 500,000 people are living in 64 towns and villages in which independent candidates won or where no clear victory went to either of the major organizations. Some 900,000 people live in communities where elections have not yet been held" ('1.1m Palestinians live in local councils controlled by Hamas', 18 December 2005).

the number of seats proportional to their overall percentage; and one for a district list, in which candidates with the highest number of votes would gain seats, regardless of party affiliation. Voting for the national list revolved around the parties' overall popularity. Voting for the district list revolved more around the candidates' local reputation, and thus resembled the municipal elections more closely. Hamas won the vote for both lists: with a 3 per cent margin on the national list (44.5 per cent vs. Fatah's 41.4 per cent), and, unsurprisingly given Hamas' ability to enlist candidates with a strong local standing, with a 6 per cent margin on the district list (41 per cent vs. 36 per cent). But, as in the municipal elections, Hamas won its votes far more strategically than Fatah did: it secured seventy-four seats out of 132 or nearly 60 per cent, with just over 40 per cent of the total vote (CECP, 2006; FairVote, 2006). Here, the difference was not so much urban versus rural vote, although that played a part. Rather, it was down to election tactics, and it is through an analysis of these that we can learn something about Hamas' attitude towards elections.

That Hamas did particularly well in urban areas can be interpreted in a number of different ways. At one level, it suggests that Hamas appeals particularly to urban voters (which in the Palestinian context includes both towns and refugee camps). This fits well with the thesis that Islamism is a modern phenomenon, facilitated by the twin processes of modernisation and urbanisation (see Chapters 2 and 7). A PSR exit poll conducted during the legislative elections indeed found that Hamas received greater support in cities (49 per cent) and refugee camps (48 per cent), and limited support in rural areas. A January 2006 NEC poll similarly found that support among respondents for Hamas, immediately after the legislative elections, was significantly higher in towns (43 per cent) and refugee camps (45 per cent) than in villages (36 per cent).[3]

The survey I conducted in 1997 among students at the Islamic University in Gaza found an even more pronounced discrepancy.

---

3 Although, unlike other Palestinian pollsters, NEC conducts polls by telephone, its website remarks that no significant difference has been observed in responses between households with and without telephone (http://www.neareastconsulting.com/surveys/ppp/files/20060129-ppp-en-pr.pdf.

Hamas supporters were twice as likely as Fatah supporters to live in refugee camps (28 per cent vs. 16 per cent), and a significantly higher proportion of Hamas supporters lived in Gaza City (43 per cent vs. 34 per cent). In sharp contrast, Fatah supporters were twice as likely to come from villages (13 per cent vs. 8 per cent) or smaller towns (33 per cent vs. 17 per cent). Although this finding cannot be generalized, because it involved students studying at the Islamic University in Gaza, rather than a territory-wide sample covering all age groups and economic sectors, it does suggest that Hamas' activists—many of whom are students—may be concentrated in urban rather than rural areas.

This leads me to a second interpretation, namely that Hamas did well because of greater organisational presence in towns and refugee camps. Most of the headquarters of Hamas' most successful charities are situated in towns or refugee camps. When the Muslim Brotherhood re-emerged in the 1970s, it did so in areas that had been neglected by other, existing institutions—the refugee camps, the deprived areas in Gaza's urban quarters, and those areas where the nationalist factions or traditional institutions did not have a presence (Milton-Edwards, 1996: 101-2). In villages, traditional institutions were typically well-established. Moreover, Fatah enjoyed better access than Hamas to the traditional elites who were more likely to be still in control of the local religious and charitable networks in the villages than in the towns.

This differential access to the traditionally powerful clans may also help to explain why Fatah did considerably better in the villages—and less well in towns. It is generally acknowledged that clan loyalties play a significant role, particularly in municipal elections with their increased focus on local issues (cf. Makovsky, 2004; *International Herald Tribune*, 'Hamas's election foray may be a turning point', 4 January 2005). During elections, clan members face considerable pressure to vote according to the wishes of their clan elders who make tactical alliances with a particular political faction.

In the villages, Fatah's alliance with some of the more powerful clan elders is strong. At the same time, clan elders are more likely to be powerful in the villages than in urban centres where people are subject to a far greater variety of political influences and networks.

Clan relations, though still strong, are thus more likely to be diluted in urban centres than in villages, offering Hamas greater opportunities for persuading voters to dissent from the clan's preferred vote or establish direct relations with voters. In addition, given Hamas' greater institutional presence in towns, it has a better chance of gaining a clan's loyalty in town centres since it has more to offer in return.[4]

Hamas' greater institutional presence in urban centres also affects its capacity for creating electoral alliances. Before the municipal elections, Hamas, though influential and capable of raising crowds of tens of 1000s, did not match Fatah's capacity to enlist candidates. With its control over the security services, the civil service, the municipalities, it's own grassroots institutional network and its long-standing clan and business alliances, Fatah had little trouble finding electoral candidates with a well-established affiliation with the faction. Hamas, by contrast, had to actively recruit among sympathetic non-members to boost its numbers, placing a considerable strain on Hamas' capacity to compete territory-wide. In this sense, too, Hamas' success in the towns can be attributed to its greater institutional presence there, and the fact that towns have a higher population concentration, facilitating a greater electoral 'return' for a similar amount of campaigning effort.

That logistical considerations were significant was underlined by one of Ramallah's newly-elected Hamas councillors who observed that "if they [Fatah] had held all these municipal elections at once, as they were supposed to, we would never have been able to compete. ... But first they held 10, then 20, and by dividing them up they allowed us to concentrate our efforts and organize ourselves, village by village" (*San Francisco Chronicle*, 'Hamas proving it's politically shrewd', 29 January 2006). It is thus precisely the fact that the municipal elections had been spread out over a year that enabled

---

4 This is not to say that Hamas did not succeed in gaining votes in the villages. In al-Shiyukh, near Hebron, it defeated Fatah's list, despite the latter being supported by one of the PA's local clan-strongmen (*Ha'aretz*, 'Hamas expected to benefit', 3 May 2005). Moreover, alliances with the powerful clans did not always prove decisive. In the West Bank town of Qalqilya, Hamas won against Fatah's list of clan elders and businessmen (*Ha'aretz*, '400,000 Palestinians expected to vote today', 5 May 2005).

Hamas to concentrate its efforts and build up electoral strength. And it is precisely in the larger towns that Hamas was most successful in gaining (or maintaining) the loyalty of the larger clans (cf. *Ha'aretz*, 'Popularity suddenly important for Hamas', 9 May 2005).

Hamas' success in the larger towns is also indicative of something else. In both the municipal and legislative elections, Hamas displayed great electoral savvy in maximising its resources. This showed in Hamas' early municipal successes in what were considered Fatah strongholds. But it also showed in the way it selected its electoral candidates, both in terms of who it selected, and how many.

While Fatah's leadership was mired in internal rivalries, making deals with clan elders, and selecting candidates on the basis of the faction's debt to them, including many "linked to financial corruption and abuse of power" (*Jerusalem Post*, 'Hamas victory boosts chances', 18 December 2005), Hamas' leadership was busy developing a programme and list which, in the words of Hamas' West Bank campaign manager, Farhat Assad, "won the confidence of the voters" (Kalman, 2006b). Using "scientific methods based on our study of the polls" to shape his faction's election platform, Assad found that "the polls all said the people's first concern was about corruption, and then the security situation. ... And they showed that 25 percent of the people cared about religion". More than Fatah, therefore, Hamas showed acute awareness that gaining power in an electoral system depends on winning the grassroots vote, which, even though Palestinian elections are influenced by clan affiliations, depends to a considerable degree on presenting a platform people can identify with.

In response to the polls—some reportedly conducted by an in-house polling unit (Tamimi, 2007)—Hamas shaped its election campaign, within the bounds of its ideological framework, around the themes that it thought people would most identify with, and at the same time best exposed Fatah's weaknesses. Its election slogan, and the name of many of its electoral lists, 'Change and Reform', spoke directly to people's main concerns about lawlessness and corruption, and constituted a stab at Fatah whose vague nationalistic list names, by contrast, reinforced the belief that, as Litvak (2005) observed, it "lacked a social agenda, subordinating it to the national struggle and postponing its articulation to the day after liberation".

At the same time, it neatly drew attention away from Hamas' lack of a clear programme on Israel and the peace process, enabling swing voters opposed to Hamas' position on Israel to vote for Hamas. In the same vein, Hamas' election manifesto omitted any direct reference to the destruction of Israel, instead calling for "a free and independent Palestinian state with sovereignty over the whole of the West Bank, Gaza Strip and Jerusalem, without concession of any span of the historic land of Palestine" (Hamas, 2006: 1; ICG, 2006a: 22).[5]

Even list names emphasising Hamas' resistance record still focused on domestic discontent with Fatah and on ordinary people feeling left out of the decision-making process. A striking illustration of this is the slogan "partners in blood, partners in decision-making" (*Daily Star*, 'Hamas challenges Fatah in elections', 6 May 2005), a sentiment that was echoed in Hamas' election manifesto, which promised to work towards "decentralisation, the delegation of authority and sharing in the process of decision-making" (Tamimi, 2006: 279).

A second way in which Hamas responded to the popular desire for change was to use its municipal election victories to showcase what it would do if elected elsewhere. Because the municipal elections were staggered, and legislative elections imminent, Hamas had an extra stimulus to deliver soon. In Bidya, for instance, a West Bank village, which had held elections in December 2004, the Hamas councillors had, within four months of coming to power, already begun replacing "the town's ancient network of water pipes, which leaked an estimated 45 per cent of the town's water yearly", had bought new transformers "to boost the town's flickering electricity", and had

---

5   This phrasing allowed both those advocating total liberation, and those in favour of a two-state solution to identify with Hamas' manifesto, as the latter can interpret the last half as a moral, rather than a political, claim to the historic land of Palestine. It appears in the manifesto that was submitted to the official election committee but does not appear in all versions (cf. Tamimi, 2006: 174-5). Tacit acceptance of a two-state solution is nevertheless suggested by the absence of electoral references to the destruction of Israel (including in street graffiti; ICG, 2006a: 19), and has been elaborated upon subsequently in the National Conciliation Document (2006), the Mecca Agreement (2007) and numerous articles (cf. Mish'al and Haniyyah [Haniya] in *Guardian*, 13 February & 6 June 2007).

increased tax revenues to pay for water and electricity ten-fold. This contrasted sharply with Fatah's previous rule during which "little was accomplished as facilities crumbled" (*Jerusalem Post*, 'Hamas, Fatah battle for soul of a town', 1 April 2005).

In al-Shiyukh, near Hebron, the newly elected Hamas council had already built a new entrance to the town, and put up streetlamps (so that "people can now see where they are going and feel safer") within the first half year of their tenure (*Jerusalem Post*, 'From bullets to ballots?', 15 July 2005). In Deir al-Balah, a town in the Gaza Strip, the Hamas-led council "reinforced the roads, they cleaned the beaches, they decorated the streets with flowers and lights" within months of coming to power (*San Francisco Chronicle*, 'Disengagement Diary Observations', 10 August 2005).

That Hamas was acutely aware both of the popular demand for concrete changes and of the symbolic capital of reputation was further underlined by the fact that Hamas not only organised squads of volunteers to clean up Gaza's streets prior to local elections—showcasing what it would do when in power as well as building rapport by encouraging locals to join in—but that it filmed the cleaning operations for use as promotional material during its election campaign (*Jerusalem Post*, 'From bullets to ballots?', 15 July 2005). It is thus little surprise that voters, across the territories, stated that they had voted for Hamas, because, in the words of one 51-year old woman from Rafah refugee camp in the Gaza Strip, "We want clean streets and new projects, like sewage treatment, and our destroyed homes to be rebuilt. I believe Fatah will monopolize everything like they have done before" (*Daily Star*, 'Hamas challenges Fatah in elections', 6 May 2005; see also *New York Times*, 'Palestinian Landslide', 28 January 2006; Kalman, 2006a; *Jerusalem Post*, 'On Allah's ticket', 14 June 2005; *Daily Star*, 'Hamas challenges Fatah', 6 May 2005).

The success of Hamas' policy to gain confidence was helped by its reputation of incorruptibility, accountability and efficiency, against Fatah's reputation of corruption and inefficiency. Hamas' widespread network of charities similarly played an important role, both by cementing Hamas' reputation as efficient and accountable and by offering services that made people beholden to Hamas (even though affiliated charities are typically careful to be seen to offer services to anyone in need, and not just those who support it; Gunning, 2000: 326; Pharmaciens sans frontières, 1998; Wheeler, 1998).

A third indication of both Hamas' awareness of its dependence on gaining votes, and its superior understanding of electoral tactics, and the depth of its grassroots support concerned its policy of only putting forward the number of (district) candidates it believed could win, given its strength of support in the district—even if this meant contesting less seats than those available for election. In sharp contrast, Fatah typically nominated too many candidates for the number of votes it could garner, a situation made worse by the entry of endless disgruntled Fatah affiliates as independents, following disagreements within Fatah over who was to represent the party. The result was that votes for Fatah were spread out over too many candidates, thereby facilitating Hamas' win. While only eleven of Hamas' fifty-six district candidates remained unelected, only seventeen of Fatah's sixty-six were elected (CECP, 2006).

In Jerusalem, against Hamas nominating four candidates for four available district seats, Fatah and Fatah independents tabled thirty candidates (*San Francisco Chronicle*, 'Hamas proving it's politically shrewd', 29 January 2006). Hamas won the four seats. In Gaza, Hamas ran five candidates for eight available seats and won all five with 37 per cent of the vote. Fatah ran eight candidates, and won no seats, despite gaining 32 per cent. In Tulkarem, Hamas won two of three seats with 27 per cent of the vote, having run two candidates only to concentrate the vote (and supporting a highly popular independent with close ties to Hamas for the third seat). Fatah ran three candidates and won no seats, despite polling higher at 34 per cent. In Nablus (see Table 1), Hamas won five out of six available seats with 38 per cent, having only put forward five candidates. Fatah won one seat, despite gaining 37 per cent of the vote, having run six candidates (FairVote, 2006).

That Hamas was able to calibrate its number of candidates to its (expected) electoral support underlines the sophistication of the surveys with which Hamas ran its campaign. But it also reveals the level of discipline within both the organisation and the wider Islamic movement, enabling Hamas to control how many candidates were put forward. By contrast, Fatah had become so internally fractional-

Table 1 District List for Nablus' 6 legislative seats (CECP, 2006)

No.	Candidate	Affiliation	Votes	Seats
1.	Ahmed Ahmed	Change & Reform	44,957	Seat
2.	Hamid Kdier	Change & Reform	43,789	Seat
3.	Mahmoud Alaloul	Fatah movement	39,746	Seat
4.	Reyad Amleh	Change & Reform	39,106	Seat
5.	Husni Borini Yaseen	Change & Reform	39,056	Seat
6.	Dawood Abo-Seir	Change & Reform	36,877	Seat
7.	Ghassan Shakaa	Fatah movement	35,397	
8.	Moawiah Masri	Independent	33,561	
9.	Ahmad Edealy	Fatah movement	32,118	
10.	Sarhan Dwikat	Fatah movement	30,958	
11.	Isam Abo Baker	Fatah movement	29,766	
12.	Dalal Salameh	Fatah movement	26,952	
13.	Ahed Abu-Goolmy	PFLP	17,221	
14.	Majida al-Masri	Independent	14,568	
15.	Jamal Aloul	Independent	12,277	
16.	Ghassan Hamdan	Independent	11,242	
17.	Maher Fares	Independent	10,122	
18.	Ismat Shakhshir	PFLP	7,726	
19.	Hani al-Masri	Independent	6,641	
20.	Ismat Sholy	PFLP	6,288	
21.	Munib Yaish	Independent	2,850	
22.	Waleed Dwiekat	Independent	2,292	
23.	Fayez Zaidan	Independent	2,290	
24.	Feda Abu Hanood	Independent	1,810	
25.	Noman Mashayek	Independent	1,604	
26.	Fathi Buzieh	Independent	1,449	
27.	Jamal Salman	Independent	1,067	
28.	Nabegh Kanan	Independent	758	
29.	Ziad Kayed Zanoon	Independent	548	
30.	Ahmed Hawamdeh	Independent	532	

ised that it could not control its affiliated independents. The disregard for finding out the strength of electoral support, meanwhile, suggests that the leadership did not sufficiently concern itself with discovering what levels of popular support Fatah enjoyed.

Hamas and public opinion

The above analysis suggests that Hamas is acutely aware of the power of public opinion within the Palestinian electoral system. That this reflects a broader attitude towards public opinion can be gleaned from numerous incidents in which Hamas made an about-turn when it realised its position was unpopular. One telling illustration is the response of a Hamas mayor from a West Bank town to the challenge posed by a group of 'secular' women (Perry, 2005). The day after election, the mayor had come into his new office to hang up a list of do's and don'ts visitors should observe. One of these stipulated that women wear the *hijab*. When word got out, a group of secular women supporters who had voted for Hamas because of its municipal agenda, marched into the mayor's office, telling him that they had not elected him to be forced to wear the *hijab* to his office and that they would not vote for him again if he did not remove the list. The mayor promptly complied.

When the Qassam Brigades fired rockets into Israel after an accidental explosion at a Hamas victory ceremony killed twenty-one in September 2005, the organisation rapidly backtracked when it realised the general public blamed it for Israeli counter-attacks (ICG, 2006a: 40; Associated Press, 'Hamas leader says group will halt rocket attacks against Israel', 25 September). When its criticism of the November 2005 Rafah border agreement proved highly unpopular, Hamas made an about-turn, even deciding to attend the signing ceremony (ICG, 2006a: 40). Hamas' decision to declare a unilateral ceasefire in June 2003 was similarly influenced by shifts in the public mood as evidenced by its canvassing public opinion prior to the declaration (see Chapters 4 and 6).

Apart from the last incident, all of the above occurred during the year of municipal elections, when Hamas was acutely aware that it could not afford to alienate the electorate. Hamas' decision to halt its rocket attacks, for instance, occurred only days before the third round of municipal elections. Even the 2003 ceasefire consultations can be seen as linked to the elections, since they took place in the context of negotiations between Hamas and Fatah over greater political participation (Chapter 6). Hamas' behaviour during this period can therefore not automatically be taken as indicative of the movement's behaviour generally. However, it does suggest that, within an electoral system where elections are held regularly, and Hamas' power is to a large extent dependent on gaining votes, Hamas is likely to pay close attention to shifts in public opinion—which is one of the reasons it won repeatedly in student and professional union elections during the 1990s and why Klein concludes that "in practice, Hamas' leadership has deferred to public opinion in the interpretation of the national interest" (2007: 444).

This does not mean that Hamas necessarily heeds public opinion. During the mid-1990s, Hamas continued with its policy of armed attacks against Israeli civilians, even though public support for these operations, as measured by surveys, was a mere 20-30 per cent (cf. CPRS Polls 13-22, 1994-6). Hamas may moreover be less inclined to heed public opinion if it operated in a different political context. But, within the political opportunity structure currently in place in Palestine, Hamas has a clear incentive to heed public opinion.

Hamas and alliance-building

Equally significant is the fact that Hamas has been willing to compromise, or at least fudge, its core message, and to put forward eligible non-member candidates instead of party members, where it deemed it advantageous to do so. Its 'Reform and Change Coalition' in Nablus illustrates this eloquently. According to the new mayor, 'Adli Ya'ish, Hamas' list contained only two "official Hamas members", the remaining thirteen being formally non-affiliated professionals. Others disputed this claim, saying that apart from the mayor, all were considered to be Hamas affiliates sharing the organisation's Islamist goals (*Jerusalem Post*, 'A pragmatic mayor for Nablus', 21 December 2005)—in other words, belonging to the wider Islamic movement.

The mayor himself, though, is widely acknowledged to be an outsider (*ibid.*). A businessman whose family, one of the old notable families of Nablus, owns the local Mercedes-Benz dealership, he is well-known for his charitable work, and his good relationship with the Israelis. One of his long-term friends is an Israeli businessman with whom, only months before the election, he agreed in principle to establish a local programme promoting coexistence with Israel among Palestinian school children. Ya'ish was first approached by Fatah. But when Hamas asked him to lead its list, he agreed to run on a Hamas ticket.

What is intriguing about this, and indeed other, alliances is that both need each other. Ya'ish was unlikely to have won on a Fatah ticket. One local specifically told the *Jerusalem Post* that "he would not have voted for him if he had run on the Fatah list", given Fatah's long record of corruption and nepotism (*ibid.*). However, Hamas would also arguably have been less successful without Ya'ish who brought to the table not just local popularity and a reputation for efficiency, honesty and charitable work, but also non-partisanship, clan affiliations and the votes of many who might otherwise not have voted for Hamas. Nablus had long been a Fatah stronghold (cf. *Jerusalem Post*, 'Hamas victory boosts chances in parliamentary elections', 18 December 2005). Hamas' success was in part dependent on winning the votes of the non-aligned and disillusioned Fatah supporters.[6] It was more likely to do so with a non-partisan list leader—particularly one Fatah had deemed acceptable—than a highly partisan Hamas activist. Ya'ish's membership of the traditional elite was similarly important, given the influence of clans in municipal voting, as was his reputation for cooperation with Israeli authorities, suggesting that a Hamas council would continue to cooperate with the authorities on matters such as water, electricity and sewerage. Finally, Ya'ish brought in votes from Nablus's non-Muslim population—the Christians and Samaritans—whom he had regularly helped as treasurer of a special emergence committee established during the al-Aqsa Intifada (*ibid.*).

Ya'ish represents an entire class of non-members who ran on a Hamas ticket. In the West Bank town of Tubas, neither of the two main factions put up their own lists but allied themselves to independents (*Ha'aretz*, 'PA names winners', 27 December 2004). In al-Shiyukh, the head of Hamas' list, Yusuf Halaika, was previously identified with Fatah as an Arafat appointee (*Ha'aretz*, 'Hamas expected to benefit from public's frustration with PA', 3 May 2005). In Nablus, a sitting member of the Legislative Council, previously affiliated with Fatah, and a representative of one of the cities' old families, Mu'awiyah al-Masri, was persuaded to run as a Hamas ally in the legislative elections, as was the deputy chairman of the previ-

---

6   In earlier municipal rounds, PSR polls found high percentages of un-decided voters. Its December 2005 exit poll found a considerable percentage of those voting for Hamas not describing themselves as Hamas supporters: 42 per cent categorised themselves as Hamas supporters, 59 per cent stated they had voted for Hamas. PSR polls conducted in March and September 2005 similarly found that 17-20 per cent of respondents said they were un-decided.

ous Legislative Council, Hasan Khraisheh, a non-aligned member from Tulkarm who had frequently opposed Fatah, although both were officially listed as 'independent' (*Ha'aretz*, 'Hamas aims to win 60 percent of PLC seats', 11 December 2005; CECP, 2006).

Hamas also made cross-religious alliances. I already alluded to Nablus' mayoral candidate bringing in the Christian and Samaritan votes. In Gaza, Hamas made an alliance with a Christian legislative candidate, Hussam al-Tawil, although the candidate denied that he was on a Hamas ticket, suggesting instead that he was supported by all parties (Aljazeera.net, 'Christian candidate on Hamas ticket', 23 January 2006; *Ha'aretz*, 'Hamas aims to win 60 percent of PLC seats', 11 December 2005). In Bethlehem's municipal elections, Hamas made a winning alliance with a Christian Marxist from the PFLP who shared Hamas' disdain for corruption, and who brought to the table a large section of the Christian vote, plus the re-assurance that Hamas would not allow its Islamist agenda to jeopardise the historic coexistence and cooperation between the town's Muslims and Christians (*Wall Street Journal*, 'Odd Allies: Bethlehem Mayor Courts Hamas, Stirring Up Region', 23 December 2005).

While strengthening Hamas' electoral chances, alliance-building creates a particular set of tensions for Hamas, in terms of how far it can push its own agenda, emphasising that Hamas is not a fanatical, ideologically rigid organisation, incapable of compromise. While there are clearly boundaries beyond which Hamas is less likely to stray, it seems to recognise that gaining political influence involves compromise in which pragmatic gains must be balanced against losing ideological purity. Particularly intriguing in this respect is that a number of its allies, including Taweel (Aljazeera.net, 'Christian candidate'), Ya'ish (*Jerusalem Post*, 'Pragmatic mayor') and Batarseh (*Wall Street Journal*, 'Odd Allies'), support co-existence with Israel and oppose Hamas' method of targeting Israeli civilians—although this is perhaps less surprising in the context of Hamas councillors having set aside ideological convictions to do business with their Israeli counterparts in order to keep municipal services flowing (*Jerusalem Post*, 'Civil Aministration to cooperate with Kalkilya's Hamas council', 17 May 2005; 'From bullets to ballots?', 15 July; 'Kalkilya Hamas talks electricity with Israelis', 28 December).

Equally intriguing is that Hamas has a long record of having been trusted by those one might expect to be wary of Hamas' Islamist agenda, such as Christians, secularists and Marxists. Hamas' victories in Ramallah's Chamber of Commerce elections are a case in point, as Ramallah contains a high percentage of Christian and secular businessmen. The same can be said of Hamas' repeated Student Council victories at Bir Zeit, the most secular of Palestinian universities. Pragmatic calculations encouraged Hamas to woo these voters, and make cross-ideological alliances. It is nevertheless significant that Hamas opted for this path, rather than insist on ideological or religious purity like the more *takfiri* Islamists elsewhere, and that it honoured its contractual commitment to these voters to the extent that they, or others like them, decided to re-elect Hamas candidates in subsequent elections.

Religion, Virtue and Symbolic Capital

Religion plays an important part in Hamas' depiction of itself towards its electoral constituency. But how exactly does it affect Hamas' symbolic capital? How does it affect Hamas' political programme? Does religion make Hamas less democratic, in the narrow sense of being responsive to public opinion and recognising the authority of a popular mandate?

If scholars such as Hoffman and Huntington are right, religion should play an important role, and one which would make Hamas inherently anti-democratic (Chapter 1). Some of the earlier studies of Hamas and the Palestinian Muslim Brotherhood indeed singled out Islam (or at least Hamas' interpretation thereof) as a key factor preventing Hamas from embracing 'true' democracy (cf. Nüsse, 1998: 74-8, 180; Abu-Amr, 1993: 18; Usher, 1995a: 78; Ahmad, 1994: 55-7). However, this conclusion sits uncomfortably with the above analysis of Hamas' electoral practices, as well as with later studies of Hamas (cf. Mishal and Sela, 2000; Hroub, 2000). Even if we find that religion plays an important role, it does not seem to have prevented Hamas from participating in electoral politics, considering the interests and concerns of its electoral constituency and recognising that formal legitimacy within the occupied territories is primarily derived from elections.

That a commitment to Islamism does not necessarily equate with a rejection of democracy is one of the key findings of Grant and Tessler whose 1999 survey of political and religious attitudes in the Palestinian territories found not only that just 24 per cent of respondents believed Islam and democracy to be incompatible, but that "those who support political Islam …. are actually more likely than others to believe that a political system based on Islamic law can be democratic" (Grant and Tessler, 2002: 16). This is not to say that Islamists are inherently democratic. Grant and Tessler's findings paint a more complex picture. But it does suggest, not only that support for political Islam does not automatically result in rejection of democracy, but that political Islam may in fact help to increase support for democracy.

In the previous chapter, we saw how religion provided Hamas leaders with symbolic capital which could then be translated into political capital through elections. However, we also found that Hamas' leadership is dominated by secular professionals, and that much of their 'religious' capital in fact concerns 'secular' capital such as a reputation for incorruptibility.

Religion plays a similar role in Hamas' relationship with its wider constituency. Hamas self-consciously portrays itself as having a religious identity. Hamas' election slogan, 'Change and Reform', is a reference to two Qur'anic verses encouraging personal development (Kalman, 2006b). Hamas' election rallies typically featured religious music, interspersed by passages from the Qur'an, and its election manifesto for the 2006 legislative elections was sprinkled with Qur'anic verses and Hadiths (*San Francisco Chronicle*, 'Hamas turns focus to political campaign, 26 January 2005; *Jerusalem Post*, 'Hamas kicks off summer election campaign', 27 March 2005; 'Hamas Election Manifesto' in Tamimi, 2006: 274-94). Mosques were central sites for Hamas' election campaign, reinforcing the message that Hamas is inspired by Islam and its leaders are 'true' Muslims—until it signed a code of conduct in January 2006 which "banned electioneering in mosques and churches" (*Ha'aretz*, 'Hamas signs pact on code of conduct', 9 January 2006).

161

References to 'Islam is the solution' and 'the Qur'an is our constitution' were commonplace. When the Hamas Cabinet was sworn in, Hamad al-Bitawi, one of Hamas' newly-elected legislators, shouted triumphantly: "The Koran is our constitution, Mohammed is our prophet, *jihad* is our path and dying for the sake of Allah is our biggest wish" (*Jerusalem Post*, 'Hamas cabinet approved in 71-36 vote', 28 March 2006). The al-Aqsa Mosque in Jerusalem, the third holiest place in Islam, was displayed prominently at election rallies, as well as in posters of 'martyrs', in party offices and in homes (although Fatah also uses this symbol).[7]

Religious knowledge, piety and charitable activity, or occupying an official position in religious institutions all play a role in determining an electoral candidate's chances of success. However, mirroring Hamas' internal make-up, most candidates are professionals with a secular education, and what symbolic capital they derive from religion primarily concerns the secular skills and social capital associated with these attributes.

In the most detailed analysis to date of the seventy-four Hamas legislators' careers, the Washington Institute for Near East Policy lists only twelve as having affiliations with mosques, four as 'imams' (which comes closest to the Western term 'cleric'), one as being involved in a religious court, and three as members of *zakah* (religious tithe) committees (WINEP, 2007; see also KAS, 2006). Many more legislators are involved in their local mosques, and have (some) religious knowledge. But their symbolic capital is not primarily defined by mosque affiliation or religious expertise.

Even those affiliated with 'religious' institutions perform largely 'secular' functions. *Zakah* committee members are responsible for deciding how to disburse *zakah* donations. 'Religious' courts are responsible for applying family and personal law. The twelve listed as having mosque affiliations are all otherwise employed as professionals.[8] Only the four imams are professionally defined by their mosque affiliation.

---

7   In nearly all the homes I visited, a model of the al-Aqsa Mosque—invariably made by the interviewee during his time in prison—stood in a prominent place.

8   WINEP left Muhammad Abu Tair's profession blank; Hamas' No.2

Although around a third of Hamas' legislators have studied Islam, they have done so primarily in a modern university setting. Most have studied Islamic law or Islamic studies rather than the more purely 'religious' subjects of 'fundamentals of religion' and *'da'wah'* (the Islamic term for preaching).[9] Most of those who have studied religious subjects have jobs in the university or charity sector, rather than in 'traditional' religious institutions.

The make-up of Hamas' first Cabinet reveals an even greater predominance of engineers, medical doctors and 'secular' university professionals. Of the twenty-five Cabinet members, only four studied Islamic law and none studied *'daw'ah'* or 'fundamentals of [Islamic] religion' (WINEP, 2007; BICOM, 2006; JMCC, 2006).[10]

Hamas' municipal councillors similarly have a predominantly 'secular' education and 'secular' careers. In Nablus, Hamas' list consisted of seven engineers, four doctors, a lawyer, a teacher and only two (religious) *shaykhs* (*Jerusalem Post*, 'Pragmatic mayor', 21 December 2005). In al-Bireh, the list included civil society activists, engineers, physicians, ex-political prisoners and other professionals, all "carefully selected based on aptitude and public service record" (palestine-info.co.uk, 'Hamas ready for Bireh municipal elections', 13 November 2005). In Sa'ir, the candidates consisted of two teachers, two businessmen, a statistician, a local administrator, and an architect (*Jerusalem Post*, 'On Allah's Ticket', 14 June 2005).[11]

That the majority of Hamas' candidates are professionals may not be a true reflection of the movement's utopian values. It is possible

---

(national list) has been in prison for most of his professional life.

9 Out of the seventy-four, twenty-two have studied Islamic *shari'ah*, *da'wah* or fundamentals of religion (WINEP, 2007). Five have studied one of these topics besides a social or natural science such as politics or development. A further four have studied (contemporary) Islamic studies.

10 One other studied comparative religion, one jurisprudence.

11 Similar profiles can be found for the municipalities of Dahariyah, al-Shiyukh, Obadeiah, Qalqilya, Deir al-Balah (*Ha'aretz*, 'Hamas blasts arrest of municipal candidates', 20 December 2004; 'Hamas expected to benefit from public's frustration with PA', 3 May 2005; *Christian Science Monitor*, 'Hamas gains grassroots edge', 27 December 2004; 'Hamas gains Palestinian political clout', 9 May 2005).

that, in line with those who claim that Hamas pursues a theocracy, Hamas would have preferred to see more religiously-educated candidates or candidates from the religious establishment if it did not have to heed electoral calculations. To compete for votes in a society where 'religious' authority has long lost its political clout (in a formal sense), and where the main political factions have been dominated by secular professionals, running a list dominated by clergy would mean taking a political risk. There are, however, at least three factors militating against Hamas pursuing cleritocratic goals.

Hamas' internal leadership profile closely resembles the profile of its electoral candidates: professionals, educated at secular institutions, with only a handful affiliated with traditional religious institutions. If Hamas were to increase the number of religiously educated or clerical candidates, it would not only risk marginalising its internal leadership but also find it difficult to find enough candidates of sufficient calibre whose loyalty to Hamas could be ensured.

Hamas also appears to recognise that 'religious' expertise is only one form of expertise and that 'religious' scholars do not necessarily make good politicians—as illustrated by the experience of Lebanon's Hizballah and the Jordanian Brotherhood, both of which examples Hamas has studied closely (Tamimi, 2007). The least we can infer from the profile of Hamas' candidates is that, under present conditions, Hamas does not unconditionally privilege religious expertise over other, more secular forms of expertise, and that it does not insist legislators have religio-legal expertise. That the majority of Hamas' candidates have secular expertise that is particularly useful for running a (quasi)-state suggests, however, that, in an electoral environment where candidates are judged by their performance, Hamas deems secular expertise and political capital more important than religious expertise. That the majority of those who have studied Islam have studied Islamic law—in a country where one of the main sources of law is Islamic law—rather than religion more broadly, only underscores this point.

Its political theory also encourages Hamas to privilege political over religious authority. In Hamas' theoretical framework, legislators in an Islamic state do not have to be religious scholars or have religious expertise. Having a popular mandate is placed above all else, and the legislative council is expected to include a wide range of expertise to enhance good governance. Political theory is in part a reflection of wider social and political structures and influences, and is thus fluid. But it also has a momentum of its own, shaping what can be considered acceptable, and thus making it more difficult for those who might argue for increased religious expertise to change Hamas' practice.

That the majority of Hamas' electoral candidates are not characterised by religious expertise does not deny the importance of religious capital, in its broadest sense. Hamas candidates typically enjoy what the *New York Times* aptly called "reputations for probity and piety" ('Hamas Surges In West Bank', 17 December 2005). However, what appears to appeal to voters is Hamas' reputation for integrity, public-spiritedness and efficiency, rather than religiosity *per se*. It seems that because Palestinians believe religious observance inspires these 'secular' virtues that association with religion increases one's symbolic capital.

This reading is supported by the findings of opinion polls. A February 2006 JMCC poll found, for instance, that almost half of all respondents (43 per cent) said that they had voted for Hamas in the 2006 election in the hope of ending corruption. A combined total of 30 per cent had done so for political or socio-economic reasons.[12] Just 19 per cent of respondents stated that they had voted for Hamas for 'religious reasons'.

Religiosity is also an inadequate predictor of voting patterns. According to the PSR Exit Poll (February 2006), a significant percentage of those who considered themselves 'somewhat religious' (38 per cent) or 'not religious' (19 per cent) said they had supported Hamas in the 2006 elections, while nearly half of those who considered themselves religious (48 per cent) did *not* support Hamas. The figures for Fatah were 40 per cent, 44 per cent and 49 per cent respectively. Thus, although there appears to be a correlation between not supporting Hamas and considering oneself 'not religious', this correla-

---

12 Improve living conditions (10.7 per cent), Hamas' political agenda (11.8 per cent), and curb Fatah's control over the government (7.5 per cent).

tion is not all-determining, while for the 'religious' and 'somewhat religious' the correlation is negligible.

Even those who cited 'religious reasons' appear in part to have been influenced by secular considerations. One voter told Aljazeera. net that she voted for Hamas because it had helped her "become closer to God" ('High turnout at Palestinian polls', 25 January 2006). However, she added that she had done so also in gratitude for the financial help she received for her studies. Hamas' candidate for the Nablus mayorship won primarily because of his reputation for integrity, efficiency and giving to charity. But this reputation was linked in both his and the voters' mind to his being "a religious man" who "pray[s] five times a day" (*Jerusalem Post*, 'Pragmatic mayor', 21 December 2005; see also *New York Times*, 'Fatah Fights To Beat Back a Rising Hamas', 23 January 2006). As one Nablus voter put it: "We want our leaders to be people who fear God ... We were Fatah supporters but we are demanding new faces" (*Christian Science Monitor*, 'Why Hamas is gaining in Palestinian polls?', 25 January 2006). This voter associated 'fearing God' with integrity. That this is not unusual in a Palestinian context is suggested by the fact that 33 per cent of those who responded to my 1997 survey at the Islamic University in Gaza similarly chose 'integrity' as the term best defining religion for them. Thus, the electoral value of religious capital derives in part from the 'secular', or in Stout's terminology (Stout, 2004: 26), civic virtues associated with religious observance.

Religion also plays an important cultural role in the creation of symbolic capital. Many of those I interviewed said they supported Hamas because they came from religious families, and thus felt affinity with Hamas' religious character. Tamimi similarly suggests that one of the reasons Hamas won the 2006 election was the increasing Islamisation of Palestinian society (Tamimi, 2006: 221). Familiarity and interaction with Hamas members attending one's local mosque would increase voters trust in Hamas as an organisation, or in particular Hamas candidates. But here too, what seems to create symbolic capital are the cultural and moral connotations and the familiarity associated with mosque attendance, rather than religion *per se* (to the extent such a distinction can be made).

Religion and Hamas' Political Programme

A second issue concerns the impact of religion on Hamas' political programme. This is not the place for a comprehensive analysis of Hamas' changing political programme and the role played by religion therein. Suffice it to make two tentative observations on the basis of a reading of Hamas' election manifesto: though Islam informs aspects of Hamas' political, and in particular its social programme, it is only one influence and source of authority among others; and the way Islam is interpreted is influenced by the wider socio-economic and political context within which Hamas operates.

Islam provides one of the frameworks for Hamas' political programme which is reflected in both the selection of its priorities and in the content of its proposals. Its election manifesto, for instance, promises to "establish Islamic Shari'ah as the main source of legislation in Palestine", and devotes an entire section on "the Subject of Admonition and Guidance" (preaching and other religious issues). It calls for Islam to be the foundation for education, on the grounds that it "dignifies the human being [by] striking a balance between individual rights and community rights". And it undertakes to "shield women with Islamic education" to ensure that their "independent personality" is based on "chastity, decency and observance" (Tamimi, 2006: 280-6).

However, the bulk of Hamas' election manifesto reads like that of any 'secular' political party. Its focus on housing, health, agricultural policy, improving education and scientific research, increasing government efficiency and reigning in the security agencies is not ostensibly influenced by religion. Islam plays an important background role, for instance, in the way Hamas calls for "an agricultural credit system to replace the interest-based system" (the Qur'an forbids usury), or in its emphasis on family values. But it is only one framework amongst others—Hamas' focus on preserving national rights, for instance, is as much informed by nationalism and its rivalry with Fatah, as it is by a religious interpretation of the conflict—and it informs less positions than one would expect from Huntington and Hoffman's predictions.

A good illustration is Hamas' position regarding women, which neither Islam nor local religio-cultural traditions can fully explain. Religion informs its position on inheritance and polygamy, for instance, which are explicitly derived from (locally) dominant and culturally reinforced interpretations of the Qur'an and the Hadith which buttress existing inequalities between men and women (al-Zahhar, 1998b; Musa, 1998a; Women's Islamic Bloc I, 1998). But its election manifesto and its female candidates seek to reduce existing inequalities, calling on women to become more active politically—in the words of Huda al-Qrenawi, seventh on the national legislative list, "women didn't come into life only to be man's servant" (WINEP, 2007)—and promising to increase job opportunities for women (Tamimi, 2006: 286). Intriguingly, these positions were also justified with reference to Islam, most eloquently by Jamila al-Shanti, third on Hamas' national list, who stated in the run-up to the 2006 election that "there are traditions here that say that a woman should take a secondary role—that she should be at the back, but that is not Islam. Hamas will scrap many of these traditions. You will find women going out and participating" (WINEP, 2007).

That this is not just empty rhetoric can be gleaned from numerous observations. Hamas' female municipal candidates in the West Bank village of Obadeiah put it into practice by refusing to run within the protective confines of the quota system, instead contesting the elections in direct competition with the other male candidates (*Christian Science Monitor*, 'Hamas gains grassroots edge', 27 December 2004).[13] In Nablus, Hamas' municipal list had more women candidates than any of the other lists (*Jerusalem Post*, 'Pragmatic mayor'). At the legislative level (CECP, 2006), Hamas has six female legislators—two less than Fatah—but this may have more to do with availability and cultural traditions than policy (cf. NDI, 2005a). Since its election victory and the success of its female candidates, Hamas has furthermore followed the example of its 1996 political off-shoot, Hizb al-

---

13 Hamas candidates in al-Mighraqa (North Gaza) similarly won outright, without needing the quota (NDI, 2005b) and others may have done similarly.

Khalas, by allowing women to sit on its *Shura* Council and setting up a women's affair committee (Hroub, 2007).

All but one of Hamas' female candidates elected in 2006 were professionals or community activists in their own right (WINEP, 2007). Of the six, one had a doctorate, three held bachelors degrees. Two were lecturers, one a journalist, one a physics teacher, and one a community activist. Only one appeared to be primarily defined as the mother of martyred sons (all of whom had engaged in paramilitary activities). Many of Hamas' female municipal candidates similarly ran for election on the basis of their charitable work, their professional skills or their involvement in the community (*Jerusalem Post*, 'Pragmatic mayor'; palestine-info.co.uk, 'Hamas ready for Bireh municipal elections', 13 November 2005; *Christian Science Monitor*, 'Hamas gains grassroots edge', 27 December 2004)—and not simply as "the manufacturer of men" charged with "taking care of the home and raising the children according to Islamic concepts and values", as Hamas' 1988 Charter had it (Mishal and Sela, 2000: 186-7). More telling still, many of the female supporters I spoke with in the 1990s credited Hamas with having given them the courage, opportunity and sometimes financial aid to break with tradition and persuade their families to allow them to attend university.

More research is needed to probe the relationship between Hamas and women, and how this has evolved over time (Hamas' 1988 Charter, for instance, advocates a far more conservative approach to women in public life; Mishal and Sela, 2000: 186-7). But, whatever the reasons behind Hamas' adoption of certain attitudes, its programme cannot be characterised as a rigid, unchanging literalist interpretation of Islamic scripture, while some of its political positions clearly constitute a break from prevailing cultural attitudes, particularly among those most likely to vote for Hamas. *Ha'aretz*, for instance, remarked that "one of the most prominent characteristics of the current [Hamas] election campaign" was precisely "the expanded role of women, despite the limitations of religion and tradition" ('Hamas aims to win 60 percent of PLC seats', 11 December 2005). Nor is this a recent development. In the late 1990s, Hamas joined Marxist and secularist feminists in raising public awareness of the prevalence of honour killings and early marriage, both of which practices it condemned (Sarraj-Mattar, 1998; Qassim, 1998a, 1998b; Radwan and Emad, 1997; Rugi, 1998; Abu Shannab, 1998d; al-Zahhar, 1998b; Hamad, 1998b; Women's Islamic Bloc I, 1998; Women's Islamic Bloc II, 1998; 'Nasr', 1998; 'Iyad', 1998). Its female activists staged debates, some in conjunction with the Ministry of Health, to discuss women's rights and warn of the dangers of early marriage (Muslim Girls Association, 1998; Women's Islamic Bloc I, 1998; Women's Islamic Bloc II, 1998). *Al-Risalah* (11 June 1998: 11) explicitly denounced honour killings as un-Islamic.

In most of these cases, Hamas' position is explicitly framed as having been inspired by Islam—even while the traditions it opposes are similarly sanctioned with reference to Islam by those who practice them (cf. al-Zahhar, 1998b). This suggests two things: the fact that Hamas portrays itself as Islamic is not an adequate explanation for why Hamas has adopted a specific programme since Islam can be, and has been, interpreted in contradictory ways; and Islam, and Hamas' explicit reliance on it, does not automatically prevent Hamas from adopting socially innovative positions which can be said to further the process of democratisation, at least in terms of increasing political participation. This is not to deny the tensions between Hamas' programme and international human rights norms, or the continued prevalence of patriarchal traditions. What seems clear, though, is that Hamas does not necessarily interpret Islam conventionally or in accordance with Western stereotypes (a point which should be obvious but unfortunately is not).

More broadly, Islam, rather than being an obstacle, appears to encourage electoral participation, at least in the way Hamas interprets it. Hamas leaders self-consciously point to Islam as one of their main inspirations for promoting electoral participation (Chapter 3). They critique Western liberal democracy for its denial of the religious origins of democracy, and argue that the essence of democracy is an Islamic invention, transmitted to Europe through contact between Renaissance and Islamic scholars. Qur'anic injunctions and early Islamic traditions are used to justify elections, consultations, the rule of law, separation of powers and the notion of a social contract. In this, Hamas merely confirms Grant and Tessler's finding that political Islam in Palestine increases the likelihood that people believe democracy and Islam to be compatible.

Given that Islam can be interpreted as both an inspiration for democracy (as Hamas does) and as its antithesis (as some other Islamist groups do), Islam itself cannot be seen as a cause of or an obstacle to Hamas' electoral participation. How Islam is interpreted appears to depend largely on the context and life experience of those who do the interpreting, as well as on the availability of particular interpretations. In this, Hamas appears to corroborate Burgat's suggestion that "the function of 'divine' law [and, by extension, of Islam's sacred texts] is not dissimilar to that of the 'natural law' or 'general principles' in Western thought" and that, despite the Qur'an being more prescriptive, reason and interpretation play a decisive role (Burgat, 2003: 132-7).

Because reason and interpretation are in turn influenced by socio-economic and political context, analysis of this context appears to be more useful in explaining Hamas' political programme, than analysis of some reified notion of Islam—although one cannot adequately explain Hamas' programme without also understanding Hamas' interpretation of Islam. The emphasis in Hamas' election manifesto on freedom of expression, curbing security agencies or making government more accountable is far better explained by Hamas' position in the Palestinian polity as a long-term opposition faction, than by its purportedly religious character. This is not to deny that Islam informs Hamas' understanding of freedom, and the proper role of security agencies, or that Hamas' emphasis on accountability is partly inspired by its interpretation of Islam. The two explanations are not necessarily at odds. But the fact that Hamas presents itself as a religiously-inspired faction does not adequately explain why Hamas has focused on these issues, and not others.

More broadly, analysis of socio-economic factors can provide useful insights into Hamas' political programme. I will return to this in Chapter 7. Relevant here, though, is the fact that Hamas' emphasis on participative democracy, or on the notions of representation and accountability can be in part explained by the socio-economic position of its constituency, and the impact of particular aspects of modernisation on it, such as university education and the weakening of the traditional landed elite. Hamas' critical position towards institutionalised religion, and in particular its readiness not to automatically accept religious authority, can be made more intelligible by the fact that much of Hamas' leadership is drawn from the urbanised professional and university-educated strata of society. Its support for democracy can similarly be (tentatively) linked to its being a movement of lower and lower middle class origins, with sufficient organisational and financial resources to be autonomous from the state and the ruling elite—just as its championing of women's participation is profoundly intertwined with the high levels of support it has among Palestinian women (cf. PSR PLC Exit Poll, February 2006; NEC, January 2006; Hilal, 2006), and the increased role of women in Hamas' political campaigns (which is itself in part a response to the incarceration and assassination of male activists).

Religion and Bourdieu's 'Mystery of Ministry'

Where Hamas' use of religion is more likely to undermine democratic practices is in the dynamic of Bourdieu's 'mystery of ministry'. Religious knowledge, piety and religiously-inspired charitable work all help to cement a relationship of loyalty and identification between Hamas candidates and voters which, mirroring the dynamic within Hamas, can impede critical judgement. The voter quoted above who had voted for Hamas because it had increased her faith and paid for her education may have been able to critically scrutinise Hamas' programme. However, the debt she feels to Hamas makes it harder for her to be critical.

This dynamic is aided by the use of religious terms such as '*haram*' (unlawful according to Islam), used for instance to dissuade people from voting in the 1996 elections (*Jerusalem Times*, January 12, 1996: 7), or to denounce the consultation programme on women's rights (Hammami and Johnson, 1999), as this precludes debate by invoking the full weight of the divine authority embedded in the term, and its connotations wih hellfire and damnation (a classic example of symbolic violence).[14] Giving sermons in mosques similarly can serve to

---

14 See discussion of centrality of afterlife in discussions with Hamas supporters and sympathisers, Chapter 4.

encourage this dynamic, if this is done to foreclose debate or prevent people from articulating their own interests. The use of mosques in itself can enhance political participation, by enlarging political space (particularly in the absence of readily available public spaces) and by drawing more people into the political process (as Hamas arguably did in the lead-up to the 2003 ceasefire). But to the extent that the political message becomes overwritten by the religious authority that comes from giving a sermon, it negates the value of consent, and pushes politics into the realm of 'recognition' (of what is divinely right, and thus leaving no room for dissent), rather than that of 'voluntary will' (revolving around an individual's own decision, and allowing for debate and dissent).[15]

A good illustration of this dynamic—although it is too soon to tell whether this is an anomaly or representative of Hamas' attitude towards religious authority now that it is in power—is the example of Qalqilya's town councillors enlisting the offices of the local mufti (the highest religious office in Qalqilya) to give its decision to ban an international music festival official religious backing (ICG, 2006a: 14; bbc.co.uk, 'Hamas council bans music festival', 1 July 2005). The newly-elected councillors decided to ban the international festival on the grounds that it encouraged (unmarried) men and women to mix, and that such mixing was '*haram*' in Islam. The mufti, who appears to be close to the councillors, weighed in to increase the council's authority.

Not only has such behaviour been rare since Hamas' coming to office, but even in this case, the council sought to legitimise its decision with reference to both the social and the divine contract. As well as declaring the festival '*haram*', Qalqilya's council argued that the festival would offend the sensibilities of the majority of Qalqilya's conservative citizens, and that Hamas would be dishonouring its contractual relationship with Qalqilya's voters if it did not ban the festival. The ban, a council spokesman said, was "democratic because it reflected the wish of the majority", adding that "we were elected by a segment of the people that wants us to preserve the conserva-

---

15 I borrow this distinction from Riley's commentary on Hegel (Riley, 1982: 192).

tive values of the city. ... The prevailing values reject mixing of the sexes" (Associated Press, 'Palestinians Debate Whether Future State Will be Theocracy or Democracy', 13 July 2005; bbc.co.uk, 'Hamas council bans').

Whether a majority of citizens indeed opposed the concert is irrelevant. Within a representative democracy, the council is correct to argue that it has a mandate to decide on behalf of the electorate. Even if the electorate did not agree in this specific instance, by voting for this council it has transferred its right to decide to the council (cf. Sartori, 1987: 110; Birch, 1993: 74-6). As long as the council's electoral programme included the preservation of the city's conservative values, it is acting democratically. Similarly, the mufti's intervention on behalf of the council is not in itself a violation of the contractual principle, as long as the decision was taken by the council. Only if the mufti's intervention was intended to foreclose debate, is the contractual principle undermined. In this instance, the councillors and the mufti appear to have used the religious authority of both the term '*haram*' and the mufti's position in part to stifle opposition beyond what employing the contractual argument could achieve.

However, the impact of such a dynamic is less in the case of those whose identity is not defined by being a Hamas supporter, than it is among Hamas members. The Nablus voter quoted earlier who said he wanted to see 'new faces' and leaders who 'fear God' is less likely to suspend his judgement just because Hamas leaders appears to be more God-fearing. If Hamas has not delivered by the next elections, or if the self-sacrifice of Hamas leaders has not led to an improvement of the situation, he may well decide not to vote for Hamas. Because this voter's identity is not defined by Hamas, he is less likely to succumb to a Hamas leader's appeal to adopt his perspective on trust, whether for the sake of the organisation's unity, the nation or God. For this man, the argument that, in Bourdieu's words, "if I am an incarnation of the collective ... and if this group is the group to which you belong, which defines you, which gives you an identity, ... you really have no choice but to obey" (Bourdieu, 1991: 211-2), does not hold as strongly as for committed Hamas members. Only when Hamas succeeds in representing itself as the embodiment of 'authentic' Islam, or more broadly, of 'authentic' Palestinian nationalism or the 'authentic' resistance, will it be able to draw such voters more deeply into the dynamic of the 'mystery of ministry'.

Violence and Symbolic Capital

Finally, what role does violence play in the creation of symbolic capital? What role does it play vis-à-vis the elections?

Any such analysis must be placed in the profoundly violent setting in which Hamas operates. Occupation, the violent practices of the Israeli army and Jewish settlers, the plethora of resistance factions, clan militias and criminal gangs, and their violent practices, combined with the widespread availability of arms, the relative weakness of central authority structures and the existence of violent clan traditions, have all served to create a political environment in which violence is commonplace.

Violence plays a significant role both in Hamas' discourse and symbolism, and in its overall identity as a 'security provider'. At issue is not whether Hamas actually delivers increased 'security'. Rather, it is the perception among both its leaders and its supporters that Hamas' violent record is an important part of what makes it a legitimate political faction in the Palestinian arena—in other words, that given the perception of a threat to existence, violence-as-protection is a valued commodity (see Chapter 4).

That violence is considered a valued (electoral) commodity can be gleaned from the prevalence of symbolic references to violence during Hamas' 2004-6 election campaigns. During election rallies, references to the resistance—and in particular to Hamas' role in 'forcing' the IDF (Israeli Defense Forces) out of Gaza—were commonplace, as were posters of Hamas' martyrs, including those who had carried out suicide bombings (cf. *San Francisco Chronicle*, 'Hamas turns focus to political campaign', 26 January 2005; 'Hamas, Fatah turn to politics after pullout', 21 August 2005). Large campaign posters depicting "horsemen with blood dripping across their conquered territory" behind the pictures of Hamas' assassinated leaders adorned election podia (*Christian Science Monitor*, 'Will Hamas change course?', 1 February 2006). Hamas candidates in Nablus launched their campaign from the home of assassinated bomb-maker Yahya

'Ayyash, thus capitalising on the symbolic capital of one of the Brigades' most famous martyrs (*Jerusalem Post*, 'Bombing the ballot', 6 January 2006).

In the lead-up to the municipal elections of May 2005, the anniversaries of the assassinations of Yassin and al-Rantisi in March and April were the occasion of large election rallies while the widows of assassinated Hamas leaders played a prominent role in both municipal and legislative campaigns (*Ha'aretz*, 'Hamas grooms itself to win', 1 May 2005; *Jerusalem Post*, 'Hamas kicks off summer election campaign', 27 March 2005). When the first Hamas Cabinet was sworn in, Hamad al-Bitawi, a Hamas legislator, shouted: "jihad is our path and dying for the sake of Allah is our biggest wish" while Prime Minister Haniyyah emphasized that his cabinet's programme was "born straight from the embryo of resistance" (*Jerusalem Post*, 'Hamas cabinet approved', 28 March 2006).

The symbolic centrality of Hamas' record of violence in elections is nothing new. Especially in student elections, references to violence have been prominent, particularly at the height of the al-Aqsa Intifada. After winning the 2001 elections for al-Najah's student council, Hamas allegedly celebrated its victory by vowing, gruesomely, that its "military wing, ... would reward Hamas supporters for the victory by carrying out a major suicide attack against Israelis" (*Jerusalem Post*, 'Hamas wins student elections at An-Najah University', 13 November 2001). During Bir Zeit's 2003 student council elections, a pro-Hamas candidate was alleged to have boasted in a public debate with his pro-Fatah rival: "Hamas activists in this university have killed 135 Zionists. How many did Fatah activists from Bir Zeit kill?" (*Jerusalem Post*, 'Hamas wins election on Israeli bodycount ticket', 11 December 2003). During the same election, Hamas activists blew up models of Israeli buses in honour of the Qassam Brigades' exploits—although this must be seen in the context of Fatah activists, belonging to a faction officially engaged in the peace process, blowing up models of Jewish settlements.

However, references to violence form only part of Hamas' electoral repertoire. During the 2004-6 municipal and legislative campaigns, much of the emphasis was on Hamas' non-violent contributions to society, and its domestic programme, which focused on issues of social justice and good governance. Hamas candidates typically campaigned on lists whose names referred to non-violent domestic themes, such as 'Change and Reform'—rather than the more militant-sounding 'Martyrs' Bloc' which Fatah used among others (*Ha'aretz*, '400,000 Palestinians expected to vote', 5 May 2005; Litvak, 2005a). At rallies, the *Jerusalem Post* noted, "the telltale models of burning Israeli buses and other symbols that were staples of previous gatherings" were largely lacking ('Hamas kicks off summer election campaign', 27 March 2005). Of the twenty subject headings in Hamas' 2006 election manifesto only two focused on issues related to the resistance—and then only emphasising the liberation of "the West Bank, Gaza Strip and Jerusalem" (with merely an oblique reference to not conceding "any span of the [rest of the] historic land of Palestine").[16] In contrast, seventeen headings concerned Hamas' domestic programme, starting, unsurprisingly, with "administrative reform and fighting corruption" and ranging from "educational policy" and "the Palestinian woman" to "youth", "housing policy" and "human rights organisations" (Tamimi, 2006: 274-94).

One of the reasons Hamas focused its electoral programme on its (non-violent) domestic programme was that it did not need to emphasise its resistance record. It was on display during numerous victory rallies staged to celebrate the withdrawal of Israeli troops and settlers from the Gaza Strip in summer 2005, complete with marching militia-men in military fatigues and rocket launchers (cf. *New Republic*, 'Power Play', 11 January 2005). It was implied in the countless posters of Hamas' martyrs which adorned streets as well as election rallies.

Meanwhile, opinion polls suggested that many credited Hamas, as the leading resistance faction, with driving the Israeli army out of Gaza. In a March 2005 poll, 75 per cent of respondents believed that Sharon's unilateral withdrawal plan was "a victory for the Palestinian armed struggle" (increasing to 84 per cent on the eve of withdrawal), while a poll conducted just prior to the withdrawal found 40 per cent crediting Hamas specifically with this 'victory' (PSR Polls 15 & 17, March & September 2005).

---

16 See note 5 (this Chapter).

Not only did Hamas have little need to highlight its resistance record but it had far more to gain from focusing on Fatah's weakest point: the absence of a credible social and political reform programme. Too great a focus on its resistance record would risk alienating the large section of undecided voters who, while disillusioned with Fatah, nevertheless supported a two-state solution. In the March 2005 PSR poll (two months before the third round of municipal elections), 81 per cent of respondents supported "reconciliation between the Palestinian and Israeli peoples after reaching a peace agreement with Israel", while the September 2005 PSR poll found that support for the establishment of a Palestinian state alongside Israel comprising the West Bank and Gaza Strip was 73 per cent. These same polls found that the percentage of un-decided respondents was 17-20 per cent while the differential between Hamas and Fatah was merely some 10 per cent. Like any election-savvy political party, Hamas thus chose to focus on what it believed would gain it the most votes.

By focusing on domestic issues it also neatly drew attention away from the absence of any realistic policy among Hamas circles regarding how to secure a viable Palestinian state. While Fatah's weakest spot was its domestic record, Hamas' was the absence of a credible alternative to Fatah's peace overtures—beyond emphasising the illegality of Israel's occupation and the right of the occupied to resist. Even though the peace process was in ruins, people still believed Fatah to be better able to secure a political settlement with Israel than Hamas. A PSR exit poll at the 2006 legislative elections found 61 per cent of respondents believing Fatah 'most able' to "move the peace process forward" (the figure for Hamas was 27 per cent).

The profile of Hamas' candidates also underlines this focus on domestic matters. While, for security reasons, it is difficult to determine with certainty whether a Hamas leader is also a major player in the Qassam Brigades, it is nevertheless striking how few Hamas candidates appear to have been Qassam commanders. If we compare the profiles collected by the Washington Institute for Near East Policy and the Konrad-Adenauer-Stiftung, only one legislator, Fathi Hammad (Northern Gaza), is identified by both as a Qassam leader. The Washington Institute lists a further three of the seventy-four Hamas legislators as having been accused of direct involvement with the resistance (WINEP, 2007).[17] The Konrad-Adenauer-Stiftung does not identify these three but identifies two other legislators (KAS, 2006).[18]

The discrepancy between these two reports underlines that this is not the final word on who has been directly involved in the resistance—let alone who is known by the electorate to have been directly involved. But, if we take these combined reports as roughly indicative of the percentage of those directly involved, particularly as the Washington Institute, with its relatively pro-Israeli leanings, is unlikely to ignore publicly available evidence of a Hamas legislator's links with the Qassam Brigades, only 5 per cent of Hamas legislators would fall under this category. The profiles of Hamas' first Cabinet members and its municipal councillors are similarly overwhelmingly devoid of references to the Brigades, although there is a somewhat greater overlap at student level.[19].

If correct, this suggests that, when appealing to the electorate for gaining political office, Hamas seeks candidates with political rather than paramilitary symbolic capital. This is particularly striking for an organisation which began as a resistance movement and whose primary goals include the destruction of Israel. There are of course

---

17 Mohammad Abu Tayr (National List, Jerusalem); Fadel Hamdan (Ramallah); Khaled Thouaib (Bethlehem). Mahmud al-Khatib (Bethlehem) is listed only as having been involved in an intra-Palestinian shooting. Spellings are WINEP's.

18 Yunis al-Astal (Khan Yunis) as Qassam member; Muhammad Rahman Shehab (Northern Gaza) as leader of the Brotherhood's 'paramilitary wing' before 1987.

19 BICOM mentioned no links (BICOM, 2006). Israeli newspapers usually did not mention links when reporting municipal elections. More links are made in the media between student leaders and the Brigades (cf. IDF, 2002; *MediaLine*, 'Hamas cell victorious in Ramallah University elections', 11 December 2003). Similarly, Ayman Taha, 1998 Student Council president at Gaza's Islamic University, was reported to have become a Qassam leader (*Associated Press*, 'Hamas remains defiant despite intense Israeli campaign', 12 September 2003; *Birmingham Post*, 'Israelis capture Hamas founder', 4 March 2003).

practical reasons militating against Hamas nominating members of the Qassam Brigades. But given that Hamas candidates risk imprisonment regardless of their links with the Brigades, and that some Brigades commanders did stand for election, as was the case in Beit Lahia (*Wall Street Journal*, 'Strained Relations: With Israel Gone, Election Splinters A Family in Gaza', 2 December 2005), these reasons cannot have been all-determining.

In limiting the number of candidates known for their resistance record, Hamas seems to recognise that expertise in resistance does not equate with political expertise, and that a career in the underground does not necessarily provide one with the political standing and networking capacity needed to do well in politics. In making this distinction, Hamas appears to be serious about the contractual nature of elections, seeking to maximise its chances of delivering on its promises—and thus increasing the chance of being (re-)elected—as opposed to honouring debts to militants.

Given the prevalence of (ex-)militants in the top ranks of other violent organisations that have turned to politics (like Sinn Fein, Hizballah, Tamil Tigers), it is noteworthy that Hamas did not capitalise more directly on the symbolic capital that comes from a career in resistance—despite opinion polls repeatedly returning high percentages of respondents positively valuing the resistance (though not necessarily its continuation). A March 2004 PSR poll found, for instance, that 67 per cent of respondents believed that "armed confrontations have helped the Palestinians achieve national rights in a way that negotiations could not" while a JMCC poll conducted shortly after the 2006 election (February) found nearly two-thirds of respondents (58 per cent) stating that armed struggle remained necessary to achieve national goals with only 39 per cent believing that negotiations alone would suffice (see also Chapter 6).

Instead, rather than using the charismatic appeal of its 'resistance heroes', Hamas has relied on the delegated capital that comes from belonging to Hamas, and by extension the Qassam Brigades, rather than on the personal capital of being a Qassam commander. A poignant illustration of this is a journalist's description of a Hamas rally:

Young men in ski masks and camouflage outfits waved guns and swirled numchucks onstage at an auditorium in El Bireh, a town in the West Bank. Women in head-to-toe *hijabs* marched to military music, holding the Koran in one hand and Hamas's green flag in the other. Even the mock rocket launchers—plastic sewage pipes painted with the colors of the Palestinian flag—appeared mildly menacing. But, when Hassan Yousef, now the mouthpiece of Hamas in the West Bank, took the podium wearing a suit and tie, he looked and sounded more like the leader of a political party (*New Republic*, 'Power Play', 11 January 2005).

The 'young men in ski masks' are there to underline Hamas' resistance record, its members' readiness to sacrifice themselves, and, significantly, the notion that Hamas will not sell out as easily to Israel as it believes Fatah has done. The person who takes to the podium as the electoral candidate is the political activist with civil society experience. The political activist takes centre-stage during elections and in the political process. But the 'young men in ski masks' and their paramilitary commanders are by no means sidelined—which is one of the reasons for Hamas' internal prevarication since its election victory.

The closest Hamas has come to directly capitalising on its members' resistance efforts is by selecting candidates with a prison record—although many of these did not have a personal resistance record but were imprisoned for belonging to Hamas. The Washington Institute lists forty-two of the seventy-four Hamas legislators as having been in prison (if we include those deported to Lebanon in 1992; WINEP, 2007). Prior to the third round of municipal elections, ninety-five Hamas activists were imprisoned by the Israeli government, thirty of which were (successful) candidates. By the end of 2005, Hamas accused Israel of having imprisoned 600 of its members (ICG, 2006a: 15; Aljazeera.net, 'Israel accused of skewing elections', 3 October 2005). In most instances, the prison record appears to be of secondary importance to the candidate's other credentials. In some cases, though, Hamas appears to have explicitly selected candidates with a prison record to highlight its commitment to Palestine and its candidates' readiness to self-sacrifice (in apparent contrast to Fatah's top leadership). The municipal list for the West Bank town of Qalqilya, for instance, was said to have included imprisoned candidates precisely to distinguish itself from Fatah's list of businessmen and clan leaders (*Ha'aretz*, '400,000 Palestinians expected to vote', 5 May 2005).

That resistance is still a core concern for Hamas is obvious. Nevertheless, Hamas' decision to field candidates with political and administrative, rather than paramilitary experience suggests that it recognises that political capital in the domestic arena is derived from having non-violent, administrative skills and professional expertise rather than from a career in the resistance. Its decision to focus its election programme more on domestic than on resistance issues, meanwhile, suggests that it recognises that the electorate is as, if not more, concerned about domestic issues as about resistance. Corroborating this, a JMCC poll taken shortly after the elections (February 2006) found that against 43 per cent of respondents stating they had voted for Hamas "with the hope of ending corruption", only 12 per cent said they had done so "because of its political agenda" (which in a Palestinian context means support for Hamas' opposition to the peace process). This does not mean that Hamas' opposition to the peace process is wholly unpopular: 39 per cent of respondents said that Hamas should continue with its operations against Israeli targets while 40 per cent stated they preferred "using both negotiations and armed struggle" to achieve "Palestinian national goals". I will return to this in Chapter 6.

Inter-Factional, Clan and Vigilante Violence

Hamas has been engaged in inter-factional violence since its inception. During the first Intifada, inter-factional violence, though at times intense, was, at least compared to the violence seen increasingly since the mid-2000s, relatively muted. Between the arrival of the Palestinian Authority in 1994 and the early 2000s, Hamas largely refrained from inter-factional violence, the odd student scuffle notwithstanding. But from the mid-2000s, interf-factional violence has become increasingly serious, suggesting that it is, at least in part, a function of the breakdown of central authority since the rise in inter-factional violence concided with the breakdown of central authority.

Much could be said about Hamas' use of violence withing a Palestinian context. But, looking at the patterns of intra-Palestinian violence leading up to and during the 2004-6 election period, three points are particularly pertinent to our discussion. First, though most of Hamas' violence has been political, part of the power struggle between Hamas and Fatah, it has not been used to directly influence elections (in sharp contrast to Fatah), nor has it, in the period before Hamas' coming to power, been directed against (civilian) government buildings. Second, much of the violence between Hamas and Fatah is driven by clan loyalties and the logic of vendettas. Finally, Hamas and Qassam militants are less often involved in violence directed against suspected immoral behaviour than during the first Intifada.

The most serious intra-Palestinian violence Hamas members have been engaged in has been violence against Fatah members. In January 2007 alone, the month before the signing of the national unity agreement in Mecca, forty-five people were killed in clashes between Fatah and Hamas. During 2006, fifty-five Palestinians were killed by Palestinian fire, most as a result of similar clashes (B'Tselem, n.d.). But even before Hamas' 2006 election victory, violence between Fatah and Hamas activists was commonplace, though on a smaller scale.

The tit-for-tat nature of the violence has been fuelled by the overlap between clan and political affiliations, giving clan vendettas a political hue while making inter-factional violence more intractable. The 2002 killing of a senior commander in the security forces, Rajah Abu Lahiyeh, for instance, was carried out by the 'Aql clan to avenge the death of Raed 'Aql, killed the previous year when Abu Lahiyeh opened fire on Hamas student supporters (*Ha'aretz*, 'Hamas, PA seek calm after top Gaza cop slain', 8 October 2002; 'Abu Mazen cannot commit suicide', 21 August 2003; 'Two killed, dozens hurt in PA-Hamas clashes in Gaza Strip', 17 July 2005). The 'Aql clan was closely associated with Hamas, and Hamas members were said to have helped in the revenge killing. Al-Rantisi, then Hamas' senior leader in Gaza, distanced Hamas from the killing, saying it concerned a feud between the 'Aql clan and Abu Lahiyeh (*Ha'aretz*, 'Hamas, PA seek calm'). However, Hamas members appear to have been involved, suggesting that clan loyalties can readily override other political or ideological objections.[20]

The above clan vendetta was exacerbated by the fact that Abu Lahiyeh had been in the (pro-Fatah) security forces while Raed 'Aql had been a Hamas activist. It thus took on political overtones. Much of the violence during 2004-6 followed a similar pattern, with funerals acting as a catalyst for further rounds of violence (cf. *International Herald Tribune*, 'Hamas and Fatah clash at Palestinian ministry', 24 April 2006; FoxNews.com, 'Hamas-Fatah Clashes Leave 12 Palestinians Injured', 9 May; *San Francisco Chronicle*, 'Fatah, Hamas followers in a series of clashes', 13 June). Because of this convergence between clan and factional loyalties, not all inter-factional violence can be unproblematically classified as political violence.

Beyond the dynamic of clan vendettas, looking more closely at the patterns of violence, there appears to be a difference in the types of targets Hamas and Fatah attack which may say something about Hamas' attitude towards authority. Where Fatah members regularly attacked government buildings or polling stations, even when Fatah was still in government, Hamas members typically attacked (pro-Fatah) security forces (including their buildings and funerals), while refraining from attacking Fatah-controlled civilian government structures.[21]

One of the reasons for this discrepancy is that Fatah typically lost more than expected in the various elections, while Hamas typically performed better than, or as well as, expected. Fatah's anger was thus

---

20 See also *Ha'aretz*, 'Feud in Gaza deepens after Palestinian police killings', 11 October 2001; Salon.com, 'Gaza melts down', 24 May 2006; 'Hamas and Fatah clash at Palestinian ministry', 24 April 2006; *Los Angeles Times*, 'Violence Erupts in Wake of Hamas Election Victory', 27 January 2006; *Boston Globe*, 'In Gaza, Palestinians fear civil war coming', 28 May 2006.

21 Cf. *Jerusalem Post*, 'More Fatah leaders quit over elections', 10 May 2005; *Ha'aretz*, 'Fatah takes most councils; Hamas wins the larger towns', 8 May; 'Two killed, dozens hurt in PA-Hamas clashes', 17 May; 'Hamas wins Al-Najah University student council elections', 29 November; Aljazeera.net, 'Palestinian police storm parliament', 3 October; 'Fatah fighters storm poll offices', 13 December; *San Francisco Chronicle*, 'Fatah, Hamas followers in a series of clashes', 13 June 2006; Salon.com, 'Gaza melts down', 24 May.

more readily directed against polling stations and, after the elections, the ministries in Hamas' control. Hamas' anger, meanwhile, was focused on the security services which had not only been used to imprison and torture them during the 1990s but had also, since Hamas' election victory, become one of Fatah's main weapons for undermining Hamas' governing ability by denying it control over the security forces that are central for maintaining law and order.

If Hamas had wished to do so, it could arguably have attacked government buildings and polling stations before coming to power. If it was strong enough to attack the Authority's security forces, it could have attacked government buildings. During the two years before the 2006 legislative elections, there were a number of occasions during which popular discontent with Fatah was such that if Hamas had decided to flex its muscles by attacking government buildings, it could have done so with relative impunity. Fatah's June 2005 decision to postpone the legislative elections was such an occasion, as was its nearly doing so again in the months leading up to the elections (cf. palestine-info.co.uk, 'Postponement of PLC elections', 29 June 2005; *Al-Ahram Weekly*, 'Elections uncertainty', 17-23 November 2005). By then, the security forces and Fatah were already so demoralised and fractionalised, that there was a ready opportunity for violence (cf. *International Herald Tribune*, 'Palestinian security in disarray, study finds', 27 July 2005). Hamas, meanwhile, had grown sufficiently in strength that it could have risked a (limited) confrontation. That Hamas did not do so is therefore significant.

Similarly noteworthy is the fact that Hamas did not use violence to influence election results (leaving aside small-scale, though sometimes deadly, scuffles between Fatah and Hamas activists, for instance over where to hang election posters; cf. *New York Times*, 'Armed Men, Lacking Jobs, Fuel Gaza's 'Violent Energy', 9 January 2006). It did not do so during the 2006 legislative elections, nor during the four municipal election rounds of 2004-5—despite Fatah loyalists repeatedly intervening violently when dismayed by election results. Nor did it do so during the student and professional elections of the 1990s. That it did not, even when it lost to Fatah, is significant.

There are various reasons why Hamas did not use violence. One factor concerns the electoral dynamic. Hamas had decided to campaign as the party of reform. One of its platforms was a critique of lawlessness and Fatah's inability to impose law and order. In the lead-up to the third round of municipal elections, Hamas leader Dr Muhammad Azal, commented for instance that "Nablus residents are tired of the armed Fatah gangs led by crime bosses and identify them not only with Fatah but with the PA's security forces." "We're losing our patience with the murders and the robberies," he stated. "The responsibility to protect residents is entirely that of the Palestinian Authority, and if it fails to protect people, we'll do it" (*Ha'aretz*, 'Hamas grooms itself to win in upcoming elections', 1 May 2005). Although Hamas has since found itself in the same position, unable to stem the lawlessness, in the context of such promises, Hamas could ill afford being seen to undermine what little law and order remained without losing the moral, and indirectly the electoral, high ground. Indeed, one of the reasons Hamas gave for ousting Fatah from Gaza's security forces in June 2007 was its concern over lawlessness, its lack of control over domestic security and its belief that Fatah stoked lawlessness to undermine Hamas' legitimacy (Rantisi, 2007; ICG, 2007b: 7-11; *Al-Ahram Weekly*, 'Gaza in the Grip of Hamas' & 'Opinions from both sides of the fence', 21-7 June 2007).

Another factor concerns Hamas' ideological aversion to *fitnah* or civil war (Mishal and Sela, 2000: 45, 55; BBC Monitoring Middle East, 'Hamas leader rejects early elections', 18 December 2006; *Jerusalem Post*, 'The invisible enemy', 13 July 2007). This aversion is in part derived from Hamas' particular interpretation of Islam, in part from its long-time position as the weaker opposition party, and in part from the recognition that *fitnah* is detrimental to the resistance, and thus serves Israel (although none of this has stopped it from engaging in limited *fitnah*). A further consideration is that intra-Palestinian violence is culturally highly unpopular, almost a taboo, and likely to affect an organisation's symbolic capital, and thus not only its self-image but also its electoral chances. One of the reasons that Hamas and Fatah agreed to a National Unity government in February 2007 was the sharp increase in inter-factional violence prior to their meeting in Mecca, and popular outcries against that violence (cf. Mish'al in *Guardian*, 13 February 2007; Tamimi, 2007). While insufficient to stop Hamas from engaging in intra-Palestinian violence, ideology, self-image, and concerns over popularity all play a constraining role.

That Hamas is reluctant to attack government buildings is also reflective of its overall attitude to government. Despite their readiness to attack security services, Hamas members typically display a deep respect for those structures of authority they consider legitimate. This is reflected in Hamas' internal practices (Chapter 4). But it is also reflected in its practice, prior to the al-Aqsa Intifada, of taking electoral complaints against Fatah to the appropriate authorities, while knowing that these authorities were controlled by Fatah (cf. Islamic Bloc leader, 1998), or in insisting on establishing a separate security force under the auspices of the Interior Ministry to break Fatah's monopoly over the security services, rather than using its existing militant cells and alliances. It is similarly reflected in the way the Hamas leadership continued to recognise the legitimacy of 'Abbas' Presidency, despite its militants overrunning the Presidential offices in Gaza when Hamas took control of Gaza in June 2007 (although other, strategic-political factors played a role in this).

To what extent Hamas' (apparent) concern with structures of accountability will survive its coming to power and its power struggle with Fatah is uncertain. That Hamas refrained from attacking (civilian) government buildings and from using violence to affect election outcomes may simply have been a function of the faction's weaker position in the Palestinian balance of power. Its readiness to step up violence against Fatah in the months leading up to the 2007 Mecca Agreement—when it was in a stronger position, and concerned about Fatah regaining the upper hand with Western support—suggests that this is imminently possible. If so, Hamas' coming to power is likely to erode the organisation's respect for (domestic) structures of accountability and the political process (cf. CBCNews.ca, 'Hamas militiamen beat Gaza protesters', 13 August 2007).

It is, however, possible that the combined force of Hamas' internal practices, its religiously-inspired aversion to *fitnah* and respect for structures, its continuing dependence on gaining votes on a law and order platform, and the imperative of keeping a united front against Israel, will stall this erosion As long as these inhibiting factors are not wholly eroded by the experience of being in power (or by the frustration of being prevented, by both Fatah and Israel and its Western allies, from exercising what Hamas members believe to be their rightful authority), Hamas members may keep their respect for structures of accountability.

The real test will come in the next round of elections. Given the financial chaos that has resulted from the boycott the international community has imposed to force Hamas to recognise Israel, and the resulting inability to make good on its election promises of increasing jobs and economic security, it is unlikely that Hamas will gain as many votes as it did in the 2006 election. Fatah, as long as it survives as a single faction, will have learned (some) lessons from its 2006 election disaster, and refrain from squandering its votes by putting up too many candidates. If Hamas loses the next elections and bows out without violence, it will have shown that an Islamist organisation is not inherently less capable of playing by the electoral rules than a 'secular' nationalist organisation. If it behaves like Fatah behaved after the 2006 election or resorts to the type of violence it engaged in during the months preceding the Mecca Agreement, it will have shown that its self-proclaimed Islamist ideals are little more than empty rhetoric.

It is noteworthy, in this respect, that Hamas members have largely abstained from another form of violence: vigilante violence against what is perceived as social and moral deviancy—although the changed opportunity structure in Gaza since June 2007 may usher in more of this type of violence. This is noteworthy both because the opportunities to do so have increased and because Hamas members and Brotherhood activists before them were accused of such violence during the 1980s and early 1990s. The '*hijab* campaign' of the late 1980s is a case in point (cf. Hammami, 1990), although Hamas members appear to have been less centrally involved than is suggested in the literature (Gunning, 2000: 142-69). The blurring of the distinction between collaborators and so-called moral deviants is another example—although here too, the available evidence suggests that, contrary to some of the wilder accusations (cf. Shahadah, 1998; Fatah PLC Member, 1998), Hamas was considered by both human rights organisations such as B'Tselem and popular rumour to be more rigorous than the other factions in ensuring that only those who were actual security risks were executed (cf. Be'er and Dr 'Abdel-Jawad, 1994: 145-7; see also Chapter 4).

Despite an increase in opportunities to engage in such violence as a result of the weakening of Palestinian security services since the outbreak of the al-Aqsa Intifada, Hamas militants' involvement in vigilante violence has been relatively sporadic. In Gaza, a young woman (later identified as a member of Hamas' Islamic Bloc at the Islamic University) was killed by militants affiliated with Hamas for publicly holding hands with a man (who turned out to be her fiancé; Hamad, 2005; ICG, 2006a: 13). In another incident, a rap concert was stopped by Hamas militants (*Times*, 'No dancing and no gays, if Hamas gets its way', 7 October 2005).

In response to such incidents, Hamas' leadership has usually distanced itself, condemning the actions of their militants. The killing of the young Gazan woman, for instance, was followed by immediate public condemnations, and calls for the perpetrators to be punished. According to Hamas spokesperson and journalist Ghazi Hamad (Hamad, 2005), Hamas leaders mediated between the family and the killers, persuading the former to deal with the murder according to *shar'iah* law, according to which the family of the victim has the right to demand the death penalty. More generally, Hamas spokesmen have dismissed rumours, reported in the Israeli press, that it has established a special unit called 'Struggle against Decay' to discipline those considered immoral, as "simply untrue" fabrications, spread by those seeking to undermine Hamas' chance in the next elections. "We are not the Taliban", said Ismail al-Ashqar, a Gazan Hamas leader. "We are an ethical movement that believes in social peace and refuses violence". Muhammad Ghazal, a Hamas leader from Nablus, similarly insisted: "We do not have a policy of interfering in the personal lives of anybody. Not now. Not tomorrow. Never" (Hamad, 2005; ICG, 2006a: 13).

Whether such statements are true is to some extent a moot point. As long as the electorate opposes such practices and political power remains dependent on electoral support, Hamas can ill afford to engage in such practices. Significantly, the general public does not seem to believe that Hamas will use violence to impose its social values. JMCC's February 2006 poll found that 70 per cent of respondents stated that they were not, or only somewhat, concerned that Hamas would "[enforce] social restrictions on the Palestinians". Only 8 per cent stated they were "very worried". This is not to deny that Hamas champions (some) socially conservative values and that it is likely to employ all the force of religion, from appeals to Islamic unity to fears of hell-fire, to persuade others of its views. But, within the current cultural climate and political structures, Hamas is more likely to employ symbolic than actual violence.

That individual Hamas members and units have become embroiled in vigilante violence is in part a function of the general breakdown of central authority, and in part of the heightened sensitivities of those engaged in resistance. As during the first Intifada, mixed-gender occasions and music festivals have come to be seen by militants as disrespectful to the dead and wounded. With the breakdown of central authority, the opportunity for vigilante violence has increased, leading to an overall increase in such violence. Members of Fatah's al-Aqsa Martyrs Brigades have similarly been involved in attacking events they disapproved of, for instance when they disrupted a concert in Nablus (*Palestine Report*, 'Festival rises from the ashes', 13 July 2005). As central authority has become further eroded by the power struggle between Hamas and Fatah, small vigilante groups have emerged, unaffiliated to any of the larger factions. In Gaza, for instance, a group calling itself Swords of Islamic Righteousness has attacked chemists and cyber-cafés on the grounds that they were believed to sell illegal drugs and enable the downloading of pornography respectively (*Times*, 'Internet cafes in the frontline of new Gaza violence', 26 December 2006).

In the context of this wider deterioration of the forces of law and order, Hamas and Qassam members have been relatively restrained. Not only have incidents involving vigilante violence been far less frequent than during the first Intifada, but Hamas' leadership has also been quicker to condemn them. Given that the opportunity to perpetrate such violence has increased, this suggests that a combination of greater internal control (compared to the first Intifada when much of the older leadership was imprisoned), greater dependence on electoral popularity, and a religiously-inspired ideology and self-image has succeeded in restraining the more violently-inclined amongst Hamas' membership. The changed opportunity structure in Gaza since June 2007 may dramatically affect this dynamic (cf. accusations of politically-fuelled vigilante violence in CBCNews.ca, 'Hamas militiamen beat Gaza protesters', 13 August 2007).

Concluding Remarks

Hamas' behaviour during the 2004-6 electoral campaigns suggests that it is acutely aware not only of what constitutes power in an electoral environment, but also of its dependence on gaining votes. Its emphasis on grassroots consultations and surveys in the shaping of its election programme and the selection of its candidates suggests that, in an electoral context, Hamas heeds public opinion—within the boundaries of its ideological commitments. It remains to be seen whether a U.S.-Israeli-sponsored peace process is capable of reconciling itself with an electoral system which can bring opponents of the peace process and American influence in the Middle East to power. But the fact that Hamas has invested so much effort in playing the electoral system well suggests that, at least in Hamas' eyes, a future Palestinian state is likely to be built around an electoral system in which power is concentrated in elected offices.

Its readiness to make alliances, even with those who support a two-state solution and co-existence with Israel, further underlines that Hamas is not fanatical and incapable of compromise, but pragmatic. Of particular interest, in this respect, is the fact that, through its alliances and its emphasis on its domestic programme, it has succeeded in gaining a significant number of votes among those who oppose important aspects of its programme. PSR's February 2006 exit poll found that 29 per cent of respondents who supported the peace process and 35 per cent of those who normally support 'independent nationalists' voted for Hamas. More strikingly still, 40 per cent of those who had voted for Hamas stated that they simultaneously backed the peace process, while 34 per cent stated that they supported "mutual recognition of Israel as a Jewish State and Palestine as a Palestinian State in a two-state context". These percentages gain in significance when contrasted with the small margins with which Hamas won the 2006 legislative elections: 3 per cent on the national list, 6 per cent on the district list. Come next election, Hamas will have to carefully consider its programme.

Religion both strengthens Hamas' commitment to democratic participation and can undermine democratic scrutiny by invoking the 'mystery of ministry' and foreclosing debate. However, though religion constitutes one of the frameworks informing Hamas' political programme, it is only one among others, and has to compete with what in a Western context would be considered secular concerns and calculations. Importantly, religion does not seem to be necessarily antithetical to democracy. Hamas' emphasis on piety can be said to strengthen democracy by encouraging civic piety and civil responsibility (see also Stout's discussion of piety in strengthening American democracy; Stout, 2004: 19-41). Much depends on how religion is interpreted which in turn is influenced by the socio-economic and political context: the socialising effect of external electoral systems, exposure to higher education, the increasing heterogenisation of Hamas' membership, the socio-economic interests of Hamas' constituency, Hamas' position as opposition party to a relatively autocratic and hierarchical Fatah. Socio-economic and political context are often better predictors of the selection and content of Hamas' political programme, than religion *per se.*

Religion plays a role in the creation of symbolic capital, as it does within Hamas. However, the majority of Hamas' electoral candidates are professionals with secular education and expertise. Few are defined by their affiliation with a religious institution. Although a third have studied aspects of Islam, the majority have specialised in Islamic law, which, for legislators in the Palestinian context, has a markedly non-religious value. In this, Hamas practises what it preaches.

Violence similarly plays an ambiguous role. On the one hand, in a context where people feel threatened, a record of political violence against 'the enemy' increases symbolic capital. On the other, Hamas does not typically capitalise directly on the violent record of its Qassam commanders, opting instead to put forward candidates with political, rather than paramilitary, symbolic capital. In this, it appears to recognise that a violent record is not necessarily good preparation for doing well in politics—just as it recognises this with respect to religious expertise.

Hamas' engagement in inter-factional violence, like Fatah's, is one of the aspects of its behaviour that can seriously undermine the democratic process in Palestine. However, it is noteworthy that Hamas' political violence has not usually been directed at the civilian structures of government, and that it has not sought to use violence to directly influence elections.

The current stalemate between Hamas and Fatah, with Hamas controlling Gaza, the Legislative Council (in theory) and one of two Cabinets, and Fatah controlling the other Cabinet, the West Bank, and the Presidency, has undermined the ability of the electoral system to centralise power and wrest it away from other contenders, such as clans, militias, partisan security chiefs and organised crime syndicates. If this stalemate continues, violence may well escalate, with serious consequences for electoral practices in the occupied territories.

That Hamas candidates are predominantly not Qassam leaders is significant if the organisation ever decides to move away from political violence. Because the personal capital of Hamas candidates does not primarily rest on direct involvement in political violence, it is, at least theoretically, easier to move away from violence. The same can be said about Hamas having more than one primary goal, enabling it to re-organise the hierarchy of its goals, and (re)present itself as primarily concerned with social justice, or introducing Islamic law, rather than violent resistance. This process is, however, not without complications. Even if personal capital is largely unrelated to the capacity to inflict violence, a considerable portion of a candidate's symbolic capital is derived from the delegated capital of belonging to a paramilitary resistance organisation. If Hamas decides to give up its arms, it can still derive symbolic capital from, in the eyes of many Palestinians, having wrested Gaza from the Israelis through armed resistance. But the memory of 'successful' violence is not the same as continuing to have the capacity to inflict violence—particularly as long as Palestinians feel that their existence is threatened.

Much will depend on the balance of power between Qassam commanders, Hamas absolutists and Hamas pragmatists. As long as the hawkish faction and the Qassam commanders hold an effective veto over the pragmatists by virtue of Hamas' tradition of consensual decision-making and the vulnerability of the peace process to violent 'spoilers', it will be difficult for the pragmatists to move away from resistance. That Hamas' political leadership contains relatively few Qassam commanders may make matters worse by increasing the chance of mutual alienation.

Another factor is the relationship between elected Hamas officials (including allies), Hamas leaders whose mandate stems from having been elected internally, and Qassam commanders. That elected candidates now have control over aspects of the structures of state, arguably increases their influence within Hamas—although the fact that they have reportedly had to step down from their positions within Hamas in an attempt to insulate the organisation from the performance of Hamas members in public office (ICG, 2007a: 25), may limit the effect of these new resources, as will the lack of control they have over the pro-Fatah security forces (which was one of the reasons behind the ousting of Fatah loyalists from Gaza's forces in June 2007; cf. *Al-Ahram Weekly*, 'Gaza in the Grip of Hamas', 21-27 June 2007).

Hamas' participation in elections is important not just for what it says about the movement's internal logic, but also for the long-term effect it may have on the movement's members. As we saw earlier, both democratisation and social movement theorists suggest that an organisation's practices have a socialising effect on the organisation's members which may affect their external behaviour—and *vice versa*. Thus, the extent to which Hamas participates in elections is important for its own sake, as it is likely to have a longer-term impact on its members' disposition towards democracy, quite apart from whether they started out as pragmatists or committed democrats.

6
HAMAS AND THE PEACE PROCESS

Where Hamas' behaviour has elicited most controversy is its violence against Israelis, and in particular against Israeli civilians. From its inception, it has attacked Israelis as part of its opposition to occupation and the succession of peace processes on offer to which I will refer as 'the peace process', despite the term's political connotations (cf. Selby, 2007). The type of violence used has changed over time, from stone throwing, knifings and shootings to kidnappings, suicide bombings and rocket attacks—and increasingly, a set of uneasy ceasefires. Throughout, though, Hamas' opposition to the peace process has been implacable. Or has it?

Rhetorically, Hamas has acted, to use Stedman's terminology (Stedman, 1997: 7-16), as a 'total spoiler', unwilling to compromise on its vision of a liberated Islamic state in all of British Mandate Palestine. Its actual behaviour has been more ambiguous. During the 1990s it staged suicide attacks which undermined the peace process and since coming to power it has refused to recognise Israel, even in the face of crippling financial sanctions. However, at various times it has refrained from attacks, most notably in the lead-up to the 1996 Palestinian legislative elections and, on and off, since March 2005. During the al-Aqsa Intifada of 2000, it was responsible for much of the carnage inflicted upon Israelis. But from early 2005, it has, notwithstanding violations, rocket attacks and various suspensions, broadly honoured a ceasefire with Israel although tensions have increased since the summer of 2007. It has not carried out suicide bombings since then—in sharp contrast to the period before—and, despite intermittently firing rockets and allowing other factions to carry out attacks, the two years since the ceasefire have seen a significant drop in the number of Israelis killed, from 108 in 2004, to 33 from March-December 2005, and 23 in 2006 (see Figure 3).

In February 2007, Hamas even went so far as agreeing to form a national unity government with Fatah on the basis of 'respecting' past agreements between the PLO and Israel (ICG, 2007a: 18-9; Mecca Agreement, 2007). Although this move fell short of full recognition of past agreements, and was made under severe pressure—following a year of financial sanctions, regional pressure, increasingly vicious Palestinian infighting and a drop in domestic support (ICG, 2007a: 27-9)—it suggests that Hamas may not be as total a spoiler as is often assumed.

Whether Hamas should be categorised as a total or a limited spoiler has serious policy implications.[1] Total spoilers, following Stedman, do not typically respond to inducement (meeting some of the spoiler's demands) or socialisation (changing the behaviour of the spoiler through a mixture of inducements and coercion). Threatening to use violence only strengthens their position, as does threatening to withdraw the support of the external 'sponsor' of a peace process. The only strategies Stedman believes to be effective are the actual use of force or the 'final train' scenario (continuing with the peace process without recognition or participation of the spoiler). However, if the total spoiler enjoys the support of a sizeable percentage of the population, even these strategies may backfire; rather than 'backlash', the result might be increased popularity.

If, however, Hamas behaves like a limited spoiler in terms of goals, intent and degree of commitment to its goals,[2] Stedman's model advocates inducement and socialisation to change the calculus

---

1 I will not here consider Stedman's third category, the 'greedy spoiler', although aspects of Hamas' search for political influence can be captured by this notion.

2 Stedman's list of qualities determining whether a spoiler is limited or total include other factors, such as the degree of leadership control and unity (Stedman, 1997: 17). These are of less relevance in terms of determining what type of spoiler Hamas is but become vital when considering the impact of internal tensions on spoiler behaviour.

of political violence. The use of force is to be carefully calibrated as it may trigger a "counterescalation of violence by the limited spoiler" and increase the popular support it enjoys.

This chapter seeks to identify the main factors shaping Hamas' behaviour towards the peace process. Following the book's general themes, of particular concern are the roles played by religion and Hamas' relationship with its wider constituency in shaping this behaviour. To what extent is Hamas' violence informed by religion, to what extent by other, political considerations? Does religious commitment make Hamas more intransigent and violent? How do changes in public opinion affect Hamas' behaviour? To what extent is Hamas' opposition to the peace process a function of intra-Palestinian rivalry, and a quest for domestic power? What role do elections, negotiations with Fatah or political inclusion play?

As before, Hamas is conceptualised as a political organisation embedded within a wider social movement, rather than as a purely paramilitary organisation. Existing analyses of Hamas' use of violence too often concentrate overly on Hamas' violence, ignoring its wider social and political context. This choice of focus is understandable given the sense of urgency inspired by the shocking nature of much of the violence. However, by focusing exclusively on violence, we risk ignoring the impact of the movement's social and political embeddedness on its use of violence. Similarly, if we wish to establish what factors may induce an organisation to become a more 'limited' spoiler, we cannot ignore the organisation's other goals and practices, since these must fill the void left by the abandonment of violence. To study Hamas' approach to violence as if it were simply a socially isolated resistance group with no domestic political ambitions and a static attitude towards violence would be to miss the tensions between Hamas' various goals, wings and constituencies, and how these affect its approach to violence and the peace process.

That Hamas' constituency is likely to be a key factor in the dynamic of violence is supported by a number of models developed to explain how political violence ends. Crenshaw, Ross and Gurr, and Weinberg and Pedahzur all argue that one of the factors that may force an organisation to desist from violence is a change in the relationship with the wider constituency it claims to represent. Of the four factors Ross and Gurr (1989: 408-10) identify as facilitating an end to violence, two concern the relationship with the organisation's constituency: 'backlash' (a decrease in an organisation's wider popularity) and 'burnout' (a decrease in its members' commitment to violent struggle). Though 'burnout' describes an internal dynamic, both factors concern the relationship between the organisation and its constituency, since membership commitment is affected by changes in the organisation's popular support, and *vice versa*. Weinberg and Pedahzur (2003: 105-18, 70n3) similarly highlight the role of backlash and burnout in encouraging violent groups to undergo a 'strategic shift' in which both goals and methods change (as opposed to a 'tactical shift' where the goals remain the same). Crenshaw (1991: 86-7), too, observes that successful counter-terrorist campaigns are more likely to succeed where targeted organisations are already weakened by internal divisions (burnout) or a loss of popular support for the movement's tactics (backlash).

Peace Process, Violence and Religion

Looking at Hamas' rhetoric vis-à-vis the peace process, we find that both religion and constituency play a central role. Mirroring Hamas' dualistic approach to authority, its opposition to the peace process has been framed in two different ways: one absolutist, deriving from divine right, and other 'eternal' categories such as inalienable human rights; the other, which will be analysed in the next section, conditional, dependent on the popular will and practical considerations concerning how to maximise the 'national interest'.

It is well established that religious symbolism and themes play a central role in Hamas' critique of the peace process (cf. Milton-Edwards, 1992; Nüsse, 1998; Hroub, 2000: 43-86). Religion informs how Hamas conceptualises the conflict, the enemy and its claims to the land. It provides justifications for its continued refusal to recognise Israel. And it provides a powerful motivational framework for those carrying out suicide attacks (Juergensmeyer, 2000: 69-78)—although this should not obscure the attacks' political and strategic rationale (cf. Bloom, 2005: 35-7).

From the start, Hamas' critique of the peace process has been grounded in a religious interpretation of the conflict. The Israeli-Palestinian conflict was depicted in Hamas' founding Charter as an epic struggle between Islam and its enemies, fulfilling the Prophet's prediction that those living in Palestine would be "in [constant] Jihad to the day of resurrection" (§34; Mishal and Sela, 2000: 197-8). The land of Palestine itself was considered to be an Islamic *waqf* (endowment) "entrusted to the Muslim generations [by its first Muslim conquerors] until Judgement Day"—although this argument was privately critiqued from the start by a number of influential leaders (Tamimi, 2007). Because under Islamic law ownership of a *waqf* passes "from the founder [of the *waqf*] to God" (Tibawi, 1978: 11), no one can renounce any part of it. In addition, and here Hamas introduced a decidedly modern twist derived from its contractual understanding of authority, any thought of renunciation was further discredited by the argument that "who, after all, has the [legitimate] right to act on behalf of Muslim generations until the Day of Judgement?" (Charter §11; Hroub, 2000: 273).[3]

Within this framework, Israeli attempts at settling the West Bank or reclaiming Jewish holy ground in Jerusalem become attacks against Islam as well as against the Palestinian people and their ancestral lands. Every mosque that is damaged in the course of the conflict is interpreted as further proof that Israel is intent on not just taking Palestinian land, but on destroying Islam itself (cf. al-Rantisi in Juergensmeyer, 2000: 73-4). One of the reasons Ariel Sharon's visit to the Haram al-Sharif compound sparked off the al-Aqsa Intifada is that this compound, which houses Islam's third holiest shrine, the al-Aqsa Mosque, has such a central symbolic place in both Muslim and Palestinian imagination. But the Intifada would not have happened if other structural and political factors had not been in place - or indeed if Sharon had not had a reputation, among Palestinians, for having been one of the prime movers behind Israeli settlement expansion, including in Jerusalem's Old City (see also Chapter 2).

---

3   The term 'legitimate' (in square brackets) is taken from Mishal and Sela's translation (181).

Religion also plays a central role in the motivation and self-identity of Hamas' activists. Many activists are recruited through the mosque, and Hamas' emphasis on Islam is an important recruiting factor. Hamas' communiqués are littered with references to the notion of Islamic warriors (*mujahidun*), and rallying cries from the Qur'an (cf. Mishal and Aharoni, 1994; http://palestine-info.co.uk, 'Communiqués'). As for the Qassam Brigades, those who carry out suicide attacks frame their missions with explicitly religious motifs, as illustrated by the video testimonies produced by Hamas' suicide bombers the night before their mission (cf. Juergensmeyer, 2000: 70-1; http://www.pmw.org.il, 'Suicide Terrorists Farewell Videos'). These videos have a political as well as a personal function, and are framed in part to attract new recruits and paint Hamas and the Qassam Brigades in a particular light. One can nevertheless conclude that religion plays a significant role in Hamas' self-image, and that of its Qassam activists.

While religion influences the way Hamas conceptualises itself, the conflict, and its enemy, it does so usually in conjunction with other narratives. The *waqf* argument, for instance, is reinforced by arguments invoking the notion of inalienable human rights and justice which are similarly influential in precluding compromise. "We in Hamas," Mish'al for instance told me (2002),

will not object to [a two-state solution] in spite of the fact that we do not accept it and do not consider it a fair solution. [...] when the Palestinian who is the son of Jaffa, Haifa, Nazareth or Beer Sheba is deprived of his right to return would this be a just solution? Now, [if we return to the 1967 borders], then you satisfy half of the Palestinians and the other half you do not satisfy; is this a fair solution? [...] as long as there is injustice and usurpation of rights, as long as a human feels that his rights are violated, he will fight. This is the lesson of history.

This argument is particularly salient for those whose ancestral lands are inside Israel. Though it is tailored to appeal to an international audience, its centrality in Hamas' rhetoric is driven by the fact that a significant number of Hamas' leaders and members are refugees from what is now Israel. It reinforces the absoluteness of the *waqf* argument, and is reinforced by those aspects of Islamic tradition that support the notion of inalienable human rights (cf. Mayer, 1999: 11-4; Dalacoura, 1998: 39-75). But it is not directly a religious argument.

Other arguments that Hamas has used invoke the principles of, among others, honour, nation, revenge and the popular mandate. The video testimonies of suicide bombers, for instance, typically invoke multiple arguments. A good illustration is a bomber stating that he and his colleagues would "make our blood cheap for the sake of God, out of love for this homeland and for the sake of the freedom and honor of this people, in order that Palestine remain Islamic ... [and] that Palestine might be liberated" (Juergensmeyer, 2000: 70).

Religion, furthermore, does not seem to determine Hamas' violent tactics, though it may be used to justify or inspire them. Hamas' decision to target civilians, for instance, was justified by Yassin (1998b) with reference to the Qur'anic notion of 'an eye for an eye':

We have the right to do unto them exactly what they are doing to us. So, if they attack the women and the children on our side, why spare their women and children? ... Let us say that he [referring to the translator] slaps me on the face, don't I have the right to slap him in the face ...? I could forgive him .... But I have the right in Islam to slap him in the face. The same [holds for our attacks on Israelis]: they attack our children, we react to their attacks.

But this justification contradicts the equally authentic command of the Prophet, that women, children and the elderly should not be targeted by Muslim armies (Kelsay, 1990; R. Peters, 1996: 33-5). Suicide tactics, though justified with reference to the notion of martyrdom, similarly contradict the prohibition in Islam against taking one's own life (cf. Mishal and Sela, 2000: 76-7; see also Kramer, 1990: 141-9). It is therefore not religion *per se* that dictates Hamas' tactics, but political and strategic considerations (such as considerations of military feasibility, or how to increase Palestinian leverage over Israel with limited resources) which influence how religion is interpreted, and which aspects are (de-)emphasised.

The targets chosen—bus stops, markets, shopping malls, cafés, discos—similarly lack religious connotation, although this is a more speculative observation, given that actual targets may not have been the intended target or may have been selected following tactical compromises. Those few that do have a religious connotation—such as the 1996 attack on the eve of the Jewish Purim festival, or the 2002 attack on Jewish pensioners having their Passover dinner—appear to have been selected to increase the feasibility and terrorising

201

potential of the attack, rather than for religious reasons. During a Jewish holiday, communities are more likely to be gathered together, increasing the chance of success. The festivities, moreover, serve to make people feel less alert and more secure, thereby increasing the impact of the bombing.

Hamas' attacks thus appear to be informed by strategic thinking (see also Mishal and Sela, 2000: 49-82, 163-71). Its actions do not suggest that this is a religious war intended to kill or convert non-Muslims, rather than a nationalist war fought over land, although one overlaid with religious meaning. Hamas leaders themselves emphasise that their struggle is not with Jews or Judaism but with an occupying state (Hroub, 2000: 50-1; al-Rantisi, 2002b; http://palestine-info.com/arabic/hamas/who/who.htm, 'A study about Hamas'). Though they undermine their position by using inflammatory quotes and espousing anti-semitic themes (cf. Nüsse, 1998: 33-41; Litvak, 2005b; http://www.memri.org), their actions back up their claim that theirs is a nationalist struggle with a religious hue rather than a religious struggle. In addition, closer analysis of the various factors driving Hamas' violence shows that its use of violence can be explained far better by looking at intra-Palestinian politics, Israeli actions and internal divisions, than by studying the religious symbolism in Hamas' rhetoric.

That religion as such cannot explain Hamas' violence can also be seen from the way other secular factions, including Marxist ones, have similarly refused to recognise Israel and have adopted Hamas' signature tactic, suicide operations, during the al-Aqsa Intifada. Religion cannot explain this. The political-strategic reasons discussed below can.

This argument is supported by Pape's finding that the most compelling explanation for the suicide bombings he analysed which took place worldwide between 1980 and 2003 was resistance to occupation, not religion. In the case of Hamas, Pape shows that the data do not support the argument that Hamas' religiously-inspired ideology can explain the rise in support for suicide tactics (Pape, 2005: 45-50). For Pape, religion plays a different role, one driven by the logic of 'religious' difference (83-92). Where the occupiers belong to a different religion, this provides a ready framework for demonising the other, and perceiving occupation in terms of a zero-sum conflict threatening both one's national and one's religious identity. This may help to explain why the Israeli-Palestinian conflict has become increasingly overlaid with religious symbolism.

Peace Process, Violence and Popular Mandate

Parallel to the absolutist arguments discussed above, Hamas has used two sets of conditional arguments: one explicitly contractual, the other about pragmatically maximising one's bargaining position and implicitly contractual. The second argument is best encapsulated in a 1994 statement of the Political Bureau which argued that "Hamas does not oppose the principle of peace. However, the peace that the government of the enemy offers is not peace but a consolidation of occupation and inequity against our people" (Hroub, 2000: 305; see also 'Introductory Memorandum', Hroub, 2000: 299). In this framework, the peace process is wrong, not because it aims for a two-state compromise, but because it is not believed to lead to a viable two-state solution, and is thus against the (presumed) national interest.

Without violence, the argument goes, Palestinians have no leverage over Israel. In the absence of a powerful neutral arbiter who can force Israel to live up to its commitments, negotiations by themselves are unlikely to persuade Israel to do so. Or, as Mish'al argued (2002), before Hamas came to power,

If we stop military operations today, how will the [Palestinian] Authority exercise pressure on Israel so that it would abide by what it is required to do? In Cairo [in the lead-up to the 1996 elections], when the Authority asked us to stop military activity, we told them: okay, now you are negotiating with the enemy, what [leverage] will you have to force Israel to give you statehood and abide by its commitments ...? ... When you negotiate for the final settlement, what cards will you have? If you stop resistance, there will be no pressure on Israel, and Israel without pressure does not give.

This argument does not concern itself with rights, divine justice, or even whether all of Palestine is liberated. It focuses on tactics, strategic calculations and how to maximise one's bargaining position (cf. also Pape, 2005: 71-3). As such, it is closer to the actions of a limited than of a total spoiler (although it could be a temporary tactical, rather than an enduring strategic shift towards compromise). Intriguingly, mirroring Israel's depiction of Hamas, this argument paints Israel as the total spoiler, one who will not be moved by inducement or socialisation, but by coercion alone. As we will see, some of Hamas' violence derives from precisely this logic.

Hamas' contractual argument revolves around the notion of a popular mandate. Within this framework, the peace process is wrong, not because of its seeking a two-state solution, but because it does not have a popular mandate and thus lacks authority. In 1995, Musa Abu Marzuq, then head of Hamas' Political Bureau, summarised this thus:

> In the past, the legitimacy of the PLO and its right of representation stemmed from its close adherence to the unchanging national rights of our people and its defence of those rights. [...] However, now that the PLO has distanced itself permanently from those [national aspirations] ... it is no longer reasonable or rational to adhere to the image of the PLO as the sole legitimate representative, particularly in the case of the clique that now exercises control over the organization. This is particularly true because the PLO never enjoyed a prior electoral mandate; had there been such a popular mandate stemming from free and democratic legislative elections to give it legitimacy, the evaluation of this matter would have differed (Hroub, 2000: 91).

It is questionable whether Hamas would have accepted the peace process if the PLO had had an explicit popular mandate to pursue it. Opinion polls suggest that, apart from a temporary dip in February 1995, a majority of Palestinians did support the peace process in its early years while a majority opposed Hamas' suicide operations (Figure 1).[4] The high turnout during the 1996 legislative elections (Mishal and Sela, 2000: 136; Zogby, 1996: 5; *Jerusalem Times*, 26 December 1996: 3) similarly suggests a high level of support for the peace process since the elections were linked, by both its proponents and opponents, to the peace process. Though technically right in saying that the PLO had no popular mandate, since no direct referendum had been held, Hamas appeared nevertheless to be out of step with public opinion. It certainly lacked a popular mandate for its own actions.

---

4   Where available, I have focused on percentages indicating support for armed attacks on civilians (as opposed to soldiers and settlers).

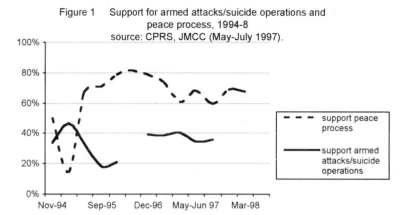

Figure 1   Support for armed attacks/suicide operations and peace process, 1994-8
source: CPRS, JMCC (May-July 1997).

It is nevertheless significant that Hamas couched its opposition to the peace process in terms of whether or not the process enjoyed a popular mandate. Its significance lies in the notion of self-entrapment (cf. Risse, 2000; Risse, 2004). Once Hamas privileges the popular will over the divine right argument, it is more difficult to reclaim the pre-eminence of the notion of God-given rights if the electorate continues to favour a suspension of rights. By referring to the notion of national interest, and placing considerations of public welfare above considerations of eternal rights, the end goal has subtly shifted, from realising a divine right to safeguarding the welfare of Palestinians. Once this argument has been used to critique Fatah for entering a peace process, Hamas is in a weaker position if it is then seen as blatantly contradicting the popular will.

Equally significant, the contractual argument has become increasingly dominant over the past two decades (see also Hroub, 2006c). During the 2006 election campaign, senior Hamas legislative candidates Hasan Yousef and Muhammad Abu Tair categorised negotiations with Israel concerning a two-state solution as legitimate if they were both "in the interest of the people" and "presented to the new parliament", the embodiment of the popular will (ICG, 2006a: 21-2). Muhammad Ghazal, one of Hamas' senior leaders in Nablus, similarly stated that, because "the Palestinian people agreed to forget 78 per cent of our land", Hamas "has accepted the 1967 borders" and is "ready to have those borders", implying that the popular will could suspend 'God-given rights' (ICG, 2006a: 20). In May-June 2006, when Hamas attacked President Abbas' proposal to hold a referendum on the peace process, the divine right argument was conspicuous for its absence (observation confirmed by Tamimi, 2007). Instead, Hamas' leaders invoked the popular mandate argument, insisting that a referendum was unnecessary—and anti-democratic—because Hamas had already won a popular mandate in the legislative elections to pursue the interests of the Palestinians as it saw fit. More significantly still, at the end of this dispute, Hamas agreed in the National Conciliation Document to put any agreement brokered between Abbas and Israel to a national referendum and abide by its outcome (ICG, 2007a: 29-30; National Conciliation Document, 2006)—although the significance of this shift was somewhat lessened by Hamas' insistence on including the Diaspora in the referendum (since Hamas believes the Diaspora to be less willing to agree to a two-state solution).

Hamas' use of a contractual logic is in part dictated by the centrality of electoral institutions and discourse in Palestinian politics. But the fact that the logic of a popular mandate has overtaken the divine right arguments prevalent in the early 1990s, suggests that Hamas recognises that, within the current Palestinian political system, the notion of divine right is insufficiently authoritative to sideline the popular will—although this dynamic may be undermined by a possible shift among Hamas' rank and file away from political back towards 'religious' arguments (Hroub, 2006c; more research is needed to confirm how widespread this shift is; in the late 1990s, anecdotal information suggested a change among the rank and file in the opposite direction).

The tension between divine right and popular mandate arguments (both of which, it has to be remembered, are rooted in religious justifications) reinforces tensions between those within Hamas who, for pragmatic reasons, favour political inclusion and are willing to accept a two-state compromise if willed by a majority of Palestinians (the 'pragmatists'), and those who oppose such a compromise on principle (for want of a better word, the 'absolutists'). These positions are influenced, though not determined, by the different contexts within which leaders operate. More of the external and paramilitary leaderships appear to fall into the absolutist camp than do internal political leaders, although the West Bank leadership was reportedly more opposed to electoral participation than their Gazan counterparts while key exiled leaders were in favour (ICG, 2007a: 25). One explanation for this is that the West Bank leadership continued to be subject to imprisonment and attack, while the Gazan leadership had had more experience of cooperating with the Fatah-led Palestinian Authority. The external leadership is arguably more concerned with the status of Palestinian refugees abroad, as they themselves are refugees and live among the refugee communities, and fear that a political compromise reached by the internal leadership might result in their marginalisation (see also Mishal and Sela, 2000: 163-7). They are also closer to the political currents in Syria and Iran, and thus more disposed to thinking that time is on their side, given changing demographics, Hizballah's rise in Lebanese politics and the growing strength of Iran and Islamist movements regionally, than those on the inside who are confronted with Israel's creeping annexation of Palestinian territories (Hroub, 2006b).

Given these internal tensions, it is significant that Hamas' public discourse has shifted away from the divine right argument (at least among the leadership). It is even more significant that it has done so concerning an issue on which one would expect Hamas to be most reluctant to abandon it. Since surveys indicate that support for a two-state solution is high (see further), there is a real possibility that a referendum would return a 'yes' vote. It is this that forces us to take Hamas' popular mandate rhetoric seriously.

Hamas and Political Violence: discerning a pattern

What factors, then, influence Hamas' use of violence against Israeli targets? What purpose does violence serve? What role do religion and Hamas' relationship with its wider constituency play?

To put this study in context, between Hamas' inception and February 2007, 1443 Israelis and 5928 Palestinians have died as a result of the conflict (B'Tselem, n.d.). In the first two years of the Intifada, Hamas' resistance was limited. But from the early 1990s onwards, it became one of the central players (Mishal and Sela, 2000: 57-112).

In 1993, it carried out its first suicide bombing but it was not until 1994 that it began to use this tactic in civilian areas (although, according to Hamas' leadership at the time, its primary targets were at that stage still the military; cf. 'Important Statement by the Political Bureau' in Hroub, 2000: 304).[5] Between 1994 and 2000, Hamas and Islamic Jihad between them carried out an average of three suicide bombings a year. When the al-Aqsa Intifada broke out, the average shot up to over twenty suicide bombings annually (Pape, 2005: 48; also Hoffman and McCormick, 2004: 268-71; ICT, n.d.). Since the 2005 ceasefire, Hamas has stopped staging suicide attacks, although even before then such attacks had become increasingly supplanted by rocket attacks for both tactical and political reasons. Although the bulk of Hamas' operations involve guerrilla-style attacks on settlements and soldiers, this chapter will focus on Hamas' suicide campaigns as a proxy for its wider resistance record.

A number of studies have looked at the relationship between Hamas' violence and the dynamics of the peace process. One of those best illustrating the assumption that Hamas is implacably opposed to the peace process (and thus a total spoiler) is the study by Kydd and Walter (2002) which concludes that Hamas' rationale for violence in the period 1993-2001 was the disruption of the peace process. This conclusion is based on the fact that most of Hamas' violence is concentrated around six major events in the peace process.

While there is no doubt that Hamas opposes the peace process and has, by its own admission, used violence to disrupt it (cf. Bloom, 2005: 24; Mish'al, 2002), Kydd and Walter leave a number of questions unanswered. Because they largely ignore the micro-context of the attacks, they assume, without much reflection, that if an attack occurs shortly before an important step in the peace process, or if it results in the disruption of the peace process, the intention was indeed to disrupt the peace process. Because they focus overly on

---

5   Bus stops, Hamas' choice of target, had military connotations. Since its establishment, Israel's national bus company had been the primary means by which army reservists had been mobilised. However, the majority of those using buses are civilians, rendering Hamas' argument less than convincing. Later attacks were carried out against explicitly civilian targets (e.g. pizzerias, shopping malls).

the peace process, they downplay the roles played by Israeli actions, intra-Palestinian rivalry and shifts in public opinion. They do not explain why violence took place when the peace process had already stalled or why Hamas at times co-operated with Fatah to facilitate the peace process. Without answers to these questions, we are in no position to decide what type of spoiler Hamas is.

To gain a better understanding, we need to study the micro-context within which violence occurred, including changes in the political opportunity structure. A good starting point is Bloom's study of Hamas' use of suicide bombing (Bloom, 2005: 19-44). Bloom critiques Kydd and Walter for pursuing a single-factor explanation and argues that three factors drove the violence: opposition to the peace process, retaliation for Israeli actions, and intra-Palestinian rivalry. Not all attacks were motivated by all three. But all three facets need to be examined to explain the timing and occurrence of violence.

The 1996 suicide bombing campaign illustrates this multi-factor dynamic particularly well.[6] In February-March 1996, four suicide bombers killed over sixty people, mostly Israelis, within the space of nine days (ICT, n.d.). Responsibility for the first three operations was claimed by Hamas, or rather members of the Qassam Brigades. The fourth was jointly claimed by Hamas and Islamic Jihad. Kydd and Walter argue that these bombings were specifically intended to undermine the peace process by driving the Israeli electorate into the arms of a more hawkish government in the May 1996 Israeli elections. However, closer analysis suggests a more complex picture.

As Kydd and Walter themselves observe, previous Hamas campaigns had failed to affect the incumbent Israeli Labour Party's commitment to the peace process (280-4). There was therefore no precedent encouraging Hamas to believe it could seriously derail the process. Rabin's assassination in November 1995 by an Israeli opponent of the peace process had arguably made Hamas aware of the deep divisions within Israeli society, which may have encouraged it to step up its efforts to exploit this division. But it was by no means clear at the time that Hamas' campaign would change the election

---

6   Bloom provides a brief analysis of this campaign but a closer analysis is
    needed to fully illustrate the multi-factor dynamic.

results. Though acting Prime Minister Peres' massive lead in the opinion polls was wiped out by the bombings, he was leading by a small margin in the weeks leading up to the elections (CNN, 'Both sides claim to win Israeli election debate', 26 May 1996; J. Peters, 1997). As Bloom rightly notes (21), Peres only lost by a fraction of a margin—less than 0.5 per cent—and then chiefly owing to an electoral boycott by Israeli Arabs who made up 20 per cent of the electorate (see also CNN, 'Israel's Arab citizens may be key to election', 22 May 1996). Peres' lacklustre election campaign also played a part, as did Netanyahu's highly effective campaign (cf. J. Peters, 1997)—both of which factors were out of Hamas' hands.

If the primary aim had been to affect the elections, it would have made more tactical sense to stage the attacks nearer the actual May 29 elections—rather than three months before, allowing Peres to regain voter confidence (see also Mishal and Sela, 2000: 211n44). Moreover, the election date, originally scheduled for November 1996, had only been set shortly before the first bomb went off, thus leaving little preparation time (*Chicago Sun-Times*, 'Peres Schedules Israeli Elections', 20 February 1996).

A better explanation for the bombings' timing is the assassination of one of Hamas' chief bomb-makers, Yahya Ayyash on 5 January 1996. The first attack took place shortly after the end of the traditional forty-day mourning period following his death, and the cell claiming responsibility for the attack both stated it was in revenge for 'Ayyash's death, and called itself 'Disciples of the martyr Yahya 'Ayyash' (Mishal and Sela, 2000: 75).

Israel's internal security service similarly concluded, having interrogated one of the organisers of the attacks, that the attacks were conceived by a "clandestine subgroup" of the Qassam Brigades, and were "most probably a direct reaction to the assassination of 'Ayyash [with] no far-reaching political goal" (Mishal and Sela, 2000: 211n44). They specifically dismissed the original claim by Israel's director of military intelligence that linked the bombings to the elections.

The contents of the leaflet distributed by the bombers similarly suggest that derailing the peace process was not the primary goal of the operation (although this would have been welcomed). Rather, it stated that the goal was to force Israel to end its practice of targeted assassinations and to "reach a truce" between the Israeli government and Hamas "through the mediation of the Palestinian Authority" (*Guardian*, "Martyr' leaves perilous legacy', 4 March 1996).

If the 1996 bombings were not primarily intended to disrupt the peace process, but were a retaliation for an Israeli assassination, Kydd and Walter's model loses some of its persuasiveness. However, the two explanations are not necessarily at odds with each other. Even if the 1996 bombings were triggered by Ayyash's assassination, they could simultaneously have served other agendas. The operations undermined the authority of Arafat who, following the January 1996 elections, had claimed to have a popular mandate to pursue the peace process—including the curtailment of armed resistance. They also sent a message to the Israeli public that Arafat could not control Hamas (which, as Kydd and Walter observe, was one of the reasons the Israeli peace camp was weakened) and, importantly, that Hamas could not be ignored (see also Usher, 1995a: 69-71).

Hamas leaders themselves admit that the underlying rationale behind Hamas' various suicide campaigns in the period 1994-6 was to "both undermine the legitimacy of the Palestinian Authority and negatively affect the peace process" (Bloom, 2005: 24). In social movement theory terms, the peace process and the establishment of the Palestinian Authority (and subsequent elections) had changed the political opportunity structure in the Palestinian territories. If the peace process had progressed according to plan, Hamas' political future could have been under threat. The aforementioned internal consultation document (Mishal and Sela, 2000: 122-30) which set out the different options for Hamas shows that its leaders were aware of the political consequences of a successful peace process for Hamas and its Brigades: limited resistance opportunities and no guarantee that Hamas would be able to translate its grassroots support into political power. Though individual attacks may have been triggered by specific incidents, the decision to respond to such incidents would have been taken against an ongoing assessment of the wider political opportunity structure.

Another factor which has typically been ignored is that the attacks also appear to have been intended to send a message to the pragmatists within Hamas that rapprochement with the Palestinian

Authority would not be tolerated. Mishal and Sela (75-6) note that the 1996 operations were supported by Hamas' external leadership because they served to disrupt the rapprochement between the internal leadership and the Palestinian Authority that had begun during discussions leading up to the 1996 election.

The internal leadership—and, intriguingly, also the leadership of the Qassam Brigades—distanced itself from the attacks, appealing to the cells responsible to cease their activities. Although this was in part a matter of self-preservation (unlike the external leadership, they and their constituency had to live with the clampdown and border closures that followed the bombings), the fact that the pragmatists called not just for a halt to the bombings but also for a return to the peace process, and that the cells responded with a leaflet demanding that the Hamas and Qassam leaderships refrain from speaking in their name, suggests that this was more than a matter of spin (Robinson, 1997: 195; CNN, 'Hamas Spokesman Calls for Renewal of Palestine Rights', 4 March 1996).

Bloom does not consider internal rivalry within Hamas. Indeed, most studies of Hamas' violence ignore this angle. It is difficult to prove that an attack is a function of internal rivalry, rather than an attempt by the internal leadership to evade censure by the Palestinian Authority. The 'terrorism' paradigm also arguably encourages one to think in terms of monolithic organisations. Yet, for the purposes of determining whether Hamas is a total or a limited spoiler, it is essential to know whether the entire leadership or only a faction stands behind the violence, and whether this internal division is likely to scupper efforts by the more pragmatic to reach a compromise.

Analysis of other suicide bombing campaigns similarly suggests that explanations are multi-factorial, and that derailment of the peace process is only one factor among others, and not always the primary aim. More specifically, in some instances violence appears to have been carried out to improve the negotiating position of the Palestinians, rather than to derail the peace process altogether.

The April 1994 suicide bombings, Hamas' first against civilians, occurred exactly one day after the traditional forty-day mourning period following the killing of twenty-nine worshippers at a Hebron mosque by an Israeli settler. They were a direct response to these killings, both in terms of timing and the explanations given at the time (Mishal and Sela, 2000: 69). They were facilitated by Hamas' increasingly close ties with Hizballah and Iran, both of which had pioneered suicide tactics in the 1980s (cf. Mishal and Sela, 2000: 65-6). However, they also occurred a month before the signing of the Cairo (peace) agreement (May 1994) and followed a string of violent incidents after the announcement of the Oslo agreement—which is why Kydd and Walter interpret them as directly targeting the peace process.

Pape (66-73) argues that the attacks may not have been intended to disrupt the peace process at all, but may have been aimed at accelerating Israel's withdrawal from Palestinian territory. Israel's withdrawal schedule had been repeatedly delayed and the attacks did indeed have the effect of speeding up Israel's exit. Subsequent statements by Hamas leaders suggest that, even if the 1994 attacks were not carried out with that goal in mind, the next series of attacks were explicitly aimed at pressuring Israel into accelerating its withdrawal and conceding more to the Palestinians. If this reading is correct, this means that, far from seeking to stall the process, Hamas sought to increase Palestinian leverage over Israel (in line with its functional critique of the peace process)—and through that, expose the flaws in Fatah's approach. Or, as Hamas leader Ahmad Bakr phrased it:

All that has been achieved so far is the consequence of our military actions. Without the so-called peace process, we would have gotten even more. ... Israel can beat all Arab armies. However, it can do nothing against a youth with a knife or an explosive charge on his body. Since it was unable to guarantee security within its borders, Israel entered into negotiations with the PLO... If the Israelis want security, they will have to abandon their settlements ... in Gaza, the West Bank, and Jerusalem (Pape, 2005: 70; the same arguments were expressed to me by numerous interviewees).

Note that Bakr focuses on the occupied territories, and not the rest of British Mandate Palestine. This may have been a ploy to persuade his Western audience that Hamas is not unreasonable. But given that other Hamas leaders had no qualms about insisting that all of Palestine be liberated, Bakr's phraseology is noteworthy—as is the fact that his justification for violence is instrumental, not religious or utopian. Equally significant is that his argument is implicitly framed in terms of who best represents the national interest of the Palestinians, suggesting that the attacks were as much a function of intra-Palestinian rivalry, and a battle for popular support, as about revenge and tactics (cf. Usher, 1995a: 69-71).

The attacks carried out during 1997 cannot be explained as attempts to derail the peace process. If anything, they appear to have been a protest against a breakdown in the process. The March bombing of Café Apropos occurred only days after Arafat had broken off negotiations in protest over Israel's decision to limit land transfers to the Palestinians and build a controversial settlement between Jerusalem and Bethlehem—leading Israel to accuse Arafat of having given Hamas the green light (Mahle, 2005: 82-3). The bombings occurred against the backdrop of an almost continuous cycle of (popular) confrontations at friction points, in response to a series of contentious Israeli policies, including the acceleration of settlement expansion and the opening of a tunnel under the Haram al-Sharif, Islam's third holiest place. The August-September bombings were explicitly linked by Hamas spokesmen to "the Israeli settlement efforts and "the "Judaization" of the Islamic holy places in Jerusalem" (Mishal and Sela, 2000: 78). They also occurred against a backdrop of increasing economic hardship as a result of the long-term border closure that followed the 1996 bombings, and can thus be seen as both a defiant gesture against border closure, and a response (conscious or not) to the increasing economic hardship.

As in the 1996 bombings, tensions within Hamas also played a part. The pragmatists among the internal leadership and the absolutists among the external and paramilitary leaderships were still debating the extent to which Hamas should collaborate with the Palestinian Authority and whether suicide operations should be suspended (following increased security operations between Israel and the Palestinian Authority). The internal leadership distanced itself from all three bombings (a reading which was supported by Arafat). The external leadership justified them as the only way to prevent further settlement expansion and the 'Judaization' of Islam's holy places (Mishal and Sela, 2000: 77-9; Hroub, 2000: 249-50; Hamami, 1997).

A number of the suicide campaigns during the al-Aqsa Intifada were direct retaliations against Israeli assassinations of Hamas leaders, rather than specifically directed against the peace process. Although Gupta and Mundra conclude on the basis of a quantitative analysis that "acts of political provocation are far better predictors of future suicide attacks than targeted assassination of the leadership of the dissident organizations" (Gupta and Mundra, 2005: 591), a number of assassination campaigns were followed, apparently in direct response, by suicide campaigns. The targeted assassination campaign of July-August 2001—during which twelve Hamas members were assassinated, including five senior leaders and a bomb-maker—was followed by successful operations in August and September, killing eighteen and wounding 234 Israelis. The autumn 2001 assassination spate—during which eleven Hamas members were killed, including four senior members and the head of the paramilitary wing in the West Bank—was similarly followed by two suicide attacks inside Israel, killing twenty-six and wounding 248 Israelis (ICT, n.d.).[7]

However, these attacks were also part of Hamas' ongoing policy of armed resistance as well as a function of intra-Palestinian rivalries. The first point needs little further elaboration, except to reiterate that suicide bombing was believed to be one of the most effective tools available to the Palestinian resistance (cf. Pape, 2005: 64-73; Gupta and Mundra, 2005: 585-90; al-Rantisi, 2002b). That the suicide attacks were a function of intra-Palestinian rivalries has similarly already been persuasively argued by both Bloom (22-31) and Hoffman and McCormick who cite intra-Palestinian competition as one of the reasons behind the phenomenal upsurge in suicide attacks, from an average of 0.24 attacks per month during the years before the al-Aqsa Intifada, to 2.6 attacks per month during the first fifteen months and 4.9 per month for the year 2002 (Hoffman and McCormick, 2004: 268-71). Indeed, they credit the formation of the al-Aqsa Martyrs' Brigades by Fatah as a direct outcome of this rivalry. Thus, it is too simplistic to depict Hamas' bombing campaigns simply as a response to Israeli assassinations. At the same time, to ignore this dimension is to miss an important dynamic.

---

7 I have only counted suicide operations inside Israel. There are other episodes revealing the same pattern.

Bloom similarly highlights intra-Palestinian rivalry—as do Gupta and Mundra (584)—but, significantly, extends her analysis beyond the factions themselves, to their relationship with the wider community. When popular support for suicide operations against civilians was low (1994-6), suicide attacks were relatively rare and Hamas was careful to link them to specific Israeli provocations so as to be able to claim 'legitimate' cause (Bloom, 2005: 24; see also Hroub, 2000: 249-50). After the outbreak of the al-Aqsa Intifada, suicide operations multiplied as factions had less need to justify them. Bloom links this shift to a change in public opinion (in social movement theory terms, a change in master frames). Polls typically found between half and two-thirds of respondents in favour (cf. PSR Polls 2-15, 2001-5). Because suicide operations had become morally and socially acceptable to a majority of Palestinians, the symbolic cost of suicide operations had decreased while ability to carry out suicide operations had become an important source of political legitimacy. Public opinion clearly played a role in this, although a changed political opportunity structure as a result of the weakening of the Palestinian Authority, the creation of new resistance organisations, greater cooperative opportunities with Iran and Hizballah (following Israel's withdrawal from Lebanon) and the increased availability of shared grievances as a result of Israeli violence, also played a part.

But this is not the whole story. Though an embedded organisation like Hamas is dependent for its long-term survival on public support,[8] it can actively affect public support for suicide bombings, using, for instance, the techniques of frame amplification and frame transformation (cf. Snow *et al.*, 1986). As Hoffman and McCormick rightly note, the Palestinian resistance organisations helped to make suicide bombing socially acceptable by bombarding the population with images of 'martyr heroes' and encouraging children from kindergarten onwards to regard self-martyrdom—and killing Israelis—as the highest honour achievable on earth (Hoffman and McCormick, 2004: 268-71; see also Levitt, 2006: 107-42). Hamas' simultaneous engagement in charitable work further legitimised suicide operations

---

8   See also Pape's argument that an organisation using suicide tactics is particularly dependent on community support (Pape, 2005: 81-3).

by increasing the overall legitimacy of the organisation—which is not to argue, as Levitt (52-79) does, that Hamas' charity network directly and routinely finances its resistance activities (for critique, see Gunning, 2007b).

However, organisations like Hamas cannot create the conditions for popular acceptance of extreme methods on their own. They can only do so within particular political opportunity structures. One of the reasons suicide operations became popular was arguably the twin perception among Palestinians that Israel responded disproportionately to Palestinian violence, and that violence was the only way forward. The first sharp rise in popular support for suicide operations—between March and December 1996, CPRS polls recorded a rise from 21 per cent to 39 per cent—occurred following a year of border closures, the stalling of the peace process, and a series of controversial Israeli policies, including the opening of a tunnel under the al-Aqsa Mosque and the building of the controversial Har Homa-Abu Ghnaim settlement. Compared to the killing of sixty-two Israelis, the punishment of an entire society of over 3.5 million people, which saw unemployment rise to 66 per cent for the first two months, and losses of 40 per cent of Gaza's and 18 per cent of the West Bank's GNP, felt disproportionate to many (Roy, 2001: 100). The comprehensive closures of 1996 caused an estimated daily loss of US$1.35m in "direct household income" alone (United Nations and the World Bank, 1997). By then, moreover, despite Oslo's stipulation that settlement expansion would be frozen, the annual increase of the West Bank settler population had tripled (Rabbani, 2001: 76). Yet the custodians of the peace process were not seen to be doing anything to change Israel's behaviour from doing so, thus increasing the sense that there were no credible alternatives.[9]

The second jump in popular support for suicide operations occurred shortly after the outbreak of the al-Aqsa Intifada. JMCC recorded a rise from 26 per cent in March 1999 to 66 per cent in December 2000. Here too, loss of faith in alternative options, and a perception that Israel responded disproportionately, played a role. By then,

---

9 Cf. Crenshaw's argument that lack of faith in alternatives can facilitate terrorism (Crenshaw, 1981: 383-4).

not only had the Camp David negotiations of summer 2000 failed (for which, contrary to certain dominant narratives, both leaderships were to blame; cf. Agha and Malley, 2001; Grinstein *et al.*, 2001), but surveys had already found in 1999 that two-thirds of respondents no longer believed that the Oslo process would result in a final agreement (cf. CPRS Polls 40-48, 1999-2000). By 2000, the number of Israeli settlers in the occupied territories had doubled to over 200,000 (Roy, 2007: 253), making a two-state solution increasingly improbable and reinforcing the perception among Palestinians that theirs was an existential conflict—which, according to Pape, significantly increases the attraction of suicide tactics (84-8). Instead of reaping a peace dividend, moreover, one in five Palestinians had slipped below the poverty line (defined as a household of two adults and four children living on less than $2.10 per day; Roy, 2001), increasing the general level of frustrated expectations. Although frustrated expectations are insufficient in themselves to 'produce' violence (cf. Piven and Cloward, 1977: 208; Lia and Skølberg, 2005; Krueger and Malečková, 2003), in such a context it is easier for violent organisations to justify extreme violence.

Escalation of violence and a sharp imbalance in casualties also played a part. Between October 2000 and mid-September 2006, the number of Palestinians killed by Israeli soldiers and settlers was 3824 (Figure 2). A fifth of these, 764, were minors. A significant percentage were civilians, although estimates vary wildly, from 87 per cent (PCHR,) through 35 per cent (ICT, 2005) to 19-43 per cent (Radlauer, 2002).[10] By contrast, during that same period 1011 Israelis were killed by Palestinians (B'Tselem, n.d.). A third of these, 314, were soldiers and just over a tenth, 119, minors. Thus for every Israeli, nearly four Palestinians were killed. For every Israeli minor, more than six Palestinian minors were killed.

A number of these minors were combatants in the sense of being engaged in (often violent) protests (see also Radlauer, 2002). But

---

10 PCHR's estimate does not fit media reports, and overestimates non-combatant casualties. ICT's estimate does not correspond to the statistics given in the same article, and differs from Radlauer's, though both are derived from the same database. Radlauer's methodology is furthermore skewed by its pro-state bias (Silke, 2004b: 16-8).

Figure 2   Number of Palestinians and Israelis killed 2000-2006
(source: B'Tselem)

that knowledge did little to dispel the impression among Palestinians that Israel's response was disproportionate, facilitating Hamas' task of making suicide operations acceptable. A good illustration of this perceived lack of proportion is Israel's 'Operation Defensive Shield'. Fifty-six Israelis were killed by the suicide bombings that triggered the operation (ICT, n.d.). Between 28 February-27 April 2002, 502 Palestinians were killed according to the Union of Palestinian Medical Relief Committees, the bulk as a result of the 'Operation Defensive Shield' (http://www.upmrc.org). The logic behind such a response may have been deterrence and eradication of paramilitary networks. The effect was radicalisation, which no amount of Hamas rhetoric could have achieved by itself.

In neither of these sudden jumps in support for suicide tactics had Hamas suddenly become more persuasive or better organised at spreading its ideology. What changed were people's diagnosis of the situation and their prognosis of how to respond. For rhetoric to be successful, it must resonate with the target group. During the mid-1990s, the situation was such that the rhetoric and practice of suicide bombing did not resonate with the majority of Palestinians. During the al-Aqsa Intifada, it did. Hamas' kindergartens, martyrdom posters and school curricula played a part, as did the suicide operations that helped to trigger border closures, invasions, unemployment and economic recession. But without Israel playing its part in helping to create the conditions for radicalisation—whether by deciding to use the army and helicopter gunships rather than riot police, to increase

219

settlement expansion rather than freeze or reverse it, or to inflict collective punishments such as house demolitions and border closures instead of targeted punishments following legal procedures—these efforts would have been far less successful (see also Gunning, 2007a: 139-40).[11] It is thus too simplistic to say, as Hoffman and McCormick do (268-71), that the Palestinian resistance organizations single-handedly created "the inverted sense of normality" within Palestinian society, which made suicide operations morally acceptable.

The above analysis suggests that Hamas' violence is a function not just of progress in the peace process, but of Israeli policies, intra-Palestinian rivalries, considerations of popular support and internal tensions. That Hamas appears to be concerned about public support already suggests that its behaviour is not wholly that of a total spoiler. But to fully appreciate the role intra-Palestinian rivalries and domestic opportunity structure play—and what this means for the extent of Hamas' spoiler behaviour—we have to shift our focus away from violence, to the dynamic behind Hamas' ceasefire declarations.

The above also confirms that Hamas' violence is predominantly political, rather than religious or sacramental. None of the key studies discussed explains Hamas' resort to violence with reference to religion, underlining that it is possible to explain Hamas' use of violence without considering the religious motivation that suicide bombers themselves typically refer to. This is not to say that religion does not play a role. But religion cannot explain the pattern of Hamas' violence in the way that the multi-level political explanation above does.

Hamas and the dynamics of ceasefire

To establish the extent to which Hamas is a total spoiler, we must look beyond violence and explore why Hamas agreed to cease violence. That Hamas has abided by various ceasefires is in itself a strong suggestion that Hamas is not a total spoiler. The earlier analysis of the different critiques Hamas has offered of the peace process, and

---

11 Cf. della Porta's discussion of the role played by types of police responses to the development of terrorism in Italy and Germany (della Porta, 1995b: 55-82.

the shift away from an absolutist religious logic to a contractual and functional one similarly implies that Hamas is becoming a less total spoiler. However, declaring a ceasefire is insufficient proof by itself, as this may simply be a ploy to re-arm, as Israel has claimed after each Hamas declaration.

Over the years, Hamas has abided by a number of ceasefires.[12] The first significant undeclared ceasefire occurred during the second half of 1995 when Hamas agreed to halt attacks to allow the Palestinian legislative election to take place. The first official ceasefire was called in June 2003, and lasted for six weeks. The longest ceasefire in which Hamas has participated lasted from March 2005 until June 2006 (violations notwithstanding) and coincided with Hamas' participation in the municipal and legislative elections. Although violations

Figure 3   Annual number of Israelis killed by Palestinians
(source: B'Tselem)

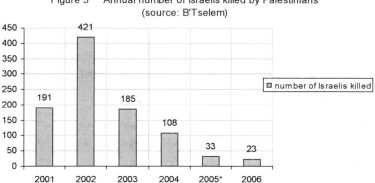

occurred and the ceasefire was suspended on various occasions, the number of Israelis killed dropped significantly following the March 2005 ceasefire declaration (Figure 3).

Only the 2003 ceasefire was officially called *hudnah*, an Islamic term which in classical times was used to denote a long-term truce between Muslims and non-Muslims. But the ceasefire in 2005, and to a lesser extent the one in 1995, followed a similar logic. The 1996

12 Crooke, who was personally involved in brokering some of the ceasefires, lists five in which Hamas participated before November 2003 (Milton-Edwards and Crooke, 2003: 16).

'ceasefire' was *de facto* rather than declared. The 2005 ceasefire was explicitly not called a '*hudnah*' but a '*tahdi'ah*' (period of calm) to differentiate it from the dismal failure of the 2003 ceasefire, and to underline its unilateral nature. I will refer to each of these episodes as a 'ceasefire'.

Opinions are divided over Hamas' intentions behind these various episodes. In both the 2003 and 2005 ceasefires, the Israeli government insisted that the ceasefire was merely an attempt by Hamas to buy time and re-arm itself (cf. http://israelnationalnews.com, 'Terrorists Say 'Ceasefire' Enables Arms Smuggling and Training', 27 November 2006; *New York Times*, 'Bombing Kills 18', 20 August 2003). In 2003, the Sharon government never accepted that a ceasefire had been declared and continued, though scaled down, its controversial policy of political assassinations (ICT, n.d.)—which was one of the reasons for its premature undoing (*New York Times*, 'Bombing Kills 18'; *Guardian*, 'Muted feelings for martyr with a grudge', 21 August 2003). In 2005, Sharon had a vested interest in maintaining a ceasefire since this would facilitate the planned withdrawal from Gaza. Israel refrained from assassinating Hamas leaders during this period, although it did assassinate resistance cadres, and imprisoned a number of Hamas leaders, both in the lead-up to the various municipal and legislative elections and after Hamas' legislative election victory. Members of organisations who broke the ceasefire continued to be targeted (ICT, n.d.).

Although Hamas has used ceasefires to re-arm itself, the notion that they are merely a ploy to buy time does not stand up to scrutiny. If this were the case, Hamas could have scaled back its activities without declaring a ceasefire. It would also not have taken ten months to be persuaded to declare a ceasefire, and then only reluctantly so, as was the case in 2003. In the event, it was not given much space in 2003 to re-group as Israel kept up its assassination and infiltration campaigns. Even so, Hamas agreed to declare a ceasefire a second time, only nineteen months after the first one had collapsed, and maintained this ceasefire even when faced with further assassinations.

In each of the three ceasefires considered, a number of factors influenced Hamas' decision. But three stand out: the prospect of increasing political influence (a change in political opportunity structure), relative military weakness (a change in resource mobilisation potential), and a shift in public opinion (a frame alignment).

The 2003 ceasefire illustrates these factors particularly well. Before the appointment of Abbas as Prime Minister, prospects for genuine power sharing were limited. While Arafat was at the helm, Hamas leaders had little confidence that a significant political role for Hamas was attainable. From the establishment of the PA onwards, Arafat had sought to sideline local leaders with a grassroots base, favouring those who were personally loyal to him (Hilal and Khan, 2004: 86-7, 97-8; Amundsen and Ezbidi, 2004: 152-4; Robinson, 1997: 179-81). According to popular rumour, the 1996 elections had been tailored to favour Arafat's nominees (cf. also Robinson, 1997: 180; Andoni, 1996: 8-9). Whether this was true, is a moot point. What matters is that many, and especially Hamas members, believed this to be true (most interviewees subscribed to this view). Municipal elections meanwhile had been repeatedly postponed, despite having been promised as an integral part of the Oslo peace process. One of the reasons unofficially cited for this decision was Arafat's fear that Hamas would do well in such elections (Smith-Polfus, 1998).

When Arafat was forced by the international community to establish a Prime Ministerial post in April 2003, the balance of power—already changing as a result of Israel's targeting the Palestinian Authority since the outbreak of the al-Aqsa Intifada, through military strikes and financial strangulation—changed further. Though Arafat was still in overall control, his power was weakened. Not only had he caved in to international pressure, but with the establishment of a separate post, internal tensions became more obvious (cf. *Guardian*, 'Palestinian Prime Minister Resigns', 6 September 2003). Fatah had already been beset by internal strife as a result of Arafat's visible physical decline. Tensions between Arafat's entourage and the local Fatah leadership had also become more explicit, particularly since the outbreak of the al-Aqsa Intifada which had allowed Fatah's grassroots cadres to regain centre stage with Marwan Barghouthi as one of their chief spokesmen (Robinson, 2001: 121-3). All this combined to suggest to Hamas that Fatah's hold on power was weakening.

At the same time, elements within Fatah, including both Barghouthi and Abbas (who was to become Prime Minister in April

2003), had begun to change tactics, seeking to persuade the traditional opponents of the peace process to agree to a ceasefire as part of an overhaul of Palestinian political structures. Given the changing balance of power, some in Fatah had come to believe that Hamas' participation was needed to increase the system's legitimacy. It could no longer afford to exclude Hamas. This process was accelerated by the threat of Fatah's grassroots cadres, led by Marwan Barghouthi, opening up parallel negotiations with Hamas (*Jerusalem Report*, 'Order in the house', 10 February 2003).[13]

Negotiations started in August 2002 with discussions over how to integrate Hamas into the PLO (cf. Milton-Edwards and Crooke, 2004b; Milton-Edwards and Crooke, 2004a; Laub, 2003; Abdallah, 2003). Barghouthi played a key part in these from his prison cell, as he could guarantee the support of the al-Aqsa Martyrs Brigades. Egypt played the role of regional broker. In January, talks stalled. The US March 2003 invasion of Iraq set negotiations back further. But when Abbas was appointed Prime Minister in April 2003, the negotiations took on a new lease of life, particularly when the US threw its weight behind the peace process by launching President Bush's 'roadmap to peace'. Abbas used this new initiative to increase the pressure on Hamas. Significantly, against US and Israeli wishes, and in recognition of his own precarious position, Abbas refused to dismantle Hamas, opting instead for persuasion and dialogue, and offering it a political future (cf. *Boston Globe*, 'Palestinians greet pact with cautious nod', 24 May 2003; *Jerusalem Post*, 'Abbas offering Hamas a spot in government', 19 June 2003).[14]

Hamas, meanwhile, faced a dilemma. Politically, it was stronger than ever before. Yet without a political system in which to participate, it had little to show for this strength. Its resistance feats had

---

13 Already in April 2002, Hamas' representative in Lebanon told me that Hamas and Fatah's middle leadership were exploring ways to reform the PLO for after Arafat's death (U. Hamdan, 2002).

14 In 2005, Abbas stated this even more categorically: "They told us you have to uproot them [Hamas]. We will not uproot. They told us you have to strike them. We will not strike. They are part of our people, and we will include them" (*International Herald Tribune*, 'Hamas's election foray may be a turning point', 4 January 2005).

served to increase its popular standing, as had Israel's relentless campaign of political assassinations against its leaders. In opinion polls, Hamas now trailed Fatah by less than five percentage points—compared to 20-30 per cent prior to the al-Aqsa Intifada. In an April 2003 JMCC poll, Hamas drew almost level with Fatah (22 vs. 23 per cent) and did so again in a June 2003 PSR poll, only weeks before the ceasefire (see also Figure 4). If Hamas agreed to suspend its armed attacks, there was a real possibility that it could translate this popularity into genuine power under Abbas and Barghouthi's envisaged power-sharing framework. Fears that a continued refusal to declare a ceasefire would result in either civil war or political marginalisation also affected the decision (a June 2003 PSR poll found, for instance, that 67 per cent of respondents feared that Hamas' refusal to declare a ceasefire would result in internal Palestinian conflict).

Militarily, Hamas and the Qassam Brigades had suffered a number of setbacks. Although still more than capable of continuing the resistance (in May and June it carried out two major suicide operations, alongside a number of attacks on soldiers and settlements; ICT, n.d.), it had become militarily weaker as a result of both Israeli counter-insurgency measures and a shift in regional support. It had lost a number of its paramilitary leaders, including regional commanders and bomb-makers, to Israel's assassination policy, although the Brigades did not suffer markedly more casualties during the period immediately before the ceasefire. According to ICT (ICT, n.d.), Hamas lost two senior and thirteen to sixteen middle- to low-ranking militants in June 2003, against two senior and between thirteen and twenty-one middle- to low-ranking deaths in May and April (these figures are speculative as some of the 'unknown' deaths may have been Hamas members). In June 2003, Israel extended its assassination policy to political leaders considered to be directly involved in the planning of suicide attacks. Weeks before the ceasefire declaration, al-Rantisi, the effective head of Hamas in Gaza at the time, narrowly escaped an assassination attempt (*Mideast Mirror*, 'Assassinating the roadmap', 10 June 2003).

However, according to those involved in the negotiations, Israel's assassination policy had been one of the reasons preventing Hamas from declaring a ceasefire during the ten months of negotiations (Milton-Edwards and Crooke, 2004b: 308; Abdallah, 2003; Laub, 2003). Because Hamas did not believe Israel would honour its ceasefire, it wished to keep open the option of retaliation. Thus, though the policy weakened Hamas (at least temporarily), it also prevented it from declaring a ceasefire. The near-assassination of al-Rantisi reportedly nearly wrecked the negotiations. In addition, on every occasion a leader was killed, Hamas succeeded in regrouping itself, returning to the struggle stronger, at both a political and a 'paramilitary' level (Gunning, 2007a: 141). It was only after the assassinations of Yassin and al-Rantisi in 2004 that Hamas' ability to stage suicide operations was seriously affected—and then primarily because of Israel's success in intercepting suicide operations (through improved intelligence penetration) rather than directly because of the threat of political assassination.[15]

Nevertheless, the intensity of Israel's assassination campaign—during the al-Aqsa Intifada, 208 suspected militants were killed across the factions besides 337 civilians in 'collateral damage' (B'Tselem, n.d.)—arguably played a role in persuading Hamas leaders that their military struggle was at an impasse, encouraging them to think of an alternative future. It is no coincidence that one of the central conditions of both ceasefires was a cessation of Israel's assassination strategy. In private, moreover, some of Hamas' senior leaders had begun to express doubts about the efficacy of their suicide bombing strategy (Milton-Edwards and Crooke, 2004b: 303). In public, Abu Shannab, one of Hamas' most senior leaders in Gaza and a leading pragmatist, stated explicitly in an interview at around that time: "Forget about rhetoric, we cannot destroy Israel. ... The reality is that Palestinians can create a state that would live by Israel. We will respect any American effort that will stop Israeli settlements and settlers, and bring the Israelis to withdraw up to the 1967 borders" (*Toronto Star*, 'The Hamas Strategy', 29 June 2003).

Regionally, Hamas' traditional supporters—the Gulf States, Syria and Iran—had each, for different reasons, become more cautious. Iran was waiting to see how the US's Iraqi campaign panned out. The Gulf States were seeking to cement their relationship with the United States,

---

15 Qassam operatives continued to attempt to stage suicide bombings but were consistently intercepted (IDF, 2004).

after the ruptures that followed 9/11. Syria, where much of Hamas' external leadership resided, had become more circumspect after the Iraq war, particularly following rumours that Washington was now pushing for regime change in Syria (*Daily Telegraph*, 'Syria now top US target for 'regime change'', 8 April 2003). Pressed by Egypt, Syria put pressure on Hamas to accept a ceasefire (Stratfor.biz, 'Hamas: Diplomatic Pressure vs. Popularity', 18 June 2003). This changed regional situation was reflected in an astonishing role reversal, with the traditionally hard-line external leadership pushing the internal leadership towards a ceasefire (cf. Laub, 2003; Abdallah, 2003).

The external leadership had also been influenced by the after-effects of 9/11. According to those involved in the negotiations, the leadership-in-exile sought to avoid being associated with al-Qaeda and other *takfiri* groups preaching global jihad against the US (Milton-Edwards and Crooke, 2004b: 304). Hamas did not seek a global *jihad* against unbelievers or the West, but the righting of what it saw as a wrong in Palestine itself. Association with al-Qaeda would both risk sidelining the Palestine question, and further complicate Hamas' relations with the EU and the US—whose pivotal role in creating a Palestinian state Hamas pragmatically acknowledged (confirming our earlier observation that religious rhetoric about the conflict being an epic battle between Judeo-Christian forces and Islam has little to do with Hamas' strategic decisions). At that stage, though the US had proscribed Hamas, the European Union had not yet done so.[16]

The third key factor was a shift in Palestinian public opinion. Until November 2002, polls had found public opinion firmly behind the resistance. In November, this began to change. Support for a mutual cessation of hostilities soared to nearly 80 per cent, and remained high through 2003 (Figure 4). The effect of this shift was muted by the fact that support for suicide operations in Israel continued to be over 50 per cent, while support for peace initiatives was gradually slipping (Figure 5). More research is needed to establish why

---

16 9/11 also affected Hamas' Western fundraising potential but because the War on Terror simultaneously served to increase Hamas' international profile, it is difficult to state with certitude that Hamas' funding was dramatically affected. According to Hamas, alternative funding sources, including Western ones, were readily available (ICG, 2006a: 23-8).

public opinion had begun to shift at this stage, and what effect Israeli and Palestinian policies had on it. But it is hardly a coincidence that

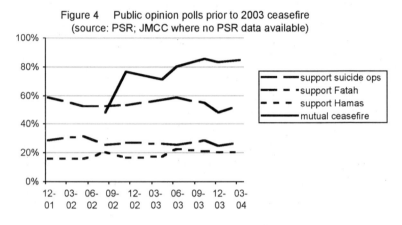

Figure 4   Public opinion polls prior to 2003 ceasefire (source: PSR; JMCC where no PSR data available)

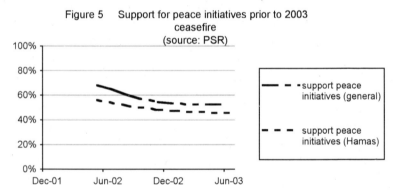

Figure 5   Support for peace initiatives prior to 2003 ceasefire (source: PSR)

the negotiations intensified at around the time that people began to overwhelmingly support a mutual cessation of violence.

Perhaps even more significant was a shift within Hamas' own constituency. Although we have no figures from before the start of the Intifada to compare with, a May 2002 PSR poll found that 56 per cent of Hamas followers supported the 2002 Saudi peace initiative (only 12 per cent behind the national average). In November 2002, PSR found 48 per cent of Hamas supporters backing President Bush's road map proposal (only 6 per cent behind the national average), and in June 2003, 45 per cent agreed that the establishment of a Palestinian state should be followed by "recognition of Israel as the state of the Jewish people". The downward trend notwithstanding, nearly half of the Hamas supporters polled backed a two-state solution. On its own, this would have been insufficient to entice Hamas into a ceasefire. But in combination with the other factors described above, this was a significant additional factor pushing Hamas towards a ceasefire.

That Hamas was indeed concerned about the opinion of its support base is corroborated by the fact that, in the lead-up to the ceasefire, Hamas leaders were seen discussing the ceasefire option with the wider population after Friday prayers (Rantisi, 2003). We have already seen the importance of consultation to Hamas' self-image and political culture. Having operated elections internally and participated in union elections for more than two decades, heeding public opinion was not an alien concept. But now that the prospect of power sharing had become more realistic as a result of the discussions with Barghouthi and 'Abbas, heeding it had become even more imperative. Because the general public was characteristically less radical than the constituencies Hamas had had to deal with in student and professional elections,[17] Hamas was pushed further to moderate its position than ever before.

The 1995 and 2005 ceasefires display the same three factors. Hroub, commenting on the 1995 ceasefire, links Hamas' decision to an increase in dialogue between Hamas and the PA, fear of civil war if Hamas were to continue its campaign, 'technical difficulties' (i.e. military weakness) and a waning of popular support for Hamas' operations (2000: 105, 249-50). Moreover, at the start of the 1995 ceasefire, there was still hope on both sides that a compromise might be found to facilitate Hamas' participation in the 1996 elections. Relative military weakness thus coincided with an opening up of

---

17 CPRS polls typically found students and professionals to be more radical than the general population (cf. polls 13, 15, 19, 22; November 1994-March 1996), as did Krueger and Malečková (2003: 125-9) and Berrebi (2003).

political opportunities which in turn encouraged Hamas to pay more attention to public opinion.

The period leading up to the 2005 ceasefire followed a similar dynamic. It was preceded by extensive talks between Abbas and Hamas, culminating in an unofficial temporary ceasefire agreement at the end of January, and an officially announced 'period of calm' in March. The first two rounds of municipal elections, meanwhile, had given Hamas an early taste of its political potential, having won approximately a third of the vote even in areas that had been billed as Fatah strongholds (Chapter 5). Militarily it had been further weakened by Israel's assassination campaign (although this had simultaneously contributed to its electoral popularity) and by Israel's success in thwarting planned attacks. The construction of Israel's security fence had also reduced its options, although it had sought to counter this by expanding its rocket facilities. It had only succeeded once in mounting a successful suicide attack against civilians inside Israel since al-Rantisi's assassination in April 2004, in Beersheba on 31 August 2004 (ICT, n.d.). The number of Israelis killed by Palestinians had dropped from 185 in 2003 to 108 in 2004 (Figure 3). Organisationally, moreover, it had suffered from the loss of a number of senior political leaders, especially in Gaza (cf. ICG, 2007a: 25)—although its participative leadership structure had enabled it to fill their places relatively seamlessly—while well over 500 Hamas and Qassam members were in prison (by April 2005, an estimated 700 Hamas associates were in prison; *Jerusalem Report*, 'Five Life Sentences Plus 20', 18 April 2005).

Opinion polls, meanwhile, continued to find overwhelming support for a ceasefire while, by the time the formal ceasefire was declared, support for suicide operations had dropped markedly—for the first time since the outbreak of the al-Aqsa Intifada—to below 30 per cent (Figure 6). Support for Islamic Jihad's Tel Aviv suicide bombing only weeks before the official agreement received 29 per cent support, as opposed to the 77 per cent the Beersheba bombing received in September 2004—although support for hypothetical suicide operations against civilians in Israel had already fallen to 54 per cent by that time (PSR polls 13 & 15, 2004 & 2005). While this poll was taken only days before the formal declaration, and more

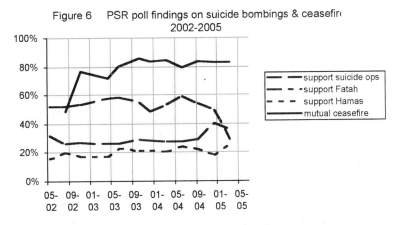

Figure 6   PSR poll findings on suicide bombings & ceasefire 2002-2005

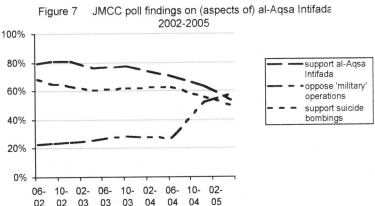

Figure 7   JMCC poll findings on (aspects of) al-Aqsa Intifada 2002-2005

than a month after the unofficial agreement, the poll both reflected an already ongoing trend away from support for the al-Aqsa Intifada (as reflected in Figure 7), and confirmed for Hamas that its unofficial ceasefire was supported by public opinion.

Within Hamas' own constituency, support for armed operations was similarly waning. The same March 2005 poll found that 53 per cent of Hamas supporters opposed the Tel Aviv bombing—in sharp contrast to September 2004, when 95 per cent of Hamas support-ers backed the Beersheba bombing. Intriguingly, though, already in September 2004, 50 per cent of Hamas supporters polled opposed the continuation of armed attacks from Gaza after Israel's withdrawal from the Strip.

Regionally, Hamas' external leadership in Syria was feeling the effect of Syria's international predicament. Already weakened by the rise of anti-Syrian sentiments in Lebanon and forced to begin withdrawing from Lebanon by the international community, Syria was also under international scrutiny over its alleged role in the February 2005 assassination of Lebanon's Prime Minister, Rafiq Hariri. Syria was in no position to be seen backing the absolutists within Hamas (cf. *Turkish Daily News*, 'Palestinian Truce Gives Best Chance Yet to Peace', 20 March 2005). Iran was similarly still wary of unnecessarily provoking the US and Israel, as rumours circulated that Washington was preparing plans for military strikes (Seymour Hersh, 'The Coming Wars', *New Yorker*, 24 January 2005). Iran's President was still the reformist Khatami. Ahmadinejad, under whose leadership Iran's foreign policy became markedly more aggressive, would not be elected until June 2005.

Reflections on the Ceasefire Dynamic

If we compare these three factors to those described by Ross and Gurr (408-10) as affecting a group's decision to end its campaign of political violence—deterrence, pre-emption, backlash and burnout—there is both overlap and difference. The public's disapproval of Islamic Jihad's February 2005 suicide bombing was a clear instance of backlash as discussed by Ross and Gurr. But even the public's swing towards a mutual ceasefire in 2002-3 can be described as backlash in the sense of affecting Hamas' electoral potential, although not in the sense of direct disenchantment with Hamas' violent tactics (public disapproval for which did not increase markedly until 2005).

Hamas' relative military weakness was in part caused by Israeli policies of deterrence and pre-emption—although changes in the level of regional support played an important part too. Israel's policies also affected popular opinion and were thus indirectly responsible for increasing the potential for backlash. That Hamas members may have been suffering from the beginnings of burnout is (tentatively) suggested by the shift visible among polled Hamas supporters towards a ceasefire, and the increasingly vigorous voice of Hamas' pragmatists expressing doubts about the strategic benefits of continued armed struggle.

None of this would have persuaded Hamas to declare a ceasefire, if Fatah and the PA had not simultaneously offered Hamas a political future. Though Fatah's decision was a reflection of the changed balance of power between Hamas and Fatah, and within Fatah, it was nevertheless pivotal that Hamas could see a political future for itself, and that its political chances could be hurt if it did not participate in the ceasefire. Because Hamas' political future would be determined within an electoral framework, the incentive to heed public opinion increased dramatically, as did the potential cost of backlash, affecting the cost-benefit calculus of whether to prioritise politics over resistance.

This was less the case in 2003 when a majority of Palestinians still supported Hamas' refusal to declare a ceasefire (PSR Poll 8, June 2003) and power sharing was nothing more than a promise. One of the reasons the ceasefire broke down prematurely was arguably that the incentives to maintain it were more prospective than concrete. But in 2005, when the municipal elections were already in full swing, and Hamas had tasted victory in some, the costs of not declaring a ceasefire were much higher. If Hamas had continued its campaign, Israel might well have postponed its planned withdrawal from Gaza (set for summer 2005), which would have caused a wave of public hostility. Conversely, Hamas could gain from Israel's withdrawal by claiming credit for having made continued occupation too costly.

Comparing the factors influencing Hamas' ceasefire dynamic with those identified as driving Hamas' violence, we find, perhaps not surprisingly, that intra-Palestinian rivalry plays a part in both. However, retaliation against Israeli attacks and opposition to the peace process play a far less prominent role in the dynamic of ceasefires. In the two months preceding both the 2003 and 2005 ceasefires (counting back from the unofficial January agreement), the number of Palestinians killed by the Israeli army was around sixty, providing ample incentive for retaliation (B'Tselem, n.d.). Retaliation thus appears to be a driving factor only when Hamas is already fully engaged in paramilitary activities (or not yet committed to a ceasefire). This reading is confirmed by Hamas having maintained its ceasefire, and extended it beyond 2005 as initially decreed, despite a steadily rising death toll for 2005 (B'Tselem, n.d.), including targeted assassinations of resistance cadres, and grassroots pressure to retaliate (cf. Aljazeera.net, 'Hamas: We are committed to ceasefire', 18 July 2005). However, in both cases, once the will to continue the ceasefire had become eroded, the logic of retaliation triggered the end of the ceasefire.[18]

Even more strikingly, both the 2003 and 2005 ceasefires were preceded by an upsurge in the peace process. The 2003 ceasefire came barely two months after President Bush had launched his 'road map to peace'. The 2005 official ceasefire declaration came six weeks after Sharon and Abbas had met, for the first time in months, and agreed to a mutual ceasefire. Hamas had already agreed, unofficially, to observe a period of calm before the Abbas-Sharon summit, to enable Abbas to broker a ceasefire with Israel (*Guardian Weekly*, 'Islamists suspend attacks on Israel', 28 January 2005). In both cases, the decision was framed implicitly as one leading to an improved two-state solution, rather than the one-state solution Hamas advocates (cf. Laub, 2003; *Chicago Tribune*, 'Palestinian factions agree to halt attacks if Israel reciprocates', 18 March 2005). This was the understanding of Hamas' prison leadership. It was also the understanding of key pragmatists among Hamas' senior leaders, most prominently Abu Shannab (who was assassinated at the end of the 2003 ceasefire). According to Fatah's senior negotiator: "If Israel agrees to fulfil its part of the *hudnah* [ceasefire] agreement, I believe we will be able to convince Hamas to engage in political dialogue and accept the principle of a two-state solution" (*Jerusalem Post*, 'Hamas, Islamic Jihad leaders prepare to announce 'hudna"', 29 June 2003).

Given that opposition to the peace process and retaliation appear to have played such secondary roles in the ceasefire decisions, intra-Palestinian rivalry and changes in the political opportunity structure seem to be the key factors influencing Hamas' decision to

---

18 In 2003, the suicide bombing that triggered the end of the ceasefire was a retaliation for the assassination of a personal friend of the bomber (*Guardian*, 'Muted feelings for martyr with a grudge', 21 August 2003); in 2005, the ceasefire ended when Hamas called for retaliation after a week in which fourteen civilians and one military leader had been killed (Avi and Amos, 2006).

suspend attacks. Military weakness and changes in regional support also played a role, particularly in 2005 when a ceasefire declaration was more likely to lead Israel to suspend its assassination policy. But since Hamas had been militarily weak before, this weakness alone cannot explain the ceasefires.

In both 2003 and 2005, increased dialogue between Hamas and Fatah had taken place prior to the declaration and prospects for power sharing were discussed (Milton-Edwards and Crooke, 2004b: 302-6; 2004a: 44-9; Kumaraswamy, 2005: 55-6; Laub, 2003; U. Hamdan, 2002, 2004). In 2005, the gains Hamas had been able to make in the municipal elections had graphically illustrated the changed political opportunity structure. For the first time since Hamas' establishment, a political framework was in place, in which the different factions could directly contest each other (beyond the union level), rather than indirectly through armed attacks on Israel. For the first time, too, Hamas had sufficient trust in both Fatah and the peace process that these opportunities would not be withdrawn at the last minute, as it had feared when Arafat was still in power. Equally significantly, Hamas' popularity had drawn level with Fatah's while support for a mutual ceasefire had intensified.

That Hamas agreed to declare a ceasefire which was explicitly linked to progress in the peace process suggests that, at least in these two instances, Hamas acted as a limited spoiler. What made this partial compromise possible is the fact that Hamas has multiple goals and is equally, if not more, interested in shaping Palestinian society as in liberating all of Palestine. A ceasefire allowed it to shelve its goal of eradicating Israel, without having to recognise Israel, while enabling it to play a central role in shaping Palestinian politics and legislation. Not agreeing to a ceasefire would have risked losing political influence.

Hamas' decision to agree to a ceasefire may be a sign of it edging closer to becoming a limited spoiler on the issue of political compromise with Israel. However, Hamas' decision may well be purely tactical, while it continues to be a total spoiler strategically. To put it differently, while Hamas' understanding of its short-term interests may have changed, its identity (as the indefatigable champion of the full restoration of Palestinian rights) may have remained the same.

Whether it is possible for an organisation to maintain such a double-act for long is questionable. Once Hamas has accepted the notion of compromise as a tactical interim goal, it becomes more difficult to return to a no-compromise stance, particularly if Hamas' supporters become convinced that compromise pays real dividends. As noted before, once Hamas begins to justify the suspension of what have hitherto been described as inalienable divine rights, with reference to a shift in the popular will, a return to the uncompromising language of divine right becomes more difficult to sustain. Hamas' leadership-in-exile may insist that Palestine is non-negotiable. But the (political) leadership inside the territories has to live with the reality that Hamas may not gain the same number of votes in the next election, particularly if Hamas cannot deliver on its domestic promises. All its careful planning and electioneering would then have been in vain, with neither a liberated, nor a reformed, nor an Islamised Palestine to show for it. The desire to secure a political future for itself within the Palestinian domestic arena thus may push Hamas towards becoming a limited spoiler at both a tactical and, eventually, a strategic level.

This is precisely what pragmatists such as Abu Shannab, Usama Hamdan (Hamas' representative in Beirut), and those close to Haniyyah suggest (Abu Shannab, 1998a; U. Hamdan, 2004; Abu Shannab in Gaess, 2002: 107-12). Within this perspective, at least as presented to the outside world, a ceasefire is a first step towards the establishment of a Palestinian state alongside Israel, and the normalisation of Palestinian society. The ceasefire is a means to maintain pressure on Israel, which, as we saw, Hamas does not believe will voluntarily give up Palestinian land. Under a ceasefire agreement, Hamas can monitor Israeli actions, and threaten to revert to resistance in case of non-compliance (which it believes will be more complicated under a full peace agreement). If Israel meets its obligations, Palestinian society will, according to this argument, grow economically stronger, which, together with an end to occupation practices, will help to de-radicalise the population and strengthen support for a permanent peace settlement, preparing the way for a full peace agreement. Following Abu Shannab (1998i-a),

This is what Shaykh Ahmed Yassin meant by a *hudnah*, ceasefire. He said: our right in Palestine is comprehensive, all of it is ours. ... We will not surrender and say yes, take it. So we will not recognise Israel, but we will accept the *status quo*. And leave everything for the future ... leave this for the next generation. If—I was discussing this even with the Israeli guards inside jail—if you allow a good Palestinian society to be beside you, the [next] generation might compromise. A person can compromise if he has a good life. He will not make problems as far as he lives well. But now we are living in a very bad condition, and we look at the other side, happy, [prosperous] and planting, so we will direct all our anger against him.

Pragmatists, like absolutists, insist that the legitimate solution to the Arab-Israeli conflict is the abolition of Israel, the return of the estimated 4.5 million Palestinian refugees living abroad (PASSIA, 2006) and the creation of an Islamic state in all of Palestine. But they claim that it is in the national interest to concede that Israel is here to stay, and to use all means at their disposal, including both political compromise and (the threat of) resistance, to create a Palestinian state in the occupied territories. Yassin's notion of a long-term *hudnah* is an attempt to balance these two logics. It does not give up its claim to the land of Palestine but it allows it to suspend this claim if the popular will believes this to be in the national interest. In the words of Ahmad Ahmad, senior Hamas legislator from Nablus: "I will negotiate for my usurped rights from the river to the sea, but I will suspend my rights over what was seized before 1967 in order to achieve all my rights that were taken after 1967" (ICG, 2006a: 20).

Within this framework, the divine right to Palestine becomes a credo, not a political programme[19]. Because this relegates the 'religious' and nationalist claims to the background, it enables the pragmatists to focus on the arguments contained in the practical critique of the peace process. Whether or not to use violence then becomes a function of whether other ways can be found to compel Israel to give the Palestinians a state based on the 1967 borders.

Whether Hamas will follow this path will depend on the relative strength of pragmatists and absolutists within Hamas, and on the environment created by the actions of the Israeli government and the international community. It will also depend on the regional balance

---

19 I am indebted to Menachem Klein for this distinction.

of power, and whether the states in favour of the Arab League's Beirut peace initiative (the Saudi plan) will outweigh the states opposed to this initiative.

For the pragmatists to continue to promote the path of compromise, the opportunity structure must remain such that it is more advantageous to compromise, than to revert to all-out resistance. If political integration is not found to pay dividends, but rather, as at present, results in a freezing of international aid and serious obstruction from the losing faction, the incentive to continue along this tactical road lessens dramatically. The June 2006 breakdown of the 2005-6 ceasefire, though triggered by a sudden rise in civilian deaths, allegedly at the hands of the Israeli army (Israel denies responsibility for the first set of casualties), was facilitated by a loss of faith in both the electoral process and the path of political compromise. Domestically, Fatah had, in Hamas' eyes, obstructed the Hamas-led legislative council and government at every turn, whether through refusing to accept Hamas' control over the security services, fuelling a breakdown in law and order, or undermining Hamas' ability to govern. Hamas contributed equally to damaging relations, by setting up a rival security service, responding to and initiating clashes, and treating the civil service as an implacable enemy. But, the key issue is that, from Hamas' perspective, it appeared as if Fatah did not honour the electoral process (cf. Rantisi, 2007).

Under these conditions, the pragmatists' argument that political participation would increase Hamas' political leverage was gradually eroded while Israel's decision to incarcerate large numbers of Hamas' elected legislators further weakened the pragmatists' position—strengthening those who never believed in either the ceasefire or political participation, and increasing the attraction of absolutist positions for pragmatists.

Faith in the electoral process was further undermined by the response of the international community. Neither Israel nor the international community (in particular the US and Europe) offered any incentives to Hamas to continue along the path of compromise, instead demanding that Hamas give up its claim to Palestine, recognise Israel and disarm, imposing financial sanctions if it did not—while openly meddling in the internal power struggle by strengthening

'Abbas' Presidential Guard (cf. *Guardian*, 'Hamas acted on a very real fear of a US-sponsored coup', 22 June 2007). If the West had treated Hamas less like a total spoiler, and instead had built on the fact that the pragmatists had persuaded the absolutists within Hamas to respect past agreements between the PLO and Israel, and that this put the pragmatists in a delicate position, more progress might have been made. Here, it is instructive to look at other peace processes and note how often governments have had to build on partial compromises to gradually bring those opposed to a political settlement on board (cf. Northern Ireland; Sri Lanka; Aceh; for details, see Heiberg, Tirman and O'Leary, 2007; see also Ricigliano, 2004).

Two final observations are in order. First, as with Hamas' recourse to violence, religion did not determine Hamas' decision to declare a ceasefire, although it played a role both in Hamas' intransigence vis-à-vis Israel, and in encouraging it to consult the grassroots. Given that all three ceasefires discussed above were declared when the peace process was progressing, religiously-inspired objections did not appear to have sufficient force to prevent Hamas from suspending its campaign—unlike, for instance, a change in political opportunity structure.

Second, displaying greater sensitivity to the popular will is no guarantee for less violence. Pressures from Hamas' grassroots constituency, for instance, appear to have played a part in the June 2006 decision to suspend the ceasefire. Salah al-Bardawil, spokesperson for Hamas' legislators, told an Israeli journalist that "people are calling us traitors" and that "we are being accused of having become a group of power-hungry people and of having forgotten the precept of jihad". According to al-Bardawil, the initial decision to end the ceasefire was taken because "we did not want to become a new version of Fatah. ... We were concerned we would lose our popularity. Therefore, we announced the resumption of the attacks" (Avi and Amos, 2006). In the week leading up to the resumption of rocket attacks, popular anger in Gaza had been boiling over. Twenty-seven people had been killed within a week, fourteen of them civilians. In addition, Israel had assassinated the head of one of the Popular Resistance Committees branches, who had just been appointed head of Hamas' alternative security force.

This highlights a fundamental dilemma in both Hamas and Israel's predicament: electoral integration does not necessarily lead to moderation. As long as the electorate is radicalised, Hamas will be encouraged to act radically, and will not have to choose between its maximalist goals and its electoral popularity. Only when the electorate becomes de-radicalised—in response to the cessation of policies such as settlement expansion, erecting security walls, economic strangulation, incarceration and targeted assassinations, and an increase in the general standard of living—may political integration have the moderating effect it is capable of by forcing Hamas to choose between political power and intransigence. Yet Israel is unlikely to drop its radicalising policies until it believes Hamas and the other resistance factions have made a strategic shift towards compromise—which is less likely to happen as long as Israel sticks to its current policies.

7

HAMAS AND DEMOCRATISATION

Over the course of the previous chapters, it has been shown that Hamas has adopted a number of democratic practices. Internally, it holds elections to select and legitimise its leadership (even though the leadership's endorsement of candidates appears to be vital). It consults its cadres and, under certain circumstances, its grassroots supporters seem to shape key aspects of its policies (even though the precise extent to which policies are shaped by the grassroots is un-clear). In the domestic arena, it participates in elections, and has by and large refrained from using violence to influence or contest elec-tion results. It has regularly been re-elected, even by tactical voters with no ideological or institutional connection to the organisation, suggesting that it takes its contractual relationship with the voters seriously enough to ensure their future support.

This is not to deny serious tensions between what is usually under-stood as 'democracy' and Hamas' practices. Hamas has used violence against fellow Palestinians, particularly in its power struggle with Fatah, but as noted previously, such violence has typically not been directed against electoral results or civilian government institutions (as opposed to security forces). It has used violence against Israelis, including civilians, both in defiance of public opinion and outside the official structures of the state, although public opinion played a role in both its decisions to mount suicide attacks and to agree to cease-fires. It has used religious arguments to foreclose dissent, in both the moral realm and vis-à-vis the peace process (although increasingly less so regarding the latter), and tensions continue to exist between its members' particular vision of 'the good life' and their commitment to heeding the popular will. Nevertheless, a sufficient number of Hamas' practices have come to conform to aspects of democracy to warrant an investigation into why such a (partial) convergence appears to have taken place.

Elsewhere in this study, I have alluded to explanations that were informed by social movement theory. Several changes that have occurred in the political opportunity structure within which Hamas operates appear to have encouraged adoption of democratic practices, although there are countervaling factors at work too. The long-standing centrality of elections in the Palestinian political system (both rhetorically and institutionally), the arrival of an indigenous Palestinian Authority in the 1990s with security forces that far outnumbered the opposition's paramilitary wings, and the relative strength of Hamas' civil society network, and through that, its grassroots support, all contributed to making compliance with the electoral game attractive, while rendering non-compliance costly. Changes in Hamas' organisational structure, ranging from the gradual heterogenisation of its membership to organisational changes, triggered by the mass incarceration of its internal leadership, also contributed to the adoption of more consultative and participatory practices. The re-alignment within the PLO, which saw the leftist factions breaking with Fatah, and siding with Hamas in opposition to the peace process, both facilitated Hamas' emergence as a mainstream opposition faction and encouraged experimentation with ideological pragmatism (at least domestically).

Other factors, such as the continued postponement of municipal elections, Arafat's autocratic leadership style, and the proliferation of armed groups during the al-Aqsa Intifada, discouraged compliance with democratic practices—as did the fact that the union elections, for long the only site of political contestation, were largely symbolic and only brought their victors limited political power. That the international sponsors of the peace process appeared to be more interested in imposing what Robinson (2001) aptly called a 'hegemonic peace' than in furthering genuine democratisation, despite the centrality of elections in the peace processes' rhetoric, also discouraged adoption of a democratic framework.

However, beyond the rise and fall of political alliances, the anti-democratic tensions within the peace process, and the particular characteristics of Arafat's practices, socio-economic changes occurred that appear to have advanced democratisation, regardless of the setbacks it has encountered. The democratisation of Palestinian politics is not a foregone conclusion. But, if one compares socio-economic developments in the Palestinian territories over the past four decades with other situations where democratisation has taken place, there appear to be a number of striking convergences.

Robinson, among others, has already shown that Hamas is a product of the ongoing processes of modernisation in Palestine (Robinson, 1997: 132-6; see also Chapter 2 of this book). What has not been explicitly considered is that Hamas is also a product of—as well as an active participant in—precisely some of those aspects of modernisation which have in various studies been linked to the process of democratisation.

Hamas, Changing Class Structures and Democratisation

I will use the work of Rueschemeyer, Stephens and Stephens (1992)—hereafter Rueschemeyer—to reflect on the impact of structural developments in Palestinian society on Hamas' constituency. Rueschemeyer's core argument is that the process of democratisation is a function of the changing balance of power between the different classes, the state and civil society, and that it is particularly likely to occur when capitalist development has led to the weakening of the land-owning class, and the emergence of a working class with the capacity for self-organisation (40-78, 269-91).

For Rueschemeyer, whether or not one supports democracy is a function of whether democracy is in one's material and political interests (57). In the cases he considers, the class habitually opposed to democratisation is the land-owning class, the class most regularly championing it the working class. The middle classes play a more ambivalent role, often allowing themselves to be co-opted by the ruling coalition. Where industrialisation has been limited and the working class is insufficiently strong, democratisation is typically the result of an alliance between the working and the middle classes.

Ideology only plays a secondary role in this model. Rueschemeyer acknowledges that ideological hegemonies can play a part (e.g. 111-5), and recognises that class interests are not an objective fact, but socially constructed (53-7). However, he consistently links ideology back to underlying class and institutional structures. Similarly, when discussing the impact of religion, Rueschemeyer suggests that it is not the content of religion but whether religious institutions are autonomous from the dominant classes that determines whether it plays a democratising role (67, 275).

Rueschemeyer's approach is unsatisfactory on a number of counts. It treats classes too homogeneously. It ignores the continuing influence of such traditional authority structures as clans, adopts an overly individualistic model and downplays the importance of alternative (such as altruistic) rationalities (cf. Marx Ferree, 1992). It does not adequately explain why working-middle class coalitions do not more often adopt authoritarian positions, and treats politics almost as a derivative of economics (see also Kim, 1994). And yet, on aggregate, the model is able to account, relatively persuasively, for why democracies in forty odd cases across different continents succeed or stall.

One might object that Rueschemeyer's model is not applicable to the Palestinian territories because they do not constitute a unitary sovereign state, their economy is disproportionately dependent on Israel's economy and international aid, and the bulk of Palestinians live outside these territories. By contrast, Rueschemeyer's cases all involve clearly defined states and a level of indigenous economic development, without a significant role for Diasporas. Although these factors clearly affect class-state-society alliances, they can arguably be accommodated within Rueschemeyer's model. Given the importance Rueschemeyer places on international alliances and economic relations, the effect of the Diaspora, dependency on Israel's economy and international aid, and the impact of neighbouring state actors (such as Egypt and Jordan) can all be relatively readily accommodated.

Occupation, and the limited nature of Palestinian quasi-state structures, fit less easily into this model but can nevertheless be accommodated by conceptualising the state as a series of separate yet interlinking components each of which affects the balance of power between the different classes and ruling elites. The focus then becomes the relationship between different classes and these fragmented state structures. Such an approach is facilitated by the fact that we are concerned here not with whether the Palestinian territories are democratising as a polity, but rather with how structural changes have affected the social movement within which Hamas is embedded. This means that questions regarding what Linz and Stepan (1996: 16-37) call 'stateness'—whether there is a sovereign state, agreement upon territorial boundaries and consensus on who constitute its citizens, without which democracy is considered impossible—are relegated to the background.[1] It is, after all, possible to have democratic developments within a polity that is not sovereign and where boundary and citizenship questions are still unresolved.

A cultural essentialist might object that Rueschemeyer's model is inapplicable because it focuses on societies with Christian majorities. A number of studies have indeed identified Islam as one of the key reasons why, unlike most other regions in the world, the Middle East has resisted democratisation (for a critical overview see Sadowski, 1993). Rueschemeyer's findings challenge this conclusion, given his suggestion that the content of religion is largely immaterial and that it is the relation of religious institutions to wider class structures that affects the prospects of democracy. Moreover, Rueschemeyer's and other structuralist-inspired models developed in a Christian or secular context have been applied, successfully, to explain variations across different Middle Eastern states (Dalacoura, 1998; Anderson, 1986; Bromley, 1994; Farsoun, 1988).

Applying this model to Palestine for the period 1967-2006, the following tentative observations offer themselves. First, although some of the processes Rueschemeyer lists as counter-democratic occurred within the occupied territories, particularly since the establishment of the PA, a significant number of Rueschemeyer's democracy-inducing processes did take place. While not all of these processes have come to full fruition, the fact that they have begun to change the class structure suggests the existence of a number of pressure points

---

1 Rueschemeyer similarly implies that democratisation requires the presence of a sovereign, autonomous state (63-9).

within Palestinian society, which, in Rueschemeyer's model, could facilitate democratisation.

Second, if we look at Hamas' place within the constellation of class, state and civil society alliances, it operates at precisely some of those pressure points from which calls for democracy have typically issued. This suggests that Hamas has not only experienced democratising pressures, which are likely to have affected both its constituency and its organisational interests, but that these are also likely to have contributed to democratisation.

Finally, although Hamas is located at a point within Palestinian society and politics where the pressure to adopt a democratic strategy is likely to be particularly strong, there are two factors which may negate this pressure to democratise, namely Hamas' continued resort to violence outside of the structures of state, and Hamas' control of a parallel welfare network both of which may be said to undermine the state consolidation which Rueschemeyer deems necessary for democratisation to succeed (although Hamas' welfare network has also provided an important civil society bulwark against the more autocratic tendencies of Fatah's state-building programme).

Starting with the first observation, we can detect a number of changes in Palestinian society, which Rueschemeyer considers to be democracy-inducing. The power of the landed elite was weakened, particularly in the period 1967-93 (although this process had already begun before the 1967 war), while the working class expanded due to the transformation of the largely agrarian workforce into a wage labour force (Chapter 2). As traditional patron-client relationships weakened, the latter became increasingly autonomous. Although lack of urbanisation[2] and industrialisation, circumscribed unionisation, and the peculiar dependency of the Palestinian economy on the Israeli economy meant that this class did not become sufficiently unified and organised to become a successful challenger to the ruling

---

2　Urbanisation has been limited in the territories. But the creation of large refugee camps, increased mobility and education, and the relative demise of agriculture have together given rise to several dynamics usually associated with urbanisation, e.g. greater population concentration, increased communication opportunities, greater exposure to different classes and non-traditional political entrepreneurs.

coalition on its own (cf. also Younis, 2000: 155), elements of this class became increasingly active in civil society during the 1970s. This process was facilitated by the emergence of a counter elite of lower class origins among the Diaspora, which affected the composition of the exiled nationalist leadership, and through them, local perceptions of the role of the different classes. A middle class similarly evolved, although the absence of indigenous development and Israel's de-development policy (cf. Roy, 1995b) served to reduce its size through emigration, particularly at the upper end of this class. Prior to the arrival of the Palestinian Authority, large sections of this class were relatively autonomous from the landed elite and the structures of state, enabling it to be active in civil society and to ally itself to the emerging working class (cf. Hilal and Khan, 2004: 72, 92-4).

For much of the 1970s and 1980s, civil society provided the type of semi-autonomous space that Rueschemeyer cites as one of the key factors facilitating democratisation. The Communist Party and resurgent Muslim Brotherhood both contributed to creating an indigenous civil society independent from state and ruling elite, as did the mushrooming of universities and professional institutions (Hiltermann, 1991; Robinson, 1997: 19-65; Mishal and Sela, 2000: 18-25). The gradual severing of links between religious structures, the state and the traditional elite, in which the Brotherhood played an important part, similarly served to enlarge the space for an autonomous civil society.

Occupation both limited civil society's options and encouraged civil society actors to become independent from existing state structures and build parallel structures to counter the negative effects of Israel's de-development policy. The indefinite suspension of municipal elections in 1980, and Israel's attempts to create a quietist alternative leadership to the emerging nationalist one, facilitated a shift from municipal councils, until then the bridge between micro-state structures and indigenous ruling elite, to civil society institutions, although it also led to the politicisation of civil society (Chapter 2). Israel's efforts at preventing the emergence of a unified national leadership similarly served to make civil society more pluralistic.

Occupation and a shared sense of threat facilitated the emergence of cross-class alliances, another key factor in Rueschemeyer's democratisation trajectory, as class interests were subjugated to the national interest. This process was facilitated by the fact that almost half of the Palestinian workforce worked for Israeli employers (Younis, 2000: 155). The adoption of mass demonstrations and strikes as resistance tactics similarly had both an equalising and a mobilising effect on society, increasing cross-class alliances and enhancing civil society's organisational potential.

From the late 1970s, the PLO, which had taken on the function of an (exiled) state-in-waiting, sought to both expand and co-opt civil society (Sayigh, 1997: 474-84, 611-3). But its leadership was far removed from the territories, and there was sufficient competition amongst the PLO's factions as well as between the PLO and other organisations, to allow for the development of a competitive civil society, and prevent the establishment of the type of hegemonic control Latin and Central American populist parties achieved (with typically negative results for the process of democratisation; Rueschemeyer, 1992: 282). The fact that the state was effectively split between Israeli and Jordanian authorities and the PLO abroad, facilitated the emergence of a relatively autonomous civil society, in spite of attempts by all three actors to subjugate it.

The establishment of the PA in 1994 as part of the Oslo Peace Process drastically changed the balance of class, civil society and state alliances. Local grassroots activists of both lower and lower middle class origin were sidelined as the returning exiled leadership of Fatah sought to impose its writ on the territories (Hilal and Khan, 2004: 86-7, 97-8; Amundsen and Ezbidi, 2004: 152-4; Robinson, 1997: 179-81). Elements of the traditional elite were brought back into the political centre as part of this internal power struggle (Robinson, 1997: 178-9). Civil society organisations, until then operating with some level of independence under the umbrella of an exiled PLO leadership, lost much of their autonomy to the Fatah-dominated PA, enabling Fatah to establish control over large sectors of civil society, in part through the creation of new quasi-state structures (Giacaman, 1998). The latter, including the security apparatus, became identified with Fatah and its allies, thus lessening its autonomy (Hilal and Khan, 2004: 83-98; Giacaman, 1998).

Fatah's ability to dominate the emerging state structures, sideline the PLO's internal opposition and, to a lesser extent, ignore domestic calls for further democratisation were facilitated by the support of Israel, the US and the EU, and in particular, by their vested interest in Fatah being sufficiently strong to suppress any opposition to the peace process (see Chapter 2). International aid enabled the PA to create a (quasi-)'rentier state', lessening its dependence on grassroots support (cf. Robinson, 1997: 198-200; Hanafi and Tabar, 2004).[3] It also facilitated the rapid expansion of security forces, enabling it to limit dissent (Hilal and Khan, 2004: 84; Robinson, 1997: 182-3). Rueschemeyer credits each of these factors as having a counter-democratic effect in other situations.

The working class was weakened in material terms by the effect of the post-Oslo border closures, causing unemployment to rise steeply, and GNI to drop sharply (cf. Roy, 2001: 100-1). Adverse economic conditions meant that large sectors of the lower class continued to be an amorphous, fragmented 'lumpen proletariat', rather than the organised, self-conscious working class imagined by Rueschemeyer. It was further weakened by the decline of the Left wing within the PLO, and the demise of the Soviet Union, which led to the discrediting of ideologies that explicitly sought to turn an unorganised lower class into a self-conscious working class. The lower classes' oppositional potential further deteriorated as a result of civil society's increasingly being dominated by NGO professionals with ties to the global international aid elite (Hanafi and Tabar, 2004: 233-6).

The middle class grew rapidly under the new Authority. But because of the nature of the new economy, their growth made them more dependent on the PA. Already fragmented geographically, sectorially, ideologically as well as organisationally, and weakened by the first Intifada (1987-93), their oppositional potential was further reduced by the control the Authority had over their employment op-

---

3   Because a 'rentier state' (Beblawi and Luciani, 1987) does not primarily depend on raising taxes due to its access to other resources (e.g. international aid and monopolies in the Palestinian case; cf. Hanafi and Tabar, 2004; Nasr, 2004), it is less beholden to its population and in a position to make key constituencies dependent on its provision of 'rents'.

portunities and the far greater organisational power of the returnees surrounding Arafat (Hilal and Khan, 2004: 91-100).

Higher education opportunities continued to expand. The number of university students more than doubled between 1994 and 1999 (Hilal and Khan, 2004: 92), offering lower and middle class students a limited autonomous space for organising dissent, as the universities became the main locus of the opposition. Some professional unions also became loci of dissent—but Fatah managed to maintain control in many. The 1990s saw the rapid expansion of internationally funded NGOs. Although the Palestinian Authority tried to control them, it only partially succeeded in doing so, thus leaving a level of autonomous space (Hilal and Khan, 2004: 98-9; Robinson, 2001: 119-20). However, because of their dependency on international aid, these NGOs both lacked the incentive to build grassroots support and were limited by the agendas of their donors.

The outbreak of the al-Aqsa Intifada changed the balance of class-state-society power again. The PA was weakened by Israeli attacks on its infrastructure, in particular its security services, and by Israel's withholding tax collected at the borders, thus severely undermining its ability to maintain order and dispense services (Roy, 2007: 266-7; Bickerton and Klausner, 2007: 346-7, 51). The Intifada also served to bring out into the open Fatah's unresolved internal power struggle, as the cadres sidelined by Arafat regained some of the influence they had lost since the first Intifada (Robinson, 2001: 121-3). Security began to break down, as clans and criminal gangs began to compete with factional militias and fractured security services. Civil society was further weakened as a result of the conflict, increasing unemployment and poverty. The conflict also increased the bargaining power of those affiliated with the various militias, which, because they were dominated by the lower and lower middle classes, strengthened the latter's position vis-à-vis the ruling coalition. But because many operated outside both civil society and the structures of state they could not easily translate this newfound strength into formal political power.

The conflict simultaneously strengthened Hamas with the effect of increasing the autonomy of civil society organisations dominated by it. Because Hamas was used to operating independently from local state structures, and maintained the backing of both its local and international funders (despite attempts by the international community to freeze its funds), its civil society institutions continued to function, making the PA increasingly dependent on it. Hamas was helped in this by its access to sympathetic international state and NGO actors, seeking to undermine the peace process or Fatah. Hamas' growing strength, coupled with the escalation of Fatah's internal tensions, further limited the Authority's power (Chapter 2).

Fatah's position was also undermined by its association with the uprising, which had led to an attenuation of international support. With Arafat's marginalisation, and eventual death, its legitimacy waned both locally and internationally. Together, these pressures made the Authority more amenable to calls for democratisation, from both inside and outside. But it also meant that the Authority was too weak, fragmented, and emaciated financially to manage the tumultuous process of democratisation. The situation was exacerbated by the close association between state structures and Fatah which meant that the security forces and the civil service were too bound up with Fatah to act as autonomous guarantors of the state (which became especially relevant when Fatah lost the 2006 election). The outcome was thus both an increase in pressure to democratise and a weakening of the state structures that were meant to oversee this process.

On balance, though obstacles to democratisation existed during the 1970s and 1980s, and increased during the 1990s, many of the changes Palestinian society experienced would, in Rueschemeyer's model, have facilitated democratisation. Key among these were the weakening of the landed elite, the expansion of the working class, the alliance between the working and middle classes and the growth of a relatively autonomous civil society—which arguably helps to explain why much of civil society during the 1970s and 1980s took on democratic characteristics, and why the first Intifada was, at least initially, a participatory grassroots phenomenon. The weakening of civil society during the 1990s also helps to explain, among other factors, why the al-Aqsa Intifada of 2000 was less participatory.

The establishment of quasi-state structures and a security apparatus under the domination of one party, and the extension of that party's control over civil society and sectors of the middle class was, in Rueschemeyerian terms, a blow to democratisation, as was the weakening of the working class. But the fact that some autonomous cross-class space continued to exist in civil society, in the form of student unions, professional associations, and charities meant that if Rueschemeyer is right, pressures to democratise continued to exist. Except for the partial recovery of the landed class, many of the underlying structural conditions which, in the 1980s, had, in this model, given rise to pressures for democratisation, remained in place. On balance, therefore, though civil society and the working-middle class alliance suffered during the 1990s, they continued to constitute a (limited) challenge to Fatah (Hilal and Khan, 2004: 91-100; Roy, 2001: 98-103).

If we now look at Hamas' place in these socio-economic shifts, we find that it is situated precisely where Rueschemeyer expects the pressure for democratisation to be greatest. Hamas resembles the type of cross-class alliance that Rueschemeyer has credited with promoting democracy elsewhere. Its members are drawn from social groups outside the ruling coalition who increased their organisational skills and resources through participation in civil society. It succeeded in mobilising members of both the lower and lower middle classes by subjugating class tensions to the demands of national liberation and religious salvation. And it similarly succeeded in creating a (limited) counter-hegemonic space, thus increasing the autonomy of its support base from the state and the ruling coalition (prior to its ascent to government).

According to Rueschemeyer's model, Hamas' constituency is precisely among those most likely to call for democracy as they stand to gain from it (both individually and collectively, thus partly bypassing the individualistic bias of the model) and have the organisational skills and resources to oppose the ruling coalition. They are, moreover, the products of precisely some of the processes of capitalist development which Rueschemeyer credits with creating the conditions for democratisation: the people whose material and political potential has increased as a result of capitalist development, greater educational opportunities and the expansion of civil society. Although the lower classes supporting Hamas are less organised than in many of Rueschemeyer's examples, and although most of Hamas' middle class supporters are from the lower end of the middle classes (especially merchants and professionals),[4] its supporters would still be prime candidates for Rueschemeyer's democratising forces since they would be major beneficiaries of democratisation.

Within Rueschemeyer's framework, Hamas can be seen as one of the factors encouraging democratisation by virtue of its location in the constellation of class, state and civil society alliances and its role in civil society. This is not to say that all of Hamas' activities advance democratisation, or that it being a force for democratisation implies that it genuinely embraces democracy. Rueschemeyer's model suggests that, through its activities in charities, elections and wider civil society, Hamas has contributed to the political mobilisation and organisational potential of those segments of society which are most likely to push for democracy, and that by operating as an autonomous force in opposition to the ruling coalition, it has helped to sustain a counter-hegemonic space and limit the power of the ruling coalition. This in turn has increased the pressure on the Authority to be held accountable and made Palestinian civil society more pluralistic. Hamas' role in creating so-called religious structures autonomous from the state and the ruling coalition is particularly significant.

Despite downplaying the importance of ideology, Rueschemeyer's model nevertheless allows for the possibility that the more autocratic aspects of Islamism's ideological legacy may have prevented Hamas from adopting a pro-democracy agenda.[5] However, the material and

---

4 NEC's January 2006 poll suggests that Hamas enjoyed both absolutely and proportionally less trust from the poorest sector ('hardship cases') than Fatah (38 per cent vs. 46 per cent), and marginally more from among those living (just) below or above the poverty line (45 per cent vs. 43 per cent, 38 per cent vs. 36 per cent). PSR's PLC Exit Poll (February 2006) suggests that Hamas has marginally more support among low income voters (46 per cent) than among mid (44 per cent) and high income voters (40 per cent), and more among merchants (49 per cent), housewives (47 per cent), professionals (46 per cent) and labourers (45 per cent) than among students (42 per cent), employees (41 per cent) and the unemployed (41 per cent).

5 Another potential for tension lies in Hamas' making Islam the main source of legislation and the effect this may have on the rights of non-Muslim citizens.

political interests of the lower and lower middle class supporters among Hamas' constituents appear to be better served by a call for democratisation than for autocratic structures since the latter would not give them the potential benefits of democratisation—particularly as they are excluded (and remain largely so, Hamas' election victory notwithstanding) from both Fatah's and the traditional elite's patronage. The fact that many of the petty bourgeoisie voted for Hamas in 2006 in protest against Fatah's alliance with rich businessmen and its attempts at establishing state-linked monopolies underscores this point (Selby, 2006; Nasr, 2004). Indeed, unlike the various authoritarian parties Rueschemeyer describes (for example, in inter-war Germany; 111-15), Hamas does not represent an alliance between the landed elite, the nation-building elite, the church and the upper middle classes—even though it has forged alliances with (pro-Jordanian) members of the landed elite and of the state-linked religious structures.[6] Nor does Hamas resemble the Latin American populist parties that Rueschemeyer discusses. In short, Hamas does not possess the structural characteristics that he found in parties that privileged authoritarian aspects of their ideological legacies.

Apart from the tension between some of Hamas' ideological positions and aspects of democratic practice, there are at least two aspects to its role in civil society that make it an obstacle to democratisation, in Rueschemeyer's model, and that may counter the democratising impact of changing socio-economic structures on Hamas. Rueschemeyer says little directly about the effects of civil society organisations creating parallel welfare structures that compete with those of the state. At one level, the presence of parallel structures should have a positive effect by limiting the state's power and forcing it to become more accountable and effective. But at another, parallel structures may undermine the state's ability to act as an autonomous actor capable of providing basic services and maintaining law and order, thus preventing it from consolidating itself and successfully managing the

---

6   There are of course other differences: Palestinian civil society was not as homogeneously penetrated as Germany's civil society preceding the inter-war period; its landed elite was much weaker; and it had stronger working-middle class alliances.

vigorous competition inherent in democracy. The success of Hamas' welfare institutions may thus have both accelerated the process of democratisation by making the PA more amenable to calls for it, and indirectly harmed democracy's prospects. The continued rivalry between Hamas and Fatah may similarly both further the process of democratisation by limiting the control of any faction over state institutions, and contribute to the fragmentation of state structures as both factions seek to increase control over them.

The second factor concerns Hamas' armed wing. Rueschemeyer observes that violence by non-state actors either undermines state consolidation (preventing states from maintaining law and order throughout the democratisation process) or triggers an excessive strengthening of the state's coercive apparatus which can then be used "to repress demands from subordinate classes for political inclusion or for material concessions" (276, 159-63, 172-3). Hamas' engagement in violence has arguably done both. During the 1990s, its violence was one factor encouraging the Authority's expansion of security services. During the 2000s, its contribution to the violence of the al-Aqsa Intifada arguably undermined state consolidation, although Israel's targeting of Palestinian security services, Fatah's infighting, and the emergence of clan and criminal gang militias also played a part, alongside the role played by Israel's border closures, security fence-building and financial strangulation.

Hamas' refusal to disband its armed wing however, must also be seen, at least in part, as a response to the failure of state consolidation. The failure of Palestinian state structures to dissociate themselves from Fatah has arguably encouraged Hamas to maintain its armed wing, as lack of faith in the impartiality of both the state's security forces and the electoral process has fuelled the belief that a militia is needed to guarantee one's political survival. Israel's failure to honour some of its key promises and enable the establishment of a viable Palestinian state has also played its part, fuelling the belief that a militia is required to secure Palestinian basic needs—particularly if the ruling coalition is believed to be compromised by its alliance with 'the enemy', or incapable of securing these needs. This then becomes a vicious cycle as Hamas' intransigence fuels both Fatah's unwillingness to create impartial state structures and Israel's reluctance to honour its promises.

In sum, though Rueschemeyer's model cannot say whether Hamas or its constituents have genuinely adopted democratic attitudes, or whether structural changes in Palestinian society will actually produce a full-scale democracy, it does suggest that Hamas has both experienced democracy-inducing pressures and operated at one of the levels within society from which pressures for democratisation typically emerge. One can quibble with this finding by pointing to the flaws in Rueschemeyer's model, or to flaws in the application of the model. But, to the extent that his model has explained other democratisation processes, Hamas' (partial) adoption of democratic practices can be said to be encouraged by wider socio-economic changes.

Hamas, Modernisation Theory and Democratisation

Though Rueschemeyer's model acknowledges the impact of changing class structures on people's perceptions by noting that class interests are socially constructed, we have to turn to modernisation theorists to develop a more detailed picture of how socio-economic development may affect perceptions. Opinions are divided over exactly how modernisation is related to democratisation. Lipset's original thesis that "the more well-to-do a nation, the greater the chances that it will sustain democracy" has been found to be both empirically accurate, and intellectually simplistic (Lipset, 1959: 75). As Przeworski (among others) has observed, though a statistical multi-country analysis will corroborate that "democratic regimes are more frequent in the more developed countries", an increase in per capita income does not necessarily lead to democratisation (Przeworski, 2003; see also, Gill, 2000: 2-3). The relationship between socio-economic development and democracy is not necessarily linear. Other factors play a role, such as whether economic wealth is dependent on state patronage. In addition, the distinction between modernity and tradition is not necessarily as sharp, nor as exclusive, as Lipset and others have painted it (Eickelman and Piscatori, 1996: 22-45; Inayatullah and Blaney, 2004: 108-16). Though modernisation theorists have attempted to respond to this critique, some of the assumptions deriving from this dichotomy still haunt their findings, such as (for example) the notion that secular mass education increases tolerance while traditional practices facilitate intolerance.

Diamond, whose revised 1992 model I will use, echoes many of the themes discussed by Rueschemeyer. Of specific interest to this analysis is his focus on political culture, and the impact of socio-economic changes on individual dispositions—something which Rueschemeyer largely ignores.

I will limit myself to discussing two of Diamond's hypotheses. One concerns the premise that educational attainment and achieving a higher economic status are key factors in producing dispositions that favour democracy (476-8). Diamond backs this hypothesis up with numerous statistical studies that have found positive correlations between educational attainment and an increase in economic status on one hand, and an increase in people's levels of tolerance, capacity to trust and compromise, and on the other their desire (and capacity) to participate politically and express dissent. Education in particular is singled out as inspiring active citizenship, a respect for minority rights, and "freedom from absolute submission to received authority" (Inkeles & Smith, quoted in Diamond: 477).

A second hypothesis concerns the role of civil society associations and their effect on people's attitudes. Those associations that are "democratic in their internal procedures of governance" are believed to instil democratic values in their members (483-5), although Diamond acknowledges that more research needs to be done to confirm this. But, quite apart from whether they advocate or practise democracy, the very proliferation of voluntary civil society associations is considered to facilitate democratisation by mobilising people, stimulating their political interests, enhancing their organisational skills and creating "a pluralistic competition of interests" (as well as providing alternative ways of redressing injustices and providing a bulwark against authoritarian rule).

Hamas draws much—though, significantly, not all—of its support from precisely those sectors of society that have been particularly influenced by the types of socio-economic change Diamond has posited as central to producing a democratic disposition: the newly educated, the upwardly mobile from among the lower and lower middle classes, and the active participants of civil society.

Hamas has benefited particularly from the rapid expansion of higher education, and draws much support from students and professionals (although, intriguingly, despite having dominated student politics for the past decade and a half, PSR's January-February 2006 exit poll found that the percentage of students having voted for Hamas in 2006 was lower, at 42 per cent, than most other categories; see note 4 above). The Brotherhood's turn towards internal elections appears to have been in part driven by the influx of students and professionals (Chapter 2). Although higher education does not appear to have increased students' tolerance during the 1980s (in this case, exposure to higher education may have caused people to feel threatened by its plurality and so reinforced prior beliefs rather than tolerance), it did increase their desire and capacity to become politically active, and to express dissent. The experience of the 1990s seems to tally more closely with Diamond's predictions regarding education's effect on levels of tolerance. The continued centrality of students and university-educated professionals coincided with Hamas' (partial) turn towards increased tolerance and ideological compromise—although other factors, such as the effects of continuing occupation, border closures and corruption on people's "life satisfaction" would in Diamond's model have undermined the effects of education (477, 486-7).

Hamas similarly draws much of its support from the petty bourgeoisie, and the upwardly mobile from among the working and lower middle classes. Here too, there may be a correlation between the rapid growth of per capita income during the 1970s and the Brotherhood's turn towards representative authority and internal elections. That economic growth subsequently stalled does not necessarily negate this correlation. A reversal in economic growth may reduce people's resources and opportunities, increase class polarisation or weaken the private sector—all of which may hamper democratisation. But what will influence democracy's long-term prospects most, in Diamond's model, is whether a process has begun that increases political awareness, readiness to compromise, and the desire and capacity of people to participate in politics, while eroding the influence of the landed elite and strengthening and widening civil society. Diamond focuses on changing attitudes, rather than economic development *per se* (486-7). In the Palestinian case, the socio-economic processes that began in the 1970s continue to affect people's attitudes and skills, even though economic growth stalled for much of the 1980s and 1990s. Student numbers, for instance, continued to expand, as did expectations of political participation. Members of the lower classes continued to have opportunities to increase their socio-economic status or become active in civil society, while the landed class never regained its prior position of dominance.

The economic decline which the Palestinian territories experienced for much of the 1990s and 2000s may, paradoxically, have contributed to the process of democratisation. Economic performance, according to Diamond, is crucial for regime maintenance, particularly if the regime in question is (semi)authoritarian (485). With rising expectations following the economic promises of Oslo, economic decline could be said to have accelerated pressures from below—particularly as the economic growth of the 1970s had already triggered some of the key dynamics Diamond cites as crucial to democratisation (a weakening landed elite, expansion of education and civil society, the emergence of a partially autonomous middle and working class). This by itself would not necessarily have resulted in greater political participation if Hamas had not also simultaneously become an increasingly acceptable alternative to those who had become alienated from Fatah (Chapter 2).

Finally, one could argue that, at least according to Diamond's model, Hamas appears to have contributed not only to the pluralisation of civil society but also to the socialisation of its members into, if not democratic, at least more participatory and contractarian values and beliefs. By simply existing outside of the structures of the PLO and the Fatah-dominated state institutions, and mobilising those who might otherwise not have been mobilised, Hamas has, within this model, contributed to the democratisation of Palestinian society. This in itself is likely to have affected its members. But, by adopting "internal procedures of governance" based on the principles of representative authority and electoral accountability, it may, following Diamond, also have actively contributed to instilling these principles into its members. Whether this is sufficient to constitute a 'democratic disposition' remains to be seen since these two notions have to compete with other, not necessarily democratic notions. Furthermore, this socialisation has arguably been undermined by internal irregularities, the continued importance of other forms of authority, and by the effect of occupation, violence and secrecy on the way these procedures have been implemented. But to the extent that these internal procedures were implemented, they may have contributed to the adoption of a more democratic attitude among Hamas' members.

There are of course other factors, which Diamond considers counter-productive to democratisation. One is the continued centrality of violence (which, historical specificities aside, Diamond links, somewhat simplistically, with lack of development). Another is Fatah's continued dominance over state institutions, economic development and parts of civil society. A third is the absence of a strong, autonomous middle class. But none of these negates the finding that many of Hamas' members and supporters come from those sectors of society which in Diamond's model are likely to have developed a more democratic disposition as a result of the socio-economic changes they have experienced (Diamond explicitly argues that such counter-democratic factors do not negate the latter's democratising potential; 477-8).

Concluding Remarks

The foregoing analysis tentatively suggests that those aspects of Hamas' practice that are democratic are not simply coincidental but to be expected, given the socio-economic changes that have occurred over the past forty years (although political opportunity structure also played a central role). This lends further credence to the argument that, regardless of potential discrepancies between Hamas' hidden and public transcripts, it is likely to promote aspects of democratic behaviour as long as wider socio-economic and political structures remain comparable.

Even if certain practices have been adopted opportunistically, they may serve to alter members' perceptions. Diamond argues this with regard to civil society organisations' capacity to socialise their members into democratic practices by adopting democratic practices internally. That thousands of Hamas supporters annually experienced the granting of authority on the basis of electoral outcomes has arguably influenced their perceptions. Rustow similarly holds that participation in electoral structures may lead to a changed disposition towards elections, regardless of whether the initial decision to participate was purely tactical (Rustow, 1970: 358-61). Alternatively, one could argue that an opportunistically chosen policy changes the calculus in such a way as to make going back on it too costly. Thus, while Hamas' leadership may opportunistically adapt its programme to woo swing voters, once enough Hamas supporters consist of these swing voters, Hamas' power base is fundamentally altered, making it harder to revert to its original programme (as long as maintaining popular support is vital to Hamas' survival).

This is not to say that Hamas will inevitably become more democratic. There are enough ambiguities in both its behaviour and the wider structural environment to warrant caution about the future. Further changes in the balance of class power, in the relationship between classes, state and civil society, or in the level, extent or pace of socio-economic development will affect the trajectory of democratisation. Failure to resolve the current stalemate between Israel and the Palestinians is likely to both impede economic development and the development of a sovereign democratic state. Yet resolution of this stalemate does not necessarily increase the prospects of democratisation if it replicates the logic of the Oslo process and uses one faction, Fatah, to impose a 'hegemonic peace'.

Failure to resolve the stalemate between Hamas and Fatah may similarly impede economic and state development—although in the long-term it may facilitate democratisation if the stalemate convinces both factions that neither can obliterate the other (as long as both continue to believe that legitimacy is dependent on maintaining popular support). Such a scenario is envisaged by Rustow, who suggests that recognition of such a stalemate is crucial in persuading the leading contenders to adopt democratic procedures to peacefully manage their conflict (355-7, 362-3). Conversely, a continuing stalemate may contribute to the fragmentation of the few state structures that are in place, thus further increasing the already high levels of lawlessness that have resulted from the breakdown of central authority.

The above analysis also provides one explanation for Grant and Tessler's finding that "those who support political Islam [in the Palestinian territories] ... are actually more likely than others to believe that a political system based on Islamic law can be democratic" (2002: 16). In Chapter 5, we saw that Hamas' support is stronger among the urban than among the rural population, and that its leadership is dominated by aspirational members of the lower middle classes with a relatively high level of education. This is precisely the section of the population that according to Diamond's model is most likely to have developed a pro-democratic disposition—a finding corroborated by Grant and Tessler's that, in Palestinian society, "pro-democracy attitudes are associated with higher education, male gender, older age, urban residence, and a higher standard of living" (16).

At the same time, the above analysis stands in tension with some of Grant and Tessler's findings. While it may help to explain why (Palestinian) men in cities are more likely to think democracy to be compatible with Islamic law, and believe Muslims and non-Muslims to have equal rights, it does not explain why they are less likely than men in refugee camps and villages to think that democracy is the best model—or indeed why in this instance men from refugee camps and villages think alike, given that refugee camps have numerous urban qualities. While it may help to explain why women in cities are more likely to believe democracy to be the best model, it does not explain why women in refugee camps are less likely to do so, given the apparently high number of women from refugee camps attending university. More research is needed on the precise impact of, for instance, Palestinian university education on students; socioeconomic changes on class, state and civil society relations; or the (transformative) interaction between clan, 'religious', electoral, state and donor practices and identities.

CONCLUDING THOUGHTS

If we were to summarise the above, the following observations offer themselves. One set of observations pertain to Hamas itself, and how we are to understand it. Another set concern how we study a movement such as Hamas. Both sets have wider relevance for the study of Islamist movements and religiously-inspired or violent political organisations more broadly.

Our analysis has shown that Hamas is a product of its environment. The timing and location of its emergence and the nature of its evolution can all in part be explained with reference to changes in the wider political opportunity structure. Hamas' membership profile, its political theory and its tactical decisions can be shown to have been shaped by the wider socio-economic changes Palestinian society has undergone, and by the particular constellation of political factions, the peculiar development of Palestinian (proto-)state structures and the political exigencies of the peace process. This is not to deny the role played by activists in affecting this opportunity structure and making the choices that they did. But Hamas' evolution cannot be fully understood outside the context of wider socio-economic and political changes.

Both in terms of these wider structures which have helped shape Hamas, and its internal dynamics, Hamas is subject to conflicting pressures. The tensions that emerged during the 1990s between internal and external, political and paramilitary, and different wings of the political leadership still haunt Hamas, and go some way in explaining why Hamas has been unable to act more decisively in the wake of its electoral victory. The tensions between different class interests and between those who benefit from continued resistance and those who do not, remain similarly unresolved.

Hamas' ideology and political theory are in part products of their environment. At the same time, they influence Hamas' practices and, through that, its environment. While Hamas is a movement of activists rather than philosophers, it is a self-consciously ideological organisation. Its ideology is neither complete nor wholly consistent. The precise shape of the Islamic state Hamas advocates is still being debated, and opinions on how to deal with Israel and Fatah diverge across the organisation, particularly following the widening of Hamas' constituency. Nevertheless, ideology has profoundly affected Hamas' political positions, its internal organisational structure and the self-image and dispositions of its members.

Comparing Hamas' political theory to its political practices, one is struck by the extent to which the two overlap. Both emphasise the importance of elections, consultation and representative authority on the one hand, and the centrality of religion, piety and religio-legal knowledge on the other. In both, representative authority is considered more important than religious authority, and political authority is differentiated from religious authority. Both circumscribe political authority with numerous checks and balances, ranging from elections and institutional separation of powers to expectations of piety and individual sacrifice. Both emphasise the importance of socialisation, and forging responsible citizens through an emphasis on community work, consultation and religious education.

As in any political movement, tensions exist between the ideal and the actual. The *Shura* Council's ability to exercise authority, for instance, is undermined by the geographical spread of Hamas' leadership, the political and financial autonomy of the external leadership, and the particular problems thrown up by Hamas being a clandestine organisation engaged in political violence. Nevertheless, political theory has shaped what Hamas members value, and what and whom they consider authoritative. A decision that can be presented as the result of a movement-wide consultation carries more weight than one that cannot, regardless of how widespread the consultation in actual fact was.

Hamas' ideology is neither inherently anti-democratic, nor anti-modern nor wholly anti-Western. It is critical of Western foreign policy in the Middle East. It is equally critical of secular democracy and its associated practices, and of secular rationality. Nevertheless, Hamas draws heavily on Western democratic notions such as the popular will, the social contract and inalienable human rights. Its political theory is deeply contractual. Authority is derived from having a popular mandate—not piety, religious knowledge or divine appointment. An Islamic state can only come about if willed by the people. Law, even Islamic law, can only be legislated by an elected legislature—not by unelected religious scholars—and revolves around a rational interpretation of both public interest and revelation.

At the same time, Hamas insists that only God's law will free people from tyranny and that only in an Islamic state will people be genuinely free. To bring this about without negating the principle of the popular will, Hamas proposes to educate society into willing an Islamic state through civic participation, consultation exercises and education. It is from this notion of a dual contract—one between God and the people, the other between leaders and led—and the conflicting visions of what constitutes freedom, that many of the apparent contradictions within Hamas' thought and practice stem. It is important, though, to emphasise that this dual contract has, certain differences notwithstanding, parallels in Western political theory in the notion of 'natural law'.

Hamas' internal practices exhibit a number of decidedly democratic principles. Formal authority is derived from regular elections—although these elections are more about conferring legitimacy and ensuring accountability than about open competition. Formal decisions are taken by elected representatives who are expected to consult the wider membership on important policy issues. Disagreement is expected to be resolved through debate, consultation and bargaining, until a majority of representatives agree on a compromise position.

Hamas' behaviour during the 2004-6 electoral campaigns similarly suggests that it is acutely aware not only of what constitutes power in an electoral environment, but also of its dependence on gaining votes. Its use of grassroots consultations and surveys in shaping its election programme and list of candidates suggests that, in an electoral context, Hamas closely heeds public opinion. It remains to be seen whether a U.S.-Israeli-sponsored peace process is capable of reconciling itself with an electoral system which can bring opponents of the peace process and American influence in the Middle East to power. But the fact that Hamas has invested so much effort in playing the electoral system well suggests that, at least in Hamas' eyes, a future Palestinian state is likely to be built around an electoral system in which power is dependent on gaining the popular vote.

Where Hamas' practices most differ from Western liberal democratic conceptions (though not necessarily actual practices) is in the role accorded to religion and violence in the creation of authority. Religion and violence play an important role in generating the symbolic capital from which Hamas and its leaders derive authority—but not as central a role as is often believed to be the case in Western circles. Religious knowledge, piety and involvement in one's local mosque all contribute to a Hamas leader's legitimacy. But formal authority within Hamas depends on whether one has been elected. The overwhelming majority of Hamas leaders and officials are secular professionals, rather than religious scholars or members of religious institutions, and the skills for which they are admired, even if they derive from piety and mosque involvement, are predominantly secular in nature. Similarly, although Hamas' ability to perpetrate violence against Israelis increases the legitimacy it enjoys among its supporters, only a handful of its leaders and elected officials have made their careers in the Qassam Brigades. The vast majority have gained political capital through their involvement in the community or in professions such as engineering, which have given them expertise relevant to government.

Religion helps to shape Hamas' overall worldview, although more research is needed to establish how exactly this dynamic works. Religion provides the discursive framework within which the conflict with Israel is framed. It provides justifications for Hamas' political positions—including, significantly, its adoption of certain democratic principles (thus burying the notion that religion is inherently incompatible with democracy). But, beyond that, much of Hamas' political behaviour cannot be explained solely with reference to religion. The bulk of its election manifesto is shaped by non-religious concerns or by its socio-economic or political position. Its behaviour towards the peace process and the patterns of its violence appear similarly to be driven more by secular than by religious calculations. And the way religion is interpreted is profoundly affected by changing political opportunity structures, socio-economic configurations and master frames.

There are various ways in which Hamas uses religion to strengthen its democratic credentials. Religious arguments are invoked to justify elections and consultation. Hamas' emphasis on piety encourages civic piety and civil responsibility. In this, Hamas' interpretation of religion is influenced by its political position as a long-time opposition party and by the socio-economic background of its membership, the bulk of which is from the lower and lower middle classes who would benefit from greater political participation.

In other ways, religion undermines Hamas' democratic potential. Religious symbolism and arguments are at times used to foreclose debate and create taboos. Religion can also be a source for justifying inequalities, for instance between men and women or between Muslims and non-Muslims, although our (all too) brief discussion of how religion manifests itself in Hamas' attitude towards women suggests that the interpretation of religion is neither static nor wholly predictable, and subject to changes in wider socio-economic and political structures (for a more in-depth discussion of Hamas' attitude towards Christians prior to the al-Aqsa Intifada, see Gunning, 2000).

More fundamentally, religion helps to conceal Hamas' ambitions for power. Part of what gives both individual leaders and the organisation legitimacy is Hamas' religiously-inspired focus on self-sacrifice, piety and divine justice. By emphasising piety and concern for divine justice, Hamas leaders draw attention away from their personal ambitions. This is not necessarily a process of deception—although it obviously can be—since leaders may well believe that they seek power for the good of the community. Given the overlap between their interests and those of their supporters, serving their own interests may further the interests of their constituency. It is, however, important to recognise the process by which this self-interest is concealed, if only because it appears to be one of the reasons why Hamas has experienced so few splits, and why internal disciplinary violence is so rare.

While internal violence is, as far as we know, rare, Hamas has been engaged in inter-factional violence and this, arguably, is one of the aspects of its behaviour that has the highest potential for undermining the democratic process in Palestine. Hamas' use of violence is in part a function of changing political opportunity structures, although internal dynamics and ideological objections also play a part. During the first Intifada, inter-factional violence coincided with weak internal controls, a demoralised nationalist movement and a relatively permissive political and ideological environment. With the creation of a central Palestinian Authority in 1994 and an increase in popular condemnations of intra-Palestinian violence, Hamas' involvement in such violence dropped. Since the outbreak of the al-Aqsa Intifada, and the weakening of both Fatah and the Authority's security forces, it has again become increasingly engaged in intra-Palestinian violence, primarily as a result of its power struggle with Fatah, although clan loyalties also play a part. However, it is noteworthy that Hamas' political violence (in a domestic context) has typically not been directed at the civilian structures of government, and that it has not sought to use violence to directly influence elections.

The current stalemate between Hamas and Fatah, with Hamas controlling Gaza, the Legislative Council (in theory) and one of two Cabinets, and Fatah controlling the other Cabinet, the West Bank, and the Presidency, has undermined the ability of the electoral system to centralise power and wrest it away from other contenders, such as clans, militias, partisan security chiefs and organised crime syndicates. If this stalemate continues, violence may well escalate, with serious consequences for electoral practices in the occupied territories.

Hamas' attitude towards the peace process is influenced by a number of contradictory factors. Its religious interpretation of the conflict has rendered compromise difficult, as has the intransigence (and influence) of the more absolutist hardliners among the external, internal and paramilitary leaderships. Yet, its gradual shift away from religious arguments towards more contractual and functional critiques of the peace process have opened up space for compromise, as has the emergence of a pragmatic leadership with greater investment in grassroots politics. Fatah's decision to open up the electoral system has increased Hamas' dependence on maintaining popular support, which in turn has increased the pressure on Hamas to consider a political compromise. Indeed, the two ceasefire declarations of 2003 and 2005 can be traced back directly to shifts in popular opinion and increased prospects of a political future for Hamas, although other factors, such as political assassinations, infiltration, and regional power shifts played significant roles too.

Hamas' readiness to make alliances in the 2004-6 elections, even with those who support co-existence with Israel, underlines that Hamas is not a fanatical faction, incapable of pragmatic compromise, but rather a pragmatic party weighing up costs and benefits. Of particular import is the fact that, through its alliances and its emphasis on domestic reform, it has succeeded in gaining a significant number of votes among those who support the peace process and are willing to recognise Israel alongside a Palestinian state.

That Hamas agreed to ceasefires which were explicitly linked to progress in the peace process suggests that, at least in these instances, Hamas has acted as a limited rather than a total spoiler. What made this partial compromise possible is the fact that Hamas has multiple goals and equal, if not greater interest in shaping Palestinian society as in liberating all of Palestine. This is not to deny the possibility that Hamas' decision was merely a tactical shift, rather than a strategic re-alignment. However, once Hamas has publicly accepted the notion of compromise as a tactical interim goal, it becomes more difficult to return to a no-compromise stance, especially if Hamas' supporters become convinced that compromise pays real dividends. The political leadership inside the territories has to live with the reality that Hamas may not gain the same number of votes in the next election, particularly if Hamas cannot deliver on its domestic promises. The desire to secure a political future for itself within the Palestinian domestic arena may thus push Hamas towards becoming a limited spoiler at both a tactical and perhaps eventually a strategic level.

For the pragmatists to continue to promote the path of compromise, the opportunity structure must remain such that it is more advantageous to compromise, than to revert to all-out resistance. If political integration is not found to pay dividends, but rather, as at present, results in a freezing of international aid and serious obstruction from the losing faction—aided and abetted by the international community—the incentive to continue along this road lessens dramatically. If the West treated Hamas less like a total spoiler, and instead built on the fact that the pragmatists were in the process of persuading the absolutists within Hamas to respect past agreements between the PLO and Israel, and that this put the pragmatists in a delicate position, the incentive to compromise would increase.

That Hamas candidates are predominantly not Qassam leaders is significant if the organisation ever decides to move away from political violence. Because the personal capital of Hamas candidates does not primarily rest on direct involvement in political violence, it is, at least theoretically, easier to foreswear violence. However, even if personal capital is largely unrelated to the capacity to inflict violence, a considerable portion of a candidate's symbolic capital is derived from the delegated capital of belonging to a paramilitary resistance organisation. If Hamas decides to give up its arms, it can still derive symbolic capital from having played a significant part in the resistance. But memory of successful violence is not the same as continuing to have the capacity to inflict violence—particularly as long as Palestinians do not feel secure, and therefore value the capacity to inflict violence on the enemy.

An added complication is the balance of power between Qassam commanders, Hamas absolutists and Hamas pragmatists. As long as the absolutists among the political leadership and the Qassam commanders hold an effective veto over the pragmatists by virtue of Hamas' tradition of consensual decision-making and the vulnerability of the peace process to violent spoilers, it will be difficult for the pragmatists to move away from resistance. That Hamas' political leadership contains relatively few Qassam commanders may make matters worse by increasing the chance of mutual alienation.

As for the prospects of democracy in Palestine, Hamas' participation in electoral structures—both internal and external—is likely to have affected its members' attitude to democracy. Hamas' extensive experience in union, and since 2004, in municipal and legislative elections is likely to reinforce the democratic aspects of its thought and practice. More fundamentally, though, if democratisation theories have any explanatory value, Hamas' adoption of (some) key democratic practices appears to be at least in part a result of structural changes in its environment. More research needs to be done to confirm this and other factors have arguably played a role. But the above analysis suggests that those aspects of Hamas' practice that are democratic are not wholly coincidental but predictable, given the socio-economic changes the territories have undergone over the past forty years. This suggests that, rather than asking the ideologically loaded and methodologically reified question 'Is Hamas democratic?'—let alone 'Is Hamas compatible with democracy?'—a more useful question is 'Under what conditions is Hamas likely to be(come more) democratic?'.

Whether Hamas will become more or less democratic, remains an open question. There are enough ambiguities in both Hamas' behaviour and structural environment, and in the theories of democratisation, to warrant caution about the future. Further changes in the balance of class power, in the relationship between classes, state and civil society, or in the level, extent or pace of socio-economic development will affect the trajectory of democratisation, as will the continued presence of private paramilitary organisations. Failure to resolve the current stalemate between Israel and the Palestinians is likely to both impede economic development and the development of a sovereign democratic state. Yet resolution of this stalemate does not necessarily increase the prospects of democratisation if it replicates the logic of the Oslo process and uses one faction, Fatah, to impose a 'hegemonic peace'.

Failure to resolve the stalemate between Hamas and Fatah may similarly impede economic and state development—although in the long-term it may facilitate democratisation if the continuing stalemate convinces both factions that neither can obliterate the other, and both continue to believe that legitimacy is dependent on maintaining popular support. Conversely, a continuing stalemate may contribute to the fragmentation of the few state structures that are in place, thus further increasing the already high levels of lawlessness which have resulted from the breakdown of central authority.

Democratisation by itself offers no guarantee that violence will end. As long as the electorate is radicalised by occupation practices, settlement expansion and economic strangulation, Hamas will not have to choose between its maximalist goals and its electoral popularity. Only when the electorate becomes de-radicalised, may political integration have the moderating effect it is capable of by forcing Hamas to choose between political power and intransigence.

Finally, a number of methodological observations can be made which are relevant not just for those studying Hamas, but for students of Islamism, (religious) social movements or violent political organisations more broadly. The above analysis has shown that moving away from a narrow fixation with violence, and from looking at Hamas from dominant state-centric perspectives, enables us to observe a much wider set of dynamics and paint a more complex picture of an organisation such as Hamas. It permits us to study Hamas' internal dynamics, where violence plays primarily a symbolic role, as well as its behaviour in electoral politics. And in the context of the peace process, it enables us to look beyond Hamas' violent tactics to the interaction between Hamas as a political organisation with the other political factions, wider society and its own differentiated internal constituencies.

It has similarly been shown that in-depth engagement with Hamas' own discourse, whether concerning the intricacies of its political ideology or its members' understanding of what makes a Hamas leader authoritative, is vital for enhancing our understanding of why Hamas acts the way it does, and how to interpret the tensions underpinning Hamas' practices. This is not to deny the importance of structural explanations, applying models from comparative politics, or complementing discourse analysis with a focus on actual practice. It is simply to underline the importance of an interpretive approach based on fieldwork and face-to-face interviews, and of taking Hamas' discourse seriously.

Equally important has been the adoption of a dialogic approach, which has sought to probe Hamas' political theory through comparison with Western political theory. Locke, Hegel, Berlin and Bourdieu have all helped to sharpen our understanding of Hamas, by suggesting similarities, raising deeper questions, and highlighting differences—vindicating Euben's suggestion that "the questions and categories of political theory are useful heuristic tools through which non-Western thinkers concerned with the moral foundations of political life may best be heard [...] enlarg[ing] the domain of political theory to include a range of human, and not merely Western, thought, practice, and experience" (1999: 158). A dialogic approach has its shortcomings. It obscures as well as enlightens. It distorts. But, if approached critically with an appreciation of the distorting influence of hegemonic discourses and cultural differences, it can increase understanding by moving beyond mechanistic structural or essentialist explanations, unearthing cross-cultural similarites and beginning to restore (some) parity across narratives in a post-colonial world.

More broadly, the above analysis has shown the usefulness of comparative political models. Social movement theory has helped in conceptualising and ordering the various influences working upon Hamas, placing Hamas within the wider social movement that sustains it, and suggesting themes to explore, such as the interaction between changing socio-economic and political structures, resources and framing. Democratisation theory has similarly provided a valuable comparative framework within which to reflect on the potential effect of socio-economic changes on Hamas and its constituencies. Both have served to situate Hamas within the context of global processes of structural change and social movement formation. In both instances, though, the theories could only be gainfully employed by problematising their reliance on the secularisation credo, while other culturally-specific factors, such as the prevailing influence of clans on politics, needed to be taken into account.

This leads me to my final methodological observation, namely the need to further problematise the secular-religious distinction. Throughout the analysis it has become clear that these terms are inadequate to convey the complexity of what is occurring. I have continued to use the terms to show that the view that Hamas is 'religious' rather than 'political' or 'secular' (as the terms are usually understood within a Western context) is simplistic and misleading. Although religion plays an important role, many of Hamas' practices are dominated by 'secular' logic or 'secular' symbolic capital. At the same time, there are some dynamics such as preaching in a mosque, the notion of an afterlife or a religious re-awakening which cannot be wholly reduced to their secular counterparts.

Moreover, what I have described as secular can be considered religious if one adopted a less restrictive notion of what constitutes religion. For Hamas, for instance, this-worldly civic activism and responsible citizenship is profoundly intertwined with religious piety, which in turn is influenced by conceptions of the afterlife. Without religion, it does not believe citizens will act responsibly. Divorcing the one from the other simply because religion has been, at least in theory, privatised and domesticated in a Western context is unsatisfactory. Developing new terms, such as Stout's 'civic piety', may offer a way out. But if we are to increase our understanding, we need to problematise these dichotomies—which calls for both a more in-depth analysis of the political and discursive structures that uphold and benefit from these distinctions (cf. Asad, 2003; Inayatullah and Blaney, 2004) and for an inter-cultural reconceptualisation of the notions of the 'political', the 'secular' and the 'religious'.

REFERENCES

News Sources

Al-Ahram Weekly (Egypt)
Aljazeera.net (Qatar)
Al-Risalah (Gaza)
Associated Press (New York)
bbc.co.uk (London)
BBC Monitoring Middle East (London)
Birmingham Post (Birmingham)
Boston Globe (Boston)
CBCNews.ca (Toronto)
Chicago Sun-Times (Chicago)
Chicago Tribune (Chicago)
Christian Science Monitor (Boston)
CNN (Atlanta)
Daily Star (Beirut)
Daily Telegraph (London)
Falastin al-Muslimah (London)
Guardian and *Guardian Weekly* (Manchester)
Gulf Daily News (Manama, Bahrain)
Ha'aretz (Tel Aviv)
Independent (London)
International Herald Tribune (Paris)
IsraelNationalNews.com/Arutz Sheva
Jerusalem Post (Jerusalem)
Jerusalem Times (Jerusalem)
Los Angeles Times (Los Angeles)

Mideast Mirror (London)
New York Times (New York)
New Yorker (New York)
Palestine Report (Jerusalem)
palestine-info.co.uk
PalToday News (Gaza)
San Francisco Chronicle (San Francisco)
Stratfor.biz (Austin TX)
Times (London)
Turkish Daily News (Ankara)
Wall Street Journal (New York)
Washington Post (Washington DC)

CITED INTERVIEWS AND CONVERSATIONS

'Abd al-Haq, Yusuf (1998). Lecturer al-Najah University, 1980s PFLP activist. Nablus, 20 May.

Abu Shannab, Ismail (1998a). Senior Hamas leader, Gaza, killed by the IDF in August 2003. Gaza, 5 May.

—— (1998b). Gaza, 16 May.

—— (1998c). Gaza, 6 June.

—— (1998d). Gaza, 13 July.

—— (1999). Gaza, 20 March.

—— (2002). Gaza, December.

Abu Zughri, Sami (1998). Hamas spokesperson and former President of Student Union, Islamic University Gaza. Gaza, 6 June.

'Ahmad' (1998). Hamas supporter and Islamic University student. Gaza, 9 May.

al-Bardawil, Salah (1998). Spokesperson Hizb al-Khalas and PLC Member. Gaza, 27 April.

al-Jarro', Yunis (1998). Lawyer and PFLP representative. Gaza, 1 June.

al-Kurd, Ahmad (1998). Director al-Salah Charity and mayor of Deir al-Balah since 2005. Deir al-Balah, 25 April.

al-Masri, 'Arafah (1998). Islamic Bloc leader and Member Student Council, Islamic University, Gaza. Gaza, 25 April.

al-Na'ami, Salah (1998). Hizb al-Khalas member, *al-Risalah* journalist, former Hamas activist. Gaza, 10 May.

al-Rantisi, 'Abd al-'Aziz (2002a). Senior Hamas leader, Gaza, killed by the IDF in April 2004. Gaza, December.

—— (2002b). Gaza, December.

al-Sourani, Raji (1998). Director Palestinian Centre for Human Rights. Gaza, 5 May.

al-Yazuri, Ibrahim (1998). Hamas founder and former Director al-Mujamma' al-Islami. Gaza, 11 June.

al-Zahhar, Mahmud (1998a). Hamas founder, PLC Member, Foreign Minister in first Hamas Government. Gaza, 23 March.

—— (1998b). Gaza, 2 May.

'Ashraf' (1998). Hamas activist (Intifada) and Islamic Bloc student member (1990s). Gaza, 16 May.

Bahr, Ahmad (1998). Hamas founder, Head Hizb al-Khalas (late 1990s). Gaza, 1 June.

Director Women's Training Centre (1998). (Female) Director and staff of one of al-Mujamma' al-Islami's Women's Training Centres. Gaza Strip, 22 March.

Dukhan, 'Abd al-Fattah (1998). Hamas founder and PLC member. Gaza, 9 June.

Fatah PLC Member (1998). Board Member Gaza Centre for Rights and Law. Gaza, 10 June.

FCO Official (2006). Foreign & Commonwealth Office. London, March.

Hamad, Ghazi (1998a). Hamas Government spokesperson and Chief Editor of *al-Risalah*. Gaza, 26 May.

—— (1998b). Gaza, 4 June.

Hamami, Jamil (1997). Senior West Bank Hamas leader. By telephone. Jerusalem, May.

Hamas and Khalas members (1999). Group interview with Hamas and Hizb al-Khalas members. Gaza, 20 March.

Hamas Cell (1998a). Group interview with former Intifada cell. Gaza, 17 May.

—— (1998b). Gaza, 26 May.

—— (1998c). Gaza, 7 June.

Hamdan, Usama (2002). Hamas spokesman, Lebanon. Beirut, April.

—— (2004). Beirut, May.

Hamdan, Yusrah (1998). Member Political Bureau Hizb al-Khalas, former student leader Women's Islamic Bloc, Islamic University Gaza (1980s). Gaza, 9 May.

Haniyyah, Ismail (1998a). Prime Minister of first Hamas Government, Dean Islamic University (1990s), Hamas student leader (1980s). Gaza, 16 May.

—— (1998b). Gaza, 12 July.

Head Islamic Bloc al-Azhar (1998). Head Islamic Bloc, al-Azhar University Gaza. Gaza, 30 May.

'Ibrahim' (1998). Director Islamist Charity and Hamas member. Khan Yunis, 7 March.

Islamic Bloc leader (1998). College of Education Student Council leader. Gaza, 7 June.

Islamic Bloc members (1998). Conversations with Islamic Bloc members at Islamic University Gaza. Gaza, 2 May.

Islamist and leftist women (1998). Group interview with Islamist and leftist women. Gaza, 16 May.

'Iyad' (1998). Hamas member. Gaza, 2 June.

'Khalid' (1998). Islamic University alumnus and non-aligned Islamist. Gaza, March.

—— (2000). Gaza, May.

Mish'al, Khalid (2002). Head Political Bureau. Damascus, April.

'Muhammad' (1998). Former Hamas cadre and Muslim Brother. Gaza, 3 May.

Musa, Yahya (1998a). Head Political Bureau Hizb al-Khalas (late 1990s), former Islamic Bloc student leader (1980s). Gaza, 4 May.

—— (1998b). Gaza, 1 July.

—— (1999). Gaza, 21 March.

Muslih, Muhammad (1998). Managing Director al-Mujamma' al-Islami. Gaza, 4 March.

Muslim Girls Association (1998). Staff at al-Jam'iyyah al-Shabbat al-Muslimat. Gaza, 24 March.

'Nasr' (1998). Hamas supporter and Islamic University alumnus. Gaza, 28 May.

Perry, Mark (2005). Director Conflicts Forum. Amman, 10 October.

Pharmaciens sans frontières (1998). Staff Gaza office. Gaza, February.

Pro-Hamas Students (1998). Informal conversations with pro-Hamas students at the Islamic University. Gaza, May-June.

Qassim, Marwa (1998a). Gaza coordinator of Women's Model Parliament, former PFLP student activist. Gaza, 19 March.

—— (1998b). Gaza, 27 May.

Rantisi, Mohammed (2003). Research assistant, Gaza. By telephone. June.

—— (2007). By telephone. June.

Salim, Jamal (1998). Senior Hamas leader, West Bank, killed by the IDF in July 2001. Nablus, 21 May.

Sarraj-Mattar, Shadia (1998). Director Women's Empowerment Project, Gaza Mental Health Project. Gaza, 10 May.

Selby, Jan (2006). Political economy of peace processes. Department of International Politics, University of Sussex. By telephone. August.

Shahadah, Ibrahim (1998). Director Gaza Centre for Rights and Law. Gaza, 10 June.

Shamma', Muhammad (1998). Director al-Mujamma' al-Islami. Gaza, 22 March.

—— (2006). Interview by research assistant M. Rantisi. Gaza, June.

Smith-Polfus, Turid (1998). Norwegian Researcher. Gaza, 27 April.

Taha, Ayman (1998). President Student Council Islamic University Gaza (1998), Qassam commander (2000s). Gaza, 30 May.

Tamimi, Azzam (2007). Founder Institute of Islamic Political Thought, London and author of *Hamas: Unwritten Chapters* (Hurst, 2006).

Turk, 'Abd al-Rahman (1998). Lecturer al-Najah University and Fatah 1980s student leader. Nablus, 20 May.

Wheeler, Linda (1998). Coordinator Mennonite Central Committee. Gaza, 17 May.

Women's Islamic Bloc I (1998). Student leaders of Women's Islamic Bloc, Islamic University Gaza. Gaza, 3 June.

Women's Islamic Bloc II (1998). Student leaders of Women's Islamic Bloc, Islamic University Gaza. Gaza, 7 June.

Yassin, Ahmad (1998a). Founder of Hamas and titular head prior to his March 2004 assassination by the IDF. Gaza, 7 February.

—— (1998b). Gaza, 8 February.

'Yusuf' (1998). Islamic Bloc leader and Member Student Council Islamic University. Gaza, 6 June.

Books and Articles

Abdallah, Hisham (2003). 'Long hard road to truce passes through Israeli prison', *Agence France Presse*, 30 June.

Abu-Amr, Ziad (1993). 'Hamas: A Historical and Political Background', *Journal of Palestine Studies*, XXII (4), Summer: 5-19.

—— (1994). *Islamic Fundamentalism in the West Bank and Gaza: Muslim Brotherhood and Islamic Jihad*. Bloomington, IN: Indiana University Press.

Abu Marzook, Mousa, and Roger Gaess (1997). 'Interview with Mousa Abu Marzook', *Middle East Policy*, V (2), May: 113-28.

Abu Shannab, Ismail (1998). 'The Islamic Approach and the Subject of Democracy [Arabic]'. Paper presented at *The case of democracy in Palestine*. Palestinian Council for Foreign Relations, Gaza. 11 July.

Adlakha, Arjun, Kevin Kinsella, and Marwan Khawaja (1995). 'Demography of the Palestinian population with special emphasis on the occupied territories', *Population Bulletin of ESCWA*, 43: 5-28.

Agha, Hussein, and Robert Malley (2001). 'Camp David: The Tragedy of Errors', *New York Review of Books*, 9 August.

Ahmad, Hisham (1994). *Hamas: From Religious Salvation to Political Transformation - The Rise of Hamas in Palestinian Society*. Jerusalem: Palestinian Academic Society for the Study of International Affairs.

al-Fenjari, Ahmed (1998). 'The system of punishment in Islam... Does it suit our present age?', *al-Risalah*, 6 April, 16, 9.

al-Husaini, Ishak (1956). *The Moslem Brethren: the greatest of modern Islamic movements*. trans. by John Brown and John Racy. Beirut: Khayat's College Book Cooperative.

al-Turabi, Hassan (1983). 'The Islamic State' in John Esposito, ed., *Voices of resurgent Islam*. New York, NY: Oxford University Press, pp. 241-51.

Amayreh, Khaled (1999). 'Hamas gains at Fatah's expense', *Al-Ahram Weekly Online*, 1-7 April.

Amundsen, Inge, and Basem Ezbidi (2004). 'PNA political institutions and the future of state formation' in Mushtaq Khan, George Giacaman and Inge Amundsen, eds., *State Formation in Palestine: Viability and governance during a social transformation*. London: RoutledgeCurzon, pp. 141-67.

Anderson, Lisa (1986). *The State and Social Transformation in Tunisia and Libya, 1830-1980*. Princeton, NJ: Princeton University Press.

Andoni, Lamis (1996). 'The Palestinian Elections: Moving toward Democracy or One-Party Rule', *Journal of Palestine Studies*, 25 (3), Spring: 5-16.

Asad, Talal (1993). 'The Construction of Religion as an Anthropological Category' in Talal Asad, ed., *Genealogies of Religion: discipline and reasons of power in Christianity and Islam*. Baltimore, MD: Johns Hopkins University Press, pp. 27-54.

—— (2003). *Formations of the Secular: Christianity, Islam, Modernity*. Stanford, CA: Stanford University Press.

Avi, Issacharoff, and Harel Amos (2006). 'Lost innocents', *Ha'aretz*, 16 June.

Avineri, Shlomo (1972). *Hegel's Theory of the Modern State*. Cambridge: Cambridge University Press.

B'Tselem (n.d.). *Intifada Fatalities*. Statistics. <http://www.btselem.org/English/Statistics/Casualties.asp>.

Barghouti, Iyad (1991). 'Religion and Politics among the Students of the Najah National University', *Middle Eastern Studies*, 27 (2), April: 203-18.

—— (1996). 'Islamist Movements in Historical Palestine' in Abdel Salam Sidahmed and Anoushiravan Ehteshami, eds., *Islamic fundamentalism*. Boulder, CO; Westview Press, pp. 163-77.

Barnett, Michael (2001). 'Authority, intervention, and the outer limits of international relations theory' in Thomas Callaghy, Ronald Kassimir and Robert Latham, eds., *Intervention and Transnationalism in Africa: Global-Local Networks of Power*. Cambridge: Cambridge University Press, pp. 47-65.

Be'er, Yizhar, and Saleh Dr 'Abdel-Jawad (1994). *Collaborators in the Occupied Territories: Human Rights Abuses and Violations*. Jerusalem: B'Tselem The Israeli Information Center for Human Rights in the Occupied Territories. January.

Beblawi, Hazem, and Giacomo Luciani, eds. (1987). *The Rentier State*. London: Croom Helm.

Beilin, Yossi (1999). *Touching Peace: From the Olso Accord to a Final Agreement*. London: Weidenfeld & Nicolson.

Benhabib, Seyla (1984). 'Obligation, Contract and Exchange: The Opening Arguments of Hegel's Philosophy of Right' in Z.A. Pelczynski, ed., *The State and Civil Society: Studies in Hegel's Political Philosophy*. Cambridge: Cambridge University Press, pp. 159-77.

Berlin, Isaiah (1969). 'Two Concepts of Liberty' in Isaiah Berlin, ed., *Four Essays on Liberty*. Oxford: Oxford University Press, pp. 118-72.

Berrebi, Claude (2003). 'Evidence About The Link Between Education, Poverty and Terrorism Among Palestinians'. Princeton University Industrial Relations Section Working Paper No. 477.

Bickerton, Ian, and Carla Klausner (2007). *A history of the Arab-Israeli conflict*. 5th edn. Upper Saddle River, NJ: Pearson Prentice Hall.

BICOM (2006). *Biographies of Hamas Cabinet*. London: Britain Israel Communications and Research Centre. <http://www.bicom.org.uk>.

Birch, Anthony (1993). *The Concepts and Theories of Modern Democracy*. London: Routledge.

Bloom, Mia (2005). *Dying to Kill: The Global Phenomenon of Suicide Terror*. New York, NY: Columbia University Press.

Bourdieu, Pierre (1986). 'The Forms of Capital' in John Richardson, ed., *Handbook of Theory and Research for the Sociology of Education*. Westport, CT: Greenwood Press, pp. 241-58.

——— (1991). *Language and Symbolic Power*. trans. by Gino Raymond and Matthew Adamson. Cambridge: Polity Press.

Bourdieu, Pierre, and Jean-Claude Passeron (1973). 'Cultural Reproduction and Social Reproduction' in Richard Brown, ed., *Knowledge, Education and Cultural Change*. London: Tavistock.

Bromley, Simon (1994). *Rethinking Middle East Politics: State Formation and Development*. Cambridge: Polity Press.

Burgat, François (1993). *The Islamic movement in North Africa*. Trans. by William Dowell. Austin, TX: Center for Middle Eastern Studies, University of Texas at Austin.

——— (2003). *Face to face with political Islam*. London: I.B. Tauris.

Butler, Judith (1996). 'Universality in Culture' in Joshua Cohen, ed., *For Love of Country: Debating the Limits of Patriotism - Martha C. Nussbaum with respondents*. Boston, MA: Beacon Press, pp. 45-52.

Carter, April (1979). *Authority and Democracy*. London: Routledge & Kegan Paul.

CECP (2006). *The Second 2006 PLC Elections: The Final Results For the Electoral Districts*. Ramallah: Central Elections Commission Palestine. <http://www.elections.ps/pdf/Final_Result_PLC_Dist_Seats_2_En.pdf>.

Chehab, Zaki (2007). *Inside Hamas: The Untold Story of Militants, Martyrs and Spies*. London: I.B. Tauris.

Cleveland, William (1994). *A History of the Modern Middle East*. Boulder, Co: Westview Press.

Cohen, Amnon (1982). *Political parties in the West Bank under the Jordanian regime, 1949-1967*. Ithaca, NY: Cornell University Press.

Crelinsten, R.D. (1987). 'Terrorism as Political Communication: The Relationship between the Controller and the Controlled' in Paul Wilkinson and Alasdair Stewart, eds., *Contemporary Research on Terrorism*. Aberdeen: Aberdeen University Press, pp. 3-23.

Crenshaw, Martha (1981). 'The Causes of Terrorism', *Comparative Politics*, 13 (4), July: 379-99.

——— (1991). 'How terrorism declines', *Terrorism and Political Violence*, 3 (1): 69-87.

——, ed. (1995a). *Terrorism in Context*. University Park, PA: Pennsylvania State University Press.

—— (1995b). 'Thoughts on Relating Terrorism to Historical Contexts' in Martha Crenshaw, ed., *Terrorism in Context*. University Park, PA: Pennsylvania State University Press, pp. 3-24.

Cullen, Bernard (1979). *Hegel's social and political thought: an introduction*. Dublin: Gill & Macmillan.

Dalacoura, Katerina (1998). *Islam, liberalism and human rights: implications for international relations*. London: I. B. Tauris.

Davies, James (1975). 'The J-Curve of Rising and Declining Satisfactions as a Cause of Some Great Revolutions and a Contained Rebellion' in Sam Sarkesian, ed., *Revolutionary Guerrilla Warfare*. Chicago: Precedent Publishing, pp. 117-41.

della Porta, Donatella (1995a). 'Left-Wing Terrorism in Italy' in Martha Crenshaw, ed., *Terrorism in Context*. University Park, PA: Pennsylvania State University Press, pp. 105-59.

—— (1995b). *Social movements, political violence, and the state: a comparative analysis of Italy and Germany*. Cambridge: Cambridge University Press.

——, ed. (1992). *Social Movements and Violence: Participation in Underground Organizations*. London: JAI Press.

Denoeux, Guilain (1993). *Urban unrest in the Middle East: a comparative study of informal networks in Egypt, Iran and Lebanon*. Albany: State University of New York Press.

Derrida, Jacques (1981). *Positions*. trans. by Alan Bass. London: Athlone.

—— (1982). *Différance*. Brighton: Harvester Press.

Derrida, Jacques, and Gayatri Chakravorty Spivak (1976). *Of grammatology*. Baltimore, MD: Johns Hopkins University Press.

Diamond, Larry (1992). 'Economic Development and Democracy Reconsidered', *American Behavioral Scientist*, 35 (4/5), March/June: 450-99.

Diamond, Larry, Juan Linz, and Seymour Lipset, eds. (1995). *Politics in Developing Countries: comparing experiences with democracy*. 2nd edn. London: Lynne Rienner.

Diani, Mario (1992). 'The concept of social movement', *Sociological Review*, 40 (1), February: 1-25.

Dunn, Ross (1996). 'Hamas withdrawal undermines Palestinian poll', *Times*, 3 January.

Eckstein, Harry, and Ted Gurr (1975). *Patterns of Authority: A Structural Basis for Political Inquiry*. New York, NY: John Wiley & Sons.

Eickelman, Dale, and James Piscatori (1996). *Muslim politics*. Princeton, NJ: Princeton University Press.

el-Awa, Mohamed (1980). *On the political system of the Islamic state*. Indianapolis, IN: American Trust Publications.

el-Awaisi, Abd al-Fattah M. (1998). *The Muslim brothers and the Palestine question, 1928-1947*. London: Tauris Academic Studies.

el Sarraj, Eyad (2002). 'Suicide Bombers: Dignity, Despair, and the Need for Hope; An Interview with Eyad El Sarraj', *Journal of Palestine Studies*, XXXI (4), Summer: 71-6.

Ephron, Dan (2005). 'Power Play', *New Republic*, 11 January.

Esposito, John (1999). *The Islamic threat: myth or reality?* 3rd edn. New York, NY: Oxford University Press.

Euben, Roxanne (1999). *Enemy in the mirror: Islamic fundamentalism and the limits of modern rationalism*. Princeton, NJ: Princeton University Press.

FairVote (2006). *It's The Election System, Stupid*. MD: FairVote Program for Representative Government. <http://www.fairvote. org/media/pep/Palestine.pdf>.

Farsoun, Samih (1988). 'Class Structure and Social Change in the Arab World: 1995' in Hisham Sharabi, ed., *The Next Arab Decade: Alternative Futures*. Boulder, CO: Westview Press, pp. 221-38.

Farsoun, Samih, and Lisa Hajjar (1990). 'The Contemporary Sociology of the Middle East: An Assessment' in Hisham Sharabi, ed., *Theory, Politics and the Arab World: Critical Responses*. New York, NY: Routledge and Center for Contemporary Arab Studies, Georgetown University, pp. 160-97.

Fay, Brian (1996). *Contemporary Philosophy of Social Science: a multicultural approach*. Oxford: Blackwell.

Friedman, R.B. (1990). 'On the Concept of Authority in Political Philosophy' in Joseph Raz, ed., *Authority*. Oxford: Basil Blackwell, pp. 56-91.

Frisch, Hillel (1993). 'The Palestinian Movement in the Territories: The Middle Command', *Middle East Studies*, 29 (2), April: 254-74.

―――― (2005). 'Has the Israeli-Palestinian conflict become Islamic? Fatah, Islam and the al-Aqsa Martyrs' Brigades', *Terrorism and Political Violence*, 17 (3), October: 391-406.

Gaess, Roger (2002). 'Interviews from Gaza: What Hamas Wants', *Middle East Policy*, IX (4), December: 102-15.

George, Alexander (1991). 'The Discipline of Terrorology' in Alexander George, ed., *Western State Terrorism*. Cambridge: Polity Press.

Ghannouchi, Rashid (1993). 'The Participation of Islamists in a Non-Islamic Government' in Azzam Tamimi, ed., *Power-Sharing Islam?* London: Liberty for Muslim World Publications.

Giacaman, George (1998). 'In the Throes of Oslo: Palestinian Society, Civil Society and the Future' in George Giacaman and Dag Lønning, eds., *After Oslo: new realities, old problems*. London: Pluto Press, pp. 1-15.

Gill, Graeme (2000). *The Dynamics of Democratization: Elites, Civil Society and the Transition Process*. Basingstoke: Macmillan.

Goldstone, Jack (2002). 'Population and security: How demographic change can lead to violent conflict', *Journal of International Affairs*, 56 (1), Fall: 3-21.

―――― , ed. (2003). *States, Parties, and Social Movements*. Cambridge: Cambridge University Press.

Graham-Brown, Sarah (1984). 'Impact on the Social Structure of Palestinian Society' in Naseer Aruri, ed., *Occupation: Israel over Palestine*. London: Zed Books, pp. 223-54.

Gramsci, Antonio (1971 [1929-35]). *Selections from the prison notebooks of Antonio Gramsci*. trans. by Quintin Hoare and Geoffrey Nowell-Smith. London: Lawrence and Wishart.

Grant, Audra, and Mark Tessler (2002). 'Palestinian Attitudes Toward Democracy and Its Compatibility with Islam: Evidence from Public Opinion Research in the West Bank and Gaza', *Arab Studies Quarterly*, 24 (4), Fall: 1-20.

Grinstein, Gidi, *et al.* (2001), 'Camp David: An Exchange', *New York Review of Books*, 20 September.

Gunning, Jeroen (2000). 'Re-Thinking Western Constructs of Islamism: Pluralism, Democracy and the Theory and Praxis of the Islamic Movement in the Gaza Strip'. Unpublished PhD Thesis. University of Durham.

—— (2004). 'Peace with Hamas? The transforming potential of political participation', *International Affairs*, 80 (2), March: 233-55.

—— (2007a). 'Hamas: Socialization and the Logic of Compromise' in Marianne Heiberg, Brendan O'Leary and John Tirman, eds., *Terror, Insurgency, and the State: Ending Protracted Conflicts*. Philadelphia, PA: University of Pennsylvania Press, pp. 123-54.

—— (2007b). 'Terrorism, Charities and Diasporas: Contrasting the fundraising practices of Hamas and al Qaeda among Muslims in Europe' in Thomas Biersteker and Sue Eckert, eds., *Countering the Financing of Terrorism*. London: Routledge.

—— (2007c). 'A Case for Critical Terrorism Studies?', *Government and Opposition*, 42 (3), Summer: 363-93.

Gupta, Dipak, and Kusum Mundra (2005). 'Suicide Bombing as a Strategic Weapon: An Empirical Investigation of Hamas and Islamic Jihad', *Terrorism and Political Violence*, 17 (4): 573-98.

Gurr, Ted (1975). 'Psychological Factors in Civil Violence' in Sam Sarkesian, ed., *Revolutionary Guerrilla Warfare*. Chicago, IL: Precedent Publishing, pp. 75-114.

Hadenius, A. (1992). *Democracy and Development*. Cambridge: Cambridge University Press.

Hafez, Mohammed, and Quintan Wiktorowicz (2004). 'Violence as Contention in the Egyptian Islamic Movement' in Quintan Wiktorowicz, ed., *Islamic Activism: a social movement theory approach*. Bloomington, IN: Indiana University Press, pp. 61-88.

Halliday, Fred (1996). *Islam and the Myth of Confrontation: religion and politics in the Middle East*. London: Tauris.

Hamad, Ghazi (2005). 'A murder in Gaza', *Palestine Report*, 20 April.

Hamas (2006). *Election Manifesto of the Change and Reform list [Arabic]*.

Hamas Leaders (n.d.). Al-Qassam Website. <http://www.alqassam. ps/english/hamasleaders/hamas.htm>.

Hammami, Rema (1990). 'Women, the Hijab and the Intifada', *Middle East Report,* 20 (3-4), May-August: 24-8.

Hammami, Rema, and Penny Johnson (1999). 'Equality with a Difference: Gender and Citizenship in Transitional Palestine', *Social Politics,* 6 (3), Fall 1999: 314-43.

Hanafi, Sari, and Linda Tabar (2004). 'Donor assistance, rent-seeking and elite formation' in Mushtaq Khan, George Giacaman and Inge Amundsen, eds., *State Formation in Palestine: Viability and governance during a social transformation.* London: Routledge-Curzon, pp. 215-38.

Hanf, Theodor, and Bernard Sabella (1996). *A Date with Democracy— Palestinians on Society and Politics. An empirical survey.* trans. by John Richardson. Freiburg: Arnold-Bergstraesser-Institut.

Hannigan, John (1991). 'Social Movement Theory and the Sociology of Religion: Toward a New Synthesis', *Sociological Analysis,* 52 (4): 311-31.

Harb el-Kak, Mona (2001). 'Pratiques comparées de participation dan deux municipalités de la banlieue de Beyrouth: Ghbairé et Borj el-Brajneh' in Agnès Favier, ed., *Municipalités et pouvoirs locaux au Liban.* Beirut: Centre d'études et de recherches sur le Moyen-Orient contemporain, pp. 157-177.

Hart, Alan (1984). *Arafat: Terrorist or Peacemaker?* London: Sidgwick & Jackson.

Hasenclever, Andreas, and Volker Rittberger (2003). 'Does Religion Make a Difference? Theoretical Approaches to the Impact of Faith on Political Conflict' in Pavlos Hatzopoulos and Fabio Petito, eds., *Religion in International Affairs: The Return from Exile.* New York: Palgrave Macmillan, pp. 107-45.

Hegel, Georg Wilhelm Friedrich (1942). *Hegel's Philosophy of Right.* trans. by T.M. Knox. Oxford: Clarendon Press.

Heiberg, Marianne, John Tirman, and Brendan O'Leary, eds. (2007). *Terror, Insurgency, and the State: Ending Protracted Conflicts* Philadelphia, PA: University of Pennsylvania Press.

Herman, Edward, and Gerry O'Sullivan (1990). *The Terrorism Industry: The Experts and Institutions that Shape our View of Terror.* New York, NY: Pantheon.

Hervieu-Léger, Danièle (2000). *Religion as a chain of memory.* Transl. Simon Lee. Cambridge: Polity Press.

Hilal, Jamil (2006). 'Hamas's Rise as Charted in the Polls, 1994-2005', *Journal of Palestine Studies,* XXXV (3), Spring: 6-19.

Hilal, Jamil, and Mushtaq Khan (2004). 'State formation under the PNA' in Mushtaq Khan, George Giacaman and Inge Amundsen, eds., *State Formation in Palestine: Viability and governance during a social transformation.* London: RoutledgeCurzon, pp. 64-119.

Hiltermann, Joost (1991). *Behind the Intifada: Labor and Women's Movements in the Occupied Territories.* Princeton, NJ: Princeton University Press.

Hizb al-Khalas (1997a). *Barnamaj Siyasi* [Political Programme]. Gaza: Prepared by Second Session of the Party's First General Conference. 11 December.

—— (1997b). 'Conference Paper' [Arabic]. Paper presented at *Political Conference for the National and Islamic Forces concerning National Relations.* 31 August.

—— (1997c). 'Conference Paper' [Arabic]. Paper presented at *Political Conference for the National and Islamic Forces concerning National Relations.* 1 September.

Hoffman, Bruce (1998). *Inside terrorism.* London: Victor Gollancz.

Hoffman, Bruce, and Gordon McCormick (2004). 'Terrorism, Signaling, and Suicide Attack', *Studies in Conflict and Terrorism,* 27 (4): 243-81.

Holt, Maria (1997). 'Palestinian Women and the Contemporary Islamist Movement', *Encounters: Journal of Inter-Cultural Perspectives,* 3 (1), March: 64-75.

The Holy Qur'an (1946). trans. by Yusuf Ali. Birmingham: Islamic Propagation Centre International.

Horgan, John (2004). 'The Case for Firsthand Research' in Andrew Silke, ed., *Research on Terrorism: Trends, Achievements and Failures.* London: Frank Cass, pp. 30-56.

—— (2006). 'Understanding Terrorism: Old Assumptions, New Assertions, and Challenges for Research' in J. Victoroff, ed., *Tangled Roots: Social and Psychological Factors in the Genesis of Terrorism.* Amsterdam: IOS Press/NATO Public Diplomacy Division, pp. 74-84.

Houlgate, Stephen (2005). *An Introduction to Hegel: Freedom, Truth and History*. Oxford: Blackwell Publishers.

Hroub, Khaled (2000). *Hamas: Political Thought and Practice*. Washington, DC: Institute for Palestine Studies.

—— (2006a). *Hamas: A Beginner's Guide*. London: Pluto Press.

—— (2006b). Paper presented at *Palestinian politics since the elections*. Chatham House. 10 October.

—— (2006c). 'Hamas's path to reinvention', *Open Democracy*, 10 October.

—— (2007). 'Hamas in government'. Paper presented at *A meeting about Hamas*. Foreign & Commonwealth Office. 17 April.

Hunter, F. Robert (1991). *The Palestinian uprising: a war by other means*. London: I.B. Tauris.

Hunter, Shireen (1995). 'The Rise of Islamist Movements and the Western Response: Clash of Civilizations or Clash of Interests' in Laura Guazzone, ed., *The Islamist dilemma: the political role of Islamist movements in the contemporary Arab world*. Reading: Ithaca, pp. 317-50.

Huntington, Samuel P. (1998). *The clash of civilizations and the remaking of world order*. London: Touchstone.

ICG (2006a). *Enter Hamas: The Challenges of Political Integration*. Brussels: International Crisis Group. 18 January.

—— (2006b). *The Arab-Israeli Conflict: To Reach a Lasting Peace*. Brussels: International Crisis Group. 5 October.

—— (2007a). *After Mecca: Engaging Hamas*. Brussels: International Crisis Group. 28 February.

—— (2007b). *After Gaza*. Brussels: International Crisis Group. 2 August.

ICT (2005). *Breakdown of Fatalities: 27 September 2000 through 1 January 2005*. Herzliya: International Institute for Counter-Terrorism. <http://www.ict.org.il/casualties_project/stats_page.cfm>.

—— (n.d.). *Database: Incidents*. Herzliya. International Institute for Counter-Terrorism. <http://www.instituteforcounterterrorism.org/apage/10583.php>.

IDF (2002). *Nablus' Al-Najah University: Breeding Ground for Suicide Bombers*. Tel Aviv: Israeli Defense Forces. 26 August. <http://www.idf.il/newsite/english/alnajah/alnajah.stm>.

—— (2004). *Successful vs. Unsuccessful (thwarted) Terrorist Attacks*. Tel Aviv: Israeli Defense Forces. <http://www1.idf.il/SIP_STORAGE/DOVER/files/6/31646.doc>.

Ilardi, Gaetano (2004). 'Redefining the Issues: The Future of Terrorism Research and the Search for Empathy' in Andrew Silke, ed., *Research on Terrorism: Trends, Achievements and Failures*. London: Frank Cass, pp. 214-28.

Inayatullah, Naeem, and David Blaney (2004). *International relations and the problem of difference*. London: Routledge.

Iqbal, Mohammed (1930). *Six Lectures on the Reconstruction of Religious Thought in Islam*. Lahore: Kapur Art Printing Works.

Irvin, Cynthia (1999). *Militant Nationalism*. Minneapolis, MI: University of Minnesota Press.

ITIC (2005). *"Charity" and Palestinian terrorism - spotlight on Hamas-run Islamic Al-Tadhamun "charitable society" in Nablus*. Special Information Bulletin. Intelligence and Terrorism Information Center. February. <http://www.intelligence.org.il>

Jarbawi, Ali (1994). 'The Position of the Palestinian Islamists on the Palestine-Israel Accord', *Muslim World*, LXXXIV (1-2), January-April: 127-54.

Jensen, Michael Irving (1998). 'Islamism and Civil Society in the Gaza Strip' in Ahmad Moussalli, ed., *Islamic Fundamentalism: Myths & Realities*. Reading: Ithaca, pp. 197-220.

JMCC (2006). *Palestinian National Authority: The PA Ministerial Cabinet List*. Jerusalem: Jerusalem Media & Communication Centre. March.

Johnson, Merwyn (1977). *Locke on freedom: an incisive study of the thought of John Locke*. Austin, TX: Best Printing.

Johnson, Nels (1984 [1982]). *Islam and the Politics of Meaning in Palestinian Nationalism*. London: Kegan Paul.

Juergensmeyer, Mark (2000). *Terror in the mind of God: the global rise of religious violence*. Berkeley, CA: University of California Press.

Kalman, Matthew (2006a). 'Fatah won the vote, but Hamas won the election', *San Francisco Chronicle*, 26 January.

———— (2006b). 'Secret democracy elevated Hamas, Underground campaign unified voters', *San Francisco Chronicle*, 19 February.

Kamali, Mohammad (1991). *Principles of Islamic jurisprudence*. Revised edn. Cambridge: Islamic Texts Society.

KAS (2006). *Result of the Palestinian legislative elections on 25 January 2006 [Die Wahlen zum Palästinensischen Legislativrat vom 25. Januar 2006]*. Ramallah: Konrad-Adenauer-Stiftung. April. <http://www.kas.de/db_files/dokumente/7_dokument_dok_pdf_8306_1.pdf>.

Keane, John (2002). 'The Limits of Secularism' in Azzam Tamimi and John Esposito, eds., *Islam and Secularism in the Middle East*. London: Hurst, pp. 29-37.

Kelsay, John (1990). 'Islam and the Distinction between Combatants and Noncombatanst', in James Johnson and John Kelsay, eds., *Cross, Crescent and Sword: The Justification and Limitation of War in Western and Islamic Tradition*. Westport, CT: Greenwood Press, pp. 197-220.

Kepel, Gilles (2002). *Jihad: the trail of political Islam*. London: I.B. Tauris.

Kerr, Malcolm (1966). *Islamic reform: The Political and Legal Theories of Muhammad 'Abduh and Rashid Rida*. Berkeley, CA: University of California Press.

Kim, Dongno (1994). 'Capitalist development and democracy: Book Review', *The American Journal of Sociology*, 100 (1), July: 267-8.

Kimmerling, Baruch, and Joel Migdal (1994). *Palestinians: The Making of a People*. Cambridge, MA: Harvard University Press.

Klein, Menachem (1996). 'Competing Brothers: The Web of Hamas-PLO Relations', *Terrorism and Political Violence*, 8 (2), Summer: 111-32.

———— (2007). 'Hamas in Power', *Middle East Journal*, 61 (3), Summer: 442-59.

Kotb [Qutb], Sayyid (1953). *Social Justice in Islam* [Al-'adalah al-ijtima'iyyah fi al-islam]. trans. by John Hardie. Washington, DC: American Council of Learned Studies.

Kramer, Martin (1990). 'The moral logic of Hizballah' in Walter Reich, ed., *Origins of terrorism: psychologies, ideologies, theologies, states of mind*. Cambridge: Cambridge University Press.

Kristianasen, Wendy (1999). 'Challenge and counterchallenge: Hamas' response to Oslo', *Journal of Palestine Studies*, 28 (3), Spring: 19-36.

Krueger, Alan, and Jitka Malečková (2003). 'Education, poverty and terrorism: is there a causal connection?', *Journal of Economic Perspectives*, 17 (4), Fall: 119-44.

Kumaraswamy, P.R. (2005). 'The Cairo Dialogue and the Palestinian Power Struggle', *International Studies*, 42 (1): 43-59.

Kydd, Andrew, and Barbara Walter (2002). 'Sabotaging the Peace: The Politics of Extremist Violence', *International Organization*, 56 (2), Spring: 263-96.

Lachman, Shai (1982). 'Arab Rebellion and Terrorism in Palestine 1929-39: The Case of Sheikh Izz al-Din al-Qassam and his Movement' in Elie Kedourie and Sylvia Haim, eds., *Zionism and Arabism in Palestine and Israel*. London: Frank Cass, pp. 52-99.

Laub, Karin (2003). 'Truce is result of 10 months of excruciating stop-and-go talks', *The Associated Press*, 30 June.

Laustsen, Carsten, and Ole Waever (2003). 'In Defense of Religion: Sacred Referent Objects for Securitization' in Pavlos Hatzopoulos and Fabio Petito, eds., *Religion in International Affairs: The Return from Exile*. New York, NY: Palgrave Macmillan, pp. 147-80.

Leca, Jean (1994). 'Democratization in the Arab World - Uncertainty, vulnerability and legitimacy. A tentative conceptualization and some hypotheses' in Ghassan Salamé, ed., *Democracy without democrats? - The renewal of politics in the Muslim world*. London: I.B. Tauris, Fondazione ENI Enrico Mattei, pp. 23-47.

Legrain, Jean-François (1990). 'The Islamic Movement and the *Intifada*' in Roger Heacock and Jamal R. Nassar, eds., *Intifada: Palestine at the Crossroads*. New York, NY: Praeger, pp. 175-89.

—— (1991). 'A defining moment: Palestinian Islamic Fundamentalism' in James Piscatori, ed., *Islamic fundamentalisms and the Gulf crisis*. Chicago, IL: American Academy of Arts and Sciences, pp. 70-87.

Levitt, Matthew (2006). *Hamas: Politics, Charity, and Terrorism in the Service of Jihad*. New Haven, CT: Yale University Press and the Washington Institute for Near East Policy.

Lia, Brynjar, and Katja Skølberg (2005). *Causes of Terrorism: An Expanded and Updated Review of the Literature*. Kjeller, Norway: Norwegian Defence Research Establishment (FFI).

Light, Margot (1988). *The Soviet theory of international relations*. Brighton: Wheatsheaf.

Linz, Juan, and Alfred Stepan (1996). *Problems of Democratic Transition and Consolidation*. Baltimore, MD: The Johns Hopkins University Press.

Lipset, Seymour Martin (1959). 'Some Social Requisites of Democracy: Economic Development and Political Legitimacy', *American Political Science Review*, 53 (1), March: 69-105.

Litvak, Meir (1996). *The Islamization of Palestinian Identity: The Case of Hamas*. Tel Aviv: Moshe Dayan Center.

—— (2005a). 'Hamas' Victory in Municipal Elections', *Tel Aviv Notes*, 26 December.

—— (2005b). 'The Anti-Semitism of Hamas', *Palestine-Israel Journal of Politics, Economics, and Culture*, 12 (2-3), December: 41-6.

Locke, John, and Peter Laslett (1960). *Two Treatises of Government*. Cambridge: Cambridge University Press.

Lukes, Steven (1990). 'Perspectives on Authority' in Joseph Raz, ed., *Authority*. Oxford: Basil Blackwell, pp. 203-17.

Lynfield, Ben (2003). 'The soft-spoken face of militant Palestinians' armed struggle', *Scotsman*, 22 August.

Mahle, Melissa (2005). 'A political-security analysis of the failed Oslo process', *Middle East Policy*, XII (1), Spring: 79-96.

Makovsky, David (2004). *Are All Politics Local? A Look at Palestinian Municipal Election Results*. PeaceWatch No. 487. Washington, DC: Washington Institute for Near East Policy. 28 December.

Marx Ferree, Myra (1992). 'The Political Context of Rationality: Rational Choice Theory and Resource Mobilization' in Aldon Morris and Carol McClurg Mueller, eds., *Frontiers in Social Movement Theory*. New Haven, CT: Yale University Press, pp. 29-52.

Maudoodi [Mawdudi], Sayyed Abulala (1955). *The Process of Islamic Revolution*. Address to Aligarh Muslim University, 1947. 2nd edn. Lahore: Markazi Maktaba Jama'at-e-Islami.

Maududi [Mawdudi], Abul A'la (1960a). *Political Theory of Islam.* Paper at Inter-Collegiate Muslim Brotherhood, Lahore, 1939. trans. by Khurshid Ahmad. Lahore: Islamic Publications.

—— (1960b). *First Principles of the Islamic State.* Résumé of a talk to lawyers and intelligentsia of Karachi, Bar Association, 1952. trans. by Khurshid Ahmad. 2nd revised edn. Lahore: Islamic Publications.

Mayer, Ann (1999). *Islam and Human Rights: Tradition and Politics.* Boulder, CO: Westview Press.

McAdam, Doug, John McCarthy, and Mayer Zald (1996). 'Introduction: Opportunities, mobilizing structures, and framing processes - toward a synthetic, comparative perspective on social movements' in Doug McAdam, John McCarthy and Mayer Zald, eds., *Comparative Perspectives on Social Movements: political opportunities, mobilizing structures, and cultural framings.* Cambridge: Cambridge University Press, pp. 1-20.

McDowall, David (1989). *Palestine and Israel: The Uprising and Beyond.* London: I.B. Tauris.

Mecca Agreement (2007). *Mecca Agreement.* Jerusalem: Jerusalem Media & Communication Centre. 8 February. <http://www.jmcc.org/documents/meccaagree.htm>.

Mernissi, Fatima (1991). *The veil and the male elite: a feminist interpretation of women's rights in Islam.* Reading, MA: Addison-Wesley.

Miles, Matthew, and Michael Huberman (1994). *Qualitative Data Analysis: an expanded sourcebook.* 2nd edn. London: Sage.

Miller, Judith (1993). 'The Challenge of Radical Islam', *Foreign Affairs,* 72 (2): 43-56.

Milton-Edwards, Beverley (1992). 'The Concept of *Jihad* and the Palestinian Islamic Movement: A Comparison of Ideas and Techniques', *British Journal of Middle Eastern Studies,* 19 (1): 48-53.

—— (1996). *Islamic Politics in Palestine.* London: Tauris Academic Studies.

Milton-Edwards, Beverley, and Alastair Crooke (2003). 'Costly choice: Hamas, ceasefires and the Palestinian-Israeli peace process', *World Today,* 59 (12), November: 15-17.

—— (2004a). 'Elusive Ingredient: Hamas and the Peace Process', *Journal of Palestine Studies,* XXXIII (4), Summer 2004: 39-52.

—— (2004b). 'Waving, Not Drowning: Strategic Dimensions of Ceasefires and Islamic Movements', *Security Dialogue,* 35 (3), September: 295-310.

Mishal, Shaul, and Re'uven Aharoni (1994). *Speaking stones: communiqués from the Intifada underground.* Syracuse, NY: Syracuse University Press.

Mishal, Shaul, and Avraham Sela (2000). *The Palestinian Hamas: Vision, Violence, and Coexistence.* New York, NY: Columbia University Press.

Mitchell, Richard (1993). *The Society of the Muslim Brothers.* Oxford: Oxford University Press.

Nasr, Mohamed (2004). 'Monopolies and the PNA' in Mushtaq Khan, George Giacaman and Inge Amundsen, eds., *State Formation in Palestine: Viability and governance during a social transformation.* London: RoutledgeCurzon, pp. 168-91.

National Conciliation Document (2006). *The full text of the National Conciliation Document of the Prisoners.* Jerusalem: Jerusalem Media & Communication Centre. 28 June. <http://www.jmcc.org/documents/prisoners2.htm>.

NDI (2005a). *Report on Palestinian Elections for Local Councils: Round One.* Washington: National Democratic Institute for International Affairs. 15 March.

—— (2005b). *Report on Palestinian Elections for Local Councils: Round Two.* Washington: National Democratic Institute for International Affairs. 29 September.

Nieuwenhuijze, C.A.O. van (1997). 'On the Prospects of Intercultural Studies and International Education' in C.A.O. van Nieuwenhuijze, ed., *Paradise Lost: reflections on the struggle for authenticity in the Middle East.* Leiden: Brill.

Norton, Augustus Richard (1995). 'Political Reform in the Middle East'. Public lecture. Magleås, Denmark. 13-14 November.

Nüsse, Andrea (1998). *Muslim Palestine: The Ideology of Hamas.* Amsterdam: Harwood Academic.

O'Leary, Brendan, and Andrew Silke (2007). 'Understanding and Ending Persistent Conflicts: Bridging Research and Policy' in

Marianne Heiberg, John Tirman and Brendan O'Leary, eds., *Terror, Insurgency, and the State: Ending Protracted Conflicts*. Philadelphia, PA: University of Pennsylvania Press, pp. 387-426.

Özkirimli, Umut (2000). *Theories of nationalism: a critical introduction*. Basingstoke: Macmillan.

Pape, Robert Anthony (2005). *Dying to win: the strategic logic of suicide terrorism*. New York, NY: Random House.

Parry, Nigel (1999). *Birzeit Elections 1999*. 24 March. <http://nigelparry.com/diary/birzeit/elect99.html>.

PASSIA (2006). *Palestine Facts: Population*. Jerusalem: PASSIA. <http://www.passia.org/palestine_facts/pdf/pdf2006/4-Population.pdf>.

PCHR (2006). *Statistics related to Al Aqsa Intifada: 29 September, 2000-updated 01 August, 2006*. Gaza. Palestinian Centre for Human Rights. <http://www.pchrgaza.org/Library/alaqsaintifada.htm>.

Peteet, Julie (1987). 'Socio-Political Integration and Conflict Resolution in the Palestinian Camps in Lebanon', *Journal of Palestine Studies*, 16 (2), Winter: 29-44.

Peters, Joel (1997). 'Under Netanyahu', *Middle East Review of International Affairs*, 1 (1), January.

Peters, Rudolph (1996). *Jihad in Classical and Modern Islam*. Princeton, NJ: Markus Wiener.

Pipes, Daniel (1983). *In the path of God: Islam and political power*. New York, NY: Basic Books.

Piven, Frances Fox, and Richard Cloward (1977). *Poor people's movements: why they succeed, how they fail*. New York, NY: Pantheon.

Post, Jerrold, Ehud Sprinzak, and Laurita Denny (2003). 'The Terrorists in Their Own Words: Interviews with 35 Incarcerated Middle Eastern Terrorists', *Journal of Terrorism and Political Violence*, 15 (1), March: 171-84.

Przeworski, Adam (2003). 'A Flawed Blueprint: The Covert Politicization of Development Economics', *Development and Modernization*, 25 (1), Spring.

Qutb, Sayyid (1980 [1964]). *Milestones [Ma'alim fi al-Tariq]*. Kuwait: International Islamic Federation of Student Organizations.

Raab, David (2003). 'The Beleaguered Christians of the Palestinian Authority', *Jerusalem Letter/Viewpoints*, 490, 1-15 January.

Rabbani, Mouin (2001). 'A Smorgasbord of Failure: Oslo and the Al-Aqsa Intifada' in Roane Carey, ed., *The New Intifada: Resisting Israel's Apartheid*. London: Verso, pp. 69-89.

Radlauer, Don (2002). *The "al-Aqsa Intifada"—An Engineered Tragedy*. Herzliya: International Institute for Counter-Terrorism. 29 September. <http://www.ict.org.il/articles/aricledet.cfm?articleid=440>.

Radwan, Eman, and Munzer Emad (1997). *Early Marriage in the Palestinian Community: Causes and Effects*. Gaza: Women's Affair Center, Research Program.

Ranstorp, Magnus (2006). 'Mapping Terrorism Research: Challenges and Priorities' in Magnus Ranstorp, ed., *Mapping Terrorism Research: State of the Art, Gaps and Future Direction*. London: Routledge, pp. 2-24.

Rapoport, David C., and Leonard Weinberg (2001). 'Elections and Violence' in David C. Rapoport and Leonard Weinberg, eds., *The democratic experience and political violence*. London: Frank Cass, pp. 15-50.

Redford, John (1996). *Yahya Ayyash: The Wages of Rage*. February. <http://world.std.com/~jlr/doom/ayyash.htm>.

Regular, Arnon (2004). 'Fatah wins vote at al-Najah University', *Ha'aretz*, 30 November.

Richardson, Louise (2006). *What Terrorists Want: Understanding the Terrorist Threat*. London: John Murray.

Ricigliano, Rob (2004). *Engaging armed groups in peace processes*. London: Conciliation Resources.

Ricoeur, Paul (1971). 'The Model of the Text: Meaningful Action Considered as a Text', *Social Research*, 38 (3), Autumn: 529-62.

Riesebrodt, Martin (1993). *Pious Passion: the emergence of modern fundamentalism in the United States and Iran*. Berkeley, CA: University of California Press.

Riley, Patrick (1982). *Will and political legitimacy: a critical exposition of social contract theory in Hobbes, Locke, Rousseau, Kant, and Hegel*. Cambridge, MA: Harvard University Press.

Risse, Thomas (2000). "'Let's Argue!": Communicative Action in World Politics', *International Organization*, 54 (1), Winter: 1-39.

—— (2004). 'Global Governance and Communicative Action', *Government and Opposition*, 39 (2), Spring: 288-313.

Roadmap (2003). *A Performance-Based Roadmap to a Permanent Two-State Solution to the Israeli-Palestinian Conflict*. Washington DC: US State Department. 30 April. <http://www.state.gov/r/pa/prs/ps/2003/20062.htm>.

Robinson, Glenn (1997). *Building a Palestinian state: the incomplete revolution*. Bloomington, IN: Indiana University Press.

—— (2001). 'The Peace of the Powerful' in Roane Carey, ed., *The New Intifada: Resisting Israel's Apartheid*. London: Verso, pp. 111-23.

—— (2004). 'Hamas as Social Movement' in Quintan Wiktorowicz, ed., *Islamic Activism: a social movement theory approach*. Bloomington, IN: Indiana University Press, pp. 112-42.

Rosenberg, Matthew (2003). 'Hamas remains defiant despite intense Israeli campaign to wipe out militants', *Associated Press*, 12 September.

Ross, Jeffrey, and Ted Gurr (1989). 'Why terrorism subsides', *Comparative Politics*, 21 (4).

Roule, Trifin (2002). 'Post-911 financial freeze dries up Hamas funding', *Jane's Intelligence Review*, 14 (5), May: 17-9.

Rousseau, Jean-Jacques (1993 [1762]). 'The Social Contract or Principles of Political Right' in Jean-Jacques Rousseau, ed., *The Social Contract and Discourses*. trans. by G.D.H. Cole. New revised edn. London: Dent, pp. 179-309.

Roy, Sara (1994). "'The Seed of Chaos, and of Night": The Gaza Strip after the Agreement', *Journal of Palestine Studies*, XXIII (3), Spring: 85-98.

—— (1995a). 'Beyond Hamas: Islamic Activism in the Gaza Strip', *Harvard Middle Eastern and Islamic Review*, 2 (1), Spring: 1-39.

—— (1995b). *The Gaza Strip: the political economy of de-development*. Washington, DC: Institute for Palestine Studies.

—— (2001). 'Decline and Disfigurement: The Palestinian Economy After Oslo' in Roane Carey, ed., *The New Intifada: Resisting Israel's Apartheid*. London: Verso, pp. 91-109.

—— (2002). 'Why Peace Failed: An Oslo Autopsy', *Current History*, 101 (651), January: 8-16.

—— (2003). 'Hamas and the Transformation(s) of Political Islam in Palestine', *Current History*, 102 (660), January: 13-20.

—— (2006). 'Humanism, scholarship and politics: writing on the Palestinian-Israeli conflict' in Sara Roy, *Failing Peace: Gaza and the Palestinian-Israeli Conflict*. London: Pluto Press, pp. xi-xxiii.

—— (2007). 'Ending the Palestinian Economy' in Sara Roy, ed., *Failing Peace: Gaza and the Palestinian-Israeli Conflict*. London: Pluto, pp. 250-93.

Rueschemeyer, Dietrich, Evelyne Stephens, and John Stephens (1992 [1996]). *Capitalist Development and Democracy*. Cambridge: Polity Press.

Rugi, Suzanne (1998). 'Commodifying Honor in Female Sexuality', *Middle East Report*, 28 (1), Spring.

Rustow, Dankwart (1970). 'Transitions to Democracy: Toward a Dynamic Model', *Comparative Politics*, 2 (3), April: 337-63.

Saad-Ghorayeb, Amal (2003). 'Factors Conducive to the Politicization of the Lebanese Shi'a and the Emergence of Hizbu'llah', *Journal of Islamic Studies*, 14 (3), September: 273-307.

Sadowski, Yahya (1993). 'The New Orientalism and the Democracy Debate', *Middle East Report*, 23 (4), July-August: 14-21.

Sahliyeh, Emile (1988). *In search of leadership: West Bank politics since 1967*. Washington, DC: Brookings Institution.

Said, Edward (1978). *Orientalism*. London: Routledge & Kegan Paul.

Salamé, Ghassan (1994). 'Introduction: Where are the Democrats?' in Ghassan Salamé, ed., *Democracy without democrats? - The renewal of politics in the Muslim world*. London: I.B. Tauris, Fondazione ENI Enrico Mattei, pp. 1-20.

Salvatore, Armando (1997). *Islam and the political discourse of modernity*. Reading: Ithaca.

Sartori, Giovanni (1987). *The Theory of Democracy Revisited*. Chatham, NJ: Chatham House Publishers.

Savir, Uri (1999). *The Process*. New York, NY: Vintage Books.

Sayigh, Yazid (1997). *Armed Struggle and the Search for State: the Palestinian national movement 1949-1993*. Oxford: Clarendon Press.

Sayyid, Bobby (1997). *A Fundamental Fear: Eurocentrism and the emergence of Islamism*. London: Zed.

Schacht, Richard (1976). 'Hegel on Freedom' in Alasdair MacIntyre, ed., *Hegel: a collection of critical essays*. Notre Dame, IN: University of Notre Dame Press, pp. 289-328.

Schad, Geoffrey (1994). 'Chronology: 16 November 1993 - 15 February 1994', *Journal of Palestine Studies*, 23 (3), April: 162-82.

Scheindlin, Dahlia (1998). 'Palestinian Women's Model Parliament', *Middle East Review of International Affairs*, 2 (3), September.

Schiff, Ze'ev, and Ehud Ya'ari (1990). *Intifada: The Palestinian Uprising - Israel's Third Front*. trans. by Ina Friedman. New York, NY: Simon and Schuster.

Schleifer, Abdullah (1993). 'Izz al-Din al-Qassam: Preacher and *Mujahid*' in Edmund Burke III, ed., *Struggle and Survival in the Modern Middle East*. London: I.B. Tauris, pp. 164-78.

Schmid, Alex, and Albert Jongman (1988). *Political Terrorism: A New Guide to Actors, Authors, Concepts, Data bases, Theories and Literature*. Amsterdam: North-Holland Publishing.

Scott, James C. (1991). *Domination and the Arts of Resistance: Hidden Transcripts*. New Haven, CT: Yale University Press.

Segal, Naomi (1995). 'Arafat is urging Palestinians to make friends with Israelis', *San Francisco Jewish Community Publications*, 3 August 2006.

Selby, Jan (2007). 'Peace Processes in an Age of Global Capitalism'. Paper presented at *International Studies Association*. Chicago. 2 March.

Shadid, Mohammed (1988). 'The Muslim Brotherhood movement in the West Bank and Gaza', *Third World Quarterly*, 10 (2), April: 658-82.

Shafiq, Munir (1998). 'On the issue of Western Democracy', *Falastin al-Muslimah*, April: 28-9.

Silke, Andrew, ed. (2004a). *Research on Terrorism: Trends, Achievements and Failures*. London: Frank Cass.

—— (2004b). 'An Introduction to Terrorism Research' in Andrew Silke, ed., *Research on Terrorism: Trends, Achievements and Failures*. London: Frank Cass, pp. 1-29.

—— (2004b). 'The Devil You Know: Continuing Problems with Research on Terrorism' in Andrew Silke, ed., *Research on Terrorism: Trends, Achievements and Failures*. London: Frank Cass, pp. 57-71.

—— (2004d). 'The Road Less Travelled: Recent Trends in Terrorism Research' in Andrew Silke, ed., *Research on Terrorism: Trends, Achievements and Failures*. London: Frank Cass, pp. 186-213.

Silverman, Hugh, ed. (1989). *Derrida and deconstruction*. London: Routledge.

Simmons, John (1992). *The Lockean theory of rights*. Oxford: Princeton University Press.

Singer, Peter (1983). *Hegel*. Oxford: Oxford University Press.

Smith, Charles (1992). *Palestine and the Arab-Israeli conflict*. 2nd edn. New York, NY: St. Martin's Press.

Snow, David, *et al.* (1986). 'Frame Alignment Processes, Micro-mobilization, and Movement Participation', *American sociological review*, 51 (4), August: 464-81.

Stedman, Stephen John (1997). 'Spoiler Problems in Peace Processes', *International Security*, 22 (2), Autumn: 5-53.

Stillman, Peter (1974). 'Hegel's Critique of Liberal Theories of Rights', *American Political Science Review*, 68 (3), September: 1086-92.

Stout, Jeffrey (2004). *Democracy & Tradition*. Princeton, NJ: Princeton University Press.

Swatos Jr., William (1989). 'Losing Faith in the "Religion" of Secularization: Worldwide Religious Resurgence and the Definition of Religion' in William Swatos, ed., *Religious Politics in Global and Comparative Perspective*. New York, NY: Greenwood, pp. 147-54.

Talmon Heller, Daniella (1994). 'The Shaykh and the Community: Popular Hanbalite Islam in 12th-13th Century Jabal Nablus and Jabal Qasyūn', *Studia Islamica*, 79: 103-120.

Tamimi, Azzam (2006). *Hamas: Unwritten Chapters*. London: Hurst.

Tarrow, Sidney (1988). 'Old Movements in New Cycles of Protest: The Career of an Italian Religious Community' in Bert Klandermans, HansPeter Kriesi and Sidney Tarrow, eds., *From Structure to Action - Comparing Social Movement Research across Cultures.* London: JAI Press, pp. 281-304.

—— (1995). 'Foreword' in Donatella della Porta, *Social movements, political violence, and the state: a comparative analysis of Italy and Germany.* Cambridge: Cambridge University Press, pp. vii-viii.

Tessler, Mark (1994). *A History of the Israeli–Palestinian Conflict.* Bloomington, IN: Indiana University Press.

Tibawi, A.L. (1978). *The Islamic Pious Foundations in Jerusalem.* London: The Islamic Cultural Centre.

Tilly, Charles (1985). 'War Making and State Making as Organized Crime' in Peter Evans, Dietrich Rueschemeyer and Theda Skocpol, eds., *Bringing the State Back in.* Cambridge: Cambridge University Press, pp. 169-91.

—— (1992). *Coercion, Capital, and European States AD 990-1992.* Oxford: Blackwell.

Tully, James (1984). 'Locke on Liberty' in Z. A. Pelczynski and John Gray, eds., *Conceptions of liberty in political philosophy.* London: Athlone, pp. 57-82.

United Nations (2001). *The Palestinian Economy: Achievements of the Interim Period and Tasks for the Future.* Geneva: United Nations Publications.

United Nations and the World Bank (1997). *Closure on the West Bank and Gaza.* Factsheet. August-September. <www.arts.mcgill.ca/mepp/unsco/closure001097.html>.

Urdal, Henrik (2006). 'A Clash of Generations? Youth Bulges and Political Violence', *International Studies Quarterly,* 50 (3), September: 607-29.

Usher, Graham (1995a). 'What kind of nation? The rise of Hamas in the occupied territories', *Race & Class,* 37 (2), October-December: 65-80.

—— (1995b). *Palestine in crisis: the struggle for peace and political independence after Oslo.* London: Pluto Press.

Waterbury, John (1994). 'Democracy without Democrats? - The potential for political liberalization in the Middle East' in Ghassan

Salamé, ed., *Democracy without democrats? - The renewal of politics in the Muslim world*. London: I.B. Tauris, Fondazione ENI Enrico Mattei, pp. 23-47.

Watt, E.D. (1982). *Authority*. London: Croom Helm.

Watt, Montgomery (1972). *The Influence of Islam on Medieval Europe*. Edinburgh: Edinburgh University Press.

Weber, Max (1964). *The Theory of Social and Economic Organization*. trans. by A.M. Henderson and Talcott Parsons. New York, NY: Free Press of Glencoe.

Weinberg, Leonard, and Ami Pedahzur (2003). *Political Parties and Terrorist Groups*. London: Routledge.

Wiktorowicz, Quintan, ed. (2004a). *Islamic Activism: A Social Movement Theory Approach*. Bloomington, IN: Indiana University Press.

—— (2004b). 'Islamic Activism and Social Movement Theory' in Quintan Wiktorowicz, ed., *Islamic Activism: A Social Movement Theory Approach*. Bloomington, IN: Indiana University Press, pp. 1-33.

Williams, Michael, and Keith Krause (1997). 'Preface' in Keith Krause and Michael Williams, eds., *Critical Security Studies*. Minneapolis, MN: University of Minnesota Press, pp. vii-xxi.

WINEP (2007). *The Palestinian Legislative Council: A Handbook*. Washington, DC: Washington Institute for Near East Policy.

Wolff, Kristin (1998). '*New* New Orientalism: Political Islam and Social Movement Theory' in Ahmad S. Moussalli, ed., *Islamic Fundamentalism: Myths & Realities*. Reading: Ithaca, pp. 41-73.

World Bank (1993a). *Developing the Occupied Territories: An Investment in Peace, Vol. 2: The Economy*. Washington, DC: The World Bank. September.

—— (1993b). *Developing the Occupied Territories: An Investment in Peace, Vol. 4: Agriculture*. Washington, DC: The World Bank. September.

Younis, Mona (2000). *Liberation and Democratization: The South African and Palestinian National Movements*. Minneapolis, MN: University of Minnesota Press.

Zogby, James (1996). 'Observing the Palestine Elections', *The Jerusalem Times*, February.

Zubaida, Sami (1989). *Islam, the People and the State: essays on political ideas and movements in the Middle East.* London: Routledge.

Zulaika, Joseba (2006). 'Read My Terror: Towards a Critical Terrorism Studies'. Keynote address at conference 'Isit Time for Critical terrorism Studies?' Manchester/Aberystwyth University. 27-28 October.

INDEX